THOMAS HOCCLEVE:
NEW APPROACHES

THOMAS HOCCLEVE: NEW APPROACHES

Edited by
Jenni Nuttall and David Watt

D. S. BREWER

First published 2022
D. S. Brewer, Cambridge

ISBN 978-1-84384-642-0

D. S. Brewer is an imprint of Boydell & Brewer Ltd
PO Box 9, Woodbridge, Suffolk IP12 3DF, UK
and of Boydell & Brewer Inc.
668 Mt Hope Avenue, Rochester, NY 14620–2731, USA
website: www.boydellandbrewer.co.uk

A CIP catalogue record for this book is available
from the British Library

The publisher has no responsibility for the continued existence or accuracy
of URLs for external or third-party internet websites referred to in this book,
and does not guarantee that any content on such websites is, or will remain,
accurate or appropriate

This publication is printed on acid-free paper

Contents

CONTENTS

Illustrations

Full credit details are provided in the captions to the images in the text. The editors, contributors and publisher are grateful to all the institutions and persons for permission to reproduce the materials in which they hold copyright. Every effort has been made to trace the copyright holders; apologies are offered for any omission, and the publisher will be pleased to add any necessary acknowledgement in subsequent editions.

Contributors

Laurie Atkinson is a Teaching Assistant and Research Assistant in the Department of English Studies, University of Durham, and MHRA Postdoctoral Research Associate for the new edition of the works of Geoffrey Chaucer in preparation for publication with Cambridge University Press. His current research, which he will be pursuing as a Teaching Fellow at the University of Tübingen from April 2022, is on early English print.

Taylor Cowdery is Assistant Professor of English and Comparative Literature at the University of North Carolina, Chapel Hill. He is currently finishing a book on the poetics of the English court poetry tradition during the fourteenth, fifteenth, and sixteenth centuries.

Helen M. Hickey is a Research Associate in the School of Culture and Communication at the University of Melbourne, Australia. Her current research interests are embodiment in literature, climate history and sensory studies.

Sebastian J. Langdell is Assistant Professor of English at Baylor University. He is currently at work on a critical edition of Hoccleve's shorter poems (the Huntington holograph poems).

Ruen-chuan Ma is Assistant Professor of English and Literature at Utah Valley University. His research interests focus on late medieval English and French literature, specifically manuscript studies (page design and codicology), reading practices (text and image, multimodality), and the reception of classical texts.

Nicholas Myklebust, an Associate Professor of medieval languages and literatures at Regis University in Denver, Colorado, specialises in early English metrical systems and the modelling of metrical change.

Jenni Nuttall is College Lecturer in Medieval English at Exeter College, University of Oxford. Her recent work has explored verse-form and literary terminology in Middle English and Middle Scots poetry.

R. D. Perry is an Assistant Professor of English and Literary Arts at the University of Denver. He specialises in medieval and early modern English literature as well as the history of philosophy and critical theory.

Michelle Ripplinger is a PhD candidate in English and Medieval Studies at UC Berkeley. She studies the relationship between ethics and aesthetics, with particular focus on the representation of women and gender in the literature of late medieval England.

Spencer Strub is Associate Research Scholar at Princeton University. His research focuses on emotion, expression, and belonging in late medieval English literature and religion.

A. Arwen Taylor is an Assistant Professor of English at Arkansas Tech University. Her research interests include the use of stylistics in the interpretation of medieval texts and medievalisms in terms of their linguistic representations of the Middle Ages.

Stephanie Trigg is Redmond Barry Distinguished Professor of English Literature at the University of Melbourne. She works on late medieval English poetry and the history of medievalism, and is currently engaged in a collaborative research project on the history of the face in literature.

David Watt is an Associate Professor in the Department of English, Theatre, Film & Media at the University of Manitoba. His research focuses on late medieval literature and manuscripts. He also studies medieval manuscripts and medievalism in Canada.

Acknowledgements

The chapters in this volume were all initially shared at a conference called 'The Making of Thomas Hoccleve', which was held in Winnipeg, Manitoba in July 2018. The conference was generously supported by a Social Sciences and Humanities Research Council of Canada Connections Grant as well as grants from Research Manitoba, the Arts Endowment Fund, and the University of Manitoba Conference Sponsorship Program. The event would not have been possible without initial support from the University of Manitoba Archives & Special Collections, the Department of English, Theatre, Film & Media, *Mosaic: An Interdisciplinary Critical Journal*, the Department of History, and the Department of Religion. We were hosted in Winnipeg by the University of Manitoba Institute for the Humanities, and we are particularly grateful to Paul Jenkins for making the conference run so smoothly that we could spend our time in dialogue with and about Hoccleve.

We are also grateful to the participants in the conference for their contributions to that dialogue and to those authors who have spent so much time since the conference responding to it by revising their presentations into the substantial chapters that appear in this book. It has been a pleasure to continue to think in new ways about how we might approach Hoccleve and his work.

We would also like to acknowledge the International Hoccleve Society for its role in shaping this volume. The society is made up of a group of people whose enthusiasm for Hoccleve is only matched by their generosity of spirit. It has been the catalyst for exciting conversations about Hoccleve for over a decade now, and it was at a gathering of society members that we initially made our plans to hold a conference and eventually publish a volume of essays. Many members of the society have helped us to reach this point. We would like to thank all of you and invite you to join us in thanking Elon Lang for having the vision to set us on this path and the determination to keep us all rowing in the same rhythm for many years.

It has been a pleasure to work with Caroline Palmer and her team at Boydell & Brewer. We are grateful for Caroline's interest in the project and for her selection of reviewers, who provided us with astute and helpful feedback. We can only imagine how difficult it has been to keep the press running so smoothly considering the challenges we have faced over the past several years, yet Caroline has consistently provided us with a clear sense of direction and purpose.

Finally, we would like to thank our families, who have not only endured our enthusiasm for Hoccleve for years but have supported our work in many ways – sometimes by encouraging us to leave it aside for a time. Thank you.

Note on Quotations

Quotations from Chaucer's works are taken from the *Riverside Chaucer*, given by conventional abbreviation and line numbers in parentheses. Quotations from Hoccleve's *Series* are taken from Ellis (ed.), '*My Compleinte*', as are quotations from Hoccleve's shorter poems where possible. Quotations from other minor works by Hoccleve not in Ellis's edition are taken from Furnivall and Gollancz (eds), *Hoccleve's Works*. Quotations from Hoccleve's *Regiment* are taken from Blyth's edition, cited by line number in parentheses in the main text. References to the constituent parts of the *Series* are given by line number in parentheses in the main text.

Abbreviations

Hoccleve's Works

C   'Complaint', in Ellis, pp. 115–30

D   'Dialogue', in Ellis, pp. 130–59

FIR   'Fabula de Quadam Imperatrice' or 'The Tale of Jereslaus's Wife', in Ellis, pp. 160–95

FMM   'Fabula de Quadam Muliere Mala' or 'The Tale of Jonathas', in Ellis, pp. 234–60

LC   *L'epistre de Cupide*

LTD   'Ars Vtillissima Sciendi Mori' or 'Learn to Die', in Ellis, pp. 196–233

MR   *La Male Regle*

RP   *Regiment of Princes*

Frequently Cited Editions

Blyth (ed.), *Regiment*: Thomas Hoccleve, *The Regiment of Princes*, ed. Charles R. Blyth (Kalamazoo, MI, 1999)

Burrow (ed.), *Complaint and Dialogue*: J. A. Burrow (ed.), *Thomas Hoccleve's Complaint and Dialogue*, EETS OS 313 (Oxford, 1999)

Burrow and Doyle (eds), *Facsimile*: J. A. Burrow and A. I. Doyle (eds), *A Facsimile of the Autograph Verse Manuscripts: Henry E. Huntington Library, San Marino (California), MSS HM 111 and HM 744, University Library, Durham (England), MS Cosin V. III.9*, EETS SS 19 (Oxford, 2002)

Ellis (ed.), *'My Compleinte'*: Roger Ellis (ed.), *'My Compleinte' and Other Poems*, Exeter Medieval Texts and Studies (Exeter, 2001)

Furnivall and Gollancz (eds), *Hoccleve's Works*: Frederick J. Furnivall and Isaac Gollancz (eds), *Hoccleve's Works: The Minor Poems*, rev. edn by Jerome Mitchell and A. I. Doyle, EETS ES 61 and 73 (2 vols, London, 1892 and 1925 (for 1897); repr. in one volume, London, 1970)

Riverside Chaucer: Larry D. Benson et al. (eds), *The Riverside Chaucer*, 3rd edn (Oxford, 1988)

Other Abbreviations

BD	*Book of the Duchess*
CT	*Canterbury Tales*
EETS	Early English Text Society
ES	Extra Series
LGW	*Legend of Good Women*
MED	*Middle English Dictionary* (online at https://quod.lib.umich. edu/m/middle-english-dictionary/dictionary)
OS	Original Series
SS	Supplementary Series
STC	*Short Title Catalogue*: A. W. Pollard and G. R. Redgrave (eds), *A Short-Title Catalogue of Books Printed in England, Scotland and Ireland, and of English Books Printed Abroad 1475–1640*, 2nd rev. edn by W. A. Jackson, F. S. Ferguson and K. F. Pantzer (3 vols, London, 1976–91)

Introduction:
Hoccleve Then and Now

Jenni Nuttall and David Watt

In the scenes of day-to-day life which the government clerk Thomas Hoccleve presents in his poetry, he is often approached by other people. Often those whom he encounters know something of him in advance, whether from prior experience or hearsay. In the *Male Regle*, the innkeepers, cooks and taxi-boatmen recognise him as a generous customer who pays promptly and well (177–84, 195–8). The old man who walks alongside Hoccleve and introduces himself in the *Regiment*'s prologue has also heard of the poet and of his literary connection with Chaucer (who had died a decade earlier). When Hoccleve tells him his name, the old man responds with recognition: 'Sone, I have herd or this men speke of thee' (1866). Hoccleve is someone known to others and discussed in his absence. Even in the 'Complaint', when he describes how some in the Westminster crowd sought to avoid him, such bystanders nonetheless reveal that they both know who he is and some part of what has happened to him (C 43–5, 64–93, 120–35). Hoccleve's reputation often precedes him, inviting many kinds of approaches even as it discourages others.

This collection of essays likewise approaches Hoccleve and his works, bringing both prior reputation and fresh eyes to bear on this most engaging of poets. Since an earlier collection of four essays on Hoccleve edited by Catherine Batt was published in 1996, Hoccleve's star has continued to rise, and he is now among the most frequently taught of fifteenth-century authors as well as the subject of many journal articles and chapters, and a growing number of monographs.[1] Many readers, not least the students who increasingly read Hoccleve's verse as part of their university degrees, find him very accessible. Students often respond with enthusiastic recognition to the confessional elements of Hoccleve's poetry, those passages in which he acknowledges his own failings and self-sabotage, his anxiety about the future, his frustrated career hopes or his precarious finances. Most particularly in an age where mental health difficulties are acknowledged more

---

[1] Catherine Batt (ed.), *Essays on Thomas Hoccleve*, Westfield Publications in Medieval Studies, 10 (Turnhout, 1996). The International Hoccleve Society compiles a Hoccleve bibliography which can be found at https://hocclevesociety.org/the-hoccleve-bibliography/.

1

readily, many of us engage very directly not only with Hoccleve's accounts of what it is to worry gloomily about the future but also his descriptions of a more acute mental health crisis and the social stigma which can result from such a temporary loss of sanity.

In a recent blog post, Brendan O'Connell of Trinity College, Dublin has written about his experiences of teaching Hoccleve remotely during a global pandemic, using the texts and translations now available on the International Hoccleve Society website.[2] Taught as part of a module on 'Surviving Trauma in the Middle Ages', Hoccleve's life and works spoke very directly to students, some of whom were contending with their own isolation, loneliness and worries. Hoccleve's candour is appealing: many readers engage with Hoccleve not despite his troubles but because of them. The same seems to have been true in his own lifetime. Moved by his account of being shunned in the 'Complaint', we might think of him as a loner, but Hoccleve gained and kept friends over the course of his life. There are many references to friendship in his poetry, not least the 'freendes' (89) who try to keep him on the straight and narrow in the *Male Regle* or the 'good frend of fern agoon' (*D* 8), a friend of many years' standing, who turns up to visit him in the *Series*. Sebastian Sobecki has argued that the *Series* is in part a work of mourning for Hoccleve's close friendship with a fellow Privy Seal clerk, John Bailey, who died in November 1420, while Rory G. Critten notes the joking marginal reference to another clerk, John Offord, in the Durham manuscript of the same text.[3]

Just as Hoccleve's openness about his mental health did not deter his friends, so his financial troubles and career frustrations did not put off patrons and readers but rather had the effect of encouraging them. By any measure, Hoccleve was a networker *par excellence*, with acquaintances and contacts running far beyond his close friends and the small group of colleagues, some named in his poetry, with whom he worked at the Privy Seal.[4] Hoccleve is well known for approaching others for help in his petitionary poems, sometimes on his own account and sometimes on behalf of others among 'my felawis of the Priue Seel' (*C* 296). These approaches reach outside of his immediate associates, colleagues and bosses: he writes not only to Henry Somer, a friend of Chaucer's who had worked his way

---

[2] Brendan O'Connell, '"Communing is the best assay": Teaching Hoccleve's Complaint Remotely', blog post online at https://hocclevesociety.org/teaching/communing-is-the-best-assay-teaching-hoccleves-complaint-remotely/.

[3] Sebastian Sobecki, *Last Words: The Public Self and the Social Author in Late Medieval England* (Oxford, 2019), pp. 65–100; Rory G. Critten, *Author, Scribe, and Book in Late Medieval English Literature* (Cambridge, 2018), pp. 63–6.

[4] For a survey of Hoccleve's network of contacts, see John J. Thompson, 'A Poet's Contacts with the Great and the Good: Further Consideration of Thomas Hoccleve's Texts and Manuscripts', in Felicity Riddy (ed.), *Prestige, Authority and Power in Late Medieval Manuscripts and Texts*, York Manuscripts Conferences Proceedings Series, 4 (York, 2000), pp. 77–101.

up in the Exchequer to become deputy to the Treasurer by 1408, and to Thomas Langley, who was first Keeper of the Privy Seal and then Henry IV's Lord Chancellor, but also (with tactful indirection at the end of the *Male Regle*) to Thomas Neville, fifth baron Furnivall, Lord Treasurer, and to Henry V himself after his Agincourt triumph (in the poem beginning 'Victorious Kyng').[5]

Despite the time Hoccleve spent in silent labour as a scribe (the physical and mental strain of which he recalls vividly for the Old Man in *RP* 988–1029), his life must thus also have been one of varied approaches and encounters, and of making contact, whether in person or through copies of his verse, with the wider world. Hoccleve sends out his verse, hopeful and perhaps confident that his poems would speak on his behalf. Another short poem asks John Carpenter (though his name is written over an erasure), Town Clerk of London from 1417, to intervene on Hoccleve's behalf in asking for more time from his creditors, some of whom want repayment urgently.[6] In return, the poem offers Carpenter not much more than its own wit, form and style, as well as the opportunity to cheer Hoccleve up. Hoccleve would be emptied of his 'heuy thoghtes' (25) and sleep better at night if Carpenter would help him. The poem flatteringly anticipates and projects Carpenter's 'goodnesse' (22) and 'good plesance' (26), though such praise would hardly surprise a wealthy and charitable man. Hoccleve's low-stakes worries and their easy resolution were, it seems, enough to warrant the poem's request and its reception. While many critical accounts of Hoccleve's self-representation understand it to be (in Lee Patterson's phrase) 'essentially strategic', Patterson argues that we should see it ultimately as 'unique, even accidental eccentricity, a peculiarity of the personality', part the result of Hoccleve's own idiosyncrasies and part the consequence of the pressures of city life.[7] Whether it is strategic or eccentric or inextricably both at once, the Carpenter poem demonstrates that Hoccleve expected such particularity, whatever its causes, to be sufficient in itself – in this case, as a note in his autograph manuscript tells us, it worked entirely as predicted.

Just as Hoccleve approached others for help, so many individuals approached him to ask him to write for them. While his reports of financial difficulties show him to be sometimes at the mercy of the willingness of others to pay his salary, he was also himself in demand as a supplier of

---

[5] J. A. Burrow provides context and chronology for Hoccleve's works in *Thomas Hoccleve*, Authors of the Middle Ages, 4 (Aldershot, 1994). For the poems mentioned, see Ellis (ed.), 'My Compleinte', p. 76 (MR, 417–24) and pp. 79–80 (ballade and roundel to Somer), and Furnivall and Gollancz (eds), *Hoccleve's Works*, p. 58 (poem addressed to Langley) and p. 62 (poem to Henry V).

[6] Furnivall and Gollancz (eds), *Hoccleve's Works*, pp. 63–4. For Carpenter, see George Shuffelton, 'John Carpenter, Lay Clerk', *Chaucer Review*, 48 (2014), 434–56.

[7] Lee Patterson, '"What is me?": Self and Society in the Poetry of Thomas Hoccleve', *Studies in the Age of Chaucer*, 23 (2001), 437–70, at pp. 438, 440.

texts, a translator and versifier in Chaucerian verse-forms and in a metre close to Chaucer's own decasyllable. Such approaches came both from influential London citizens and from members of the nobility. Hoccleve had translations of religious works commissioned by Robert Chichele, grocer and brother of a long-serving archbishop of Canterbury; by Thomas Marleburgh, a stationer; as well as by Joan FitzAlan, countess of Hereford and mother of Mary Bohun, Henry IV's first wife.[8] There are also traces of more mysterious connections such as the unnamed 'deuoute man' (D 235) who encouraged him to translate part or all of Suso's *Horologium Sapientiae*. Hoccleve also had the contacts to attract the attention of noblemen with well-evidenced literary interests, such as Humphrey, duke of Gloucester who asked the poet for 'a book' (D 532) without specifying a subject. Likewise, in an envoy poem to accompany a 'little pamfilet' (1), Hoccleve reminds Edward, duke of York that he had asked him in person 'at London' for a collection of whatever 'balades' (13), whatever short lyrics, he had to hand.[9] This encounter was not exactly a conventional moment of commission or presentation, the patron providing a text to be translated or the humble poet offering a completed work. Like the encounter between Gower and Richard II on a boat on the Thames in which the king simply asks for 'Som newe thing' so that the king can inspect 'the forme of [Gower's] writyng', Hoccleve was free in these instances to decide what to write and what to give.[10] The form of Hoccleve's writing was equally interesting to patrons in its own right.

The precise dynamics of other approaches are harder to reconstruct: was Hoccleve asked to write a new mirror-for-princes work by Prince Henry or someone in his circle, or was the *Regiment* itself an approach to the prince as a means of advertising his services?[11] The text presents itself as the Old Man's convenient solution to Hoccleve's money troubles: he need only write 'a goodly tale or two' (1902) for the prince to trigger a generous response. Characteristically, the work Hoccleve produced was not a short narrative, but a combination of long autobiographical prologue and main text constructed 'plotmeel' (2053), that is, short selections translated from three advice texts synthesised in Hoccleve's own arrangement. Whatever the *Regiment*'s particular origins, Hoccleve was clearly adept at judging what sort of approach to make in his poetry, allowing him to navigate the shifting sands of a Lancastrian politics constantly destabilised both by

---

[8] Ellis (ed.), 'My Compleinte', pp. 53–63 (see n. 245), 82–7 (see n. to title), 88–92 (see n. 1).

[9] Furnivall and Gollancz (eds), *Hoccleve's Works*, pp. 49–51.

[10] John Gower, *Confessio Amantis*, ed. Russell A. Peck (3 vols, Kalamazoo, 2000), vol. 1, p. 67 (first recension prologue, lines *51 and *53).

[11] For an influential account of the *Regiment*'s genesis, see Derek Pearsall, 'Thomas Hoccleve's *Regement of Princes*: The Poetics of Royal Self-Representation', *Speculum*, 69 (1994), 386–410.

the after-shocks of Richard II's deposition and its own internal rivalries.[12] Moreover, Hoccleve's poetry might also be valued by Lancastrian readers for its near-Chaucerian versification and repurposings of much of Chaucer's rhetoric and style. Yet despite his indebtedness to Chaucer, Hoccleve very noticeably avoids certain of Chaucer's favoured genres – he does not write dream vision, conventional love lyrics (the poem in mock-praise of his lady is more evidence of Hoccleve's habitual misogyny than of anything else), refrain lyrics of Boethian advice, or any continuations or imitations of Chaucerian narratives. Whether it was seen as close to Chaucer's verse or different in genre and subject if not in style, Hoccleve's poetry was nonetheless desirable to those interested in vernacular verse to a degree which allowed him a certain freedom over its content and approach.

Driven by the New Historicism of the 1980s and 1990s which re-evaluated literary works in their social, historical and intellectual contexts, many readings of Hoccleve's works have probed whether he is capable of an independent political voice (with much debate about by what means and how overtly he offers correction, deflection or critique of Lancastrian imperatives), or whether, as Larry Scanlon has argued, Hoccleve remains a defender of royal interests and religious orthodoxy, though certainly a nuanced and sophisticated writer.[13] We might wonder which relationships or alignments felt most important to Hoccleve. Did he feel more strongly allied with his fellow clerks working anonymously within the machinery of Crown government, or with those in power above them? Or, despite his professional identity, did he nonetheless in some important way feel 'clergial' (as he describes the footsteps in which he follows at *RP* 2150), a member of the first estate whose role was to advise, exhort and care for the souls of the laity? In the face of these competing alignments, modern roles such as 'laureate' or 'spokesman' or 'publicist' cannot easily capture Hoccleve's position vis-à-vis the Lancastrian Crown. Some of Hoccleve's poems which refer to public occasions and events may be in fact anti-occasional; they are topically occasioned but not for or about the ceremonies they use as their prompts.[14] We also cannot discount the possibility of the virtual and the vicarious, in which addresses to Henry V or Sir John Oldcastle are imagined as much for other audiences as they are for their notional addressee or

---

[12] See especially Paul Strohm, *England's Empty Throne: Usurpation and the Language of Legitimation, 1399–1422* (New Haven, 1998); Robert Meyer-Lee, *Poets and Power from Chaucer to Wyatt*, Cambridge Studies in Medieval Literature, 61 (Cambridge, 2007); and Jenni Nuttall, *The Creation of Lancastrian Kinship: Literature, Language, and Politics in Late Medieval England*, Cambridge Studies in Medieval Literature, 67 (Cambridge, 2007).

[13] Larry Scanlon, 'Nothing But Change and Variance: The Problem of Hoccleve's Politics', *Chaucer Review*, 48 (2014), 503–23. Footnote 1 of Scanlon's article offers a useful survey of work on Hoccleve's politics.

[14] Jenni Nuttall, 'Thomas Hoccleve's Poems for Henry V: Anti-Occasional Verse and Ecclesiastical Reform' (2015), published online at 10.1093/oxfordhb/9780199935338.013.61 (Oxford Handbooks Online).

subject. Patronage itself could become an in-joke for a coterie audience. If David Watt and Rory G. Critten are right that the *Series* is a text written predominantly for a Westminster readership, the 'envoy' to Joan Neville, countess of Westmorland was perhaps, as Sebastian Sobecki has suggested, 'a joke at the expense of the countess', a wilfully inappropriate dedication following the misogyny of the preceding tale.[15] Hoccleve challenges us not to impose our assumptions onto him, but rather, through flexible and open-minded approaches, to contemplate new possibilities of commission, patronage and reception.

Hoccleve's Reception History

Approaching Hoccleve and his works thus requires us to become comfortable with a certain amount of ongoing uncertainty and dissonance, to acknowledge that many elements might appear to be in contradiction and to be open constantly to the revision of our assumptions. Hoccleve, too, understood the inherent mutability of personae and poses across the course of a literary career. After a passage of misogynist humour in the *Series*, the unnamed Friend asks how things are between Hoccleve and his wife. Hoccleve says that she would be unimpressed if he should 'pleye a soleyn' (D 724), meaning to play the part of an unmarried person, perhaps particularly a celibate cleric (from whom antifeminism might be stereotypically expected). *Soleyn* also perhaps conveys some of its other meanings of 'sullen', 'lonely' or 'morose' – how dare Hoccleve claim this when he has companionship at home? Hoccleve accepts that to write verse is inevitably to 'pleye' various parts, to reshape and reposition himself, performing different roles for the appreciation of different audiences. And if Hoccleve defied easy categorisation in his life, his posthumous reputation has proved equally malleable. Subsequent generations have remembered, misremembered and reinvented 'Hoccleve'. Given the lack of early printed editions of his works, one might once have assumed that Hoccleve was largely forgotten until the small edition of six poems published by George Mason in 1796 and Thomas Wright's 1860 edition of the *Regiment*.[16] Yet, as Dallas Simpson's 2001 PhD maps out in its chronological survey of allusions, Hoccleve remained a figure known to literary history throughout the centuries after his death.[17]

---

[15] David Watt, *The Making of Thomas Hoccleve's* Series (Liverpool, 2013), pp. 33–9, 54–9; Critten, *Author, Scribe, and Book*, p. 58; Sobecki, *Last Words*, p. 96.

[16] *Poems by Thomas Hoccleve, Never Before Printed*, ed. George Mason (London, 1796); *De regimine principum: A Poem*, ed. Thomas Wright (London, 1860).

[17] Dallas Fullerton Simpson, 'An Annotated Critical Bibliography for Five of the 15th-Century English Chaucerians: Thomas Hoccleve, John Lydgate, George Ashby, Thomas Norton, and Stephen Hawes' (2 vols, unpublished PhD dissertation, Australian National University, 2001), vol. 1, pp. 5–10, 20–5, 33–9, 62–237.

Tracing his fate from the later fifteenth century to the later nineteenth century reveals the range of approaches which Hoccleve and his works attracted. When compiling Cambridge, Trinity College, MS R. 3. 20 in the 1430s, the scribe and anthologist John Shirley knew Hoccleve's name and occupation.[18] He introduces *L'epistre de Cupide* as 'a lytel traytis [treatise] made and compyled by Thomas Occleue of þoffice of þe priue seel' (p. 116). As we might expect given Shirley's packaging of elite culture for wider audiences, he presents *L'epistre* as a poem which models courtly behaviours and language, demonstrating 'þe maners and þe conuersacions booþe of men and wymmen conuersantes [i.e., 'dwelling'] in þis lytell yle of Albyone' (p. 116). In the *Book of Curtesye*, a conduct book written for children in the second half of the fifteenth century, Hoccleve's *Regiment* takes its place alongside Gower's *Confessio Amantis*, all of Chaucer's works and Lydgate's 'volumes [...] large and wyde' (386) in the reading list of books a young reader is advised to explore. The author celebrates the 'writing playne' (360) and 'goodly langage' (353) by which Hoccleve makes his 'exortacion' (353) for princes to be virtuous.[19] Praising such boldness in speaking to those in power, he is one of four 'faders Auncient' (400) who were (in a phrase echoing Hoccleve's own praise of Chaucer) 'Founders in oure langage' (432), rather than the more usual triumvirate of Gower, Chaucer and Lydgate.

Despite the *Book of Curtesye*'s enthusiasm for the *Regiment*, neither this poem nor the *Series* were printed during the sixteenth century, though two of Hoccleve's poems did find their way into Thynne's 1532 edition of Chaucer (*L'epistre*, plus a lyric addressing Henry V and the Knights of the Garter as one of the items following the table of contents, neither attributed to Hoccleve).[20] Hoccleve's posthumous reputation was often entangled with Chaucer's. In John Speed's full-length portrait of Chaucer for Thomas Speght's 1598 edition, Hoccleve is named as Chaucer's 'Scholar', positioning him as a student learning from a teacher.[21] Speght correctly attributes *L'epistre* to Hoccleve rather than Chaucer in his introduction, as well as citing the lines in praise of Chaucer from the *Regiment* (4992–9, 1958–74, 2077–107).[22] Both Speght's précis of the text and his headnote to *L'epistre* draw on Shirley's *incipit*, adding to this a reference to Hoccleve's apology in the *Series* for any offence taken by women readers of *L'epistre* (though

---

[18] On Shirley and his work on this manuscript, see Margaret Connolly, *John Shirley: Book Production and the Noble Household in Fifteenth-Century England* (Aldershot, 1996), pp. 69–101.

[19] *Caxton's Book of Curtesye*, ed. Frederick J. Furnivall, EETS ES 3 (London, 1868), cited by line number.

[20] *Workes of Geffray Chaucer Newly Printed* (London, 1532), fols 371rb–4ra (*L'epistre*) (STC (2nd edn) 5068).

[21] Megan Cook, *The Poet and the Antiquaries: Chaucerian Scholarship and the Rise of Literary History, 1532–1635* (Philadelphia, 2019), pp. 38, 170–3.

[22] *The Workes of our Antient and Lerned English Poet, Geffrey Chaucer*, ed. Thomas Speght (London, 1598), sigs C1r, C1v–C2r, D2r (STC (2nd edn) 5078).

Speght locates this in the 'Complaint' rather than the 'Dialogue', suggesting perhaps that his knowledge of the *Series* was not firsthand). Speght's edition thus claimed *L'epistre* for Hoccleve, though not always convincingly for all of its readers. In introducing his 1718 modernisation of *L'epistre*, George Sewell assigns it to Chaucer on the authority of the antiquary John Leland, even though he acknowledges that some editions give it to Hoccleve. Sewell discounts 'the common story of Occleve's Recantation', turning Speght's editorial intervention into a popular myth which can be passed over in favour of more scholarly evidence.[23]

Other half-remembered stories about Hoccleve's reputation as a petitionary poet may have led to Chaucer's 'Complaint to his Purse' being ascribed to him by Speght ('Th. Occleue to his empty purse').[24] This attribution ('Th. Ocleue. in. Chaucer', i.e., Hoccleve in an edition of Chaucer's works) was repeated by the essayist Sir William Cornwallis in one of his *Essayes of Certaine Paradoxes* (1616) which provocatively argued 'That it is good to be in debt'.[25] Cornwallis introduces Hoccleve as 'That Poet Laureat' who forfeited his laurel wreath by writing a poem to his purse to keep him from penury. This mistaken attribution was not the only misapprehension about Hoccleve to circulate in the centuries after his death. Thanks to the Tudor polemicist John Bale, he also enjoyed a historical cameo as a leading Wycliffite rather than a defender of religious orthodoxy.[26] Bale's *Scriptorum Illustrium Maioris Brytanniae Catalogus* (1557), a collection of biographies of British writers, describes a Hoccleve who is learned and eloquent, considered the leading poet after Chaucer and, like Chaucer, responsible for the upgrading of literary English.[27] Yet Bale, misconstruing a reference by the chronicler Thomas Walsingham which names an 'Oklefe' as one of Wycliffe's followers, also gives the information that Hoccleve followed Berengarius's heretical teachings on transubstantiation. Simpson suggests that Bale wilfully conflated the two identities, Walsingham's heretic and our Privy Seal poet, for reasons of religious propaganda.[28] In Anthony Cade's

---

[23] George Sewell, *The Proclamation of Cupid: Or, A Defence of Women* (London, 1718), preface (no pagination). Sewell's attribution is discussed in Elon Lang, 'Thomas Hoccleve and the Poetics of Reading' (unpublished PhD dissertation, Washington University, 2010), pp. 209–12.

[24] *The Workes of our Ancient and Learned English Poet, Geffrey Chaucer, Newly Printed* (London, 1602), fols 320–1 (STC (2nd edn) 5080).

[25] Sir William Cornwallis, *Essayes of Certaine Paradoxes* (London, 1616), no pagination (STC (2nd edn) 5779).

[26] Bale's references to Hoccleve have been discussed by Nicholas Perkins, '"Heer Y die in thy presence": The Rewriting of Martyrs in and after Hoccleve', *Review of English Studies*, 69, issue 288 (2018), 13–31, at pp. 18–19.

[27] John Bale, *Scriptorum Illustrium Maioris Brytanniae Catalogus* (2 vols, Basel, 1557–59), vol. 1, p. 537. Bale's information about Hoccleve is summarised by Simpson, 'Annotated Critical Bibliography', vol. 1, pp. 91–2.

[28] Simpson, 'Annotated Critical Bibliography', vol. 1, pp. 8–9, 90.

Iustification of the Church of England (1630) Hoccleve has a counter-factual existence as university debater: 'Thomas Ocleue, maintained the doctrine of Wiclife and Berengarius, publikely in the schooles at Oxford, 1410'.[29]

While access to Hoccleve's works in print was limited, allowing errors like this to proliferate, it is clear that he continued to be read in manuscript, from which short extracts could be cited. The Tudor historian John Stow owned a copy of Hoccleve's *Regiment* and the Durham manuscript of the *Series*.[30] In the 1570 edition of his *Summarye of the Chronicles of Englande* entry for 1401, Stow quotes a single stanza of the *Regiment* (*RP* 532–9) which explains how England's dirty streets have no need of brooms because they are swept by the excessively voluminous sleeves of fashionable young men.[31] Stow quotes Hoccleve in order to make a similar point about supposed moral decline in Elizabethan England, where outrageous fashions are likewise preferred over the more moderate dress of more virtuous men. Stow's citing of Hoccleve as a historical source encouraged others to follow suit. The 1614 edition of William Camden's historical collection *Remaines Concerning Britain* plagiarises Stow's 1570 *Summarye* by citing, in a section on historical dress, 'Hoccliue [...] a master of that age' on the 'long pocketting sleeves' of Henry IV's reign (though omitting Hoccleve's apostrophe exhorting England to 'stande upright' (*RP* 537) and banish such luxury).[32] Later editions of Camden's *Remaines* published after 1623 have further material added, and, in the 1657 version, a much longer section of the *Regiment* (414–560) is given, attributed to Oxford, Bodleian Library MS Laud misc. 735 (identifiable via its former shelfmark K. 78 which is noted in the margin), a manuscript containing both the *Regiment* and the *Series*.[33] With donations to libraries by antiquarian manuscript collectors such as William Laud, Chancellor of Oxford University and Archbishop of Canterbury under Charles I, Hoccleve's works were available to those with access to the relevant libraries or who could acquire manuscript copies for themselves.

The poet Sir William Browne, for example, owned a copy of the *Regiment* (Oxford, Bodleian Library, MS Ashmole 40, which he read and annotated in detail) and also the Durham manuscript of the *Series*.[34] Having acquired

[29] Anthony Cade, *A Iustification of the Church of England* (London, 1630), p. 186 (STC (2nd edn) 4327).

[30] Burrow (ed.), *Complaint and Dialogue*, p. x; R. F. Green, 'Notes on Some Manuscripts of Hoccleve's *Regiment of Princes*', *British Library Journal*, 4 (1978), 37–41, at p. 41.

[31] John Stow, *A Summarye of the Chronicles of Englande* (London, 1570), fols 252r–v (STC (2nd edn) 23322).

[32] William Camden, *Remaines Concerning Britain* (London, 1614), pp. 234–5 (STC (2nd edn) 4522).

[33] William Camden, *Remaines Concerning Britain* (London, 1657), pp. 197–201. The manuscript source is identified in a marginal note on p. 197. R. W. Hunt, Falconer Madan and P. D. Record, *A Summary Catalogue of Western Manuscripts in the Bodleian Library* (7 vols, Oxford, 1895–1953), vol. 2, part 1, p. 64.

[34] Michelle O'Callaghan, *The 'Shepheard's Nation': Jacobean Spenserians and Early Stuart*

this holograph from Stow's library, Browne framed the entirety of the 'Tale of Jonathas' in a pastoral setting in his 1614 *Shepheards Pipe*.[35] Boyd Brogan has demonstrated the full extent of Browne's intertextual engagement with the whole of Hoccleve's *Series* in the *Shepheards Pipe*'s Second Eclogue.[36] It ends with a brief note that the tale is Hoccleve's and 'was neuer till now imprinted'. Browne tempts his readership with the thought that if Hoccleve's work proves attractive to them, he would be encouraged 'to publish the rest of his workes, being all perfect in my hands'. While this demand did not materialise, other antiquarians also made transcriptions from Hoccleve's work in manuscript. The Oxford scholar and librarian Richard James transcribed Hoccleve's 'To Sir John Oldcastle', spurred by his interest in the historical Oldcastle's links to Shakespeare's Falstaff.[37] James compiled a set of scholarly notes on Hoccleve's poem, very much in defence of Oldcastle as a proto-protestant but without much criticism of Hoccleve or his poem despite its own attacks on Oldcastle and Lollardy.[38] James also mentions Hoccleve in a Latin poem on the marriage of Charles I and Henrietta Maria in 1624. The lyric celebrates the alliance of France and Britain by reference to other poets who had already praised such a subject. Hoccleve's relevance is explained in a marginal note: 'Erat Chauceri discipulus et magno in libri desiderio fertur videndi regna Galliæ & Britanniæ firma pace vnita' (Hoccleve was a disciple of Chaucer and reveals in his books a strong desire to see the kingdoms of France and England bound together in a stable peace).[39] James refers to the pacifism of the concluding section of the *Regiment*, evidencing an independent reading of Hoccleve from the brief references available in print.

With antiquarian interest in his life and works ongoing, Hoccleve took his place in seventeenth- and eighteenth-century histories of poetry. *Theatrum Poetarum* (1675), compiled by Milton's nephew Edward Phillips, was an alphabetical list of mostly English poets. It records that Hoccleve was 'a very famous English Poet in his time', though his reputation is based on the passages in praise of Chaucer and his role in the preservation of the portrait of Chaucer: 'so much the more famous he is by being remember'd to have been the Disciple of the most fam'd Chaucer'.[40] The 'Life of Geoffrey

---

Political Culture, 1612–25 (Oxford, 2000), pp. 123–5.

[35] William Browne, *The Shepheards Pipe* (London, 1614), no pagination (STC (2nd edn) 3917).

[36] Boyd Brogan, '"Some Other Kind of Lore": Satire and Self-Governance in Spenserian Poetry', *Studies in Philology*, 114 (2017), 67–96.

[37] Richard James's Oldcastle transcription is discussed in more detail in Perkins, '"Heer Y die"'.

[38] Oxford, Bodleian Library, MS James 34. For a description, see *Summary Catalogue of Western Manuscripts*, vol. 2, part 2, p. 768. For an edition of James's transcription and notes, see *The Poems etc., of Richard James*, ed. A. B. Grosart (London, 1880), pp. 133–99.

[39] Anon., 'Spenser Allusions', *Studies in Philology*, 109 (2012), 353–530, at pp. 383–4.

[40] Edward Phillips, *Theatrum Poetarum, Or, A Compleat Collection of the Poets* (London, 1675), p. 233.

Chaucer' published in John Urry's 1721 edition of Chaucer's works gives a brief description of Hoccleve as Privy Seal clerk, follower of Chaucer, 'one of the politest Wits in England', Oxford alumnus and supposed Wycliffite, as well as a sophisticated reading of *L'epistre* as both 'a curious defence of, and at the same time an artful satyr upon women'.[41] Elizabeth Cooper's *Muses Library* (1737), the first published anthology of early English poetry, devotes a page to Hoccleve.[42] Cooper reports that she has not been able to achieve even 'a Sight' of Hoccleve's *Regiment*, though (presumably from a Chaucer edition) she gives lines 1958–72, the lament on Chaucer's death, which she calls 'tender and pathetick'. She gives an interesting account of Hoccleve's precarious yet potentially very favourable literary reputation in the first half of the eighteenth century: 'By some he is highly applauded, by others not so much as mention'd'. Hoccleve also takes his place in Thomas Tanner's *Bibliotheca Britannico-Hibernica*, an alphabetical Latin encyclopedia of British authors up to 1700, based on John Leland's unprinted *De scriptoribus* but much expanded and improved, which was published in 1748, thirteen years after Tanner's death. In his entry on our poet, Tanner follows Bale in praising Hoccleve and gives an extensive list of works and manuscripts, and (as Simpson shows) drew on his own reading of the *Regiment* for various details.[43]

In the second half of the century, there are further promising signs that Hoccleve was both being read and given his due place in Britain's literary history. Hoccleve is included in Pope's 1769 sketch for a literary history of English poetry, listed under the 'School of Chaucer', and also appears in Thomas Gray's notes towards a history of English poetry which Gray sent to Thomas Warton in April 1770, again in a list of poets who were influenced by Chaucer.[44] Warton thanked Gray for his notes, comparing them favourably with Pope's scheme which he had also been sent.[45] But Warton proved disastrous for Hoccleve's reputation: in his *History of English Poetry* (1774–81), Warton attacks Hoccleve mercilessly, calling him a 'feeble writer' on little evidence.[46] On the basis of the titles of some of his poems, Warton claims for Hoccleve a 'coldness of genius' (meaning his temperament and/

---

[41] *The Works of Geoffrey Chaucer*, ed. John Urry (London, 1721), in 'The Life of Geoffrey Chaucer' (no pagination).

[42] *The Muses Library; or a Series of English Poetry, from the Saxons, to the Reign of King Charles II*, ed. Elizabeth Cooper (London, 1737), p. 31.

[43] Thomas Tanner, *Bibliotheca Britannico-Hibernica* (London, 1748), p. 557. Tanner's entry is summarised in Simpson, 'Annotated Critical Bibliography', vol. 1, p. 94.

[44] Pope's plan is printed in Owen Ruffhead, *The Life of Alexander Pope, Esq.* (London, 1769), p. 425. For Gray's letter, see *The Works of Thomas Gray: In Verse and Prose*, ed. Edmund Gosse (4 vols, London, 1895), vol. 3, pp. 364–7.

[45] Warton's reply is printed in Alexander Chalmers, *The Works of the English Poets, from Chaucer to Cowper* (21 vols, London, 1810), vol. 18, p. 81.

[46] Thomas Warton, *The History of English Poetry* (4 vols, London, 1774–81), vol. 2, pp. 38–44, at p. 38.

or his creative power), likely to displease those who want 'invention and fancy' in their poetry.[47] Though he quotes several passages of the *Regiment*, he is dismissive of those medieval clerks (both Hoccleve and his sources) who 'presumed to dictate to kings' from the theoretical speculations of the cloister.[48] We might hope that Warton said such things because he had not really read Hoccleve, but his discussion of narratives from the *Gesta Romanorum* in volume 3 shows he had read the *Series* (from Oxford, Bodleian Library MS Selden Supra 53). He quotes several stanzas of the 'Tale of Jereslaus's Wife', though characteristically he claims that Hoccleve offers 'no sort of embellishment' to his source.[49]

Undeterred by Warton's low opinion of Hoccleve, in 1796 George Mason brought out the first printed edition of Hoccleve's poetry.[50] Mason offered a detailed and sympathetic introduction, plus notes and glossary accompanying the text of six hitherto unpublished poems (the *Male Regle*, the balade and roundel to Henry Somer and the poem on behalf of the Court of Good Company also addressed to him, the poem to Henry V beginning 'Victorious kyng', the poem to Carpenter and the poem addressed to Edward, duke of York).[51] Probably encouraged by Warton's low opinion, some of those who read Hoccleve in Mason's edition were dismissive, Joseph Ritson calling them poems of 'peculiar stupidity'.[52] By 1841, Isaac D'Israeli, in a book collecting together interesting vignettes of literary history, could give an account of disagreements among Hoccleve's readers, many following Warton's lines of attack but others (such as Sharon Turner in his *History of the Middle Ages*) finding that Hoccleve 'has not had his just share of reputation'.[53] D'Israeli calls Hoccleve a 'shrewd observer' of his society and a 'playful painter' of court life in *L'epistre*, though he follows Warton in claiming that he is 'bare of ornament' stylistically.[54]

Such verdicts might have condemned him to further criticism, but Hoccleve continued to catch the eye of readers in various ways. In September 1814, Wordsworth wrote to advise Robert Anderson, the editor of *A Complete Edition of the Poets of Great Britain* which had been published in 1792–95, on authors who could be included in a more comprehensive

---

[47] Warton, *History of English Poetry*, vol. 2, p. 38.

[48] Warton, *History of English Poetry*, vol. 2, p. 39. Warton quotes *RP* 2038–53, 2077–93, 2101–7 and 1958–74 (vol. 2, pp. 41–4).

[49] Warton, *History of English Poetry*, vol. 3, pp. lvi–lvii, lxxxiii–lxxxvi. Warton quotes *FIR* 1–7, 309–11, 337–54 and 365–78.

[50] On this first printed edition of Hoccleve's poetry, see J. A. Burrow, 'An Eighteenth-Century Edition of Hoccleve', in Geoffrey Lester (ed.), *Chaucer in Perspective: Middle English Essays in Honour of Norman Blake* (Sheffield, 1999), pp. 252–66.

[51] Mason (ed.), *Poems by Thomas Hoccleve, Never Before Printed*.

[52] Joseph Ritson, *Bibliographica Poetica* (London, 1802), pp. 60–3, at p. 63.

[53] Isaac D'Israeli, *Amenities of Literature* (3 vols, London, 1841), vol. 1, pp. 305–11, at p. 306.

[54] D'Israeli, *Amenities*, vol. 1, pp. 308, 310.

version. After suggestions relating to Skelton and Turberville, Hoccleve is first on a list of poets to add to a new edition.[55] Wordsworth's enthusiasm for Hoccleve might allow us to revive the question of whether he had read Hoccleve in manuscript, perhaps in Cambridge (a suggestion first made by Stephen Medcalf in 1981).[56] Wordsworth's 'Resolution and Independence' has a speaker preoccupied by 'Dim sadness, and blind thoughts' (28).[57] He wanders on the moor, worrying about many of Hoccleve's characteristic concerns – 'Solitude, pain of heart, distress, and poverty' (35) – which may afflict him in the future. He is particularly troubled by the thought of poets whose lives often end in 'despondency and madness' (49). He then meets a mysterious old man, who seems centuries old: 'The oldest man he seemed that ever wore grey hairs' (56). The resemblances are sometimes reworked rather than mirrored: here the speaker asks the old man about his occupation of leech-gathering, the reversal of the Old Man's teasing out of the details of Hoccleve's profession in the *Regiment*.

Wordsworth's poem, if it is in part a response to Hoccleve's works, is an uncertain and rare example of Hoccleve in the hands of later writers rather than in the pages of literary historians. Other creative responses to Hoccleve and his works are more recent, the product of his increasing presence (once Early English Text Society editions became available) on university syllabi and in anthologies of Middle English literature. The British poet Peter Reading, famed for his misanthropic and anti-romantic verse, quotes two lines of Hoccleve's mock praise of his 'grotesque lady' in his poem 'Prolonged Look'.[58] The poem's prolonged look is both the speaker's cruel gaze at the changing physical appearance of a woman he has known for a long time and his glance back to Hoccleve's fifteenth-century misogyny which might somehow excuse it. More benignly, the British author Barbara Pym invents a clergyman called Archdeacon Henry Hoccleve in her 1950 novel *Some Tame Gazelle*, a character who reappears in *Excellent Women* (1952).[59] A character who is himself fond of literary allusion, Archdeacon Hoccleve's long sermon about Judgment Day in the latter novel is, in Pym's description, full of subtle allusions to the *Series*.[60] 'Resolution and Independence', 'Prolonged Look' and Pym's novels each resurrect, however fleetingly and enigmatically, one facet of Hoccleve's many-sided life and literary works.

[55] Ernest De Selincourt, *The Letters of William and Dorothy Wordsworth* (6 vols, Oxford, 1935–39), vol. 3, pp. 151–5, at p. 153.

[56] Stephen Medcalf, 'Inner and Outer', in Stephen Medcalf (ed.), *The Later Middle Ages* (London, 1981), pp. 108–71, at pp. 135–40.

[57] *The Poems of William Wordsworth: Collected Reading Texts from the Cornell Wordsworth Series*, ed. Jared Curtis (3 vols, Tirril, 2011), vol. 1, pp. 624–8.

[58] Peter Reading, *Collected Poems. 1, Poems 1970–1984* (Newcastle upon Tyne, 1995), p. 88.

[59] Barbara Pym, *Some Tame Gazelle* (London, 2009).

[60] Barbara Pym, *Excellent Women* (London, 2006), p. 69.

Approaching Hoccleve Now

Warton's authority on early English poetry did, however, spawn a long-lasting strain of belittling criticism, first of Hoccleve as a poet and then increasingly as a man, which influenced readers and shaped criticism for many decades. Frederick J. Furnivall's *Dictionary of National Biography* entry from the last decade of the nineteenth century gave much information about Hoccleve's life and works, but also reported that he 'shows no sign of humour' and that the *Regiment* is 'very poor'.[61] In introductions to his EETS editions, Furnivall, though he conveyed much of Hoccleve's charm and interest, also carica-tured the poet as a 'weak, sensitive, look-on-the-worst side kind of man', a let-down by the standards of late Victorian masculinity, opinions oft cited in Hoccleve criticism even in recent decades.[62] It has proved hard for Hoccleve to shake off such scorn: Malcolm Richardson called him 'a bungler, misfit, and perpetual also-ran' in 1986, while John Bowers catalogued the extent of his supposed 'failure' in 2002.[63] In this volume, we have discouraged our contributors from following the now rather well-worn path, in which essays on Hoccleve and his works begin with a ritual recitation of earlier critical disparagement before offering something more positive. We hope that our readers are happy to approach Hoccleve without the critical baggage which Warton's estimation and Furnivall's commentary encouraged.

We also hope our readers will see this collection as an opportunity to reflect on what more might be said about Hoccleve's life and works in light of a range of new critical approaches. We agree with Larry Scanlon's assertion that 'Hoccleve has now been firmly installed in the Middle English canon. At the same time,' he went on to write, expressing a curiosity (if not anxiety) shared by a number of critics who had done so much to promote Hoccleve's work, 'with the waning of critical historicism, it will be inter-esting to see what the future holds, inasmuch as a substantial portion of his poetry has tracked so well with historicist concerns'.[64] We do not presume to claim that this volume provides a definitive account of the future of Hoccleve criticism from Scanlon's perspective or ours, but we hope that it illustrates the vibrancy of current conversations amongst Hoccleve scholars and their relationship to recent movements in the field of literary criticism more broadly. We believe the new approaches taken in each of these chapters reflect three broad developments that, according to Joseph North,

[61] F. J. F. [i.e., Frederick James Furnivall], 'Hoccleve or Occleve, Thomas', in Leslie Stephen and Sidney Lee (eds), *Dictionary of National Biography* (22 vols, Oxford, 1921–22), vol. 9, pp. 950–1, at p. 951.

[62] Furnivall and Gollancz (eds), *Hoccleve's Works*, p. xxxviii.

[63] Malcolm Richardson, 'Hoccleve in His Social Context', *Chaucer Review*, 20 (1986), 313–22, at p. 322; John M. Bowers, 'Thomas Hoccleve and the Politics of Tradition', *Chaucer Review*, 36 (2002), 352–69, at pp. 355–9.

[64] Scanlon, 'Nothing But Change and Variance', p. 523.

have arisen in the past two decades in response to the historicist/contextu-alist paradigm that dominated the discipline for a generation.[65]

The first of the developments North describes is the return to methods of analysis associated with formal or aesthetic concerns. Hoccleve's reputation as a poet has flourished as scholars have embraced the critical movement that Marjorie Levinson describes as New Formalism.[66] In retrospect, it is unsurprising that Hoccleve scholars would embrace a model that balances literary form and historical context. Although the only monograph devoted entirely to Hoccleve in the twentieth century – Jerome Mitchell's *Thomas Hoccleve: A Study in Early Fifteenth-Century English Poetic* (1968) – concentrated primarily on versification, many of the seminal articles and book chapters that shaped Hoccleve criticism in the latter decades of the twentieth century approached the narrator's persona (including questions of voice and genre) with a careful consideration of the specific circumstances in which Hoccleve was writing.[67] John Burrow's criticism, which exemplifies such a balance, has inspired subsequent scholars while his editions have furnished them with the tools needed to build upon the foundation he provided.[68] Burrow's research into Hoccleve's life and work has not only gifted contemporary scholars a concise biography but also a more nuanced understanding of how we might approach the autobi-ographical elements in Hoccleve's verse.[69] While Burrow provided more granular detail about the historical Hoccleve, critics like Richard Firth Green, A. C. Spearing, and D. C. Greetham considered anew his role in literary history.[70] As New Historicism reached the height of its influence, Paul Strohm and Lee Patterson turned to Hoccleve's texts as key witnesses to the social, political, and historical pressures that shaped them.[71] While

---

[65] Joseph North, *Literary Criticism: A Concise Political History* (Cambridge, MA, 2017), pp. 124–94.

[66] Marjorie Levinson, 'What Is New Formalism?', *Proceedings of the Modern Language Association*, 122 (2007), 558–69.

[67] Jerome Mitchell, *Thomas Hoccleve: A Study in Early Fifteenth-Century English Poetic* (Urbana, 1968).

[68] See especially John Burrow, 'Hoccleve's *Series*: Experience and Books', in R. F. Yeager (ed.) *Fifteenth-Century Studies: Recent Essays* (Hamden, CT, 1984), pp. 259–73; 'Hoccleve and the Middle French Poets', in Helen Cooper and Sally Mapstone (eds), *The Long Fifteenth Century: Essays for Douglas Gray* (Oxford, 1997), pp. 35–49; Burrow (ed.), *Complaint and Dialogue*; and Burrow and Doyle (eds), *Facsimile*.

[69] Burrow, *Thomas Hoccleve*. See also J. A. Burrow, 'Autobiographical Poetry in the Middle Ages: The Case of Thomas Hoccleve', *Proceedings of the British Academy*, 68 (1983), 389–412.

[70] Richard Firth Green, *Poets and Princepleasers: Literature and the English Court in the Late Middle Ages* (Toronto, 1980), esp. pp. 135–67; A. C. Spearing, *Medieval to Renaissance in English Poetry* (Cambridge, 1985), esp. pp. 110–20; D. C. Greetham, 'Self-Referential Artifacts: Hoccleve's Persona as a Literary Device', *Modern Philology*, 86 (1989), 242–51.

[71] Paul Strohm, *England's Empty Throne: Usurpation and the Language of Legitimation*,

Scanlon is right to acknowledge that the contemporary status of Hoccleve's texts is a result of his writing tracking so well with the historicist concerns of authors like Strohm and Patterson, historicist concerns also informed the critical practices that emerged in response to New Historicism and that continue to orient contemporary approaches to Hoccleve.

Formalist and Aesthetic Concerns

While Hoccleve criticism had never fully abandoned formalist and aesthetic concerns, the turn to New Formalism in Hoccleve studies is perhaps most clearly reflected in two books published by Ethan Knapp and Nicholas Perkins in 2001. These books, the first monographs devoted exclusively to Hoccleve since 1968, both re-imagined the relationship between Hoccleve's poetic forms and his historical circumstances.[72] What these books have in common with each other and with other contemporary criticism is that they aimed to deliver Hoccleve's works 'from the closures they have suffered through a combination of their impulses, their official receptions, and general processes of cultural absorption' by restoring them 'to their original, compositional complexity'.[73] From our contemporary perspective, it is clear that many of the essays written on Hoccleve in the past two decades have rehearsed his critical disparagement because their purpose was to use the methods now associated with New Formalism in order to demonstrate why his work had either been misrepresented or misunderstood by those critics who had belittled it. Taken as a whole, the scholarship undertaken in the past two decades has made a compelling case for leaving the antipathy to Hoccleve behind: it now seems evident that his work engages productively with his political and ecclesiastical circumstances, literary traditions as he understood them, and the material conditions of book production.[74] Just as importantly, it is now evident

---

1399–1422 (New Haven, 1998); Lee Patterson, '"What is me?": Self and Society in the Poetry of Thomas Hoccleve', *Studies in the Age of Chaucer*, 23 (2001), 437–72.

[72] Ethan Knapp, *The Bureaucratic Muse: Thomas Hoccleve and the Literature of Late Medieval England* (University Park, 2001); Nicholas Perkins, *Hoccleve's* Regiment of Princes: *Counsel and Constraint* (Cambridge, 2001).

[73] Levinson, 'What Is New Formalism?', p. 560.

[74] On the ecclesiastical context, see especially Vincent Gillespie, 'Chichele's Church: Vernacular Theology in England after Thomas Arundel', in Vincent Gillespie and Kantik Ghosh (eds), *After Arundel: Religious Writing in Fifteenth-Century England*, Medieval Church Studies, 21 (Turnhout, 2011), pp. 3–42; Robyn Malo, 'Penitential Discourse in Thomas Hoccleve's *Series*', *Studies in the Age of Chaucer*, 34 (2012), 277–305; and Sebastian Langdell, *Thomas Hoccleve: Religious Reform, Transnational Poetics, and the Invention of Chaucer* (Liverpool, 2018). On Hoccleve and literary tradition, see especially J. A. Burrow, 'Hoccleve and the Middle French Poets', in Helen Cooper and Sally Mapstone (eds), *The Long Fifteenth Century: Essays for Douglas Gray* (Oxford, 1997),

that the formal and aesthetic features of Hoccleve's verse have made and continue to make his account of mental illness especially compelling.[75] Through their extensive engagement with Hoccleve scholarship from the past two decades, the chapters in this volume testify eloquently to its vitality and significance.

The four chapters in this volume's first section analyse Hoccleve's poetry by establishing its organising principles at the level of the line, dialogue, and structures – both formal and generic – of the *Series* and the *Regiment of Princes*. In his chapter, Nicholas Myklebust focuses on one of the most fundamental aspects of poetic form, the line of verse, by historicising Hoccleve's metrical practice. As he writes, 'the problem of describing Hoccleve's metre is in fact an epiphenomenon of neglecting properly to historicise that metre and contextualise it within its own aesthetic and material moment' (3). Myklebust shows that the sophistication of Hoccleve's poetic line has long been misunderstood because those studying it have been more interested in explaining how it fails to measure up to other models than in providing an account that understands the principles on which it functions. A. Arwen Taylor draws on an approach established in the twentieth century – speech act theory – to articulate what the *Series* tells us about the limits of the complaint as a form of conversation as well as a legal and literary form. She argues that the texts that comprise the *Series* 'are linked by their interest in social dynamics of discourse' (3). Taylor's interest in the relationship between literary structure and social exchange is shared by R. D. Perry, whose chapter argues that 'the formal organising principle of the *Series* will move by means of the vagaries of human sociability, the chance encounter with acquaintances and the variable needs of companions and employers' (13). In the last chapter in the first section, Laurie Atkinson explores the difficulty of determining an organising principle in the *Regiment of Princes*, a poem that makes a 'deliberate formal gesture towards the tradition of dream poetry' but does not actually become a dream poem (22). What can an approach that

---

pp. 35–49; Eleanor Johnson, *Practicing Literary Theory in the Middle Ages: Ethics and the Mixed Form in Chaucer, Gower, Usk, and Hoccleve* (Chicago, 2013); and Langdell, *Thomas Hoccleve*. On Hoccleve and book production, see Linne R. Mooney, 'Some New Light on Thomas Hoccleve', *Studies in the Age of Chaucer*, 29 (2007), 293–340; Helen Killick, 'Thomas Hoccleve as Poet and Clerk' (unpublished PhD dissertation, University of York, 2010); Watt, *Making of Thomas Hoccleve's Series*; Critten, *Author, Scribe, and Book*; and Jane Griffiths, '"In Bookes Thus Writen I Fynde": Hoccleve's Self-Glossing in *The Regiment of Princes* and *The Series*', *Medium Ævum*, 86 (2017), 91–107.

[75] For examples of the changing approach to illness in the *Series*, see Penelope Doob, *Nebuchadnezzar's Children: Conventions of Madness* (New Haven, 1974); James Simpson, 'Madness and Texts: Hoccleve's *Series*', in Julia Boffey and Janet Cowan (eds), *Chaucer and Fifteenth-Century Poetry*, King's College London Medieval Studies, 5 (London, 1991), pp. 15–29; Marion Turner, 'Illness Narratives in the Later Middle Ages: Arderne, Chaucer, and Hoccleve', *Journal of Medieval and Early Modern Studies*, 46 (2016), 61–87.

attends to form, Atkinson asks, tell us about Hoccleve's invocation of genre in the *Regiment*? The essays of our first section demonstrate that Hoccleve employed organisational principles that can be reconstructed through careful attention to his deployment of metrical patterns, dialogic exchanges, and the relationship between formal and generic elements.

New Modes of Reading

The three chapters in our second section each focus on the *Series*, yet they also collectively draw attention to a second major development in literary criticism over the past two decades. According to Joseph North, a dissatisfaction with the historicist paradigm has led many critics 'to make proposals for new modes of reading' and to 'related developments in the study of affect'.[76] The exchanges between Hoccleve and his Friend in the *Series* are preoccupied with reading, and they even provide an account of the design of the text being changed to assuage women upset by their reading of Hoccleve's translation of Christine de Pizan's *Epistre au dieu d'amours*. The nature of Hoccleve's relationship to Christine's work has been the subject of ongoing debate, and its urgency has been renewed by Misty Schieberle's discovery that Hoccleve copied Christine's work in his own hand.[77] Michelle Ripplinger contributes to our understanding of the relationship between these two writers by reconsidering what the figure of the woman reader might have meant for Hoccleve and his readers. She argues that he 'inflects his representations of the woman reader with critical terms which were central to late medieval debates about the nature of interpretation and the ethics of representation, especially those of surface and depth' (2). The figure of the woman reader drawn from classical and patristic tradition was associated with overly literal textual interpretation. Yet, according to Ripplinger, this figure also allowed Hoccleve to express a different kind of anxiety as he worked through his ideas about the relationship between text and moralisation: 'what if there is nothing *but* surface?' (2). By inviting this question, Hoccleve asks readers to interrogate longstanding assumptions about reading practices, namely the idea that some texts only disclose their meaning to the most sophisticated of (male) readers. Historicist reading practices likewise often assume that texts only disclose their meaning to those willing to move beyond the literal. In this sense, then, Ripplinger's chapter invites us to compare the shift in reading practices of concern to Hoccleve and the shift that Eve Kosofsky Sedgwick encouraged in the early twenty-first century, a shift away from 'the methodological centrality of

---

[76] North, *Literary Criticism*, p. 125.
[77] Misty Schieberle, 'A New Hoccleve Literary Manuscript: The Trilingual Miscellany in London, British Library, MS Harley 219', *Review of English Studies*, 70, issue 297 (2019), 799–822.

suspicion to our current critical practice', which assumes that only expert readers can uncover textual meaning, to reparative reading practices, which are much more open-ended.[78] 'What we can best learn from such reparative reading practices are, perhaps,' Sedgwick writes, 'the many ways selves and communities succeed in extracting sustenance from the objects of a culture – even of a culture whose avowed desire has often been not to sustain them.'[79] Ripplinger's essay suggests that Hoccleve not only used the figure of women to explore his anxiety about changes in reading practices but that he also imagined fifteenth-century women reading in a way that was sustaining for them.

Reparative reading practices are associated closely with developments in the study of affect because they both acknowledge and encourage feeling as a legitimate way of responding to and thinking about texts. Hoccleve's embodiment of emotion was often seen as a flaw by twentieth-century critics, but Spencer Strub and Stephanie Trigg align themselves with other contemporary critics by considering it to be a distinctive feature. Strub argues that the *Series* repeatedly returns to 'the power and fragility of the voice' in an embodied sense, 'as they are instantiated in images of swelling and bursting' (1). Strub's chapter exemplifies the value of renewed attention to emotion as a response to reading at a time when the 'paths of identification running from reader to author to narrator to character' demand our attention, even though the experience might be unsettling (3). Trigg further explores the way that the sharing of unsettling feelings – in this case, about death – between readers, authors, and characters can help us to contemplate the formation of knowledge. In the part of the *Series* called 'Learn to Die', she writes, 'Hoccleve takes us from the Disciple's desire for knowledge to a dramatic rendition of the power of feeling, across a range of bodily and mental affects, and back and forth between four speakers' (1). Trigg's account of the scene of death draws attention to the way that feelings become significant – both meaningful and important – through dynamic social interactions. Her chapter thus works alongside other recent scholarship to show how Hoccleve's poetry is both enhanced by and enhances our understanding of contemporary approaches to affect and the history of emotion.[80]

---

[78] Eve Kosofsky Sedgwick, 'Paranoid Reading, Reparative Reading, or, You're So Paranoid, You Probably Think This Essay Is About You', in her *Touching Feeling: Affect, Pedagogy, Performativity* (Durham, NC, 2003), pp. 123–51, at p. 125 and pp. 150–1.

[79] Sedgwick, 'Paranoid Reading, Reparative Reading', at p. 125 and pp. 150–1.

[80] For related readings, see Amy Appleford, 'The Sea Ground and the London Street: The Ascetic Self in Julian of Norwich and Thomas Hoccleve', *Chaucer Review*, 51 (2016), 49–67; and Holly A. Crocker, 'Engendering Affect in Hoccleve's *Series*', in Glenn Burger and Holly A. Crocker (eds), *Medieval Affect, Feeling, and Emotion*, Cambridge Studies in Medieval Literature, 107 (Cambridge, 2019), pp. 70–89.

The Expansion of Conceptual Frames

The diverse approaches taken by the chapters in this volume's final section reveal some of the tensions underlying the third major development that North identifies: the expansion of conceptual frames that have come to be associated with disciplinary specialisation. On the one hand, these chapters show the value of what North calls the scholarly approach insofar as they employ the specialist literary practice of close reading to analyse evidence drawn from their author's extensive knowledge of Hoccleve's life and work. On the other hand, they also reveal their commitment to what North identifies as generalist criticism insofar as they are committed to moving beyond literary questions. Drawing on a flourishing critical tradition that connects Hoccleve's life as a writer to his writing of life, these chapters remind us that Hoccleve criticism has long engaged with specialist literary concerns while also asking what it means to study an author who constantly reminds readers of the dynamic relationship between his lived life and his literary, bureaucratic, and scribal work. In the first of these chapters, Taylor Cowdery sets the *Formulary* (a large collection of Privy Seal documents that Hoccleve collected near the end of his life) in conversation with the poet's life and poetry.[81] Cowdery argues that 'aspects of Hoccleve's realism – in particular, his self-presentation as an abject petitioner, his figuration of power in bureaucratic terms, and his depiction of setting – all have their corollary in the literary tropes of the Privy Seal office' (2–3). Moreover, he argues, the bureaucratic forms that Hoccleve used in his everyday writing informed the scope and scale of his attention: they can help us to understand both his literary forms and his everyday experience. Helen Hickey is likewise concerned with imagining Hoccleve's everyday experience of the world. Her chapter draws on Guillemette Bolens's concept of kinesic intelligence to explain how readers can use their own embodied experience to empathise with Hoccleve when responding to images of the body in motion. These two chapters share the formal concerns explored in this volume's first section, inviting readers to draw conclusions about Hoccleve's writing life as well as his poetic achievement. While their approach depends on their specialisation as literary scholars, these chapters also engage in what North calls generalist criticism when they suggest that we might gain greater insight into Hoccleve's experience of the world through their approach.

The final two chapters also connect their specialist literary approach, especially the practice of close reading, to concerns normally associated with generalist criticism. They are connected to each other insofar as

---

[81] On this tradition, see Burrow, 'Autobiographical Poetry in the Middle Ages', 389–412; Knapp, *Bureaucratic Muse*; A. C. Spearing, *Medieval Autographies: The 'I' of the Text* (Notre Dame, 2012); Sobecki, *Last Words*; and Sebastian Sobecki, 'MS Harley 219, the *Gesta Romanorum*, and Hoccleve's Poetics of Autobiography' (forthcoming).

they both identify the sacramental as an idea that permeates Hoccleve's poetic practice. Ruen-chuan Ma focuses his attention 'on Hoccleve's use of illumination, in both a codicological and spiritual sense, to curate literary legacy' (1–2), both Chaucer's and ultimately his own. Drawing on and contributing to the growing body of recent criticism that establishes strong connections between literary and material forms, Ma demonstrates that Hoccleve's experience of making books in late medieval London encouraged him to see 'the codex as a unique site of memorialisation through curation' (3), thanks especially to the practice of illumination and the imagery associated with it. Sebastian Langdell, on the other hand, argues that reading Hoccleve's minor works alongside his major ones (major in the sense that they are both longer and more widely-known) can illuminate the way that 'even the most seemingly secular production can be sacramentally infused' (2). This final chapter provides an apt conclusion for the volume as a whole insofar as it shows that there is still much to be gained by considering Hoccleve's work as a whole as a productive context for the study of individual poems. After all, the collection of his poems that he made at the end of his life reveals not only the range of his thematic and poetic concerns but also his capacity for curating a literary legacy which will allow later generations to read across and through his works.

It seems fitting that the approaches taken to Hoccleve in this book should reflect vibrant ongoing dialogues about Hoccleve as well as broader conversations in literary theory. His work is often explicitly or implicitly in dialogue with both English poets like Chaucer and Gower as well as continental writers like Ovid, Guillaume de Machaut, Eustace Deschamps, Henrich Suso, and Christine de Pizan (to name only a few). His two longest poems, the *Regiment of Princes* and the *Series*, employ dialogue as a structural principle and reflect aspects of his discussions with others about aspects of life and death in late medieval London. These dialogues seem especially intimate because they so often reflect his personal concerns, touching on the difficulty of acquiring writing material, of settling on suitable material for a patron, or on the possible responses of readers whom he assumes will be various. He recognises that his legacy will be determined by the way others respond to the words he has written in books, often in his own hand. The approaches reflected in this volume each grant those words at least some of the 'mercy and indulgence' (*RP* 5460) that Hoccleve asks for in the words from the compiler of the book at the end of the *Regiment of Princes*. The critical generosity exemplified by the approach of the chapters in this volume reflects developments in literary criticism more generally and Hoccleve studies in particular. While this volume aims to provide a sense of the range of approaches currently being taken in Hoccleve studies, we know it is not fully representative. That is a sign to us of the vibrancy of this field today. Ultimately, then, we hope that this volume will engage productively in a broader conversation about Hoccleve and the possibilities for expanding the geographical and temporal frames through which we read his work as we continue to ask what he might have to say to those who approach him now.

Part I

Form in Context

1

Historicising Hoccleve's Metre

Nicholas Myklebust

Since Frederick Furnivall edited Thomas Hoccleve's poems for the Early English Text Society in the final decade of the nineteenth century, historians of English metre have struggled to make sense of the poet's idiosyncratic repertoire of rhythms. For seven or eight lines at a time, the metre may scan identically to that of John Gower or Geoffrey Chaucer, with five offbeats strictly alternating with five beats to a count of ten syllables. That metre may then seem abruptly to abandon its template and briefly adopt something akin to the verse principles of *Pearl* or *Piers Plowman* only to shapeshift again to resemble nothing whatsoever in literature, English or otherwise. What logic one gleans from the metre can appear clumsy and haphazard, leaving an impression less of an organised system than a riddle of contradictory cues. Hoccleve's penchant for rhythms that both invoke and refuse comparison with other accentual-syllabic prosodies of the late fourteenth and early fifteenth centuries has long posed a unique problem: because Hoccleve's metre cannot persuasively be reconciled with any known metrical system, it must be allowed its own category. It is simply too much itself to be anything else. And yet that metre also seems to be too much of everything else to observe internally consistent verse principles or surpass mere pastiche. How then to proceed with a description of that metre when it offers both too little and too much?

One may reasonably reply that such a question fails to identify relative to what or whom Hoccleve's metre offers 'too little' or 'too much'. Is the metre primarily a species of Chaucer's decasyllable? Of Machaut's *vers de dix*? Of Marlowe's pentameter? As this essay will argue, the problem of describing Hoccleve's metre is in fact an epiphenomenon of neglecting properly to historicise that metre and contextualise it within its own aesthetic and material moment. Much of the confusion surrounding Hoccleve's metrical line issues not from the internal complexity of the line itself (complex though it is) but rather from diachronic narratives imposed on the metre anachronistically that situate it exclusively in positivist taxonomies that read Chaucer, for instance, as an antitype to all later types and late medieval English decasyllabic verse as prototypical pentameter. When one reads Hoccleve's metre synchronically relative to the aesthetic pressures and interests of the first decades of the fifteenth century, an alternative description emerges in which Hoccleve's metre is not confused or derelict – not an exemplum of late medieval decadence – but a logically consistent innovation on prosodic models circulating through Lancastrian metrical communities. Rather than a parrot's garbled imitation, Hoccleve's metre more accurately represents a well-formed sentence in an expanding conversation of voices. It is elastic; it is responsive to its interlocutors; and it is situational – that is, most intelligible in the context of its circumstance, in which poets writing after the death of Chaucer reorganised a single metrical grammar consisting of three constraints to produce varied and variable alternatives to Chaucer's and Gower's experiments in the English long line.

However, Hoccleve's metre cannot be uncoupled from the history of its critical reception, and any attempt to view the metre synchronically must first begin by surveying prior attempts to describe the metre diachronically as an interregnum in metrical progress ruled on one side by Chaucer and on the other by personalities such as George Gascoigne. And although scattered commentary on Hoccleve's metre appears before 1890, it was Furnivall who elected to judge that metre explicitly by the example of Chaucer and so catalysed a cascading series of negative reactions to Hoccleve's art. The poets were in close social and linguistic proximity, and Hoccleve not only appealed to the authority of Chaucer, but he also wrote thousands of lines concordant with Chaucer's decasyllable. For Furnivall, the decision to use Chaucer as a metrical yardstick must have been uncontroversial. Ten Brink had recently demonstrated the clarity and precision of Chaucer's verse, and as early as 1890, Chaucer offered something of an independent variable by which to control the analysis of dependent, minor poets.[1] When measured against Chaucer, Hoccleve's metre sounds starkly irregular with frequent runs of two weak syllables between beats and a clutter of adjacent, clashing stresses. As a result, Furnivall dismissed Hoccleve's versification as whimsical and undisciplined, a sentiment later echoed by George Saintsbury and adopted uncritically by generations of scholars predisposed to fit the square Hocclevean peg in the round Chaucerian hole.[2] M. C. Seymour offers a lucid survey of their collective odium: 'In the first half of the twentieth century [Hoccleve] is largely praised for his chattiness, damned for his false metre on indefensible grounds, and generally and patronisingly denied any competence in his craft.'[3] From these early appreciations came a predictable

---

[1] Bernhard Ten Brink, *Chaucers Sprache und Verkunst* (Strassburg, 1885), pp. 97–123.

[2] Frederick J. Furnivall (ed.), *Hoccleve's Works I. The Minor Poems*, EETS ES 61 (London, 1892), p. xli. Cf. Frederick J. Furnivall (ed.), *Hoccleve's Works III. The Regement of Princes*, EETS ES 72 (London, 1897), p. xvii; George Saintsbury, *A History of English Prosody from the Twelfth Century to the Present Day* (3 vols, New York, 1966), vol. 1, p. 144.

[3] M. C. Seymour (ed.), *Selections from Hoccleve* (Oxford, 1981), p. xix. Cf. Eleanor Hammond, *English Verse between Chaucer and Surrey* (Durham, NC, 1927), p. 55; H.

script: Hoccleve's metre fails to produce the patterns of its exemplar, and in botching his imitation, Hoccleve recklessly travestied Chaucer's invention and precipitated, with John Lydgate, fifteen decades of metrical desuetude.

A handful of recent perspectives have challenged this portrait by attending to features of Hoccleve's metre that may, in fact, show internal consistency. None of these readings, however, has succeeded either in producing a complete description of Hoccleve's metre or in adequately contextualising that metre in its historical moment. Seymour's characterisation of the metre as 'technically simple' ignores the stunning array of rhythmic combinations in Hoccleve's lines as well as their systematic exclusion of other, specific rhythms, an error repeated in Norman Davis's reasonable statement that Hoccleve's verse 'is generally the five-stress line' of an English decasyllable.[4] John Burrow and Judith Jefferson have worked assiduously from the holograph manuscripts only to conclude that although the metre is syllabically regular and painstaking in its management of final –e, the rhythm is nevertheless inconclusive, with a Gallic disinterest for the placement of the beat.[5] Such speculations offer no insight into the role stress plays in the metre and remain agnostic about the textual and historical significance of Hoccleve's accomplishment. More perniciously, they retain a misleading assumption from earlier, dismissive accounts of Hoccleve's metre that clouds rather than clarifies the principles of Hoccleve's art and prevents critics from historicising its practice: they presume the metre is an imitation that aims to duplicate precisely the metre of Chaucer; where it fails to do so, it is flawed.

Because these studies also take Chaucer's metre as the starting point of a tradition that grew inexorably into the verse of the Tudors rather than as one metre competing with many at a time when metrical customs had not yet been cast, they reinforce rather than erode our most durable assumptions about the supposed decline of late medieval English metre. In order not to rehearse this narrative of fifteenth-century collapse, it is imperative both to contextualise Hoccleve's metre with respect to the Chaucerian model he inherited and to situate the peculiar rhythms of his art among the art of his contemporaries, whose own innovations in the English

---

S. Bennett, *Chaucer and the Fifteenth Century* (Oxford, 1954), p. 150; Jerome Mitchell, *Thomas Hoccleve: A Study in Early Fifteenth-Century English Poetic* (Urbana, 1968), p. 97.

[4] Seymour (ed.), *Selections from Hoccleve*, p. xix; Norman Davis, 'Notes on Grammar and Spelling in the Fifteenth Century', in Douglas Gray (ed.), *The Oxford Book of Late Medieval Verse and Prose* (Oxford, 1985), p. 494. See also E. G. Stanley, 'Chaucer's Metre after Chaucer, I. Chaucer to Hoccleve', *Notes and Queries*, 234 (1989), 11–23.

[5] See J. A. Burrow, 'Hoccleve and Chaucer', in Ruth Morse and Barry Windeatt (eds), *Chaucer Traditions: Studies in Honour of Derek Brewer* (Cambridge, 1990), pp. 54–61, at pp. 54–6; Judith Jefferson, 'The Hoccleve Holographs and Hoccleve's Metrical Practice: More Than Counting Syllables?', *Parergon*, 18 (2000), 203–26; and J. A. Burrow, 'Scribal Mismetring', in A. J. Minnis (ed.), *Middle English Poetry: Texts and Traditions* (York, 2001), pp. 169–79.

decasyllable offer insight into a culture of competition with, not imitation of, Chaucer's metre.

Our confused reception of Hoccleve's verse stems not from its failure to replicate Chaucer's line but rather from its strategic revision of that line. Statistical study of the total Hoccleve corpus confirms that the poet practised a rigorously controlled program of matching strong syllables to strong metrical positions, precisely as Chaucer had done, but also incorporated licences from his contemporaries into his own verse to craft precisely the rhythms that troubled Furnivall, prompting him to mistake an elaboration on Chaucer's model for an ineptitude at copying it. Such rhythms, replete with clashing stress and double offbeats, or runs of two weak syllables between beats, conspicuously do not appear in Chaucer's line of alternating weaker and stronger syllables and speak to the influence of other early fifteenth-century treatments of the English decasyllable on Hoccleve's metrical style.

Tracing these prosodic figures from Hoccleve to their source in John Walton, canon of Osney, whose verse translation of Boethius in 1410 marks a watershed moment in the history of English prosody, reveals a counternarrative to the tale of hesitating, weak-willed poetasters populating a period of stale imitation.[6] In the synchronic interplay of fifteenth-century poets lies clear evidence of another history of late medieval English art, one that dispels the longstanding impatience with which critics regard Hoccleve's metre and falsifies any notion that its art is reducible to a stilted ventriloquism of Chaucer's voice. Indeed, a careful audit of Hoccleve's metre confirms, first, that metrical grammars operative in the early fifteenth century were at least as responsive to one another as to prior models, such as Chaucer's, with Hoccleve drawing on Walton's example as much as, or more than, Chaucer's, and, second, that signature rhythms shared between Walton and Hoccleve prefigure the modern iambic pentameter and testify to a profound innovation in medieval metre-making.[7]

The first step in any reconstruction of Hoccleve's metre, then, must be a description of the prosodic model on which he experimented and with which his own metre so commonly is mistaken: Chaucer's alternating decasyllable. The metrical template for Chaucer's ten-syllable, five-beat line is markedly spare: weak syllables alternate with strong syllables, with no more and no less than one weak position separating the metrical beats that fall on the line's even positions:

---

[6] On Walton's life and manuscripts, see Brian Donaghey, Irma Taavitsainen and Erik Miller, 'Walton's Boethius: From Manuscript to Print', *English Studies*, 5 (1999), 398–407.
[7] A metrical grammar consists of the total system of constraints and rules in a poet's prosody. These constraints and rules are ranked in a hierarchy from least to most violable, and the ranked constraints act as something of a sieve for the poetic output, determining which rhythms are well formed and which are ill formed.

```
x  /  x  /  x  /  x  /  x  /
```
The tendre croppes, and the yonge sunne (CT I.7)

Final *–e*, or schwa, a reduced vowel in Middle English phonology that often appears at the ends of words, keeps the line perceptually salient, or recognisable, by ensuring that the grammatical constituents most eligible to receive a beat occur at an ideal distance from one another, thereby minimising conditions that lead to beat subordination and loss, where adjacent strong syllables, for instance, may tempt a reader to hear four beats rather than five:

```
  x  /  x  /  x  /   x   x   /
```
*The tendre croppes, and the **yonge sunne**

↓

```
  x  /  x  /  x  /   x  /  x  /
```
The tendre croppes, and the **yonge** sunne[8]

When strong stresses occur in adjacent positions in the metrical line, readers may struggle to perceive them as distinct, stable prosodic units. Because *yonge* immediately precedes the noun *sunne*, despite its strong stress the adjective will be demoted from a beat to an offbeat:

```
  x  /  x  /  x  /   x   .   /
```
The tendre croppes, and the **yonge sunne**

An intervening offbeat clarifies the status of each stress as a beat by enhancing the contrast between weaker and stronger syllables. And because schwa represents the weakest possible syllable in late Middle English, it offers maximal contrast with both the preceding and the succeeding strong syllables, or beats, in the line:

```
  x  /  x  /  x  /   x  /  x  /
```
The tendre croppes, and the **yonge sunne**

From this use of schwa comes the clear, regular movement from weak to strong syllables in an alternating metre of ten syllables and five beats.

---

[8] In this formalism, an x represents a metrical offbeat; a / represents a metrical beat; an * represents an unmetrical line or ill-formed rhythm in the metrical grammar; and an → represents a reorganisation of the prosody and can be glossed as 'becomes' or 'turns into'. A . placed in the scansion indicates a heavy, stressed syllable that has been demoted from a beat to an offbeat. Such demotion naturally occurs in a clash following an inversion, in which the metrical beat moves from an even to an odd position in the line.

Chaucer's line owes much of its clarity to this strict refusal to disturb the alternation of weaker and stronger syllables, whether by placing two strong syllables next to each other in a potential clash, as in the first scansion, or by allowing two weak syllables, or offbeats, to run together, as in the second. In the example above, if the schwa on *yonge* is not counted, the line is unmetrical in Chaucer's grammar on account of the clash between *yonge* and *sunne*. By counting the schwa metrically and therefore preventing the clash, the line easily produces a well-formed rhythm. However, if schwa is not counted, and if the clash persists, the second strongly stressed word will subordinate the first and the line will lose a beat altogether. These conditions – adjacency of strong syllables and adjacency of weak syllables – equally threaten the movement from offbeat to beat, and both rely on schwa to act as a buffer between target syllables in the line, maintaining an optimal distance between its beats and rendering the rhythm effortless to parse. The boundaries between its units are unequivocal.

To preserve maximal contrasts between weaker and stronger syllables, Chaucer's metre blocks stress clashes and double offbeats; his metrical grammar prohibits anapests as well as trochees and spondees, and it naturally precludes their combination. (This constraint also governs the grammars of Gower and Lydgate.)

```
    x   /   x   /   x   /   x   /   x   /
Short was his gowne, with sleves longe and wyde (CT I.93)
    /   x   x   /   x   /   x   /   x   /
*Shorter his gowne, with sleves longe and wyde
  x   x   /   /   x   /   x   /   x   /
*In a short gowne, with sleves longe and wyde
    /   x   .     /   x   /   x   /   x   /
*Short the black gowne, with sleves longe and wyde
```

Chaucer's template overlaps considerably with Hoccleve's metre, which also promotes an even alternation between weaker and stronger syllables to a count of ten. However, a small, systematic set of differences confirms that the metres, despite common outputs, are not identical specimens, and this recognition of difference plays a crucial role in evaluating rhythmic licences. What may be expressive in one metre may be ungrammatical in another, even if both metres mostly tolerate the same sets of rhythms.

For instance, in order to determine whether or not Hoccleve and Chaucer share a metre, one must confirm that Chaucer's metre and Hoccleve's accept and exclude the same sets of rhythms. One metre will not tolerate rhythms that the other excludes, or if one metre does permit rhythms refused by the other, then the metres are different, even if their constraints substantially overlap.[9] Two metres may map to the same template; but it is important

---

[9]   This formulation is logically necessary to avoid the fallacy of the transposed

to note that what a line cannot do matters as much, or more, than what it can do. And although Hoccleve's line may tolerate every rhythm Chaucer wrote, Chaucer's line does not tolerate every rhythm Hoccleve wrote. Further, one can state that a rhythm is not tolerated if it fails to occur at all, fails to occur in a statistically significant distribution, or occurs in a distribution that can always plausibly be read in more than one way. For instance, although possible inversions arise in Chaucer's metre, none occurs in a context that can be read *only* as an inversion:

> x   /   x   /   x   /   x   / x   /
> Trouthe **and** honour, fredom and curteisie (*CT* I.46)
> /   x   /   x   /   x   /   x   /
> **Blesse** the hous from every wikkid wight (*CT* I.3484)

In the first instance, because the line begins with two monosyllables, and because *honour* may be stressed on either its first or its second syllable, the line is free to shift the beat to the coordinating conjunction; and in the second instance, apocope on schwa in *Blesse* renders the line headless. Whether one *should* scan the lines this way is not the point; rather, one always *can*. Nothing in the metrical line precludes such a reading. It is therefore not accurate to state that Chaucer's metre tolerates such inversions, whereas it is accurate to state that Hoccleve's does:

> / x x   /   /   x x   /   x   /
> Hadde beforn vexed my poore goost (*RP* 9)

To secure the tenth syllable – a requirement in Hoccleve's metre – final *-e* must be sounded on *Hadde*, ensuring an inversion. The schwa is not subject to apocope, as a headless line would count only nine syllables. In Hoccleve's metre, unlike in Chaucer's, such inverted rhythms, with a beat retracted to a weak metrical position, are common and unambiguous.

Still more dubious are instances of stress clash in Chaucer's metre, despite such lines as these from *Troilus and Criseyde*:

> For with **good hope** he gan fully assente (I.391)
> For of **good name** and wisdom and manere (I.880)

In both lines, a monosyllabic adjective immediately precedes a monosyllabic noun; under certain circumstances, such a construct may trigger a clash. However, it is just as possible that the beat will fall on the second preposition in the line, provoking a demotion on the adjective and placing beats on the second and fourth metrical syllables:

---

conditional, also known as confusion of the inverse, when comparing the orders of probability in a hypothesis and a data set.

```
    x   /   x    /  x  /  x/   x   /
For with good hope he gan fully assente
```

In such a case, whether the line tolerates a clash or triggers a demotion depends on the inclusion or exclusion of a related subset of rhythms: if the grammar tolerates double offbeats, then it also will tolerate a clash. (Indeed, one may plausibly claim the two rhythms are in a complementary distribution and therefore, like allophones or allomorphs, they are in fact realisations of a single underlying principle.) By contrast, if the grammar excludes double offbeats, it also will exclude clashes on the grounds that (1) a metrical pause is required to resolve the clash; (2) such a pause will group the preceding two offbeats together as constituents of a single metrical unit; and (3) this action will reorganise the line to include a triple rhythm. Indeed, in *Troilus and Criseyde* I.391, not only does the rhythm, if clashing, induce a double offbeat, but the metrical pause also adds an *implied* offbeat to the line, giving it eleven syllables and an excess of metrical content, a distribution nowhere attested in the work of Chaucer:

```
                    (x)
   x    x    /    P    /   x  /  x/  x   /
[For with good]    [hope]he gan fully assente
```

At first glance, beat subordination – the other solution to a clash – may sound artificial or stilted, especially to modern readers. However, because any monosyllable may carry a beat, as a metrical beat is distinct from phonological stress, and because Chaucer's grammar privileges alternation at the strictest level possible, when subordination can occur, it *will* occur, provided the demotion does not violate the rules of Middle English phonology.

Still less likely in Chaucer's verse is an inversion preceding a clash, combining the retracted beat of a trochee with the full stop of a spondee:

```
  /  x  .  /
*Ful of fals sterres heuene is alle alihte
```

Chaucer's inversions consistently coincide with monosyllabic strings in which the placement of the beat is variable, disyllables are licensed for stress shift, or inflected disyllables are eligible for apocopation, suggesting that Chaucer's verse excludes these rhythms and, further, indicating that despite the two metres operating from a template of ten syllables alternating in prominence from weak to strong, Chaucer's metre fails to permit two signature rhythms of Hoccleve's metre: double offbeats and clashing stress. In Chaucer's verse, the figures are too few or too prone to multiple interpretation to fall within a category of permissible rhythms.[10] Such comparisons raise important questions about the proper methods for reconstruction of historically remote metres that resemble each other and interact with and inform each other.

Comparing Chaucer's metre with Hoccleve's, one must ask how the former's exclusion of rhythms attested in the latter guides the reconstruction of either or both metrical templates. In particular, given the absence or consistently ambiguous presence of clashing or inverted rhythms in Chaucer's verse, how can one explain its resemblance to Hoccleve's? One promising approach identifies the constraints shared by the metrical systems and assigns a rank to each constraint.[11] In the cases of Chaucer and Hoccleve, one can infer the presence of three such constraints: an alternating constraint requiring that the line maintain a maximal contrast between weak and strong syllables; a syllabic constraint requiring a fixed number of syllables per line; and a boundary constraint requiring structural asymmetries between left and right edges of metrical cola, an intermediate level of prosodic structure between the syllable and the metrical line.[12] The first constraint ensures an output of lines that promotes maximal perceptual salience of beats and offbeats. The second enforces the number of constituents in a line capable of bearing a beat or an offbeat. And the third guarantees that the beginnings of metrical structures will be laxer than the endings. All three constraints will be present in both Chaucer's and Hoccleve's metres, but each metre will rank the constraints differently. Lower-ranked constraints will be more violable than higher-ranked constraints, and if occasions arise in which constraints are in conflict, the line will violate the lower-ranked constraint to preserve the higher-ranked constraint. Such a hypothesis accounts for the rhythms shared between Hoccleve and Chaucer as well as those tolerated only by Hoccleve.

---

[10] See Thomas Cable, 'Issues for a New History of English Prosody', in Donka Minkova and Robert Stockwell (eds), *Studies in the History of the English Language: A Millennial Perspective* (Berlin, 2003), pp. 125–52; Donka Minkova and Robert Stockwell, 'The Partial-Contact Origins of English Pentameter Verse: The Anglicization of an Italian Model', in Dieter Kastovsky and Arthur Mettinger (eds), *Language Contact in the History of English* (Bern, 2001), pp. 337–63.

[11] See Donka Minkova, 'Constraint Ranking in Middle English Stress Shifting', *English Language and Linguistics*, 1 (1997), 135–75; Chris Golston, 'Constraint-Based Metrics', *Natural Language and Linguistic Theory*, 16 (1998), 719–70.

[12] Cf. Bruce Hayes, *Metrical Stress Theory: Principles and Case Studies* (Chicago, 1995), pp. 13–47.

Table 1.1. Chaucer's constraint hierarchy.

	ALT	SYL	BND
Inversion	*!		
Clash	*!		
Double offbeat	*!		
Headless line		*	

Table 1.1 shows the hierarchy of constraints in Chaucer's metrical grammar by arranging the three constraints – alternating, syllabic, and boundary – from least violable to most violable moving from left to right. A star under a constraint indicates a violation. A star with an exclamation mark signals an ungrammatical violation, or a violation that the *metrical* grammar (rather than the linguistic grammar) cannot tolerate. Here a missing syllable at the beginning of the line causes no problem, as the grammar tolerates a violation of the syllabic constraint, which is ranked lower than the alternating constraint. However, a clash, inversion, or double offbeat is not permitted, as each violates the highest-ranked constraint. The ordering of constraints determines what rhythms are permissible in a metre and what are not. Meta-analysis of all major studies of Chaucer's metre since 1850 and collation of all metrical variants in the earliest six witnesses of the *Canterbury Tales* evidence a line in which the violation of lower constraints alters only the number of syllables in a line but does not obscure the optimal contrast between stronger and weaker syllables that gives the rhythm its clarity and legibility:

```
   /   x   /  x  /  x   /   x   /
Alle the days of povere men been wikke (CT IV.118)
  / x   x   /  x  /  x  /   x    /
*Alle the days of povere men been wikke
   x   /   x  /  x  /   x   /   x  /
Alle days of povere men been wikke, I rede
   /   /   x  /  x  /   x   /   x  /
*Alle days of povere men been wikke, I rede
```

A hierarchical ranking of constraints explains unique features of the Chaucerian style, such as its high incidence of headless lines but low incidence of broken-backed lines. In the former, the line deletes an offbeat at its beginning, and in the latter, the line deletes an offbeat in its middle. However, in the latter, deletion triggers a clash, violating the highest-ranked constraint in the hierarchy. Such a violation would be rare or non-existent. But in the former, offbeat deletion impairs the syllable count but does not affect the alternation of beats and offbeats, violating the second, lower-ranked constraint and not the first, highest-ranked constraint. Such a violation would be perfectly acceptable. One may therefore describe Chaucer's metrical template as a rigorously enforced alternating metre that permits violations of the syllable count subject to a distributional restriction ensuring all violations occur only at the beginning of the metrical line. Furthermore, no runs of successive weak syllables may occur, as these rhythms also violate the alternating constraint that governs the metrical grammar. In Chaucer's metre, there is only the elastic clockwork of a metronome variously paced to match different speeds of human speech.

By contrast, Table 1.2, the constraint hierarchy for Hoccleve's metre, shows that whereas violations of the alternating constraint are permissible, as that constraint ranks last among the three, a line lacking an initial weak syllable is not permissible, as it violates the highest-ranking, syllabic constraint:

Table 1.2. Hoccleve's constraint hierarchy.

	SYL	BND	ALT
Inversion			*
Clash			*
Double offbeat			*
Headless line	*!		

Because Hoccleve's metre, like Chaucer's, features both a syllable count of ten and a regular alternation of weaker and stronger syllables, and because these resources do not co-occur in English vernacular verse prior to Chaucer's decasyllables in the 1370s, one can assume that Hoccleve's metre derives from, even if it does not strictly imitate, Chaucer's. The question to ask, then, is not whether Hoccleve's metre and Chaucer's share common features; they do. Neither is the question how well or exhaustively the derived metre matches its donor, as any reconfiguration of constraints in the metrical grammar will provoke a mutation in the metrical genotype. Instead, precisely *how* does Hoccleve's metrical grammar adjust the ranking of those constraints also present in Chaucer's hierarchy? This question provides a clear basis on which to determine how the metres relate: what rhythms do they mutually tolerate and what rhythms do they differently exclude according to the ranking of common constraints? The set of excluded or non-overlapping rhythms offers a metrical profile for each poet, and that profile situates one poet's experiment in the context of the other's and allows for reconstructions that are historically contextualised.

When tested as a constraint hierarchy derived from Chaucer's, Hoccleve's metre becomes logical and consistent. Indeed, in appropriating Chaucer's metre, Hoccleve seems to have made only a very minor adjustment to the hierarchy; and yet this adjustment explains the extraordinary difference in the poets' styles. All metrical lines in the Hoccleve corpus follow logically from a single change to Chaucer's constraint hierarchy. Rather than placing an alternating constraint at the top, as the least violable principle, Hoccleve's metre demotes the constraint on maximal contrasts and promotes to the top of the hierarchy the syllabic constraint. As a result, Hoccleve's metre tolerates an entirely new and striking set of rhythms excluded by Chaucer and excludes a signature rhythm permitted by Chaucer: whereas a headless line may be perfectly acceptable in Chaucer's verse, it is flagrantly unmetrical in Hoccleve's. The first line of the *General Prologue*, then, for Hoccleve, is out of bounds:

```
  /   x   / x /   x   / x   /
Whan that April with his shoures soote (CT I.1)
```

Moreover, holograph evidence confirms Hoccleve intended every line to have ten syllables and that orthographic final –*e* must be sounded when it does not undergo elision, as before another vowel or h.[13] When orthographic –*e* does not meet the criteria for elision, it must be metrically counted, even if the resulting rhythm triggers an inversion:

```
 x   / x  /  / x / x  x    /
If that us list for to sue Thy grace (RP 739)
   / x  / x  x   /   x  /   x   /
Of his owne free wil and lust, that whan (RP 1152)
```

From these principles, one can deduce that non-alternating lines, as in an inversion, are real in Hoccleve's verse but also that they are entirely expected given the metre's re-ranking of the constraints inherited from Chaucer. Indeed, the syllabic constraint is so sensitive that even when a simple transposition in the line will produce a smoother rhythm, Hoccleve declines the option if the result threatens the syllable count:

```
   x  / x  /  x  /   x   / x  /
Yee make me and me putte atte werre (D 819)
   x   / x  /   x  / x  x  / x  /
*Yee make me and putte me atte werre
```

In the transposed construct, the orthographic –*e* on *putte* precedes a consonant and so cannot be apocopated according to the rules of Hoccleve's metre; being sounded, the schwa pushes the syllable count to eleven.

Because it is ranked lower than the syllabic constraint, the alternating constraint is more violable in Hoccleve's metre, and when a rhythm places

---

[13] See Burrow (ed.), *Complaint and Dialogue*, pp. xxxv–lv; and John Bowers, 'Hoccleve's Huntington Holographs: The First "Collected Poems" in English', *Fifteenth-Century Studies*, 15 (1989), 27–51.

the two constraints in conflict, the higher ranked of the two prevails. It is no surprise, then, that every line in Hoccleve's corpus contains ten syllables but only most lines are strictly alternating. The lower-ranked alternating constraint may fail and the verse remain metrical, as in the example above, or in the following line in the *Regiment of Princes*:

```
    x   /   /   x   /  x   x   /    x   /
And pees, sore is meeved therwith; but we (5319)
```

Here an inversion precedes yet another inversion, triggering a double offbeat and rendering the line impossible to scan as an instance of Chaucer's metre. The inversion and double offbeat both are sanctioned as long as they cause the line neither to exceed a count of ten syllables nor to shrink or swell the number of beats in a line beyond five. Of course, this is not the case in Chaucer's metre, where no violation of the alternating constraint is permitted. But despite being ranked below the syllabic constraint in Hoccleve's metre, alternation is no less a requirement and therefore no less a part of the line. The poems may furnish us with rhythms that sound rather more Miltonic than Chaucerian, but that, of course, is the point: Hoccleve's metre is not Chaucer's; it is a competitor that strategically reorganises the rules of an inherited form to make its art both different and differently possible.

And although Hoccleve's strategy targets a precise mechanism in Chaucer's metre and modifies that mechanism only slightly, demoting alternation and promoting the syllable count, one should not infer that the consequences of this reorganisation are minor or superficial. It is not as though Hoccleve's re-ranking of constraints resembles the mere rearrangement of objects in a still life painting. On the contrary, Hoccleve's experiment approximates a new approach to perspective itself. The constraints are closer to, say, colour and plane – the building blocks of a representation of space – than to any coordination of objects in that space. In a line of accentual-syllabic verse, one may think of syllable count and the placement of beats as fundamental axioms of the logical order of rhythm. One may focus primarily on the count, in which case irregular-ities in the placement of beats may surface as local flourishes; or one may focus primarily on the placement of the beats, in which case a playfulness with the syllable count will serve as an expressive resource. Every line will have both constraints, just as every painting will include at least one colour and its plane, but priority given to one or the other distinguishes a Rothko from a Pollock or a Picasso from a Dali. The strictly alternating rhythms of Chaucer's verse issue from the poet's adoption of maximal contrast as the single most important feature of his rhythm. But rather than use beat to control variations in syllable count, as Chaucer had done, Hoccleve reversed the order, using consistency in the count of syllables to control rhythmic variation. In this respect, Hoccleve's metre may strike its reader as somewhat French. John Burrow describes it as 'careful [...] about the syllable count' but with 'uncertain' rhythms.[14] Because he dismisses the possibility that Hoccleve's verse may follow strict rules concerning the distribution of stressed syllables and metrical beats – rules, as it happens, that follow naturally from a demotion of the alternating constraint in Chaucer's template – Burrow insists that there can be little doubt that the 'general metrical rule for Hoccleve, as for his French contemporaries, concerned the number of syllables, not the distribution of stresses'.[15]

The presence of an alternating constraint in Hoccleve's metrical grammar contradicts this claim. Indeed, double offbeats and clashing stress could not consistently co-occur in lines of five beats in Hoccleve's poetry *unless* the verse prioritised both the number of syllables and their organisation into alternating offbeats and beats. With no constraint on the distribution of stress, for instance, the verse could not rule out swathes of four-beat lines mixing freely with five-beat lines – a pattern that does not occur.

Subtler still, Hoccleve's verse deploys a radical inversion, or a retracted beat immediately preceding a stress clash in the same metrical colon:

/   x   .   /   / x   x   /   x   /
Stonde in hard plyt. Sone, be waar, rede I (*RP* 1733)

The signature fall-and-full-stop movement of a radical inversion is utterly without precedent in the metres of Chaucer and Gower. Moreover, later poets, such as Lydgate, who also rank the alternating constraint above the syllabic constraint, as Chaucer did, excluded these radical inversions from their lines and, despite their own distinctive contributions to English prosody, these poets did not capitalise on the aesthetic potential of a retracted beat followed by a clash. It is not until Sidney, in fact, a century and a half later, that the figure resurfaces in English poetry:

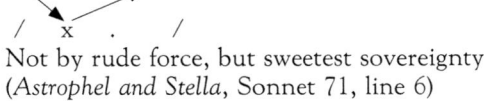

/   x   .   /
Not by rude force, but sweetest sovereignty
(*Astrophel and Stella*, Sonnet 71, line 6)

Not only do such figures require a constraint on the distribution of stresses in the line, so that the clash occurs at the rightmost boundary of a metrical colon (confirming such a constraint is active in Hoccleve's metre), but such figures are unattested in the verse of every poet of the period with one exception: John Walton, whose *De consolatione philosophiae* dates to 1410,

---

[14] J. A. Burrow, 'Hoccleve and the Middle French Poets', in Helen Cooper and Sally Mapstone (eds), *The Long Fifteenth Century: Essays for Douglas Gray* (Oxford, 1997), p. 38.
[15] Burrow (ed.), *Complaint and Dialogue*, p. xxvii.

the *terminus post quem* for Hoccleve's *Regiment of Princes*.[16] Moreover, only John Walton seems to have licensed double offbeats and clashes to occur individually as well, as the metrical grammars of Gower, Chaucer, and Lydgate all proscribe against these rhythms both isolated and combined.

What, then, is the relationship of Walton's verse to Hoccleve's? Did Hoccleve read some circulated manuscript of Walton's translation and merge its style with his? Did the poets stumble independently upon the same innovation in a case of convergent evolution? There is no direct evidence in the provenance of the manuscripts to confirm the first hypothesis, however likely it may be. Several of the earliest manuscripts of Walton's poem were owned by various families in London during Hoccleve's lifetime, and the scribe of Cambridge, Fitzwilliam Museum, MS McLean 184, who copied both *De consolatione* and the *Regiment*, seems to have ascribed authorship of both poems to one person, albeit an anonymous author, owing to their similarities of style.[17] However, even the second hypothesis of convergent evolution relies on tacit or intuitive, if not explicit, knowledge shared by members of a metrical culture. Such tacit knowledge would be all the more expedient in Hoccleve's case, for although Hoccleve's metrical grammar does not prevent rhythms such as radical inversions from occurring, neither does it readily facilitate them. By ranking the syllabic constraint above the boundary constraint, Hoccleve's metre weakens the role of the metrical colon, or the intermediate level of structure between the syllable and the line. Located between the tactile percept of the syllable and the abstract, intellectual construct of the line, the colon offers a boundary marker and resource for rhythms such as radical inversions. In such rhythms, a displaced beat threatens the clarity of the line itself; to restore the line's clarity, the colon effects an alignment to match the reorganised sequence of beats and syllables with the template on which readers rely to identify the line correctly as an instance of a given verse design. Such rhythms as radical inversions tend not to occur organically in weak cola, and it is therefore likelier that Hoccleve first encountered the robust, angular rhythms elsewhere and rigged them to his rather liquid metre than that Hoccleve engineered them himself without the benefit of example.

Whatever the case, and however Hoccleve came upon his discovery, double offbeats and stress clashes are conspicuously rare in Hoccleve's works prior to 1410, which antedate 81.3 per cent of these rhythms; and no instance of a radical inversion – Walton's signature – appears anywhere in

---

[16] Scholars date the poem by its references to John Badby's burning in March of 1410 and its dedication to Prince Henry, who became king on 21 March 1413. Documents from the Exchequer confirming payment owed to Hoccleve for his work as a clerk in the Privy Seal office place the latest possible date at 1411.

[17] Mark Science (ed.), *Boethius: De consolatione philosophiae*, EETS OS 170 (London, 1927), p. xiii; Noel Kaylor, 'John Walton's 1410 Verse Translation of the *De consolatione philosophiae* in the Context of Its Medieval Tradition', *Fifteenth-Century Studies*, 6 (1983), 121–48; and Donaghey et al., 'Walton's Boethius'.

Hoccleve's verse prior to the circulation of Walton's manuscripts in London in 1410. In Hoccleve's *L'epistre de Cupide*, several lines contain either a double offbeat or a clash, for instance, and such lines mark a departure from Chaucer's and Gower's decasyllable:

<pre>
          /   /
And with good herte sette hem in the weye (47)[18]
  /   x x   /
Shewe me grace, and I shal euere be (30)
</pre>

And yet none combines them:

<pre>
  /   x   .   /
*Shewe good herte, and I shal euere be
</pre>

After the *Regiment*, however, one sees a marked increase in both triple rhythms and clashes and the first radical inversions:

<pre>
  /   x   .   /   x   /   x / x /
Senek saith how the kyng Antigone (RP 3536)
    x   . / / x   x /   x   /
Sore wole it trouble myn innocence (D 326)
   / x   .   / x   /   x /   x /
Of the world, vertu gooth so faste abak (LTD 570)
</pre>

Not only does the incidence of radical inversion rise sharply after 1410, but distribution of the figure through Hoccleve's line also becomes more flagrant, with adjacent beats obstinately housed in non-overlapping intonational phrases, as in line 570 of 'Learn to Die'; function words placed in the fourth metrical position to attract a beat despite functioning as an enclitic to a host, as in line 326 of the 'Dialogue', or as the proclitic of a new phonological phrase, as in line 3536 of the *Regiment*; and, most intrusive, three consecutive strong stresses, with two beats and a third beat demoted to an offbeat, straddling two phonological phrases, as in line 570 of 'Learn to Die'.

It would therefore seem that after 1410, Hoccleve's line increasingly absorbs rhythms characteristic of Walton's *De consolatione*, although, it

---

[18] One may reasonably scan this line with a retracted beat instead of a clash, as in the case of Chaucer's 'For with good hope he gan fully assente' (*TC* I.391). Indeed, the syntactic structure of the sentences preceding the clash is nearly identical. However, more important than the possibility of an alternative scansion in Hoccleve's case is the possibility of the scansion indicating a clash; either is appropriate for Hoccleve whereas only the former is permissible for Chaucer. Moreover, lines such as line 326 of the 'Dialogue' demonstrate that Hoccleve undoubtedly did write lines with clashing stress, and these clashing rhythms overwhelmingly occur precisely in the position of 'good herte' in *L'epistre de Cupide* line 47 – that is, in the third and fourth, or else in the fourth and fifth, metrical positions in the line.

is important to note, Hoccleve never risks imitation. His style remains characteristically his own: purposefully halting. For instance, although the incidence of inversion nearly doubles in a span of ten years, the style of the inversions also changes. In poems preceding the *Regiment*, inversions align with the beginning of an intonational phrase:

```
        /   x   x  / x  / x   / x   /
IP | | [Lordes reconforten in sundry wyse] (MR 336)
        /   x   x   /   x  / x  / x /
IP | | [Wikkid and feers and ful of crueltee] (L'epistre 153)
```

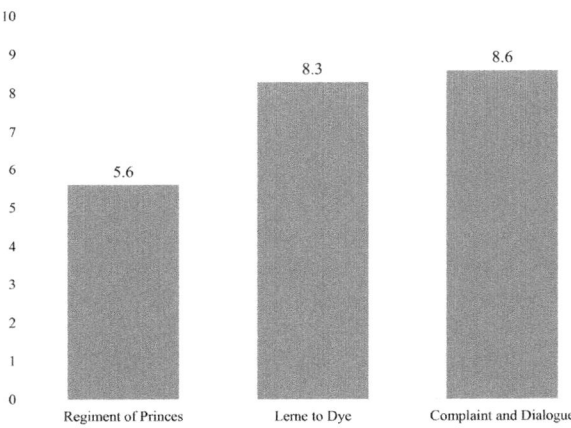

Figure 1.1. Incidence of inversion per 100 lines in
Hoccleve's verse.

Beginning with the *Regiment*, and continuing to the end of Hoccleve's career, inversions migrate away from phrasal boundaries, or else they align with boundaries lower on the prosodic hierarchy, such as the clitic group, where the cues for parsing the line's structure are finer and more fragile:

```
   x   /  x   /  /   x   /   x   x   /
And thogh it hem pynche sharply and sese (C 346)
   /   x  /  x  x/  x  /  x   /
And or asshen into hir eerthe also (LTD 855)
```

This later style of inversion diverges noticeably from Walton's, which is much less prepared to abandon alignment with phrasal boundaries. Nevertheless, the strong correlation between higher incidence of inversion in Hoccleve's work and the introduction of Walton's translation suggests, if nothing else, that Hoccleve capitalised on a metrical form that had no precedent in Chaucer or Gower and, through Walton, served as an expedient prosodic emblem of Boethian meditation.

Where did these figures come from, and why did Hoccleve adopt them, with increasing confidence, as a signature licence of his metrical style? In the case of Walton, the circumstances seem clear. Where Chaucer used grammatical options to avoid stress clashes, Walton expanded the role of apocope to provoke them, erasing the buffer between strong stresses (i.e. final –e) and collapsing the distance between those stresses, stimulating a clash. For instance, where Chaucer inflects the weak adjective in order to separate adjacent strong syllables, Walton often refuses the inflection: with each syllable in the figure increasing in prominence, the line establishes a rising rhythm that peaks on the fourth syllable of the metrical cadence:

And broght my blisse **and my bone cheefe** all bace (I.8)[19]

Because clashes and inversions both violate the alternating principle Chaucer ranked at the top of his constraint hierarchy, one does not find them in his poetry. However, a mere thirty-five lines into the prologue of the first book of *De consolatione*, these figures not only appear; they also combine to form a radical inversion, the most marked and jarring rhythm available to an early fifteenth-century poet. Furthermore, Walton neatly forestalls any alternative scansion of the line that would mollify the disturbance: syncope of the middle vowel of *Antecrist* is not possible; there are no final vowels to apocopate; and the word is emphatically not a candidate for stress shift:

/ x . /
Antecrist will pursue þeym þerfore (Prologue 35)

Walton crafts an even more disruptive form of radical inversion in Book IV that has no analogue in Hoccleve's verse prior to 1410 but appears later in 'Learn to Die':

/ x . / x / x / x /
Well and ground, bothe lord and kyng is he (IV.1471)
/ x . / x / x / x /
Of the world, vertu gooth so faste abak (*LTD* 570)

---

[19] All citations of Walton are from Science (ed.), *Boethius: De consolatione philosophiae* (Oxford, 1927).

Walton's handling of plural adjectives throughout the poem confirms that the schwa on *bothe* is sounded, presenting a problem for the alternating constraint, with three syllables crowded into one intonational phrase and the final seven syllables housed in another. Ordinarily this division would not be a problem, but the stressed monosyllable *ground*, in a weak position, struggles fully to subordinate to the following strong stress, because that beat lies in a different phrase:

Well and ground, bothe lord and kyng is he

The phrasal boundary falls between two strong beats (*ground* and *bothe*), preventing the reader from cleanly subordinating *ground* to the following stress. However, by bracketing the syllables, readers can oppose the line's metrical structure to its prosodic structure:

```
     /   x    .      /   x  /  x  /  x  /    scansion
[[[Well and] [ground, both]] [[e lord] [and kyng] [is he]]]  bracketing
  |_____|        |_____|   prosody
```

No other metrical text of the period warrants this repair strategy, as no other text presents such a baroque rhythm. It is remarkable, then, to find precisely this rhythm, with precisely the same repair strategy, in Hoccleve's 'Learn to Die'. Mutual discovery of such a rhythm is possible, if unlikely; mutual deployment of that rhythm across intonational phrase boundaries to provoke an unprecedented style of readerly problem-solving is possible only in the mathematical sense.

A similar improbability concerns radical inversions immediately followed by a retracted beat and a double offbeat:

```
     /   x    .     /   /  x  x  /  x  /
Stonde in hard plyt. Sone, be waar, rede I (RP 1733)
   /  x    .     /   /  x  x  /  x  /
Putteth false hope out of youre hertes clene (DCP I.327)
```

To modern ears, these lines sound canonical. The rhythms are not difficult to parse, and poets as diverse as Shakespeare and Shelley have used them. They are typical effects in a line of iambic pentameter. But Chaucer, Gower, and Lydgate did not write in iambic pentameter; they wrote in iambic decasyllables, metres that sound and look alike but differ in their ranking of constraints.

Table 1.3. Walton's constraint hierarchy

	BND	ALT	SYL
Inversion		*	
Clash		*	
Double offbeat		*	
Headless line			*

Because the alternating constraint is demoted, the metre permits clashes, inversions, and double offbeats, as does Hoccleve's. However, because the alternating constraint here outranks the syllabic constraint, Walton's metre also permits headless lines, as Chaucer's metre does but Hoccleve's does not.

The critical trigger for these rhythms – again a device only rarely exploited by Hoccleve prior to 1410 – is apocope. In both Walton's 'Putteth **false** hope out of youre hertes clene' and Hoccleve's '**Stonde** in hard plyt. Sone, be waar, rede I', an orthographical –e licensed by the poet's phonological grammar must be cut from the metrical count. The rising cadences so typical of Walton's heavy line, and, for that matter, Sidney's, also require liberal apocopation of inflectional and etymological schwa:

And when þe prou**ince þat highte Cam**panye (I.417)
These ben lo cau**ses of right grete** vigour (I.941)
And some men wenen þat þis question (V.222)
And ma**ny a pore man** and anguyschous (I.403)

Striking final –e on the plural adjective *some* in V.222 establishes a rising cadence that peaks on the first syllable of the verb, whereas apocope on *pore* in I.403 induces a metrical pause between the second and third beats in the line: 'And many a **pore [P] man** and anguyschous': In Walton's verse, 1.5 per cent of lines contain at least one of these rhythmic figures, all excluded from Chaucer's metre and all permitted in Hoccleve's.

Like Hoccleve, Walton followed Chaucer in observing strict grammatical fidelity in the use of final –e and, in particular, in exploiting the weak adjective as a metrical resource: 'And certaynly þe **firste** þing it esse' (I.639). Walton's treatment of the weak adjective, however, is not an exception but a rule in his generally conservative approach to final –e in late Middle English grammar, preserving, for instance, word-final schwa on weak verbs in the first person singular past tense (as in '"Lo of this forseid good?" I **seide**, "ʒys"', III.149) as well as on plural *ja*-stem adjectives and weak feminine nouns, all features of both Chaucer's and Hoccleve's fastidious grammatical systems:

Vntrewe names of þinges for to witen (II.1011)
And so his herte was right wel y-esid (IV.1640)

Where schwa occurs in Walton's poem, then, it is always licensed. But unlike both Hoccleve and Chaucer, Walton's metre liberally apocopates, with 70 per cent of all cases of final *-e* unsounded. By contrast, Chaucer's metre apocopates in approximately 50 per cent of cases. Higher rates of apocope in the metre cultivate the conditions for stress clash, particularly in a weak adjective, where Walton eliminates schwa in 13 per cent of cases compared with Chaucer's 3.5 per cent in the Hengwrt manuscript of the *Canterbury Tales*. In fact, the different attitudes of Hoccleve and Walton toward apocope offer additional indirect evidence for the hypothesis that Hoccleve, in 1410 or 1411, may have read a manuscript of *De consolatione*. Hoccleve's grammatical wariness ensures that he and Walton, had they independently created radical inversion, would have appealed to very nearly contrary metrical principles in order to do so. Because of his requirement that no line contain fewer than ten syllables, Hoccleve treated inflections with a prescriptive flair: if the grammar permits them, and if the orthography indicates them, the metre must count them. Walton, by contrast, freely leveraged inflectional decay as a resource to be recruited rather than a corruption to be contained. In fact, the prosodic heft of his slow, muscular line issues from an exaggerated use of apocope to curate metrical conditions maximally amenable to stress clash.

Whether independently engineered by Walton and Hoccleve or reciprocally appropriated, these rhythmic devices speak to a metrical culture of bold experiment and careful attention in the first decades of the fifteenth century in England – indeed, a market of exchange values in which the revision of prior and contemporary metrical models served as a proxy capital for vernacular authors in competition for increasingly subtle and complex formal codes. Hoccleve's metre evolved in response to ecological pressures in a cultural niche. A notable pressure, of course, came from the example and authority of Chaucer. Another, less conspicuous pressure came from Walton, an unwitting collaborator in the invention of the post-Chaucerian Boethian begging poem. Metrically intelligent poets like Hoccleve and Walton, free merely to approximate other metres, seized on overlapping formal cues and used each poet's own radical equivocation against him to rewrite the decasyllable according to their own interests. The constraints that defined the decasyllable lay at the nexus of those linguistic features that were, in the act of writing, already, or else fast becoming, obsolete and yet still acceptable in formal literary contexts, in which case Hoccleve's revisions of other metres seem less intractable than inevitable. By tampering with competing models, Hoccleve crafted a signature practice of re-scripting grammatical relics in order, paradoxically, to foreground his own modernity and to inscribe in the echo-effect of their metres a competition disguised as petition. As Ethan Knapp explains, 'the cultural energy for this revision stems from Hoccleve's partisan membership in a new, emergent class of secularised bureaucrats. It stems also from the world of textual production they inhabited, not the court of love but the court of chancery', where texts are 'neither initially the product, nor in the end, the responsibility of any one author'.[20] It is somewhat ironic, then, that efforts to understand Hoccleve's art – to reconstruct its particular logic – place such authority on the holograph manuscripts, as though they, in some exemption from the processes of textual production, offer critics precisely the singular product and sole responsibility refused by the bureaucratic culture of Hoccleve's own world.

From the holographs – lures of definiteness that they are – one can deduce that each line of Hoccleve's metre will have ten syllables; that a written final -e will be sounded and therefore metrical unless conditions for elision are met; and that, in the manner of the *vers de dix*, the line will culminate in a phrasal accent. These are good and necessary deductions, but they do not tell the inner life of the metre because they fail properly to historicise it. How does the line populate that count as it moves toward culminative accent? The poems themselves flatly contradict the claim that Hoccleve 'tended to let the rhythms within his lines look after themselves, as the French did', or that the distribution of beats is normative and nothing more.[21] But the holographs cannot move reconstruction beyond their own textual limitations. Instead, one must look to the synchronic plane of Hoccleve's own culture of mutual exchange. The periphery must move outward to encompass the orbits of other influences rather than collapse further into the authority and end of the author's autograph.[22]

[20] Ethan Knapp, *The Bureaucratic Muse: Thomas Hoccleve and the Literature of Late Medieval England* (University Park, 2001), p. 42. See also J. A. Burrow, 'The Poet as Petitioner', *Studies in the Age of Chaucer*, 3 (1981), 61–75.

[21] Martin J. Duffell, '"The Craft so Long to Lerne": Chaucer's Invention of the Iambic Pentameter', *Chaucer Review*, 34 (2000), 269–88, at p. 284.

[22] Cf. John Bowers, 'Hoccleve's Two Copies of *Lerne to Dye*: Implications for Textual Critics', *Papers of the Bibliographical Society of America*, 83 (1989), 437–72.

2

Speech Acts and Conversation in the Series

A. Arwen Taylor

Hoccleve's *Series* is not an obviously unified work. Its elements represent a variety of genres and the structure of the whole – in keeping with its title – depends largely on its sequence. The texts are not an anthology that could be easily re-ordered, but a set of poems arranged into a coherent sequence via the framing narrative that is also, at times, a part of the collection. Indeed, when the name 'Series' was first attached to the text in print by E. P. Hammond, it was given as a description used 'for convenience' rather than a clear attempt to title this 'partially-linked set of poems and prose moralizations'; the easiest way to label it was evidently to note that, whatever the content of texts, they do have an order to them.[1] Thus the opening 'Complaint', Thomas's solitary articulation of his grievances and anxieties, leads directly into the 'Dialogue', in which Thomas is joined by a friend who reads his complaint and responds to it.[2] In their subsequent conversation, Thomas agrees he will delay his intended next project, a translation of Suso's *Horologium Sapientiae* (here titled 'Lerne for to Die', *D*

[1] E. P. Hammond, *English Verse between Chaucer and Surrey* (Durham, NC, 1927), p. 69.
[2] I follow here the growing convention of using 'Hoccleve' to refer to the historical person, and 'Thomas' to refer to the poetic speaker who narrates his poetry, although the distance we should understand between Thomas the character and Hoccleve the person remains unsettled. A. C. Spearing argues that Hoccleve is close enough to the poetic speaker that it seems unnecessary to call the figure a 'persona', while still using the term 'autography' rather than 'autobiography' to stay short of 'reading Hoccleve as a whole self back into a text in which he appears as a fragmented subject': *Medieval Autographies: The 'I' of the Text* (Notre Dame, 2012), p. 174. Jenni Nuttall points out that the *Series* represents events that apparently occurred at around the same time Hoccleve composed his balade to Henry Somer in a much different tone: 'The *Series* depicts a melancholic, socially isolated poet, deeply conscious of his own mortality and undertaking his final poetic work (*D* 239–4), while the balade to Somer presents a persona full of wit, *joie de vivre*, and sociability. It is not that one work falsifies the other or renders it inauthentic. Such juxtapositions simply remind us that Hoccleve's self-presentation is inevitably partial and purposeful, temporary rather than defining, always to be read in the light of its context and circumstance': 'Thomas Hoccleve's Poems for Henry V: Anti-Occasional Verse and Ecclesiastical Reform', *Oxford Handbooks Online* (2015), published online at 10.1093/oxfordhb/9780199935338.013.61.

47

206), until after he has translated a fabula from the *Gesta Romanorum* as an apology to women offended by his earlier writing. Following these four texts, the Friend re-appears to request that Thomas translate another fabula, this time one censorious of women, which becomes the fifth and final text of the *Series*. The five texts are thus not only 'partially-linked' by their inclusion within a frame narrative, as scholars handily recognise, but more specifically, set into their sequence by the flow of a conversation that periodically takes up text selection and thus determines the further entries in the *Series*.

While at least some structural links in the *Series* are evident, unifying thematic concerns are harder to come by, though scholars have worked to identify resonances that persist from poem to poem. For example, Hisashi Sugito explores how the use of the terms *taste* and *savour* allows the 'Complaint', 'Dialogue' and 'Learn to Die' to address common themes of experiential knowledge and the limits of language; Karen Winstead finds 'substantial unity of design and purpose' in the *Series*'s self-mocking account of the nature of women, especially in the connection of the 'Dialogue' to the two *fabulae*.[3] David Watt shows how the book's awareness of its own process of book-making haunts and holds the *Series* together. In examining this text as both thematically occupied with and structured by conversation, I build upon this last argument in particular. As Watt notes, the '*Series* is not the book that Thomas initially planned to make', because it changes 'as he tries to anticipate the needs and objections of potential readers' and changes more 'when a friend reads the text and suggests alterations'.[4] That is, not just the book production itself, but the conversations he has about it, both literal and imagined, inform the structure and creation of the text. I focus here on these structuring effects, as the *Series* narrates its own construction as both participating in and responding to conversation. Conversation makes up much of the substance of the text even as it motivates its creation; what begins as an anxious meditation by a speaker in isolation – and notably excluded from conversation – continues to accrue text upon text as a result of that speaker's invitation back into conversational exchange. The *Series*, I argue, is shaped by these conversational currents, and its texts are linked by their interest in the social dynamics of discourse. While the text is often discussed in terms of the metatextual qualities that keep it intermittently focused on itself as a text, it has so far gone undiscussed that these effects are bound up in a specifically conversational structure and thus an interest in how language makes changes in the world – that is, in speech acts.[5]

---

[3] Hisashi Sugito, 'Rereading Hoccleve's *Series*: The Limits of Language and Experience', *Journal of Medieval Religious Cultures*, 39 (2013), 43–59; Karen Winstead, '"I am al othir to yow than yee weene": Hoccleve, Women, and the *Series*', *Philological Quarterly*, 72 (1993), 143–55.
[4] David Watt, *The Making of Thomas Hoccleve's Series* (Liverpool, 2013), p. 2.
[5] James Simpson, for example, explores the effect of heightened reality in the frame narrative created by the *Series*'s description of its own composition: 'Madness and Texts:

The social functionality of language is thus a persistent concern of the text, emerging both as an interest in the way that language performs, or fails to perform, its intended actions, and a related care for the productivity of conversation. The opening 'Complaint' makes a fraught attempt to change social realities through language although, as a complaining speech act, it is not entirely successful. In its failure to accomplish what Thomas wants from it, however, that speech act catalyses a longer conversation and, concomitantly, the spiralling production of a longer text. Reading the *Series* in terms of conversation and speech acts allows us to see it as a text unified by this concern with language in its distinctly social character; the sequence balances its apprehension over the shiftiness of individual speech acts with an investment in the fluidity and generativity of conversation, allowing meaning to arise from open-ended and interactional language play. If the *Series* is thematically erratic in its content, it is so because it follows the discursive logic of conversation.

Speech Acts and Conversation

Conversation is generally treated by linguists as a turn-taking event that balances a need to accomplish tasks such as the exchange of information with an interpersonal interest in creating rapport.[6] Relevance and context are central concerns of conversational analysis. H. P. Grice noted that in order for interlocutors to participate in a conversation, as a 'rational, cooperative activity', they rely on an expectation that utterances will be, among other things, relevant to what is being discussed.[7] The context of an utterance is therefore essential to its interpretation, and in conversation, the 'sequential progression of interaction' means that 'each utterance is formed by a prior context and it also produces a context for a next utterance' – every utterance up to any given point is a part of the context that makes

---

Hoccleve's *Series*', in Julia Boffey and Janet Cowen (eds), *Chaucer and Fifteenth-Century Poetry*, King's College London Medieval Studies, 5 (London, 1991), pp. 15–29. Ethan Knapp, who describes the *Series* as 'organized only as a loose anthology with no real conclusion', finds in its 'self-referential meditation on writing' a 'sophisticated meditation upon the irresolvable fragmentation of the self': *The Bureaucratic Muse: Thomas Hoccleve and the Literature of Late Medieval England* (University Park, 2001), pp. 161, 163.

[6] See, for example, Rebecca Clift, *Conversational Analysis* (Cambridge, 2016), for an overview of the cross-disciplinary field of Conversational Analysis.

[7] Quoted in Deirdre Wilson and Dan Sperber, *Meaning and Relevance* (Cambridge, 2012), p. 3. Wilson and Sperber expand the significance of relevance in communicating, pointing out that 'the very act of communicating raises precise and predictable expectations of relevance' and that, in terms of comprehension, hearers know to 'Follow a path of least effort' as they interpret, and then 'Stop when your expectations of relevance are satisfied': *Meaning and Relevance*, pp. 6–7.

the next utterance interpretable.[8] Conversation, which can be analysed in terms of its discrete speech acts, thus contributes to the establishment of 'felicity conditions' that allow a speech act to function.[9]

Speech act theory originates in the work of J. L. Austin, whose *How to Do Things with Words* first observes that a philosophy of language must account not just for language's capacity to refer to the world, but to take action within it. Austin points out that some utterances are 'performative' rather than 'constative', in that they seek not to describe a state of affairs, but to create that state; e.g. 'I hereby name this ship the *Queen Elizabeth*' does not just describe such a ship, but changes the world so that a ship named the *Queen Elizabeth* now exists. Of course, in order for this performative speech act to work, it must be uttered under a certain set of conditions, by a person whose agreed-upon role is to perform this naming (and perhaps also ritually break a bottle on the bow).[10] Austin describes speech acts thus performed, under the right conditions to make them effective, as 'felicitous', and points out that certain conditions must likewise be in place for any speech act to perform as it has the potential to do.[11] Austin further distinguishes the 'locution', the linguistic form itself, from the 'illocution', the kind of act that the utterance of this form might accomplish. Both are then distinct from the 'perlocution', the effect that a speech act has.[12]

---

[8]   Nguyen Van Han, 'Contrast and Critique of Two Approaches to Discourse Analysis: Conversation Analysis and Speech Act Theory', *Advances in Language and Literary Studies*, 5 (2014), 155–62.

[9]   The unit of analysis most often used in Conversational Analysis theory is, however, the adjacency pair or the turn (see, for example, Clift, *Conversational Analysis*, pp. 68–73), an approach that can be seen as redressing a gap in speech act theory: that not all utterances which contribute to a conversation clearly have some kind of illocutionary force, though they may function instead to smooth the negotiation of turns and turn-taking in conversation.

[10]   The *Queen Elizabeth* example is Austin's. On the matter of infelicities, he goes on: 'Suppose, for example, I see a vessel on the stocks, walk up and smash the bottle hung at the stern, proclaim "I name this ship the Mr. *Stalin*" and for good measure kick away the chocks: but the trouble is, I was not the person chosen to name it.' In such a case, 'We can all agree (1) that the ship was not thereby named; (2) that it is an infernal shame': *How to Do Things with Words*, ed. J. O. Urmson and Marina Sbisà, 2nd edn (Oxford, 1962), pp. 5 and 23.

[11]   Austin initially describes performative utterances as 'felicitous or not': *How to Do Things with Words*, p. 22. John Searle then elaborates on specific felicity conditions germane to particular kinds of speech acts: *Speech Acts: An Essay in the Philosophy of Language* (Cambridge, 1969), pp. 55–71.

[12]   Austin (*How to Do Things with Words*, p. 106) elaborates on the difference between perlocution and illocution in part by introducing the matter of intention: 'Since our acts are actions, we must always remember the distinction between producing effects or consequences which are intended or unintended; and (i) when the speaker intends to produce an effect it may nevertheless not occur, and (ii) when he does not intend to produce it or intends not to produce it it may nevertheless occur. To cope with complication (i) we invoke as before the distinction between attempt and achievement.'

However, near the end of *How to Do Things with Words,* Austin determines that his initial distinction between constative and performative speech does not really hold: any utterance has, upon closer inspection, some performative force. A felicitous performance of the utterance 'I hereby name this ship the *Queen Elizabeth'* does make a particularly ritualised, remarkable change in an object's identity: a ship has now been named. However, the utterance 'Is this ship the *Queen Elizabeth?'* also performs a social action: a question has now been asked. (Simply paraphrasing the question as 'I hereby ask: "Is this ship the *Queen Elizabeth?"'* puts it in line with the grammatical expectations of a performative speech act.) Concepts such as illocutionary force and felicity are in fact relevant to the understanding and effect of any utterance.

Furthermore, this type of analysis can be extended to efficacious language used not only in a spontaneous 'ordinary language' context, but in crafted poetic contexts as well. Literature, as the critic J. Hillis Miller has observed, is also 'a way of doing thing with words' and therefore constitutes 'speech that acts', in its many attendant affects both within and without its universe of discourse.[13] Miller points out several ways that speech act theory might apply to literature: for one thing, literature often represents speech acts performed by characters interacting in its fictional universe; for another, the language used in a literary work (or even the literary work taken as a whole) might be legible as a speech act, directed to, or at least intercepted by, a reader.[14] Reading the *Series* with such speech act effects in mind, and considering its speech acts within their conversational contexts, both exposes the effects of discrete utterances within the fiction of the text and allows us to evaluate the text's concerns over its own interlocutorial engagement with its audience.

Complaining

The speech act giving Thomas trouble at the beginning of the *Series* is, of course, the complaint. Complaining has a long and rich tradition in medieval literature, one to which Hoccleve is no stranger, and in the range of Hoccleve's complaints we find examples of various modes of literary

---

[13] J. Hillis Miller, *Speech Acts in Literature* (Stanford, 2001), pp. 1–2.

[14] Perhaps the most important illocutionary effect of fiction, though not one I apply here, has to do with the creation of the fiction itself. As Gregory Currie points out, when making a statement of fiction, a speaker 'wants to get the audience to make-believe the proposition uttered'. That is, fictional literature acts by creating its fictional world, so that when Chaucer tells us that twenty-nine pilgrims came to the Tabard Inn, or Hoccleve describes the arrival of and conversation with a friend, the language creates a cognitive impression of those people, that place and the whole scenario: 'Works of Fiction and Illocutionary Acts', *Philosophy and Literature*, 10 (1986), 304–8, at p. 304.

complaining. His 'Conpleynte Paramont', for example, is a lament in the voice of Mary, addressed widely and non-specifically: the vocative turns from God the Father to the Holy Ghost, to Gabriel, Elizabeth, Christ himself, the moon, stars and firmament, and more, as Mary expresses her grief over the death of her son. This is literary complaint in the vein that Lee Patterson describes in terms of the 'emotionalism that complaint takes as its special province, the claim it makes upon the affect of both speaker and audience'. Patterson points out that such complaints make only 'self-cancelling' claims, 'useless' by design; that is, they are not meant to inspire change in the world, only to mourn what is evidently intransigent.[15] Indeed, Hoccleve's Marian voice cannot be taken as sincerely intending to undo the death of Christ (though the reader is ironically aware that that death will nonetheless be undone), only as an expression of her yearning and sorrow. This is not to say the poem has no illocutionary effects at all – as a text it is presumably meant to inspire greater devotion in its readers – but that the complaining speech acts of the first-person voice of the poem do not evidently aim to bring about recompense or restoration.[16]

Compare this with, for example, the balade Hoccleve writes to King Henry asking for the money he and his colleagues are owed. In this case, the poem is directed to a particular audience and for a particular end; Hoccleve invokes his 'sharp distress' and worry that debt will force him 'to trotte vn-to Newgate' (8), not just to garner sympathy, but because he aims to accomplish something concrete and specific – he wants Henry to pay up.[17] Rather than functioning as a literary complaint, this short poem reflects the rhetoric of medieval legal *pleinte*, which Wendy Scase sums up as 'the expression of a grievance as a means of initiating litigation'. *Pleinte* is always addressed to someone who can act to resolve the speaker's injury or loss, rather than simply asking a reader to witness a speaker's suffering and empathise.[18]

These two modes of medieval complaining align remarkably well with modern linguistics research into the complaint as a speech act, in which complaint is divided into two pragmatic types: direct and indirect. The

[15] Lee Patterson, 'Writing Amorous Wrongs: Chaucer and the Order of Complaint', in James M. Dean and Christian Zacher (eds), *The Idea of Medieval Literature: New Essays on Chaucer and Medieval Culture in Honor of Donald R. Howard* (Newark, 1992), pp. 55–71.

[16] See Jennifer E. Bryan, 'Hoccleve, the Virgin, and the Politics of Complaint', *Proceedings of the Modern Language Association*, 117 (2002), pp. 1172–87, for a discussion of Hoccleve's Marian complaint in terms of its devotional functions.

[17] Furnivall and Gollancz (eds), *Hoccleve's Works*, p. 62.

[18] Wendy Scase, *Literature and Complaint in England 1272–1553* (Oxford, 2007), p. 1. Scase argues the two modes – legal plaint and literary complaint – intersect, as 'the culture of judicial plaint interfaces with, and helps to shape, literature (p. 2). She also observes that given Hoccleve's employment at the Privy Seal and experience of writing diplomatic letters, warrants and other documents, it is no surprise that rhetoric from legal petitions and dictaminal writing would make its way into Hoccleve's literary output (pp. 179–81).

difference rests on both the purpose of the complaint and the felicity conditions that bolster it. The central felicity condition for a complaint to function is that something has gone wrong: the complainer has been disappointed, injured, or aggrieved. In a direct complaint, as in a legal *pleinte*, the speaker addresses some entity that has the capacity to make redress, often the same party that caused the wrong to begin with; a direct complaint typically has an official or legalistic quality, as it may also be performed in a 'complaint department' such as a human resources or customer service office (e.g. 'my manager makes me work unpaid overtime' or 'the television I purchased won't turn on'). By contrast, indirect complaints function like most literary complaint, directed at a powerless third party who has no ability to fix a problem, but who can instead validate the speaker's frustration. The point of an indirect complaint is to build rapport – to commiserate, vent, garner sympathy (notice that both examples given in the parenthetical above would still be felicitous if spoken to a friend who can do nothing to fix the problem).[19] Both direct and indirect complaints balance an expressive illocution (i.e. this is how I feel about what's happened) with a requesting illocution (i.e. this is what I want someone to do), but direct complaints typically emphasise the request over the expressive, while indirect complaints typically emphasise the expressive over the request.

The complaint, or complaints, of the 'Complaint' can be read as either direct or indirect, or as something intriguingly in between, depending how we understand the felicity conditions that apply to the poem, and especially how those conditions function relative to its audience and interlocutors. The central wrong done that motivates the complaint, that allows it to exist as this type of speech act at all, has to do with Thomas's reputation: he has been ill and recovered, but people seem not to trust his recovery. This complaint runs up against two distinct difficulties in terms of felicity conditions. For one thing, it is not clear who precisely is responsible for this harm or where he might take his complaint to demand redress. That is, there is no complaint department that handles rumour, gossip and misunderstanding; all one can do is to try and address gossip as it arises in occasional contexts. Thomas is injured by a general category of 'Men' who do not believe in his recovery, so that 'No wiȝt with me list make daliaunce' and 'The worlde' treats him as a stranger (C 64–70). He sees 'chere abaten and apalle' on the faces of the Westminster crowd in general (C 74) and overhears how 'manie oone' (C 85) are discussing the likely return of his illness; he quotes not an individual, but a 'þei' who have said that 'Whanne passinge hete is [...] trustiþ this, / Assaile him [Thomas] wole aȝein that maladie' (C 92–3). Even when individual voices emerge from the nebulous *they* doing him injury, Thomas is not able to enter the conversation to contradict the claims made about him. He

[19] Diana Boxer, 'Complaints: How to Gripe and Establish Rapport', in Alicia Martínez-Flor and Esther Usó-Juan (eds), *Speech Act Performance: Theoretical, Empirical and Methodological Issues* (Amsterdam, 2010), pp. 163–79.

hears one speaker describe his brain as 'ful bukkish' (C 123) and another remark that there is 'no sadnesse [soundness] in his heed' (C 125–6), while yet another describes how he holds himself and moves oddly, his feet 'ay wauynge to and fro' and his eyes darting to the corners of the room (C 131–3). Because of this purported oddness in his behaviour, even if he were to make his complaint where it is most relevant, to the individuals doing him harm, he is justly worried that he would not be taken seriously: he will not be believed to be a reliable reporter of his own condition.

This impasse exposes a tacit felicity condition that troubles the root of any speech act – that the speaking subject must be not only sincere (as John Searle emphasises in his anatomising of speech acts) but sane, that is, that their perception can be trusted.[20] Because Thomas's unwellness affected his memory and wit, he cannot fulfil this condition to assure a listener of his own recovery and cognitive capacity; a madman cannot be trusted to claim his own sanity. Thus he returns home, worried that he might 'answere amys' and be harmed more by it:

> Whatso þat euere I shulde answere or seie,
> They wolden not han holde it worth a leke.
> Forwhy, as I had lost my tunge keie,
> Kepte I me cloos, and trussed me my weie. (C 141–5)

He recognises that anything he could say would be without value to these interlocutors; therefore, he locks his tongue and keeps himself close, holds back his speech and abandons the social context for it. Moreover, he is mindful that since he has recovered, he has often had reason to be angry, but his anger, too, must remain unexpressed lest it be misconstrued as further evidence of madness:

> Sithen I recouered was, haue I ful ofte
> Cause had of anger and inpacience,
> Where I borne haue it easily and softe,
> Suffringe wronge be done to me, and offence,
> And not answered aȝen, but kepte scilence,
> Leste þat men of me deme wolde, and sein,
> 'Se howe this man is fallen in aȝein.' (C 76–82)

The felicity conditions at play make any efficacious speech act virtually impossible. Because he cannot fulfil the condition that he is (in his interlocutors' perception) a sane subject whose basic apprehension of the world can be trusted, any speech act he attempts is vulnerable to the perceived possibility that he is still mad; he is forced into silence not because he has lost access to speech, but because in this social context, he has lost access to illocution.

The complaint of the poem is thus, in fact, multiple overlapping complaints, about not only Thomas's situation, but the (im)possibilities

---

[20] Searle, *Speech Acts*, p. 60.

of complaint itself. His initial complaint is directed at God, who visits men with illness and loss of goods – and, says Thomas, 'he forȝat not me' (C 39). This develops into the poem's core complaint about gossip and reputation, bemoaning others' misunderstanding of Thomas's condition and their refusal to trust his recovery. But in and around this lament, a further meta-complaint begins to emerge about the failure of complaint itself and about Thomas's inability to make his complaint where it counts, to the interlocutors most responsible for his injury. Thomas would like to participate in the conversations he hears around him, to refute the claims being made and object to speakers' characterisation of him. But he cannot manoeuvre the felicity conditions into place in order to make such a speech act possible; any direct complaint he might want to make in the real social context where he is struggling cannot be accomplished, given the felicity conditions that would be necessary for that complaint to succeed.

The Friend's arrival, then, allows Thomas to distil the felicity conditions for his speech act down to the more manageable situation of speaking in person to a single interlocutor. The Friend's relationship to this complaint is unclear: we do not know to what extent the complaint's accusation touches him, whether he is a part of the problem (since the offending party in this case includes anyone in the demographic Thomas might interact with), or whether he is an ally from whom Thomas wants only sympathy and understanding. Intriguingly, the Friend doesn't respond as either offender or ally; he neither takes up an implied request for rapport, nor answers as if he has any power to offer redress. Sidestepping both roles, he instead cuts to the basic felicity condition of any complaint, as mentioned above, denying that there is even a problem:

'Howe it stood with thee leide is al aslepe,
Men han forȝete it. It is oute of mynde.
That þou touche therof I not ne kepe.
Lat be, þat reede I, for I cannot finde
O man to speke of it.' (D 29–33)

Whether or not this is intended to be comforting, the Friend's description of the situation recasts the kind of speech act that Thomas can be attempting with the 'Complaint': if Thomas is wrong, and his illness has mostly been forgotten by the community around him, then the illocution of the 'Complaint' cannot succeed. If the Friend is right, the poem becomes legible as the anxious ravings of a paranoid neurotic, rather than a legitimate response to an injurious circumstance. At this point, as readers substantially separated from the circumstances that occasion the complaint, we are confronted with our lack of access to the social reality about and into which Thomas speaks; with two perspectives of the situation, we have no way to judge between them.[21]

---

[21] Of course, this reading situation is further complicated by the fact that readers must balance, with the two characters' accounts of a fictional situation, an awareness of the historical reality undergirding it, in which the historical person Thomas Hoccleve does

Conversing

Conversation constitutes a central concern of the 'Complaint', both as part of the problem and as the longed-for solution. Thomas both craves conversation and resents it; he has been hurt by the content of the conversations he overhears but hurt even more by his exclusion from them. He mourns that 'commynynge is the best assay' (C 217) of one's character and fitness, and is sure that, if he could only 'commvne of thingis mene' (C 218), he could make his true condition clear. In a particularly melodramatic moment, he bids 'adieu, farwel' (C 267) to his good fortune: 'Sithen welny eny wiȝt for to commvne / With me loth is, farwel prosperite' (C 269–70). He despairs, briefly, that with no chance to explain himself, no communion with his peers, he will sink into misfortune and misery; he recognises *commvning* as essential to a prosperous and well-lived life.[22]

Before he is actually invited into a conversation, he has one modelled for him by the book he turns to near the end of the 'Complaint'. Hoccleve renders a passage from this book (Isidore of Seville's *Synonyma*) in which a suffering man describes the anguish of his life, mourning that he was even born and wishing to die.[23] His lament inspires a visit from Reason, who tells the suffering man to more stoically endure his trials, to 'Wrastle [...] aȝein heuynesse / Of the worlde, toublis, suffringe and duress' (C 342–3). Thomas says he is consoled by the 'speche of Reason' (C 315), but in fact, he reports the whole conversation, giving the suffering man's first-person account of his own misery before he includes Reason's rebuttal. This culminates in Reason's instruction to the man to 'Not grucche and seie, "Whi susteine I this?"' (C 363) – not to complain but instead to repent and pray. It is significant that Thomas encounters not only a doctrinal argument from Reason, but the experience of a complaining person: a man who is able to articulate his own complaint, and have it heard and answered by another speaker, even if the answer isn't either the redress or rapport he might have wanted. That is, all of this works as a model onto which Thomas can project himself, as a complainer who needs an interlocutor to hear his complaint, and perhaps rein in and redirect his energy.

---

appear to have suffered a period of severe mental illness. See J. A. Burrow, 'Thomas Hoccleve', in Michael C. Seymour (ed.), *Authors of the Middle Ages: English Writers of the Late Middle Ages*, vol. 1 (Aldershot, 1994), pp. 185–248, at p. 210.

[22] For the purpose of this reading, I focus on the word *communing* in its conversational sense of 'conversing, discussing, conferring, negotiating', but the word includes a range of broader possible meanings, including that of sharing goods or possessions, Christian fellowship, the Eucharist, and a deeper or more spiritual sense of communion.

[23] A. G. Rigg, 'Hoccleve's *Complaint* and Isidore of Seville', *Speculum*, 45 (1970), 564–74. See also J. A. Burrow, 'Hoccleve's *Complaint* and Isidore of Seville Again', *Speculum*, 73 (1998), 424–8.

The Friend's arrival just after Thomas has been dwelling on the conversation between a complaining man and his allegorical visitation casts the Friend in a parallel role as a figure who appears in a critical moment to respond to a suffering person's distress. The Friend seems to position himself as someone outside the dynamic of injury and complaint in which Thomas is caught, as if he is not a part of the discursive situation, only someone 'listening in' on an exchange. But the detachedness of his response might also be taken as a part of his effort to move past the core problem of whether Thomas has been wronged by others' gossip and allow the Friend to take on his crucial role in the 'Dialogue', that of an idealised interlocutor for a person badly in need of conversation.

The Friend offers the chance to participate in the kind of conversations that are precisely the source of Thomas's angst, conversations about his illness and recovery and his related social situation. In so doing, the Friend creates felicitous conditions for Thomas's complaint; the speech act he could not fully accomplish in the previous text can now be performed, even if the Friend is not fully receptive to it. He does this, for one thing, by simply engaging with Thomas as a single interlocutor, allowing him to make his complaint to a simple, clear audience. As Roger Ellis notes in the introduction to his edition of the *Series*: 'for Hoccleve, conversation, like relationships, can only function satisfactorily on a one-to-one basis, as a purely temporary alleviation of a basic isolation'.[24] Thomas earlier found himself overwhelmed and silenced by the proliferation of voices speculating about his mental wellness; for now, he seems to speak comfortably only with this single friend. This gives him a chance to make some critical conversational moves: to make the case for his own mental wellness and self-knowledge, to push back against counterarguments, and to eventually convince an interlocutor of his position.

The Friend's resistance to the 'Complaint' is simultaneously frustrating and opportune, in that it provides an opening for Thomas to make a satisfying response to things that have hitherto been said *about* him rather than *to* him. Thomas expresses astonishment that his Friend has apparently not really appreciated either his complaint, or his report of the situation that necessitated the complaint's composition. He may be 'lewide', he says, but he is not completely 'dote', and goes on: 'I woote what man han seide and seien of me / Her wordis haue I not as ʒit forgote.' And, he emphasises, 'þat þing þat I here, / Can I witnesse and vnto it referee' (D 36–7, 48–9). Though the Friend's initial pushback may read as a species of gaslighting, denying that Thomas can accurately perceive his own reality, it is precisely the pushback the Friend offers that creates the opportunity for Thomas to assert and claim his own experience. Thomas can now felicitously articulate a position that he was unable to assert in the previous social

[24] Ellis (ed.), '*My Compleinte*', p. 41.

situations he describes: that he knows himself and his own experiences and ought to be trusted to report them accurately.

Similarly, as the conversation turns to Thomas's next writing project, Thomas is both enabled and required to defend his scholarly capacity. The Friend's doubts about Thomas's intention to take up a new project strike chords uncomfortably similar to those that Thomas has overheard from his detractors: that his health cannot be trusted and he is likely to slip back into mental illness. The Friend explains that Thomas's mind is like a hearth after a fire which, although the fire has been put out, may still be 'of the fyr warm, thogh no fyr be seene' (D 312). Likewise, although 'past be the grete of thy seeknesse / Yit lurke in thee may sum of hir warmnesse' (D 314–15). The Friend evokes again the problem that Thomas may not be aware of his own fragility; worse, if his brain may still be 'warm' with his madness, then since he has no other instrument by which to measure his relative sanity, presumably he will have to lean on others' evaluations to grasp his own condition. Not only may Thomas still be ill, the Friend suggests, but he will be unable to know it if he is.

Again, Thomas is pushed to defend his own mental competence and scholarly ability, asserting to the interlocutor denying it that 'My sclendre wit feel I as sad and stable / As euere it was at any tyme or this' (D 366–7). The Friend is not immediately convinced and the two bat the matter back and forth for a hundred lines further, the Friend claiming that it was the 'laborious busynesse' of 'studie' (D 381, 379) that brought on his illness before, and Thomas responding that it was not study that caused his breakdown, but that it is useless to search excessively 'of the cause' (D 431), and that he does not feel compelled to take counsel from someone 'of a soothe him list nat learned be' (D 465). By now, Thomas has become quite pointed, accusing the Friend of giving advice he has not earned the right to give, and pointing out how little the Friend must trust him. Thomas invokes the very conversation he and the Friend are having as evidence of his sanity:

> Han yee aght herd of me in communynge
> Wherthurgh yee oghten deeme of me amis?
> Haue I nat seid reason, to your thyngynge?' (D 470–2)

Here Thomas points up the most important value this conversation has for him: through it he not only claims, but demonstrates, that his illness has passed and his reason has returned. The inability to enter into and perform within the conversations that he described in the 'Complaint' robbed him of precisely this opportunity, to not only argue back against others' misconceptions, but to demonstrate their wrongness.

The Friend, as he persistently doubts and undermines Thomas through the first half of the 'Dialogue', may or may not be an especially good friend. He is, however, an invaluable interlocutor. At last he concedes that he has 'taastid' Thomas enough, and finds him in 'good plyt' (D 487) such that he is able to say that 'I woot wel thow art wel ynow' (D 488). This last speech act takes on an especially remarkable performative function: Thomas has been plagued, no longer by a mental or physical illness, but by a kind of discursive and social unwellness, an inability to speak in accordance with conditions that would make his speech felicitous. Here at last his wellness is given locutionary acknowledgement and he is confirmed, in social reality, as not only a mentally healthy person, but as an efficacious interlocutor. By telling him that 'I believe you are well enough', the Friend in a social sense *makes* Thomas well: he confirms Thomas's ability to make an effective argument, to use language well in social space. In communing with his Friend, Thomas can do what he could not with the Westminster crowds: persuade another of his health and mental capacity, by both the argument he makes, and the fact that he is able to make a reasonable argument at all. The frustration of one egregiously failed speech act, the complaint, is resolved into a full conversation that more generously shifts the grounds of discourse, granting the interlocutorial site of disagreement as an opening for Thomas to reclaim himself as an able and knowing person.

Speech Acts and Text Acts

As the 'Dialogue' turns away from Thomas's health and to the question of text selection, the question of speech acts evolves into what I provisionally call 'text acts', that is, the overall force and effect that a text has as it is taken up by readers.[25] The Friend reminds Thomas to consider the rhetorical and political stakes that emerge, and have emerged, as he creates and distributes his writing, and so their discussion is particularly occupied with the kinds of interpersonal effects that Thomas's writing will have. That is, they recognise that Thomas's work will not only convey meaning but will constitute actions – doing things with words – and that he would therefore do well to consider what kinds of social effects he is willing to have his texts make available, i.e. the text acts these poems might perform. The selection of texts for the remainder of the *Series* is thus occupied with the ways that these texts will contribute as moves within a broader conversational dynamic, emerging not just from the immediate, literal conversation between Thomas and the Friend, but in terms of their awareness of a broader 'conversation' unfolding between Thomas and his readers. The coherence of the *Series* lies in these negotiations, through which the texts are not so much unified in theme or purpose as they are linked by a common set of contingencies alongside

---

[25] In this I am developing Miller's point that a 'speech act in literature' might describe 'a possible performative dimension of a literary work taken as a whole': *Speech Acts in Literature*, p. 1. That is, like any speech act, a text has the capacity to effect a change in the world, altering social realities in ways that depend upon its perlocution and felicity.

Thomas's desire to effect certain kinds of text acts through the works he chooses to translate.

Each text, each time it is read, produces a new speech act situation: the illocutionary potential of the text is met with a reader whose expectations, knowledge, previous encounters with Hoccleve and his writing, interpretive habits, etc. all inform the conditions that delimit and undergird the text's effects. The perlocution of a written text – the effect it has as it is read, which may or may not align with its illocutionary intent – is not necessarily more difficult to control than that of a speech act, but crucially, there is less possibility of repair if it goes awry. In a spoken conversation, a speaker can assess perlocutionary clues and determine that their speech act has not performed as intended, and thus adapt their next entry in the conversation to clarify the previous one. But a written text cannot be so flexible; to respond to readers who construe it in ways its author does not prefer, the author generally has no recourse but to produce another text. The 'conversation' among author, text and reader is thus elongated and in those longer spaces between illocution and perlocution, interpretation and response, grows Thomas's anxiety that the language he produces may not produce a perlocution he wants. He has, therefore, some understandable interest in the kinds of text acts his writing will make available.

Thomas hopes, for example, that 'Learn to Die' will have specific salutary effects for both himself and his readers. He anticipates being able to 'clense [...] sumwhat by translacioun' his own guilt (D 216), but hopes further that:

> Many another wiȝt eke thereby shal
> His conscience tenderly groope,
> And wiþ himseilfe acounte and recken of al
> That he hath in this liff wrouȝt, greet or small. (D 219–22)

His interest in 'Learn to Die' lies in how it will act upon readers, whom he expects will not only learn from their encounter with the text, but be turned to particular psychological and spiritual actions, probing their own conscience and evaluating their works – the text will alter their internal reality. As evidence of the text's efficacy, he goes on to meditate on his own ageing and prospective end, the heaviness he feels as he contemplates changing fortune and the inevitable loss of everything in death (D 246–87). Since death comes for us all, he says, should one not make provision for it so that 'we may stande in conscience cleer?' (D 294). He thus demonstrates exactly the effect he expects his translation to have. Just pondering a translation of the text has put him in mind of the response one ought to cultivate as death approaches – the text has therefore already had its desired effect on him, and he would thus be a particularly appropriate translator of it for others.

In setting up 'Learn to Die' as the *Series*'s third text, Hoccleve seems to be following a thematic progression in the conversational complexity of the whole work. In the 'Complaint', the speech act is performed alone, in a mode of self-occupation and self-disclosure; the 'Dialogue' adds an interlocutor to that dynamic, now portraying two speakers in conversation. The allegorical 'Learn to Die' will add representational complications to these dynamics of complaint and dialogue, in that in this case the speakers' exchange is both a literal conversation between speakers and a metaphorical 'conversation' that represents the moral psychology through which a disciple might approach wisdom, or a dying man encounter death. Just as the 'Dialogue' has echoes of complaint within it, 'Learn to Die' includes both complaint, from the figural man 'dyying and talkyng' (*LTD* 86), and dialogue which shifts among three speakers – the disciple, the dying man and Wisdom. Each text adds to the kinds of speech act and conversational structure used in the preceding text – or would, if 'Learn to Die' were indeed the third text in the *Series*.

But the developmental neatness of that structure is forestalled by the Friend, who informs Thomas that some of his readers are angry, and so a better next move would be to write something to mollify them. That is, both the literal conversation he is having locally, and the broader 'conversation' he is having with readers through his writing, interrupt and defer this more orderly progression of texts. Thomas, it turns out, had already accumulated various discursive responsibilities before this project started. His earlier poetic endeavours, if we trust the Friend's account, have offended women, and so there is another kind of penance and rehabilitation he needs to attend to before he can attempt the one promised by 'Learn to Die'. Whatever he intended to convey with his earlier translation of *Epistre au dieu d'amours*, the perlocutionary upshot was apparently one of reproach; his female readers 'nat foryeue haue ne foryite' (*D* 672) but are 'swart wroth and ful euele apaid' (*D* 755). Thomas objects that he was merely a 'reportour', not an 'auctour' (*D* 760-1), and that he 'to hem thoghte ne repreef ne shame' (*D* 773): his illocution was not intended as censure, even if the poetry has been taken that way. He avers of his text that whoever 'lookith aright therin may see / Þat they me oghten haue in greet cheertee' (*D* 777), but this attempt to put responsibility back on the reader only highlights that basic difficulty with the text act, that if one's meaning goes awry, it is not a straightforward matter to simply clarify it and move on with the conversation. Thomas seems annoyed to discover how far out of his control textual perlocution is, but eventually concedes that he needs to make some effort to repair it, and thus takes as his next translation the 'Fabula de Quadam Imperatrice Romana' from the *Gesta Romanorum*, rather than his intended penitential project.

This first fabula certainly has the illocutionary potential to function as the kind of text act Thomas needs, depicting its female character as both extraordinarily virtuous and extraordinarily victimised. The empress is kidnapped, threatened, assaulted and accused and then eventually given the deeply satisfying moral revenge of being allowed to extract a confession from each of her male abusers while holding over them her power to heal. The story makes patient virtue mostly female and cruel vice mostly male, and includes moments at which the narrator interposes himself to reprove such vicious men:

Yee men, whos vsage is, women to greeue,
And falsely deceyue hem and bytraye
No wonder is thogh yee misshape and cheeue
God qwyte yow wole and your wages paye
In swich wyse þat it yow shal affray. (FIR 722–6)

Moreover, the allegorical moralisation of the fabula is literally an afterthought, another consequence of conversational vagary. It is only included at all because when the Friend reads it, he points out that it lacks the moralisation he expects, and he offers Thomas a copy of the book that includes the allegorising gloss. The allegorical reading is thus offered only at a delay, allowing us to see that the poem is perfectly satisfactory as a non-allegorical defence of women. Thomas was clearly satisfied with it un-moralised, or moralised only implicitly, as a sympathetic depiction of patient female suffering; it makes more sense as an apology to women absent its allegorical gloss.

On the other hand, Hoccleve sets the fabula up by undermining its illocutionary potential in advance, as a text that will 'axe pardoun' and purge his guilt (D 816, 825–6). The felicity conditions on apology include an especially stringent sincerity condition – the apologiser needs to (be understood to) sincerely believe they have done something wrong for the apology to be heard as anything but hollow.[26] But Thomas is expressly not apologetic, only worried; he protests throughout that he has been misunderstood, that as a translator he cannot be at fault for what the original text says. His choice to translate the fabula is thus made in 'dredde' (D 799), not any sincere admission of guilt, and he wraps up the 'Dialogue' still contending his innocence, asking for pardon from women 'thogh I nat trespace' (D 816). So while the fabula may be read in isolation as a pro-female apologia, set into the context of the whole work, it is clear that Thomas (and maybe Hoccleve) wants to have it both ways, apologising and making amends even as he denies the need for either.

This need not be taken as evidence that Hoccleve – or Thomas – misapprehends the basic structure of speech acts. On the contrary, his simultaneous assertion and denial of the intended illocution of the first fabula arises from

---

[26] Austin points out that the 'spiritual' dimension of a speech act such as promising is less significant than the words themselves, in that if one has promised, one can't get out if it by claiming insincerity after the fact (How to Do Things with Words, p. 10). The apology strikes an interesting contrast, in that 'just' speaking the words of an apology will be deemed inadequate, an empty 'lip service' to apology, if the hearer does not also have an impression that the speaker is genuinely contrite.

the same workings of conversation that have governed the structure of the *Series* thus far: speech acts are always contingent and always multiple, dependent for significance on audience and context, the conversation in which they are uttered. By framing the fabula in this way, Hoccleve does his penance (a reparatory offering of a thousand lines of poetry is not nothing, after all) while also saving face, and laying bare a perlocutionary conundrum always at work in apology: who can ever be sure that an apologetic speaker really means it? And the perlocutionary possibilities of this complicated text act are potentially generative for further textual production, opening up multiple possible trajectories in the implied conversation with his readers – one can imagine him being asked to clarify or apologise for his semi-apology, or even being lauded and asked to write more. But we are not privy to the female readers' response; instead, it is again his conversation with the Friend that determines his next course of writing.

The second fabula, 'Fabula de Quadam Muliere Mala', makes the unexpected, though conversationally plausible, twist of inverting the text act of the first fabula. Thomas begins this final poem with the ironic assertion that he thought he was done writing – 'This book thus to han endid had Y thought' (FMM 1) – having lined up his three intended texts, with the addition of the recommended fabula. But his Friend makes yet another appearance, and as is so often the case in the *Series*, he has read something that affected him greatly. He wants it translated, this time with an intended audience of 'yong men' (FMM 9) in hopes it will 'par cause hem riot to forber' (FMM 10) and constrain them from seeking the company of prostitutes. The Friend is looking for a text to serve as a warning and remonstrance for a young male audience, but Thomas still has his female readers in mind, and is worried that he will be known as a 'double man' (FMM 40) if he agrees to this, pointing out the contradictions between the Friend's earlier advice and what he wants done now. But the Friend is convinced, and convinces Thomas, that the difference in audience will allow him to pull off this reversal: virtuous women reading will, he says, understand that it is written only against 'wikkid wommen' (FMM 60) – its illocution impugns only that hypothetical audience – and so his upstanding female readers will not take it to be censorious toward themselves.

Just as the conversation preceding the first fabula subverts that text as an apology, this conversation works to soften the condemnatory illocution of the second fabula and absorb its discursive risks. Thomas is able to offload the responsibility for producing this text onto not only the Friend, but the conversation itself; by including their conversation ahead of the text, he not only offers an argument for making this fabula a part of the *Series*, but more importantly, allows us to see Thomas in the process of being persuaded by that argument. Readers are thus offered a justification for its inclusion, but also shown how and why that reasoning was conversationally convincing. Thomas's justifiable concerns about the text as a social object are ameliorated insofar as the text's existence is made the consequence of a conversation, an extension of the discursive relationship between Thomas and his Friend.

This dynamic of conversation as a remedy for the trouble with speech acts is essential to the logic of the *Series*, which is presented as emerging from a conversation fuelled by, among other things, anxiety about how language functions socially, particularly on the level of individual speech acts. And like a conversation, it does not progress according to an organised plan, but rambles and twists, circles back on itself or tries alternative pathways, accreting texts because the speakers have carried the conversation in those directions. In this way, the *Series* is able to assemble a range of themes, topics and genres that are made coherent because they are produced through the conversation between Thomas and his Friend, and linked as illocutionary moves in the conversation Thomas has with his readers. The text thus exhibits how speech act and conversation interact: though individual speech acts may be unreliable, they do not occur in isolation. The development of conversation around them allows a speaker to accommodate their failings and gaps – and to produce more speech acts in doing so, acts themselves subject to the instability of language deployed in contingent and shifting social contexts. Just as speech acts both proliferate in conversation and proliferate that conversation, the conversation in and around the *Series* motivates its accrual of texts; in this sense the *Series* is not only open-ended, but unfinishable. Thomas comes into the fifth text noting his own surprise that he is still writing, but there is no structural reason for this one to be the final text either. As long as there is the possibility of further conversation, no speech act, and no text act, is final.

3

Hoccleve and the Logic of Incompleteness

R. D. Perry

The focus of this essay is the formal organising principle of Thomas Hoccleve's *Series*.[1] By 'formal organising principle' I refer to the means by which the work organises itself, how it imagines its parameters – the way in which it begins and the possibilities with which it may end – and the logic that governs the work as it proceeds.[2] This concept has been discussed, simply, as a work of art's 'organisation'. For instance, F. R. Leavis diagnoses T. S. Eliot's difficulty in creating a poem – *The Waste Land* – based on a modern 'mode of consciousness' as stemming from such consciousness's 'lack of organising principle, the absence of any inherent direction', causing Eliot to turn to mythological imagery to provide his poem with such an 'organising principle'.[3] The assumption is that a work of art should have an 'organising principle' that shapes the work of art in an 'inherent direction' even when the mind that produces it or that the work of art imitates does not.

As something that shapes the artwork, the formal organising principle has sometimes gone under the name of the work's 'structure', as with Barbara Herrnstein Smith: 'it will be useful to regard the structure of a poem as consisting of the principles by which it is generated or according to which one element follows another'.[4] For her, structure can be 'both formal and thematic', but the name 'structure' is complicated by the fact that formal

---

[1] This essay is dedicated to Lyn Hejinian, on the occasion of her retirement.
[2] The idea is related to Martin Heidegger's hermeneutic of formal indication, by which an experience discloses its meaning as you are having it. Similarly, the formal organisational principle of the text is one that the text discloses as it proceeds: Martin Heidegger, *Being and Time*, trans. John Macquarrie and Edward Robinson (New York, 1962), especially pp. 52–4. For a discussion, see Lawrence J. Hatab, 'The Hurdle of Words: Language, Being, and Philosophy in Heidegger', in Michael Bowler and Ingo Farin (eds), *Hermeneutical Heidegger* (Evanston, 2016), pp. 262–82.
[3] F. R. Leavis, *New Bearings in English Poetry: A Study of the Contemporary Situation*, new edn (London, 1950), p. 95.
[4] Barbara Herrnstein Smith, *Poetic Closure: A Study of How Poems End* (Chicago, 1968), p. 4.

and thematic structures do not necessarily need to correspond.[5] A ballade by Geoffrey Chaucer, like 'Lak of Stedfastnesse', has a formal structure of three rhyme royal stanzas with an envoy, and a thematic structure in which the speaker increases anxiety about the state of worldly affairs before, in the envoy, asking Richard II to set things right.[6] To discuss that work's formal organising principle, one would need to talk about the complex ways the formal and thematic structures interact. Recognising the formal organising principle of a work, then, is an important part of formalist criticism writ large. As Christopher Cannon reminds us, using a terminology derived from Chaucer, form 'allows analysis to build a bridge between the immaterial and material: "form" is necessarily the "werk" seen in terms of the "thoughte" behind it, the brute physicality of some things as it is rooted in the realm of ideas conceived in some mind'.[7] If the 'brute physicality' discloses an artwork's structure, the formal organising principle describes the contours by which the 'some mind' renders the thing's 'brute physicality', the mould that confines the structure into a particular shape.

Every artistic work will have a formal organising principle – it's an important part of what makes art quite literally 'work' for both the artist and the audience – although some will be much harder to see than others.[8] Hoccleve's *Regiment of Princes*, for instance, could rely on the 'mirror for princes' genre to provide it with a formal organising principle – albeit a conventional and externally-imposed one – but the ramble of the first half seriously undermines such a structure, and so it does not have as obvious a formal organising principle as the *Series* does; the need for the autobiographical prologue to be so long and to cover so many different topics is not obvious to the reader. The *Series*, though, is quite open about its formal organising principle: the formal organising principle of the *Series* is the framing dialogue through which Hoccleve and his friend decide on which inset texts Hoccleve produces and in which order. In the *Series*, because the formal organising principle constitutes the narrative frame of the work, announcing 'this is how I am constructed', the work itself is the story of its

---

[5]   Smith, *Poetic Closure*, 6.

[6]   *Riverside Chaucer*, p. 654. For a reading of 'Lak of Stedfastnesse' that emphasises its capacity to critique and attempt to reform Richard II, see Paul Megna, 'Chaucerian *Parrhesia*: World-Building and Truth-Telling in The Canterbury Tales and "Lak of Stedfastnesse"', *postmedieval*, 9 (2018), 30–43.

[7]   Christopher Cannon, 'Form', in Paul Strohm (ed.), *Middle English*, Oxford Twenty-First Century Approaches to Literature (Oxford, 2007), pp. 177–90, at p. 178. Cannon's theorisation of form takes a great deal from Marxist theory, but it likewise makes use of Heideggerian aesthetics, as he specifically discusses in *The Grounds of English Literature* (Oxford, 2004), pp. 3–10.

[8]   See the theoretical discussion by John David Rhodes: 'Belabored: Style as Work', *Framework*, 53 (2012), 47–64; and, for a more directly literary one, Maura Nolan, 'Style', in Brian Cummings and James Simpson (eds), *Cultural Reformations: Medieval and Renaissance in Literary History* (Oxford, 2010), pp. 396–419.

own creation.[9] Chaucer's work plays with this formal organising principle at points, revealing he is working from a hidden authoritative text in *Troilus and Criseyde* or that he is on a pilgrimage and will simply 'reherce' the tale-telling competition in the *Canterbury Tales* (I.732). Indeed, as such poems make clear, investigating a formal organising principle will involve outlining what Caroline Levine refers to broadly as 'narrative', the articulation of which will risk that dreaded 'heresy of paraphrase'.[10] As Levine makes clear, a close attention to the plot of a work like Hoccleve's *Series* does not simplify it, but reveals the formal organising principle in all of its 'irreducible complexity'.[11]

But, one can only 'nearly' include Chaucer, because what he is doing is somewhat different than Hoccleve. In order to attend to that difference, one must first think through Chaucer's formal organising principle in the *Canterbury Tales* and what opportunities it presents to him. Chaucer's tale-telling game – his formal organising principle as he begins his work – allows for an immense variety of genres and styles to be incorporated into his poem. But, Chaucer also alters that formal organising principle with the inclusion of the *Canon's Yeoman's Tale*, which transforms the game from a set number of tellers and tales to a game that is, logically speaking, illimitable; this new formal organising principle means that Chaucer's *Canterbury Tales*, in short, are not just incomplete, but *incompleteable*. Hoccleve's *Series* reveals to us both what Hoccleve learned from the formal organising principle of the *Canterbury Tales* as well as what he saw that he could do differently. Like the *Canterbury Tales*, Hoccleve's work strives for variability in terms of content and the capacity to expand more or less indefinitely. As such, it too is incomplete, or at least not complete in a way that its form dictates, and this flirtation with incompleteness has ramifications for its physical instantiations. Ultimately, the difference between the *Canterbury Tales* and the *Series* will come down to the ways in which they relate to the material conditions of textual production: Chaucer was interested in what it could do for him, and Hoccleve was interested in the way that he was a part

---

[9]   Such self-conscious performances of an artwork's making are not necessarily rare. It is a favourite trick of nineteenth-century fiction, from the depositions that make up Wilkie Collins's *Moonstone* to the archive that is Bram Stoker's *Dracula*, but the same formal organising principle is found in many places and in different artistic media, such as Diego Velázquez's *Las Maninas*, which is a painting about Velázquez painting that painting. Deborah McGrady discusses their popularity in late medieval France in 'The Rise of Metafiction', in William Burgwinkle, Nicholas Hammond and Emma Wilson (eds), *The Cambridge History of French Literature* (Cambridge, 2011), pp. 172–9.

[10]   Caroline Levine, *Forms: Whole, Rhythm, Hierarchy, Network* (Princeton, 2015), p. 19. The phrase 'heresy of paraphrase' is Cleanth Brooks's, another critic concerned with 'structure', from the title of the final chapter in *The Well-Wrought Urn: Studies in the Structure of Poetry* (New York, 1970), pp. 192–214. Levine discusses Brooks's work at length; see Levine, *Forms*, pp. 24–48.

[11]   Levine, *Forms*, p. 20.

of it. Attending to how these material conditions give rise to the *Series* asks us to reassess what it means to be a writer and a reader of texts for someone in Hoccleve's position, as writing and reading collapse into one another in a continual process of production and consumption, redefining the boundaries of what may be considered one's life and one's work.

The Incomplete *Canterbury Tales*

With the *Canterbury Tales*, Chaucer inscribed the formal organising principle into the text itself, so that – like the *Series* – the story of the text's unfolding is the narrative of the text's creation. Chaucer meets up with twenty-nine pilgrims (the number is actually less certain than the text would have you believe) at the Tabard Inn and they set off on their way to Canterbury, playing as they ride a tale-telling game organised by Harry Bailly, the Tabard's host and their guide. Each pilgrim, so the Host says, will tell two tales on the way to Canterbury and two tales on the way back, at which point they will be judged on which tale provides the 'best sentence and moost solaas', and the winner will have 'a soper at oure aller cost' back at the Tabard (I.798–9). Of course, Chaucer came nowhere near completing the roughly 120 projected tales, and that is one of the primary reasons we understand the *Tales* to be an incomplete work, left unfinished at the author's death. This judgement about the incompleteness of the *Tales* has been contested, most forcefully by Larry Benson, who says 'we have the work in what Chaucer regarded as its final state; unfinished, unrevised, and imperfect as *The Canterbury Tales* may be, Chaucer was finished with it'.[12] Benson does not quibble with the way that the formal organising principle of the *Tales* sets things up, but he insists Chaucer had given up any notion of completing that task.

The issue with Benson's assessment is that Chaucer alters the formal organising principle along the way, and he alters it in such a way as to render unintelligible any judgement of the *Tales* as 'finished'. Chaucer plays fast and loose with the tale-telling game throughout: it seems as if chance will govern the order, only to have the dictates of feudal hierarchy assert themselves when the Knight draws the straw and kicks off the tale-telling game; chance however reasserts itself, when the Miller replaces the Monk as the second tale-teller, allowing the tales to proceed according to the vagaries of social interaction and personal grudges between the characters; the order of the tellers that Harry Bailly tries to regulate is continuously violated and keeps being revised as different pilgrims tell their tales; other pilgrims are

---

[12] Larry Benson, 'The Order of *The Canterbury Tales*', *Studies in the Age of Chaucer*, 3 (1981), 77–120, at p. 81. Benson puts a good deal of weight on the internal evidence of the Retraction as Chaucer's signal that he was done writing the *Tales*.

interrupted and are unable to finish even the one tale they try to tell (and it is not clear what status those tales have in the game – do they count as a turn?); what even constitutes a tale is never exactly made clear (for instance, does the Wife of Bath's prologue count?).

But, the only catastrophic violation of the tale-telling game – the one that requires us to reassess how the text is being constructed – does not occur until rather late in the text (under the Ellesmere ordering, at least). Once the Canon and his Yeoman encounter the pilgrims and the Canon's Yeoman tells his tale (after his shady master runs off), then the *Tales* are operating under a different formal principle of organisation. Once the Canon's Yeoman has his say, that is, no longer is Chaucer simply reporting on the tales told by the thirty or so people who left the Tabard Inn: he is reporting on their tales *and those things said by the people they may meet along the way*. At that point, no longer is he planning to 'reherce' 120 tales, but a potentially infinite number (at least in practice): the pilgrims can always meet more people; there are always more tales to tell. At this point, the *Tales* move from a text that is incomplete because of Chaucer's death, to a text whose production could only end by Chaucer's death (if then – but more on that in a moment). This capacity for illimitable expansion is what ultimately renders the *Canterbury Tales* incompleteable.

So why might Chaucer have made this change? What good does an incompleteable text do him? One answer, and an important one when thinking about Hoccleve's relationship to Chaucer, is that an incompleteable text allows Chaucer to accede to the material conditions of textual production.[13] There is ample evidence about Chaucer's concern with the means by which his texts are produced; 'Adam Scriveyn' is about the instability of textual production, or – if one objects to 'Adam Scriveyn' for whatever reason – the stanza at the end of *Troilus and Criseyde* about 'diversite' of English and the threat that someone might 'myswrite' or 'mysmetre' his poem is another recognition about the vagaries of manuscript creation and circulation (V.1793–6).[14] The formal organising principle of the *Canterbury Tales* is

---

[13] Reading the *Canterbury Tales* as a response to late medieval English textual culture, especially the proliferation of the vernacular manuscript miscellany, is nothing new. See (although they don't exactly use those words) Helen Cooper, *The Structure of the Canterbury Tales* (Athens, GA, 1983), pp. 8–90; and Donald R. Howard, *The Idea of the Canterbury Tales* (Berkeley, 1976), pp. 56–74. For the tension between manuscript studies and formalism, especially in its New Critical guise, see Robert Meyer-Lee, 'Manuscript Studies, Literary Value, and the Object of Chaucer Studies', *Studies in the Age of Chaucer*, 30 (2008), 1–37. Interestingly, recent returns to considering the form of the *Canterbury Tales* as a whole have come from the direction of manuscript studies. See Robert Meyer-Lee, 'Abandon the Fragments', *Studies in the Age of Chaucer*, 35 (2013), 47–83; and Alexandra Gillespie, 'Are *The Canterbury Tales* a Book?', *Exemplaria*, 30 (2018), 66–83.

[14] 'Adam Scriveyn' has been a particularly controversial text ever since the addressee was identified as Adam Pinkhurst in Linne Mooney, 'Chaucer's Scribe', *Speculum*, 81 (2006), 97–138. For one of the best responses to the identification and the controversy,

another instance of Chaucer confronting this material fact and, rather than making a complaint about it, accepting the material conditions under which he is working and trying to get them to work for him. Of course, the two other instances, 'Adam Scriveyn' and *Troilus and Criseyde*, are concerned with local instances of mismetring or miscopying, whereas the *Canterbury Tales* tackles textual instability at a much larger scale. An incompleteable text accepts that an author's work will change, sometimes drastically, as it circulates in a manuscript culture; it allows for variation, for things to be changed, left out, or especially added to it as it moves through the world. In fact, the incompleteness of the text elicits additions, as individuals try to make the text complete, or at least more complete. The various scribal links between the tales attest to the fact that people will naturally want to complete an incomplete text, as do the additions of *Gamelyn* to complete the *Cook's Tale* or Hoccleve's own *Story of the Monk Who Clad the Virgin* becoming the *Ploughman's Tale*, not to mention those works that want to complete the pilgrimage itself and so imagine the pilgrims at Canterbury and starting on their return journey, like John Lydgate's *Siege of Thebes* and the *Canterbury Interlude and the Merchant's Tale of Beryn*.[15]

Perhaps the most important thing that an incompleteable text like Chaucer's can do is allow the author to confront his or her mortality. The text will necessarily change once it has left Chaucer's hands, and once he has died then all sorts of people can do whatever they want with it, as Lydgate and others in fact did. Chaucer accepted that fact and made what seems like an authorial problem into a formal solution. In short, Chaucer created a form that not only anticipated that the text would change after he died but also licenses those changes. The *Canterbury Tales* allow for expansion, validating attempts at completion and extension by virtue of the work's formal organising principle. Those extensions need not be by Chaucer, nor do they need to be done during his lifetime; manuscript and early print culture makes it easy enough to add to texts, and Chaucer's work fully accepts

---

see Alexandra Gillespie, 'Reading Chaucer's Words to Adam', *Chaucer Review*, 42 (2008), 269–83.

[15] Some of these scribal links from London, British Library Lansdowne MS 851 and Royal MS 18. C. II, Hoccleve's *Story of the Monk Who Clad the Virgin*, and the *Canterbury Interlude and the Merchant's Tale of Beryn* can be found in John M. Bowers (ed.), *Canterbury Tales: Fifteenth Century Continuations and Additions* (Kalamazoo, 1992), pp. 41–53, 23–39, and 55–196 respectively. For *Gamelyn*, see Stephen Knight and Thomas Ohlgren (eds), *Robin Hood and Other Outlaw Tales* (Kalamazoo, 1997). For Lydgate's poem, see John Lydgate, *The Siege of Thebes*, ed. Robert R. Edwards (Kalamazoo, 2001). Studies on *Gamelyn* and incompleteness, from the point of view of a textual critic, include A. S. G. Edwards, 'The *Canterbury Tales* and *Gamelyn*', in Christopher Cannon and Maura Nolan (eds), *Medieval Latin and Middle English Literature: Essays in Honour of Jill Mann* (Cambridge, 2011), pp. 76–90; and Timothy Stinson, '(In)Completeness in Middle English Literature: The Case of the *Cook's Tale* and *The Tale of Gamelyn*', *Manuscript Studies*, 1 (2017), 3–22.

that fact, allowing for new work to circulate as a part of it, fully under the purview of its original design.[16] Chaucer, in other words, creates a formal organising principle that uses a fake instance of contingency (the random addition of a new character to the pilgrimage frame and the story-telling game) in order to incorporate real historical contingency into his text – in its most innocuous form as the vagaries and uncertainties of manuscript culture, but also including that most inevitable of contingencies, death itself. Much of late medieval English literature is in some sense a response to death, and Sebastian Sobecki has read the *Series* in that way as well; the formal organising principle of the *Canterbury Tales* suggests that it should be understood as one of those responses.[17] But, if the *Canterbury Tales* is Chaucer's response to his inevitable death, then we should understand the *Series* as almost its opposite: it is Hoccleve's response to the way that he lives.

The Incomplete *Series*

In many ways, the *Series* is Hoccleve's version of the *Canterbury Tales*. This point has been made before, perhaps most memorably by Ethan Knapp's characterisation of the opening of the *Series* as the *Canterbury Tales* 'transposed into a substantially more bitter key'.[18] Indeed, the form of the *Series* reveals Hoccleve to be a very astute reader of Chaucer's work, as well as very much his own poet.[19] After all, as my focus on form instead of tone will show, Hoccleve would have had to be an astute reader to so nearly duplicate

---

[16] *Gamelyn* is a case in point for manuscript culture. On early print culture, see Megan Cook, *The Poet and the Antiquaries: Chaucerian Scholarship and the Rise of Literary History, 1532–1635* (Philadelphia, 2019), especially in her discussion of Chaucer's works in folio, pp. 17–43.

[17] For broader readings of the relationship of late medieval English literature to death, see Amy Appleford, *Learning to Die in London, 1380–1540* (Philadelphia, 2014); and D. Vance Smith, *Arts of Dying: The Making of Literature in Medieval England* (Chicago, 2020). On the *Series*, see Sebastian Sobecki, *Last Words: The Public Self and the Social Author in Late Medieval England* (Oxford, 2019), pp. 65–100. Arguing, as I do, that the *Series* is about Hoccleve's mode of living is in no way a contradiction of Sobecki's point, for it is in his life that Hoccleve mourns John Bailey's death.

[18] Ethan Knapp, *The Bureaucratic Muse: Thomas Hoccleve and the Literature of Late Medieval England* (University Park, 2001), p. 164. Sebastian Langdell nicely tempers this assessment into a 'minor key': *Thomas Hoccleve: Religious Reform, Transnational Poetics, and the Invention of Chaucer* (Liverpool, 2018), p. 11 and the discussion following. For an earlier articulation, see J. A. Burrow, 'Hoccleve's *Series*: Experience and Books', in R. F. Yeager (ed.), *Fifteenth Century Studies: Recent Essays* (Hamden, CT, 1984), pp. 259–73.

[19] For a long time the predominate way of understanding Hoccleve was as Chaucer's follower who was not his own poet. The most influential version of this is Seth Lerer, *Chaucer and His Readers: Imagining the Author in Late-Medieval England* (Princeton, 1993). A much more agential reading of Hoccleve is found in John M. Bowers, 'Thomas Hoccleve and the Politics of Tradition', *Chaucer Review*, 36 (2002), 352–69. See also the

the formal ordering principle of the *Tales*. Like Chaucer's poem, Hoccleve's *Series* is a story collection tied together by a narrative frame, one not organised by an artificial game – as Boccaccio's *Decameron* is or as the *Tales* are at their beginning – but one which instead proceeds in a pell-mell order governed by what seems like chance, as the *Tales* are, from the drawing of straws, to the outbursts of personal attacks and narrative payback, to the random encounter with the Canon's Yeoman. And like the *Tales*, it becomes hard to tell when a work that proceeds by way of chance would naturally come to its conclusion. It is in the form that chance takes in his formal organising principle that Hoccleve shows his own poetic strengths.

The first thing to point out is that, like the *Canterbury Tales*, the *Series* is variable and open-ended. It can carry on indefinitely and incorporate an incredibly wide variety of individual texts within it, from lyric reflections to moralised fables to work in the *ars moriendi* tradition, both in prose and verse. The formal organising principle of the work relies upon two strategies as a means of expansion. First, as David Mills has pointed out, the agent of that extenuation and variability is the figure of Hoccleve's friend: 'the Friend becomes the means of randomising the work and deferring its closure'.[20] The relationship of character to plot is as old as literary criticism, only it is usually a means of closing the work off, as when, for instance, the tragic character finally realises the terrible predicament he is in.[21] Here, though, the character of the Friend serves the formal organising principle by allowing for continual elaboration and variation.[22] It begins with the 'Complaint' in which Hoccleve reveals his mental illness and recovery, and he laments the difficulty he has had reintegrating with society ever since. Society then comes to him: a 'good frende of ferne agoon' (*D* 8) knocks at Hoccleve's door at the end of the complaint, thus beginning the 'Dialogue'. From here, the Friend becomes the impetus for generating texts. The Friend rejects Hoccleve's complaint and asks him to circulate something else, and it is the Friend who recalls that Hoccleve owes a book, apparently on a topic of his choosing, to Humphrey, duke of Gloucester. After some debate about what Hoccleve should write for the duke, it is the Friend again who suggests that Hoccleve also needs to write something that serves as recompense for the bad things he said about women in his earlier *L'epistre de Cupide* and who decides that Hoccleve can do double duty, writing this penitential

---

broader discussion in his *Chaucer and Langland: The Antagonistic Tradition* (Notre Dame, 2007), pp. 183–215.

[20] David Mills, 'Voices of Hoccleve', in Catherine Batt (ed.), *Essays on Thomas Hoccleve* (Turnhout, 1996), pp. 85–107, at p. 99.

[21] Understanding plot through characterisation, as well as the figure of Oedipus behind the example, is found in Aristotle, *Poetics*, in Jonathan Barnes (ed.), *The Complete Works of Aristotle*, vol. 2 (2 vols, Princeton, 1984), pp. 2316–40.

[22] Sebastian Langdell has read the Friend as a key to the *Series*'s polyvocality as well as an embodiment about the dangers of misreading: *Thomas Hoccleve*, pp. 11–34.

work in praise of women for Humphrey, based on the dubious premise that Humphrey likes 'With ladyes to haue daliance' and so 'this book wole he shewen hem par chance' (*D* 706–7).[23]

It is in the 'Dialogue', then, that the formal organising principle of the *Series* takes hold and provides us with a model for how the work will proceed: the Friend, the avatar of the public world, will venture into the private space of Hoccleve's dwelling and cause him to produce texts to be taken back out into the broader social world that the Friend inhabits much more easily than Hoccleve can. For the rest of the *Series*, then, the inset stories are punctuated by the Friend who, as one says in the Deep South, 'just drops by for a visit'. This is true for whole stories themselves as well as for parts of them. When Hoccleve finishes the story of the Roman empress, from the *Gesta Romanorum*, the Friend reappears and Hoccleve gives him the tale to read. The Friend likes it but wants a 'moralizynge' end to it (*FIR* 934); Hoccleve says there is none, but the Friend recalls one from the original, fetches the book and reads it to Hoccleve, leaving the book with Hoccleve so that he can translate the moralisation into prose, which he does. After this, the prosimetrum form of the fourth part – the first part of Henry Suso's work, titled here 'Lerne for to Die' (*D* 206), and then a prose version of 'The Celestial Jerusalem', 'the ixe lesson which is rad / In holy chirche vpon a[ll] halwen day' (*LTD* 925–6) – looks like Hoccleve simply following the lead of what his friend wants. While the fourth part has no introduction, its appearance has been already explained in the 'Dialogue', in which Hoccleve tells the Friend that 'haue I purposid to translate' Suso's work, incited to do so by an unnamed 'deuoute man' (*D* 206–11, 235). At the beginning of the fifth part, the Friend once again serves as the impetus and means for Hoccleve to create an entire inset work: the Friend asks Hoccleve to translate another story from the *Gesta Romanorum*, about a wicked woman, to serve as a lesson to the Friend's fifteen-year-old son. Hoccleve worries that this will anger the women that Hoccleve was supposed to appease with the first *Gesta Romanorum* translation, but the Friend assures Hoccleve that good women will not mind stories about wicked ones, that such stories will

---

[23] The back and forth here is deeply indebted to Chaucer's work, especially to the prologue to the *Legend of Good Women*, which features a similar assignment of penance, and to the *General Prologue* of the *Canterbury Tales*, from which Hoccleve borrows language to excuse his writing. For the relations between these texts, see Langdell, *Thomas Hoccleve*, pp. 35–63. I also discuss this correspondence at length in the second chapter of my dissertation: 'Chaucer's French Tradition: Coterie Poetics in Late Medieval England' (unpublished PhD dissertation, University of California, Berkeley, 2016). For further readings, see Lee Patterson, '"What is me?": Self and Society in Hoccleve's Poetry', *Studies in the Age of Chaucer*, 23 (2001), 437–70; and Jonathan Stavsky, 'Hoccleve's Take on Chaucer and Christine de Pizan: Gender, Authorship, and Intertextuality in the *Epistre au dieu d'amours*, the *Letter of Cupid*, and the *Series*', *Philological Quarterly*, 93 (2014), 435–60.

not reflect poorly on them. Hoccleve accepts the argument and borrows the Friend's copy of the story, translating both it and its moralisation.

It is important to add that, while the Friend allows for variety and a means of extending the work, he is less a means of fully 'randomising' the *Series* than he might appear. The Friend is merely a figure of fake contingency, much as the Canon's Yeoman is: the Friend 'randomly' drops by Hoccleve's dwelling to start the proliferation of texts; it just so 'happens' that the Friend remembers Hoccleve's earlier obligation to Humphrey and will need, as it turns out, something to teach his son. None of the Friend's activities are actually contingent, of course. Hoccleve has decided to include them and he uses the narration of them to drive his text on. Even so, the Friend still incorporates a figure of contingency into the work, which will then proceed not according to, say, the virtues Humphrey needs to be a good leader and the stories appropriate to them, such as John Gower might create (as he had listed stories under the organising rubric of sin and virtue in the *Confessio Amantis*, for example) or what a kind of sequel to the *Regiment of Princes* might produce. Instead, the formal organising principle of the *Series* will move by means of the vagaries of human sociability, the chance encounter with acquaintances and the variable needs of companions and employers.

The other major means by which the formal organising principle of the text continues the narrative is through gender difference and misunderstanding.[24] On this point the text is thoroughly indebted to Chaucer's *Legend of Good Women*, which makes an offence against women a means of producing an ever-expanding series of texts. There is no indication, either in Chaucer's text or here in Hoccleve's, that there is any real audience behind this complaint, although one could easily imagine such. Unlike Chaucer's text, however, there is not even really a fictional audience behind the complaint in the *Series*; whereas Chaucer is directly confronted by the God of Love and Queen Alceste, Hoccleve is simply left to take his friend's word for it that there is an audience of upset women. The complaint of the unspecified female audience, then, is at the border of history and literary trope, much like the way that in France, and almost contemporary with Hoccleve, the legitimate historical complaint about the treatment of women found in the Christine de Pizan-centred *Querelle de la Rose* becomes something closer to a fictive game producing an expanding number of texts

---

[24] On this aspect of misunderstanding, see Langdell, *Thomas Hoccleve*, pp. 35–40. Much more could be written about gender in the *Series*. Interestingly, two of the most important treatments deal with masculinity. See Isabel Davis, *Writing Masculinity in the Later Middle Ages* (Cambridge, 2007); and Holly A. Crocker, 'Engendering Affect in Hoccleve's *Series*', in Glenn D. Burger and Holly A. Crocker (eds), *Medieval Affect, Feeling, and Emotion* (Cambridge, 2019), pp. 70–89. For an important discussion of these angry female readers, see Michelle Ripplinger's 'Hoccleve's *Series* and the Unanticipated Woman Reader' in this volume.

with the *Querelle de la Belle Dame sans Merci*.[25] As with the second *Querelle*, whether or not the outrage surrounding *L'epistre de Cupide* is historically accurate, its primary function in the *Series* is not to allay or redress the terms of the complaint, but to work in tandem with the character of the Friend as a means of producing more and more material. Taken together, the Friend and the outraged female readership could very well push the narrative well beyond where it ends. Indeed, the Friend's persistent meddling combined with the sheer number of medieval texts that would outrage female readers means that the formal organising principle would not necessarily end at some natural point, but, like the *Canterbury Tales*, could become a kind of infinite regress, another incompleteable text.

The formal organising principle of the *Canterbury Tales* is intimately tied to their incompleteness, so is the same true of the *Series*? Hoccleve's work, after all, does make some concluding gestures, but just how definitive are they? Nominally, the *Series* ends with a typical fifteenth-century envoy, inspired by Chaucer's *Troilus* – with a 'Go, small book' – and dedicated to 'my lady of Westmerland' with the instruction 'to plese hir wommanhede do thy might' (*FMM* 733–40).[26] The manuscript evidence both for the reintroduction of the framing device before the second *Gesta Romanorum* selection and for the concluding envoy is far less stable than the appearance of the work in both modern editions would at first suggest. If one takes a maximalist view of what counts as the *Series*, it survives, wholly or in part, in eleven manuscripts.[27] This number requires qualification, though, because it includes any manuscript that contains any part of the *Series*.[28] A set of

[25] For the *Querelle de la Rose*, see Eric Hicks (ed.), *Le Débat sur le 'Roman de la Rose': Christine de Pisan, Jean Gerson, Jean de Montreuil, Gontier et Pierre Col* (Geneva, 1996). For an English translation, see David F. Hult (ed. and trans.), *Debate of the Romance of the Rose* (Chicago, 2010). For the *Querelle de la Belle Dame sans Merci*, see Alain Chartier, Baudet Herenc and Achille Caulier, *Le Cycle de la Belle Dame sans Mercy: Une Anthologie Poétique du XVe Siècle* (BNF MS FR. 1131), ed. and trans. David F. Hult and Joan E. McRae (Paris, 2003). For an English translation, see Joan E. McRae (ed. and trans.), *Alain Chartier: The Quarrel of the Belle Dame sans Mercy* (New York, 2004).

[26] J. A. Burrow points out that this is Joan Neville, née Beaufort, countess of Westmorland: *Thomas Hoccleve* (Aldershot, 1994), p. 28. The relationship of Hoccleve to the Chaucer family, and what bearing that might have on the relationship between the *Series* and the *Canterbury Tales* is a topic that would benefit from further exploration.

[27] The holograph manuscripts can be found in Burrow and Doyle (eds), *Facsimile*. A discussion of the non-holograph manuscripts, which informs what follows, is contained in the fourth appendix in Ellis (ed.), *'My Compleinte'*, pp. 276–7.

[28] A more qualified accounting of the *Series*, one that would account for only those manuscripts with the frame and all the stories, reduces the number to six: the Durham holograph manuscript, discussed below; Coventry, City Records Office, MS Accession 325/1; Oxford, Bodleian Library, MS Bodley 221; Oxford, Bodleian Library, MS Laud misc. 735; Oxford, Bodleian Library, MS Selden Supra 53; New Haven, CT, Yale University, Beinecke Library, MS 493. As I will discuss shortly, this list needs even further qualification, because only the Durham holograph has the concluding envoy.

manuscripts lacks the frame narrative, because they contain only the latter parts of the work, either the Suso translation, or the *Gesta* narratives, or both in the case of London, British Library, Royal MS 17. D. VI. From the point of view of latter copyists, it certainly makes sense that, without the opening complaint and dialogue, the frame becomes altogether extraneous and is simply dropped. However, one of the holograph manuscripts, one of the earlier two at that – San Marino, Huntington Library, MS HM 744 – contains the Suso translation without the frame.[29] This possibly earlier instance of circulation for a portion of the *Series*, combined with the fact that certain selections of it continued to circulate independently, is a potent reminder that works that come to make up the *Series* may well have predated Hoccleve's conception of the work as a whole, no matter what the narrator says in the 'Dialogue'. Like the *Canterbury Tales*, then, the *Series* could have exhibited a sort of centripetal force on Hoccleve's earlier work, incorporating what were once individual works into a loose whole.[30] Furthermore, as a compositional process, the *Series* could have continued to absorb Hoccleve's other works until his death, or even after.[31] What is more, like the *Canterbury Tales*, the *Series* may have even come to incorporate the works of other authors. Such is nearly the case with John Lydgate's *Dance of Death*, which comes to survive in four predominately complete manuscripts of the *Series*: Oxford, Bodleian Library, MS Bodley 221; Oxford, Bodleian Library, MS Laud misc. 735; Oxford, Bodleian Library, MS Selden Supra 53; New Haven, CT, Yale University, Beinecke Library, MS 493. Had Lydgate been less famous, or the *Dance of Death* had a more constrained circulation, it could have been to the *Series* what *Gamelyn* is to the *Canterbury Tales*.

That the *Series* could continue to expand is further suggested by the fact that the concluding envoy to the work exists in only one manuscript, the Durham holograph: Durham, University Library, MS Cosin V. III. 9. This manuscript situation gives the envoy a peculiar authority. On the one hand, its existence in a holograph manuscript means that its authority is unimpeachable; Hoccleve meant for it to be there. On the other, the fact that all other manuscripts of the *Series*, even if they contain the entire frame narrative, lack the envoy means that the work stands on its own quite well without it; the envoy is superfluous to the work taken as a whole if

---

[29] For a dating of the holograph manuscripts, see Burrow and Doyle (eds), *Facsimile*, pp. xx–xxi.

[30] The fact that it appears that the *Knight's Tale* and the *Second Nun's Tale* are mentioned in the *Legend of Good Women* (F420–6 and G408–16) suggests that at least those two works predate the *Canterbury Tales* as a project and are later subsumed into the larger work.

[31] The *Canterbury Tales* came to contain the *Tale of Gamelyn* after Chaucer's death, allowing that work to survive in twenty-five *Canterbury Tales* manuscripts, and only in those manuscripts. For a thorough discussion of this situation, see the essays by Edwards and Stinson cited in note 15.

so many other manuscripts do not need it. There is no evidence that, in contrast to what occurred with the *Canterbury Tales*' abruptly terminated *Cook's Tale*, the scribes were the least bit concerned that the text ended where it did. This situation is complicated by the fact that it is impossible to know if the exemplars of the manuscripts lacked the envoy. As they were copies, and not intended as gifts for Lady Westmorland, the scribes may well have dropped the envoy if it did exist in their exemplar. It may be that only the Durham holograph manuscript was meant to be given to Lady Westmorland, and so Hoccleve added the envoy only to that manuscript. It fits perfectly on the last folio of the manuscript, but it was clearly no afterthought, beginning with the illuminated initial 'G' of 'Go, small book' that fits the pattern of illumination that the rest of the manuscript has. The ownership of the manuscript does not help us, as there is no evidence that Joan Beaufort, countess of Westmorland in fact received this copy that Hoccleve dedicated to her.

The content of the envoy likewise participates in this tension between being part of and separate from the *Series*. The whole envoy is as follows:

> Go, smal book, to the noble excellence
> Of my lady Westmerland, and seye
> Hir humble seruant with al reuerence
> Him recommandith vnto hir nobleye
> And byseeche hir on my behalue and preye
> Thee to receyue for hir owne right,
> And looke thow in manere weye
> To plese hir wommanhede do thy might. (FMM 733–40)

Then, in the lower right-hand corner, Hoccleve has written 'Humble seruant / to your gracious / noblesse' and signed it 'T. hoccleue' (FMM 741). In terms of *mise en page*, then, the envoy both continues as things have been – a final, though very short, addition to a multi-segment work – and it sets itself apart as requiring a final signature out of the way of the rest of the text. In terms of content, it recalls the anxiety about doing something to appease and honour the women angered at *L'epistre de Cupide*, as discussed in the 'Dialogue', and yet it is emphatically addressed only to one woman, with the Chaucerian echo in its opening especially appropriate to her heritage – as one of the legitimated children of John of Gaunt and Katherine Swynford, she was Chaucer's niece by marriage. In short, the style of the envoy is perfectly appropriate for the occasion – a dedication to one's social better – and fitted expertly to the work it concludes, recalling the look and tone of what has preceded it. But it is, crucially, still outside of that work, an addition, appropriate but not essential to the work as a whole.

There is nothing, in other words, preventing Hoccleve from making another copy of the *Series* that drops the envoy and adds further material. As I have mentioned, there is a surviving instance in one of Hoccleve's own manuscripts where a singular inset text from the *Series*, 'Learn to Die', exists on its own, a text that would reappear in its new setting as the fourth part of the *Series* in one of Hoccleve's later manuscripts – and, in fact, this is the only extant example we have of Hoccleve recopying one of his works.[32] In terms of the work's formal organising principle, it would be completely licit for Hoccleve to do a more complex version of that, and the fact that 'Learn to Die' has no frame narrative proceeding it, having been introduced only through the discussion in the 'Dialogue', is a testament to just how easily the *Series* incorporates disparate materials as a means of continuation. Indeed, such form of continuation is already imagined as part of the work's mode of proceeding. After 'Learn to Die', the prologue to the second *Gesta* story begins:

> This book thus to han endid had Y thought,
> Bur my freend made me change my cast.
> Cleene out of þat purpose hath he me broght. (FMM 1–3)

This is the moment where the Friend reappears, says that he has a story that he would love translated for his fifteen-year-old son, and persuades Hoccleve to continue his work. In terms of the work's narrative, this reappearance of the Friend justifies continuing the work into a fifth part and retroactively legitimises the fourth. Hoccleve implies that he has finally translated the work he said he would in the 'Dialogue' and so should be done with this project. It is just when he thinks he is finished, though, that his friend makes him change direction and alter 'þat purpose' (FMM 3). Here we see, then, the means by which Hoccleve could continue his text well beyond the limits under which it currently extends. If there were no final envoy – and I have argued that we should take the finality of the envoy with a grain of salt – then one might expect perhaps another text and then another, added to the text as it now stands by some variation of these three lines, with Hoccleve continuously explaining that 'I thought I was done, but then my friend showed back up'.

As with Chaucer, the result would be – and to a certain extent already is – an open-ended text, one that has similar benefits to the one Chaucer creates: it is a formal organising principle that allows for maximum variety in terms of the internal contents of the work – any genre could potentially fit within it – and it allows for indefinite expansion – you can always return to the text and add more. In a discussion partially about her own poetic practice and partially about the work of other contemporary poets, Lyn Hejinian's 'The Rejection of Closure' puts the benefits of an open text this way:

---

[32] I should note that this claim would be altered by Linne R. Mooney's identification of a holograph *Regiment of Princes*: 'A Holograph Copy of Thomas Hoccleve's *Regiment of Princes*', *Studies in the Age of Chaucer*, 33 (2011), 263–96. Mooney's claim has been powerfully contested: see the discussion of Hoccleve's holographs in Lawrence Warner, *Chaucer's Scribes: London Textual Production, 1384–1432* (Cambridge, 2018), pp. 115–33.

I can only begin [...] by perceiving the world as vast and overwhelming; each moment stands under an enormous vertical and horizontal pressure of information, potent with ambiguity, meaning-full, unfixed, and certainly incomplete. What saves this from becoming a vast undifferentiated mass of data and situation is one's ability to make distinctions. The open text is one which both acknowledges the vastness of the world and is formally differentiating. It is form that provides an opening.[33]

Hoccleve's work may be nominally finished; it has a final envoy. But the final envoy is arbitrary; nothing else makes the work end there: another story could be added, another quire sewn in. We can easily imagine Hoccleve's friend showing back up, telling Hoccleve 'never mind; it turns out that women were very angry about that last story' (and I imagine they would be!) and asking Hoccleve to translate something new in order to do penance. According to the formal organising principle of the work itself, it could keep expanding in just this way. The only possible roadblock might be Hoccleve's eventual death and, in that way, we might think of Chaucer's *Canterbury Tales* and Hoccleve's *Series* in the terms that Anne Middleton uses to talk about William Langland's work, where the writing of the poem is the writing of a life.[34] Even so, as we have seen with Chaucer, the poem could still continue; another 'friend' of Hoccleve's could have picked up where he left off. In part, Hoccleve's relative lack of fame may have prevented that from happening. Should he have achieved the status of John Lydgate, in which he is mentioned alongside Chaucer and Gower as poetic forebears into the early modern period, we may well have had continuations to the *Series*. But there are other reasons the *Series* may not have been continued by other authors, and one of them has to do with the way the text presents authorship.

Opening the *Series*

The obvious incompleteness of the *Tales* is different from the notional incompleteness of the *Series*, and that difference tells us in what essential way Hoccleve's formal organising principle is different from Chaucer's. Hoccleve makes explicit something Chaucer leaves implicit: that the

---

[33] Lyn Hejinian, *The Language of Inquiry* (Berkeley, 2000), pp. 40–58, quoting from p. 41.
[34] The idea first appears in incipient form in Anne Middleton, 'Narration and the Invention of Experience', in Larry D. Benson and Siegfried Wenzel (eds), *The Wisdom of Poetry: Essays in Early English Literature in Honor of Morton W. Bloomfield* (Kalamazoo, 1982), pp. 91–122. It reaches its fully articulated form in two further essays by Middleton: 'William Langland's "Kynde Name": Authorial Signature and Social Identity in Late Fourteenth-Century England', in Lee Patterson (ed.), *Literary Practice and Social Change in England, 1380–1530* (Berkeley, 1990), pp. 15–82; and 'Acts of Vagrancy: The C Version "Autobiography" and the Statute of 1388', in Steven Justice and Kathryn Kerby-Fulton (eds), *Written Work: Langland, Labor, and Authorship* (Philadelphia, 1998), pp. 208–317.

open-ended nature of their texts is enabled by the conditions of manuscript production in late medieval England. Chaucer's understanding of his material culture only occasionally rises to the surface of his texts, in his complaints about miscopying or his invitation to the easily offended reader in the prologue to the *Miller's Tale* to 'Turne over the leef and chese another tale' (*CT* I.3177). Hoccleve's *Series*, by contrast, is thoroughly embedded in the material conditions of its production. David Watt has written incisively about this, specifically about the importance of booklets to the structure of the *Series*, the opportunities and obstacles that Hoccleve navigates using booklet production.[35] But Hoccleve is doing more than making brilliant use of his scribal position: Hoccleve combines two of the most widely commented upon aspects of his poetry – his notoriously bureaucratic milieu and the insistent materiality and textuality of his imagination – in order to produce a narrative form that is open to the contingent and the potential.[36] In so doing he redefines what it means to be a writer and a reader from where he is sitting.

The thoroughly textual nature of the *Series* is not apparent in its opening; we have no real coordinates to determine what the textual situation of the 'Complaint' is. Are we meant to imagine, for instance, the first-person speaker engaging in oral lamentations?[37] It is not until the opening of the 'Dialogue' with Hoccleve's friend that the reader realises, retrospectively, that the opening complaint we have just read is something that was written down: 'And riȝt anoon I redde hym my compleinte' (*D* 17). This moment is not the only time that such a retrospective textualisation occurs; at the end of the first story from the *Gesta Romanorum*, before the moralisation, Hoccleve hands his friend the physical copy of the text we have just been reading: 'My tale anoon Y fette, and he it nam / Into his hand and it al ouersy' (*FIR* 957–8). The delayed temporality of the Friend's reception of Hoccleve's work, and our realisation that we read what Hoccleve wrote down before the Friend does, is something that Watt points out as made possible by booklet production.[38] That's certainly true, but it also alters

---

[35] David Watt, *The Making of Thomas Hoccleve's Series* (Liverpool, 2013), especially pp. 65–102.

[36] For the most sustained engagements with Hoccleve and the bureaucracy, see Knapp, *Bureaucratic Muse*; Langdell, *Thomas Hoccleve*; and Sobecki, *Last Words*. For Hoccleve's material and textual mode of thought, see Burrow, 'Hoccleve's *Series*'; Watt, *Making of Thomas Hoccleve's Series*; James Simpson, 'Madness and Texts: Hoccleve's *Series*', in Julia Boffey and Janet Cowen (eds), *Chaucer and Fifteenth-Century Poetry*, King's College London Medieval Studies, 5 (London, 1991), pp. 15–29; and finally, in a slightly different register, Taylor Cowdery, 'Hoccleve's Poetics of Matter', *Studies in the Age of Chaucer*, 38 (2016), 133–64.

[37] To a certain extent, this point is mitigated by the self-conscious 'I braste oute on þe morwe and þus bigan' (*C* 35) and the following rubric 'Here endith my prolog and folwith my compleinte'. But these are not definitive obstacles to my argument here; they say nothing about taking out a pen and writing, for instance.

[38] Watt, *Making of Thomas Hoccleve's Series*, pp. 89–93.

our sense of authorship and what kind of reception is imagined here. The 'Complaint' prepares readers for a radically personal text, only for the 'Dialogue' to then subsume Hoccleve's personality into an impersonal network of textual production and circulation, something along the lines of the Privy Seal, where one might assume both the Friend and the texts he possesses originate.[39] But, like any good *aufhebung* (the Hegelian process that both cancels a concept even as it retains it at a higher, more complex level of understanding), Hoccleve's personality is not abolished in this subsumption, but is preserved as something both personal and impersonal. That tendency is why the Friend asks immediately upon reading the 'Complaint' not 'did you really feel that way?' but 'Hast þou maad þis compleint forth to goo / Among þe peple?' and why Hoccleve answers 'What ellis?' (*D* 23–5). For Hoccleve and his friend, for those involved in the textual culture of the Privy Seal, *that is what texts do*.

That assumption, governed by their position in the material production of textual culture, also helps explain the formal organising principle of Hoccleve's *Series* – why it proceeds by the contingent coming and going of persons (patrons and compatriots alike), why the ending feels largely arbitrary, and why it has the capacity for nearly infinite expansion, despite no one taking up the mantle. Those general qualities of contingency, arbitrariness, and indefinite expansion are also the ones that govern textual production in a bureaucratic office. Chaucer's incompleteness is one that imagines a literary posterity, that someone will come along, realise the text is not finished, and will set about adding to it. Hoccleve's incompleteness is more immediate and embedded in its own culture than that. The *Series* imagines release and reception within the bureaucratic culture of the Privy Seal, whose members after all have been instrumental to the production of Hoccleve's poetry all along. Chaucer gives us a text that depends on a certain textual culture in order for him to create it. Hoccleve gives us something closer to a text produced by that textual culture itself, and one that culture could continue to produce. Which is to say, as several commentators on Hoccleve have done, that authorship in the *Series* is produced by a community, a 'communal assemblage as a collaborative form' as Ethan Knapp would have it.[40] As Isabel Davis has argued, 'by Hoccleve's time [...] labour and labouring communities have become the natural subject of masculine autobiography'; to speak about himself, Hoccleve has to speak about the other male scribes that make up his community of workers.[41] For Holly A. Crocker, the *Series* is an 'aesthetic endeavour that ultimately provides Thomas with a socially restored masculinity', something that can only be achieved through the 'dialogic practice of communal (self) creation

---

[39] On bureaucracy and the Privy Seal, especially in regard to the *Series*, see Knapp, *Bureaucratic Muse*, pp. 159–84.

[40] Knapp, *Bureaucratic Muse*, p. 183.

[41] Davis, *Writing Masculinity in the Later Middle Ages*, p. 142.

that the friend explicitly connects to poetic composition'.[42] Such a milieu might also ironically explain why no one continues the *Series*: they had their own work to do.

This vision of communal authorship has another ramification: this community of authors is also a community of readers. Hoccleve's friend does not just ask him to write things; he reads what Hoccleve has written. Both Hoccleve and the Friend, moreover, expect others to read Hoccleve's work as well; that assumption is what lies behind the question and answer regarding the circulation of the 'Complaint', and even, outside of the world of the text, what inspired Hoccleve to construct the *Formulary*, that compendium of scribal documents that he could be sure his fellow scribes would read and then write out.[43] Such an expectation is, as should be already clear, the product of class and occupation. As opposed to the nobility that are the patrons and dedicatees of works, one can expect other Privy Seal clerks to read what you write. Hoccleve might not have been able to count on Henry V reading the *Regiment of Princes*, nor Joan Neville reading the *Series* – even if we want to give them both the benefit of the doubt and assume that they did – because reading is an idiosyncratic quirk of the nobility, something some of them do but in no way a prerequisite of their position. In contrast, clerks, and Privy Seal clerks especially, both read and write; if, as Davis claims, autobiography is about work for late medieval men, then reading and writing is what makes these men who they are.

I stress what may seem like an obvious point of these scribes as readers because it has some bearing on the 'open text' as it is described, once again, by Lyn Hejinian:

> The 'open text', by definition, is open to the world and particularly to the reader. It invites participation, rejects the authority of the writer over the reader and thus, by analogy, the authority implicit in other (social, economic, cultural) hierarchies. It speaks for writing that is generative rather than directive. The writer relinquishes control as a motive. The 'open text' often emphasizes or foregrounds process, either the process of the original composition or of subsequent compositions by the readers, and thus resists the cultural tendencies that seek to identify and fix material and turn it into a product; that is, it resists reduction and commodification.[44]

I would quickly caution that Hoccleve's openness is not quite as radically egalitarian as Hejinian describes; he doesn't anywhere suggest that doing away with the nobility might be a good idea, nor is his relationship to women untroubled. But, Hoccleve's concerns in the *Series* are levelling in

---

[42] Crocker, 'Engendering Affect in Hoccleve's *Series*', p. 71.

[43] For an edition, see Elna-Jean Young Bentley, 'The *Formulary* of Thomas Hoccleve' (unpublished PhD dissertation, Emory University, 1965).

[44] Hejinian, *Language of Inquiry*, p. 43.

their own way, preoccupied as he is throughout much of the text with the general public, represented by the community of the Privy Seal office, or with the universal applicability of *ars moriendi* literature. As for the rest of what Hejinian outlines here, these formal concerns are much more clearly descriptive of what Hoccleve is after as well. His interest in the reader is not only embodied by the alterations and demands that his friend makes about his text, but also in his consternation with what the audience of female readers make of his work. The fact that the *Series* 'invites participation' is, I think, precisely what is being registered in these discussions by Crocker, Davis, and Knapp of it having a kind of communal authorship. Not only does it, like the *Canterbury Tales*, allow its readers to continue adding to it; it seems as if that is already what has happened for it to come into being in the first place. It is the Friend's reading of the 'Complaint' in the 'Dialogue' that causes the Friend to encourage Hoccleve to write something else. It is reading a text that produces more texts, reading that sets the *Series* in motion. In this way, further discussions of the communal authorship of the *Series* should likewise take into account its communal readership.[45]

More importantly for my focus on the formal organising principle, though, is the fact that the *Series* is, as Hejinian describes the 'open text', processual. For Hejinian, 'open texts' would tend to have the kinds of formal organising principle described at the beginning of this essay, works that are concerned with the narration of their own creation. This is because they want readers to continue that work, to further narrate the creation of even more text. Hejinian finds in this process a means to resist commodification, that works against the conditions of production dictated under capitalism. Thinking on Hoccleve, one can find in the *Series* something else, a means of taking back, at an early moment in the rise of capitalism, the simple equation of life with work. The mode of critique takes the form not of revision – like Middleton's Langland – but of production itself.[46] That is, Hoccleve thinks that his life is reading and writing, but that is the good news. It is what his friend has found as a means of soothing his anxious mind, and it is what affords Hoccleve continual meaningful contact with his friend, as well as those audiences that are only mentioned – Duke Humphrey, Lady Westmorland, the group of unnamed offended female readers – or only implicit – the Privy Seal scribes as a whole. One could pessimistically read this as a disciplinary technique, a means of making Hoccleve conform himself to a variety of repressive social strictures, and no doubt it is in part that. But, reading and writing in an ongoing process that approximates the work of a bureaucratic office is also the means by which Hoccleve creates his last, and in my view, most complex aesthetic achievement. Hoccleve has produced a sort of 'open text' that can collapse what it means to be a writer and what it means to

---

[45] Once again Ripplinger's essay in this collection provides a possible direction for further consideration.
[46] Middleton, 'Narration and the Invention of Experience'.

be a reader. He has made a poem that he can show to his fellow Privy Seal clerks and say 'this is what we do', to point out that if they are in the process of making with one another the bureaucratic document known as the government of England, at least they are also producing together and reading for each other something like the *Series*.

4

A 'troubly dreme drempt al in wakynge': Hoccleve's Nearly-Dream Poem

Laurie Atkinson

This essay reappraises the peculiar experiments in genre and form in Thomas Hoccleve's *Regiment of Princes*. Lines 1 to 2016 of the *Regiment* represent a purposeful reworking of one of late medieval England's most favoured, but eventually outmoded, poetic forms: dream-framed first-person narrative. In what follows, the genre-bending first section of the *Regiment* is considered as a development of, and an alternative to, the dream poetry of Chaucer and his French predecessors and contemporaries. Central to my analysis is an understanding of form as the manifestation in text of an 'originating thought' of the poet.[1] Hoccleve, like Chaucer, adopts a dream-framed form in order to dramatise the processes of poetic composition. However, where Chaucer seems primarily interested in the situation of his works in relation to other authors and texts, Hoccleve's reconfigurations in the *Regiment* betray a more immediate concern with the position of his writing relative to contemporary political and religious discourses, and the insertion of his quasi-autobiographical textual double into a properly functioning system of Lancastrian royal patronage. Beginning by discussing the *Regiment*'s formal elements and its genre, I then delineate some of the key narratorial features of Middle French and Chaucerian dream poetry in order to make the case that Hoccleve's distinctive self-authorising strategy in the *Regiment* involves both an imitation and a pointed refusal of Chaucer's dream poems.

The *Regiment* has presented modern critics with a number of formal difficulties. The first is its lack of proportion. Almost two-fifths of the *Regiment*'s 5463 lines comprise its first-person narrative in which a poet-narrator – later identified by the name 'Hoccleve' (1864, 1865) – walks out from his home at Chester's Inn and encounters a 'poore old hoor man' (122). The narrative's ostensible purpose is to provide a fictionalised account of the historical author Hoccleve's compilation of the mirror-for-princes treatise that follows.

---

[1] The phrase is Christopher Cannon's: 'Form', in Paul Strohm (ed.), *Middle English*, Oxford Twenty-First Century Approaches to Literature (Oxford, 2007), pp. 177–90, at p. 182.

That treatise begins at line 2017, with a Prologue dedicating the work to Prince Henry, the future King Henry V. Most manuscripts use a rubric to mark another transition at line 2156. While they vary a little, these rubrics generally indicate that the prologue has come to an end and the *Regiment* proper is about to begin: 'Explicit prologus, de principum regimine; incipiendo de fide observanda' [the prologue to the *Regiment of Princes* here ends; the beginning [of the section] concerning the keeping of faith].[2]

A second difficulty for critics of the *Regiment* arises from the first: its two main parts seem inconsistent. The *Regiment* proper (lines 2156 to 5463) conforms to the pattern of the late medieval mirror for princes, yet it is little over half the story. The *Regiment*'s first section was considered by scribes and readers to be integral to the whole: all but one of the *Regiment* manuscripts include lines 1 to 2016.[3] Faced with such evidence, one cannot help but ask: *why* did Hoccleve and his fifteenth-century audience consider this quasi-autobiographical first-person narrative to be an appropriate introduction to the *Regiment*'s didactic core?

This raises a third difficulty facing the critic of Hoccleve's *Regiment*: the impossibility of assigning the Dialogue with the Old Man to a stable literary genre.[4] The narrative invokes many of the conventions of medieval dream poetry – especially Chaucer's – but also betrays obvious differences.[5] Nicholas Perkins writes that the 'time of the encounter (morning), its place, and Hoccleve's [i.e. the poet-narrator's] solitude and troubled psychological state all suggest the topoi of a dream-vision'; and yet, as the poem progresses, 'Hoccleve [...] overturns the reader's expectation of the scene'.[6] The concerns of Hoccleve's poet-narrator and his Old Man belong to Lancastrian England rather than to a dream otherworld; the locale of their dialogue is not some *locus amoenus* but a field near the Strand; and, as if to jolt readers to their senses long before they reach critical REM, the poet-narrator of Hoccleve's nearly-dream poem never falls asleep. There is also an important structural difference: the Dialogue with the Old Man is not a self-contained first-person narrative like Chaucer's *Book of the Duchess* or *Parliament of Fowls*; it functions instead to frame a different kind of text, the *Regiment* proper. The combination of these differences renders the opening of the *Regiment* somewhat resistant to close comparative analysis.

---

2 The rubric quoted is from London, British Library, MS Arundel 38, fol. 39v.

3 Oxford, Bodleian Library, MS Rawlinson poet. 168 is the only complete *Regiment* manuscript to omit lines 1 to 2016.

4 I adopt Nicholas Perkins's names for the three parts of the *Regiment*: the Dialogue with the Old Man (1–2016), the Prologue (2017–155), and the *Regiment* proper (2156–5463). See Perkins's justification in *Hoccleve's* Regiment of Princes: *Counsel and Constraint* (Cambridge, 2001), pp. 178–85. This is a departure from Charles R. Blyth's edition, in which the first 2016 lines of the *Regiment* are named as the Prologue.

5 For an early formulation of this point, see C. S. Lewis, *The Allegory of Love: A Study in Medieval Tradition* (London, 1936), pp. 238–9.

6 Perkins, *Counsel and Constraint*, pp. 179, 180.

What follows is an analysis of the motivations for, and implications of, the *Regiment*'s deliberate formal gesture towards the tradition of dream poetry, an analysis that adopts the approach to textual form proposed by Christopher Cannon.[7] Form, Cannon observes, can be understood not only as 'the idea that precedes the thing' or, alternatively, as 'the attribute that gives things their distinctive being', but rather as 'the *in*forming of raw materials according to the script of some idea, as the *forming* of an object guided by some thought'.[8] When applied to textual form, this theory 'necessarily defines every contour that might be discerned in a text, not just as a clue to an originating thought (or set of them), but as a version of it'.[9] What, then, in Cannon's terms, can the form of Hoccleve's *Regiment* tell us about the 'originating thought' that guided its design?

This return to form promises to augment the current, predominantly historicist, understanding of Hoccleve's preoccupations in the *Regiment*. The Dialogue with the Old Man has usually been read alongside *La Male Regle de T. Hoccleue* and the narrative frame of the *Series* as an instance of Hoccleve's experimentation in the self-promotional opportunities of autobiographical poetry.[10] Robert Meyer-Lee has explored the importance of Hoccleve's recognisable but never entirely artless personae for his authorial self-representation in relation to secular authority, literary tradition, and the making of books.[11] Rather than following Meyer-Lee and others in considering Hoccleve's textual identity as a strategic response to extrinsic historical circumstances, this essay approaches Hoccleve's quasi-autobiography as a strategic response to the potentialities of a particular poetic form – as a development of, and an alternative to, the dream-framed first-person narratives of Chaucer and his French predecessors and contemporaries.

The reassessment of the form and genre of the Dialogue with the Old Man here proposed – a 'biographication' of dream-framed first-person narrative – intersects with A. C. Spearing's work on narrative theory and medieval narrative. Building on earlier investigations, Spearing suggests that it may be helpful to imagine that 'extended, non-lyrical, fictional writings in and of the first person' might belong to a medieval 'super-genre' that he calls 'autography'. The Middle French *dit* is the consummate example of

7   Cannon, 'Form', pp. 177–90.
8   Cannon, 'Form', p. 177.
9   Cannon, 'Form', p. 182.
10 An approach instigated by J. A. Burrow, 'Autobiographical Poetry in the Middle Ages: The Case of Thomas Hoccleve', in J. A. Burrow (ed.), *Middle English Literature: British Academy Gollancz Lectures* (Oxford, 1989), pp. 223–46; see also Burrow's 'The Poet as Petitioner', *Studies in the Age of Chaucer*, 3 (1981), 61–75.
11 Robert J. Meyer-Lee, *Poets and Power from Chaucer to Wyatt* (Cambridge, 2007), pp. 88–124. Earlier significant studies of Hoccleve's poetic personae include David C. Greetham, 'Self-Referential Artifacts: Hoccleve's Persona as a Literary Device', *Modern Philology*, 86 (1989), 242–51; and Anthony J. Hasler, 'Hoccleve's Unregimented Body', *Paragraph*, 13 (1990), 164–83.

this kind of text in which 'there is no implied assertion that the first person either does or does not correspond to a real-life individual'.[12] In a chapter on Hoccleve's *Regiment*, Spearing takes the self-reflexive, yet inescapably textual, 'I' of the Dialogue with the Old Man as indicative of the poem's status as autography. 'The "I" of the preamble', writes Spearing, 'is a textual "I", itself fragmented, and composed out of fragments of other texts, predominantly Chaucerian.'[13] Hoccleve's specific debt to Chaucer, he argues, 'involved learning from Chaucer to do things that Chaucer had not done, and especially to apply to the first person a manner of exposing weakness (timidity, cowardice, self-indulgence) that Chaucer had only applied to third persons'.[14] Spearing is referring here to the 'free indirect style' devised for the descriptions of the pilgrims in the *General Prologue* to the *Canterbury Tales*.[15] His approach invites further enquiry into the extent to which Hoccleve's Dialogue with the Old Man directly responds to Chaucer's earlier dream-framed poems, and to the narrating personae derived from the Middle French *dits amoureux*. Chaucer's innovations in first- and third-person narration provided Hoccleve with a point of departure for his own experiments in the autography genre: they afforded both a starting point and a paradigm from which he could deliberately depart.

In the Dialogue with the Old Man, Hoccleve recreates an ostensibly Chaucerian setting and poet-narrator which deliberately disappoint the generic expectations that they evoke. The broad appeal of the dream poem to late medieval poets and readers resided in the opportunity it afforded for compositional freedom, and its claim to an allegorical significance other – and greater – than its literal meaning. However, the crucial feature that the dream-framed form offered to Chaucer, to the French *dits* (discussed further below), and to what Spearing has elsewhere described as the 'Chaucerian Tradition' of English and Scottish dream poetry, is the appearance of a poet-narrator who is presented as the textual double of the historical author.[16] In Chaucer's dream poems, the poet-narrator is essentially subordinate to the poet's metapoetic concerns. It is tempting to read the bookish 'Geffrey' of the *House of Fame* (729) as a self-deprecating representation of the historical author; yet even when assigned a name, the readerly poet-narrator of Chaucer's dream poems is first and foremost a more depersonalised figure within 'an allegory of the processes of reading and writing'.[17] This

---

[12] A. C. Spearing, *Medieval Autographies: The 'I' of the Text* (Notre Dame, 2012), pp. 1, 7; see also Spearing's *Textual Subjectivity: The Encoding of Subjectivity in Medieval Narratives and Lyrics* (Oxford, 2005).

[13] Spearing, *Medieval Autographies*, p. 169.

[14] Spearing, *Medieval Autographies*, p. 169.

[15] Spearing, *Medieval Autographies*, pp. 156–8.

[16] A. C. Spearing, *Medieval Dream-Poetry* (Cambridge, 1976), pp. 171–218.

[17] Deanne Williams, 'The Dream Visions', in Seth Lerer (ed.), *The Yale Companion to Chaucer* (New Haven, 2006), pp. 147–78, at p. 149.

figure's significance is not delimited by the known biography (then or now) of the historical Chaucer. By contrast, Hoccleve's 'biographication' of the dream poem's narrating persona in the Dialogue with the Old Man arguably has the opposite effect, re-emphasising the personal and political circumstances for the *Regiment*'s composition, and foregrounding the claim of the historical author to attention and reward. This decision pointedly to eschew the dream-framed form so favoured by the early Chaucer complicates our understanding of Hoccleve's affiliation to, and departures from, his claimed poetic father. Hoccleve's 'conjur[ing]' of Chaucer as a 'remembered presence' in the *Regiment* has been much discussed.[18] What interests me in this essay is Hoccleve's exploitation of the quasi-autobiographical potential of Chaucerian poetic form in order to establish his personal credentials as an advisor to princes.[19]

The implications of Hoccleve's engagement with Chaucer's treatment of the dream-framed form become clearer when we consider Hoccleve's awareness of a range of framed first-person writing. Boethius's *De consolatione philosophiae* is usually taken as the foremost literary analogue for the opening to the *Regiment*.[20] Critics have rightly drawn attention to the thematic similarities between the consolation offered to Hoccleve's poet-narrator, fearful that Fortune 'Aftir glad look [...] shapith her to stynge' (68), and the situation of Boethius's prisoner – towards whom 'Fortune cloudy' has already 'chaunged hir deceivable chere' (Chaucer, *Boece* I, *metrum* 1, lines 26–8). However, the Dialogue with the Old Man also engages with a wide range of late medieval vernacular traditions of dream-framed dialogue and complaint. Hoccleve was one of the copyists of another late medieval

---

[18] James Simpson, 'Chaucer's Presence and Absence, 1400–1550', in Piero Boitani (ed.), *The Cambridge Companion to Chaucer*, 2nd edn (Cambridge, 2003), pp. 251–69, at p. 258. See also A. C. Spearing, *Medieval to Renaissance in English Poetry* (Cambridge, 1985), pp. 88–110; Seth Lerer, *Chaucer and His Readers: Imagining the Author in Late-Medieval England* (Princeton, 1993), pp. 23–4 and 58–9; Sebastian Langdell, *Thomas Hoccleve: Religious Reform, Transnational Poetics, and the Invention of Chaucer* (Liverpool, 2018), pp. 64–99. For an alternative reading of Hoccleve's attitude towards Chaucer as 'a strategy for poetic usurpation', see Ethan Knapp, *The Bureaucratic Muse: Thomas Hoccleve and the Literature of Late Medieval England* (University Park, 2001), pp. 107–28.

[19] For an alternative reading of Hoccleve's engagement with Chaucerian dream poetry, see Hisashi Sugito, 'Reality as Dream: Hoccleve's Daydreaming Mind', *Chaucer Review*, 49 (2014), 244–63. Sugito also observes the formal similarities between Chaucer's dream poems and Hoccleve's Dialogue with the Old Man, though in the latter, the poet-narrator never falls asleep. Sugito proposes an interpretation of Hoccleve's 'dream' as 'not a physical one such as other poets experience, but a figurative one referring to the condition of his mind' (p. 246), with an emphasis on Hoccleve's representation of his 'unfocused state of mind' (p. 247), rather than, as in my discussion, his credentials as an advisor to princes.

[20] See, for example, Stephan Kohl, 'More Than Virtues and Vices: Self-Analysis in Hoccleve's "Autobiographies"', *Fifteenth-Century Studies*, 14 (1988), 115–27, at pp. 119–20; and Perkins, *Counsel and Constraint*, pp. 180–1.

compilatio with a narrative frame: Gower's *Confessio Amantis* in Cambridge, Trinity College, MS R. 3. 2.[21] The work of Sebastian Langdell has also demonstrated the potential Langlandian influence on the *Regiment*.[22] It was, however, the quasi-autobiographical potential of Chaucer's dream poems, in tandem with their Middle French models, which Hoccleve seems to have found especially stimulating in the Dialogue with the Old Man.

The poet-narrators that appear in the dream poems of Chaucer and many of his fifteenth-century successors conform to a recognisable type. It is a persona that is essentially derived from the Middle French *dits amoureux*, most notably the works of Guillaume de Machaut and Jean Froissart, as well as their thirteenth-century predecessor, *Le Roman de la Rose* of Guillaume de Lorris and Jean de Meun.[23] Integral to the narrative framing of the *dits amoureux*, whether presented as a dream or otherwise, is the introduction of a textual first person who is understood to be the narrator of, but also a character within, the account that follows – a clerk, but also a lover. This figure is only ever an imperfect, often ironic, representation of the historical author. Their clerkly aspect suggests a level of correspondence between the fictional narrating persona and the author for the work; their attributes as a lover, meanwhile, betray the influence of literary convention. At the opening of *Le Jugement dou Roy de Behaingne*, Machaut's *je* describes his handsome costume: he is dressed 'Coms cils qui tres parfaitement amay / D'amore seüre' [In the fashion of a man who loved most perfectly / With a constant love] (11–12).[24] Here, as in Machaut's *Dit de la Fonteinne Amoureuse*,

---

[21] See A. I. Doyle and M. B. Parkes, 'The Production of Copies of the *Canterbury Tales* and the *Confessio Amantis* in the Early Fifteenth Century', in M. B. Parkes and Andrew G. Watson (eds), *Medieval Scribes, Manuscripts and Libraries: Essays Presented to N. R. Ker* (London, 1978), pp. 163–210, at pp. 182–5. The parallels between Gower's handling of his Amans persona and the presentation of the *Regiment*'s 'Hoccleve' warrant greater attention given the juxtaposition in both works of a first-person narrative frame and (in the case of Book VII of the *Confessio*) a moral-political didactic core. On this juxtaposition, see further Charles R. Blyth, 'Thomas Hoccleve's Other Master', *Mediaevalia*, 16 (1993), 349–59, at pp. 351–2.

[22] Langdell, *Thomas Hoccleve*, pp. 100–37.

[23] See B. A. Windeatt (ed. and trans.), *Chaucer's Dream Poetry: Sources and Analogues* (Cambridge, 1982); James I. Wimsatt, *Chaucer and His French Contemporaries: Natural Music in the Fourteenth Century* (Toronto, 1993), especially pp. 77–108; and William Calin, *The French Tradition and the Literature of Medieval England* (Toronto, 1994), especially pp. 276–301. For an introduction to and discussion of the distinguishing features of the *dit*, see Jacqueline Cerquiglini, 'Le clerc et l'écriture: le *voir dit* de Guillaume de Machaut et la définition du *dit*', in Hans Ulrich Gumbrecht (ed.), *Literatur in der Gesellschaft des Spätmittelalters* (Heidelberg, 1980), pp. 151–68. On the *dit* and subjectivity in French and English poetry, see also Sarah Kay, *Subjectivity in Troubadour Poetry* (Cambridge, 1990); and Michel Zink, *The Invention of Literary Subjectivity*, trans. David Sices (Baltimore, 1999).

[24] All references to and translations of the *Roy de Behaingne* are from Guillaume Machaut, *The Complete Poetry and Music*, vol. 1: *The Debate Series*, trans. and ed. R. Barton Palmer with Domenic Leo and Uri Smilansky (Kalamazoo, 2016).

the poet-narrator is the reporter of others' experiences in love rather than his own; yet the poem ends with a re-affirmation of his vocation as a 'Loiaus amis' [true lover] (2069). In the *Fonteinne Amoureuse*, Machaut's poet-narrator is identified at the outset of the poem as a sufferer in love. He claims to write:

> Pour moy deduire et soulacier
> Et pour ma pensee lacier
> En loial amour qui me lace
> En ses las, ou point ne me lasse,
> Car jamais ne seroie las
> D'estre y [...]

> [In order to give delight and consolation to myself, and to bind my thoughts to the true love that holds me in those bonds where I shall never tire of being ...] (1–6)[25]

Given this introduction, it comes as something of a surprise when the subject of the *Fonteinne Amoureuse* is revealed to be the sorrows in love expressed by a different, princely lover, diligently transcribed by the poet-narrator in his chamber as if he is serving as a clerk to that prince. At lines 45–51, the name of the historical author, Machaut, and that of his patron, John, duke of Berry, are revealed in a cryptogram; and soon afterwards, the poet-narrator realigns his identity to that of a 'clers / Rudes, nices et malapers' [ignorant, silly, impertinent clerk] (139–40), sometime in the service of the king of Bohemia. Again, a simple correspondence between poet-narrator and historical author is not long maintained: the amorous aspect of Machaut's textual first person is returned to the fore in the dream of Venus and the prince's lady that comprises the second half of the poem.[26] Thus the *dits amoureux* adumbrate the sustained quasi-autobiographical writing of the kind elaborated in the first part of the *Regiment*.[27]

---

[25] Quotations from the *Fonteinne Amoureuse* are taken from Ernest Hœpffner (ed.), *Œuvres de Guillaume de Machaut* (3 vols, Paris, 1908–21), vol. 3; translations are taken from Windeatt (ed. and trans.), *Chaucer's Dream Poetry*.

[26] A slightly different balance is struck between the amorous and clerkly identities of the poet-narrator in Froissart's *Paradys d'Amours*. There, the poet-narrator is primarily a lover – 'Je, qui bien par amours amai' [I, who was in love indeed] (46) – and it is his own lovesickness that is assuaged by the dream of Plaisance and Esperance that follows. Auguste Scheler (ed.), *Œuvres de Froissart. Poésies* (3 vols, Brussels, 1870–72), vol. 1; translation from Windeatt (ed. and trans.), *Chaucer's Dream Poetry*.

[27] Further study is needed of the extent to which the *Rose* and its Middle French successors might have exerted a *direct* influence on Hoccleve's framed first-person narratives. Hoccleve evidently knew the former: he makes explicit reference to de Meun's *Rose* as early as 1402 in *L'epistre de Cupide* (lines 286–7). On Hoccleve's further engagement with Middle French poetry, and the *dits* in particular, see J. A. Burrow, 'Hoccleve and the Middle French Poets', in Helen Cooper and Sally Mapstone (eds), *The Long Fifteenth Century: Essays for Douglas Gray* (Oxford, 1997), pp. 35–49; Spearing, *Medieval*

The textual first persons of the *dits amoureux* are only partially referential: their portraits are painted with varying levels of detail, but they are never meant as an exact likeness. The characterisation of the poems' poet-narrators inevitably influences the reader's conception of the implied author for the work, yet they are too partial and too often undercut to be substituted for the more complex 'author-image' that is a combination of both the indexical signs that can be found in the text itself and the interpretation of those indexes by each individual reader.[28] The poet-narrator of the *dit* functions, in effect, as a narrative device whereby the historical author may attempt to mediate the reception of his/her writings – projections, in poetry, of an idealised court society, from the perspective of one of its more peripheral, though largely sympathetic, members. So, in the *Fonteinne Amoureuse*, the poet-narrator claims that he is compelled to reveal his name by a personified 'amours fine' [Fine Loving] (37) – that is, the conventions of courtly love – rather than more material concerns. The allusion to the poet's service to the king of Bohemia foregrounds a clerkly occupation close to that of the historical Machaut; yet it also recalls the role of the poet-narrator of *Roy de Behaingne* as the mediator between the wholly literary knight and lover of the first part of the *dit* and the textual double of the historical Machaut's lord and patron, John of Bohemia, at the castle of Durbuy in the second.[29] Beyond Machaut's cryptograms, these poet-narrators are rarely made the explicit namesake of the historical author; nevertheless, in their status as clerks and failed lovers, as hangers-on in court society who must observe rather than participate in the love affairs of others, they feature as an innocuous and often humorous proxy for the historical authors Machaut, Froissart, or, in his own experiments with the form, Chaucer, vis-à-vis an implied court audience.

Chaucer's adoption, and re-imagination, of the narrating persona of the *dits amoureux* in his dream visions of the 1370s and 1380s has far-reaching implications for the development of his poetics and for those of his English successors.[30] The poet-narrators of Chaucer's dream poems depart from his Middle French models, establishing features that could be imitated or refused

---

Autographies, pp. 129–208; Langdell, *Thomas Hoccleve*, pp. 52–63; Misty Schieberle, 'A New Hoccleve Literary Manuscript: The Trilingual Miscellany in London, British Library, MS Harley 219', *Review of English Studies*, 70, issue 297 (2019), 1–24; and on the reception of the *Rose* in late medieval England more broadly, Philip Knox, *The Romance of the Rose and the Making of Fourteenth-Century English Literature* (Oxford, 2022).

[28] I take my definition of the implied author from Wolf Schmid, 'Implied Author' (2013), in Peter Hühn et al. (eds), *The Living Handbook of Narratology*, http://www.lhn.uni-hamburg.de (accessed 30 July 2019).

[29] Durbuy, east of Namur in modern-day Belgium, was a castle of John the Blind (1296–1346), count of Luxembourg and king of Bohemia, whom Machaut served from the 1320s.

[30] On Chaucer's deployment and development of the first-person poet-narrator, see

in later English dream poetry.[31] For example, Chaucer emphasises the clerkly rather than the amorous identity of his narrating personae, and suggests only a loose correspondence between his textual first person and himself. As many critics have observed, Chaucer's poet-narrators are 'anxious about love rather than in love'.[32] The poet-narrator's professed study of, but lack of experience with, love in the *Parliament of Fowls* (8–9, 157–68) and *House of Fame* (627–40) foregrounds the clerkly character of Chaucer's narrating personae to an even greater extent than do Machaut and Froissart. Nevertheless, Chaucer's dream poems depart from the *dits amoureux* in their fairly limited interest in the named historical author's self-promotion. There is a marked reluctance in the *Book of the Duchess*, the *Parliament of Fowls*, and, to a lesser extent, the *House of Fame*, to deploy the poet-narrator as a claimant for the poetic skill and existing bibliography of the person who was supposed to have composed the work, whether that be the intradiegetic poet-narrator or the historical author Chaucer.[33] The poet-narrator in these early dream poems is clearly a writer of poetry – he has taken it upon himself to put into verse the report which we are reading – but he is not yet presented as a recognisable poet of established reputation like, for instance, the poet-narrator in Machaut's *Jugement dou Roy de Navarre*, who is tried before a court of love for having spoken ill of ladies in the *Roy de Behaingne*. One purpose of the historical author's textual double in Machaut's *dits* is to serve as a record of his extra-literary biography. Machaut's poet-narrators refer to (and are held accountable for) earlier works written by the historical author Machaut. The situation in the *Roy de Navarre* is analogous to that in the Prologue to Chaucer's *Legend of Good Women* and, in turn, the narrative frame to Hoccleve's *Series*, where Chaucer's and Hoccleve's textual doubles are themselves brought to account for their supposedly anti-feminist writings.[34] By contrast, the books that are encountered by Chaucer's poet-narrators in the *Book of the Duchess*, *House of Fame* and *Parliament of Fowls* are the works of classical *auctores* and continental poets. In each of the three early dream poems, Chaucer's clerkly poet-narrators are not only inept lovers but they are also as yet unproven as poets.

Chaucer's presentation of his textual doubles in this way seems connected to the subject matter of the early dream poems. The *Book of the Duchess*, the *Parliament of Fowls*, and, most overtly, the *House of Fame* are concerned

especially David Lawton, *Chaucer's Narrators* (Cambridge, 1985); Spearing, *Textual Subjectivity*, pp. 68–136; and Spearing, *Medieval Autographies*, pp. 65–98.

[31] On the concepts of 'imitation' and 'refusal' as an approach to late medieval authorship, see Robert R. Edwards, 'Authorship, Imitation and Refusal in Late-Medieval England', *Swiss Papers in English Language and Literature*, 25 (2011), 51–73.

[32] Lawton, *Chaucer's Narrators*, p. 38.

[33] See Spearing, *Medieval Dream-Poetry*, pp. 82–3; and Lawton, *Chaucer's Narrators*, pp. 52–3. The paucity of biographical detail is particularly striking in the *Duchess* given its heavy reliance on Machaut's verse, especially the *Roy de Behaingne*.

[34] See Chaucer, *Legend of Good Women* (F308–579); and Hoccleve, 'Dialogue', lines 659–826.

with the maturation of their poet-narrators – their acquisition of the poetic skill and/or the material for subsequent compositions that will see them transformed into something like the implied author for the work after their awakening from the dream.[35] Whereas Chaucer may not promote his name as explicitly as Machaut and Froissart, he certainly adopts the ironic distance that they establish between the poet-narrator and implied author.[36] By highlighting the difference between the blinkered view of the poet-narrator *within* the text and the critical – though still hardly omniscient – perspective of the implied author (and audience) outside it while stripping the poet-narrator of almost any biographical detail or bibliographical attribution that might identify him with the historical author, Chaucer effaces nearly all evidence of his own life and works from his early dream poems. His textual first person instead becomes the vehicle for more speculative reflections on poetic composition.

This changes in the Prologue to the *Legend of Good Women* (F328–34), where Chaucer names his own works – *Troilus* and his translation of the *Rose* – as the books for which his textual double is brought to trial before the God of Love. The poet-narrator is still placed at an ironic distance from the implied author: he fails to recognise Alceste as the Daisy to whom he had earlier directed his devotions (F499–551); nor is he able to defend himself against the charges of Love.[37] Nevertheless, the poet-narrator has for the first time been elevated to the status of an established poet with an extant bibliography. It is surely no coincidence that in the Prologue to the *Legend* Chaucer's poet-narrator is presented as the client of not one but two literary patrons – the God of Love within the fictional account for the composition of the work set out in the Prologue; and, in the F text, the 'quene' to whom Love bids the poet-narrator give the book 'at Eltham or at Sheene' (F496–7), usually identified as Queen Anne of Bohemia, wife of Richard II. The expanded possibility for quasi-auto-biographical self-promotion suggested by the *Legend* inspired Hoccleve. Critics have long recognised the resonance between the poet-narrator's encounter with the God of Love and the intercession of Alceste in the *Legend* and the literary criticism and commission depicted in Hoccleve's *Series*. I contend that Hoccleve's *Regiment* also shows him thinking through (and beyond) the narrative structure for which Chaucer's dream poems, including the *Legend*, provided his most immediate points of departure.

The quasi-autobiographical potential that is carried over, though suppressed, in Chaucer's *dit*-inspired *Book of the Duchess*, *Parliament of Fowls* and *House of Fame*, and developed, though still not fully realised, in the

---

[35] This transformation is most fully realised in the conclusion to the *Book of the Duchess*. The poem's last line, 'This was my sweven; now hit is doon' (1334), 'bring[s] us', remarks Lawton, 'for the first time to the poet's present [...]. Only in this closing section [...] is the narrator-persona fully reconciled with the figure of the poet' (*Chaucer's Narrators*, p. 54).

[36] See Calin, *French Tradition*, p. 285.

[37] Calin, *French Tradition*, pp. 292–3.

Prologue to the *Legend*, is recovered, and expanded, in Hoccleve's *Regiment*. Its initial situation, a dialogue between the poet-narrator and an old man, resonates with the *Book of the Duchess*. The opening stanzas of the Dialogue with the Old Man introduce a poet-narrator who reports a sleepless night spent 'Musynge upon the restlees bysynesse / Which that this troubly world hath ay on honde' (1–2). Poet-narrators who report some recent or ongoing mental disturbance are almost ubiquitous in the narrative frames of English and Scottish dream poems in the 'Chaucerian Tradition'.[38] There is no evocation in the Dialogue with the Old Man of an appropriate seasonal setting by means of an astrological description as in, for example, Lydgate's *Temple of Glas* (lines 4–9, December) and *Complaynte of a Lovers Lyfe* (lines 1–11, May) – the seasonal trope owes more to the opening of the *General Prologue* to the *Canterbury Tales* (I.1–18) than to Chaucer's dream poems *per se*. Nevertheless, there is ample evidence for Larry Scanlon's comparison of the 'moment of psychic disturbance' with which the *Regiment* begins to the insomniac opening of Chaucer's *Duchess*.[39] Both poet-narrators are solitary, doleful figures (85–98; cf. *BD* 25–7), they are distracted by 'thoght' (1–112; cf. *BD* 4–15, 28–9) and each is deprived of sleep (6–7, 71–9, 109–10, 115–16; cf. *BD*, 1–43). The reader cannot help but compare the textual first person of the opening of the Dialogue with the Old Man, like that of the *Duchess*, with the unrequited-lover-type poet-narrators of the *dits amoureux* – characters whose mental state is perfectly conducive to what in Macrobian terms would be described as a *somnium*, an enigmatic dream that requires interpretation.[40]

---

[38] The *Fonteinne Amoureuse* (61–8) and Froissart's *Paradys d'Amours* (1–12) are important continental sources for the trope. The poet-narrator of the *Parliament*, following his reading of the *Somnium Scipionis* before going to bed, is 'fulfild of thought and besy hevinesse' (89). In lines 1–43 of the *Book of the Duchess*, Chaucer's poet-narrator describes being similarly afflicted by 'so many an ydel thought / Purely for defaute of slepe' (4–5), a motif that reappears in the opening lines of Lydgate's *Temple of Glas* (1–3) and, presented explicitly as lovesickness, before Amans's complaint to Cupid and Venus in the *Confessio* (I.104–23). John Gower, *Confessio Amantis*, vol. 1, ed. Russell A. Peck, trans. Andrew Galloway, 2nd edn (Kalamazoo, 2006). All references to the *Confessio* (and translations) are to this edition.

[39] Larry Scanlon, 'The King's Two Voices: Narrative and Power in Hoccleve's *Regement of Princes*', in Lee Patterson (ed.), *Literary Practice and Social Change in Britain 1380–1530* (Berkeley, 1990), pp. 216–47, at p. 234.

[40] See Macrobius, *Commentary on the Dream of Scipio*, trans. William Harris Stahl (New York, 1952), I.iii. On Macrobius's highly influential classification of dreams, see Steven F. Kruger, *Dreaming in the Middle Ages* (Cambridge, 1992), pp. 21–32. Compare the similar move in Book I of Gower's *Confessio*. The Latin note at the moment of transition from moral commentary to exemplary first-person narrative reads: 'Hic quasi in persona aliorum, quos amor alligat, fingens se auctor esse Amantem, varias eorum passiones variis huius libri distinccionibus per singula scribere proponit' [Here the author, fashioning himself to be the Lover as if in the role of those others whom love binds, proposes to write about their various passions one by one in the various sections of this book] (Latin marginalia at I.59).

Hoccleve deploys a narrating persona with which his readers could assume familiarity, yet the 'Hoccleve' of the Dialogue with the Old Man is not merely the depersonalised lover of literary convention.

No *somnium* follows the opening stanzas of the Dialogue with the Old Man. However, the frequency with which Hoccleve compares the mental state of his poet-narrator to an unsettled dream continues to evoke the topoi of the dream poem – in part to draw attention to the poem's divergence from the expectations of the genre. Following his sleepless night, the poet-narrator recalls how 'I roos me up, for boote fond I noon' (115; cf. *BD* 38) and 'Into the feeld I dressid me in hye' (116). The narrative frame serves as the introduction to a waking encounter with an 'old hoor man' rather than 'so inly swete a sweven' (*BD* 276); yet Hoccleve is oddly obtuse when it comes to confirming that his poet-narrator is *not* in fact asleep. To the Old Man's greeting, 'Good day, sire, and God yow blesse!' (123), the poet-narrator is at first oblivious: 'But I [heard] no word, for my seekly distresse / Forbad myn eres usen hir office' (124–5). Charles R. Blyth compares the scene to the delayed reaction of the Black Knight to the poet-narrator in the *Book of the Duchess*.[41] The parallel continues in the Old Man's assessment of the poet-narrator's 'drery cheere' and 'deedly colour pale and wan' (128–9); he concludes, as does the *Book of the Duchess*'s poet-narrator of the Black Knight, that 'This man that I see here / Al wrong is wrestid, by aght I see can' (129–30), and desires to know the cause of his affliction (cf. *BD*, 448–9, 536–8).

The next lines re-enact an awakening scene that resonates with scenes in Chaucer's writing that explore the unstable boundary between the waking world and dreams. In the story of Ceyx and Alcyone in the *Book of the Duchess*'s narrative frame, Juno's messenger wakes Morpheus in his cave by blowing a horn in his ear and calling '"Awak! [...] Who is lyth there?"' (181) – the moment is echoed at the beginning of the dream core when the poet-narrator is roused by a hunting horn (344–5). Again, at the beginning of Book II of the *House of Fame*, the Eagle, having carried Chaucer's poet-narrator high into the air, 'to me spak / In mannes vois and seyde, "Awak!" / [...] / And called me tho by my name, / [...] / Right in the same vois and stevene / That useth oon I coulde nevene' (555–6, 558, 561–2).[42] Both passages seem strangely stilted; the identity of both the speaker and the addressee are made temporarily uncertain whilst voices only half heard suggest slippages between

---

[41] Blyth (ed.), *Regiment*, note to line 124.
[42] That is, the Eagle speaks in the same voice and with the same tone as one whom the poet-narrator 'could name'. Compare a further Chaucerian intertext for the scene: *Troilus and Criseyde*, I.722–56, where Pandarus commands the melancholy Troilus to 'awake', and later shakes him (I.869), discussed in Nicholas Perkins, 'Haunted Hoccleve? The Regiment of Princes, the Troilean Intertext, and Conversations with the Dead', *Chaucer Review*, 43 (2008), 103–39, at pp. 105–6. In his dialogues in particular, Hoccleve combines and mingles elements from throughout Chaucer's poetry, and not only his dream poems.

states of consciousness. The meeting of Hoccleve's poet-narrator and the Old Man has a similar effect. The Old Man, looking to rouse the poet-narrator from his melancholy stupor, addresses him sharply:

> He stirte unto me and seide, 'Sleepstow, man?
> Awake!' and gan me shake wondir faste,
> And with a sigh I answerde atte laste:

> 'A, who is there?' 'I', quod this olde greye,
> 'Am heer', and he me tolde the manere
> How he spak to me, as yee herde me seye. (RP 131–6)

As in the *House of Fame*, the command that the poet-narrator 'Awake!' marks the beginning of his instruction by a figure of authority, though without the comic overtones of the dialogue between 'Geffrey' and the Eagle. Hoccleve then extends Chaucer's strategy of only partially identifying his interlocutors. The Old Man's self-identification is promised and then denied by the contorted syntax of the redundant 'I [...] / Am heer' statement (an echo, perhaps, of the words of Juno's messenger to Morpheus: 'Hyt am I' (*BD* 186)). Nor does the Old Man ask the poet-narrator's name until over 1700 lines later, by which time the lengthy account of the poet-narrator's dwelling, occupation and marital circumstances has highlighted the absurdity of the omission. Lines 135–6 draw attention to the earlier solecism whereby the poet-narrator was able to report what the Old Man first thought of him when they crossed paths at lines 120–30 ('Than thought he thus [...]', 129). The Old Man is said to have told the poet-narrator 'the manere / How he spak to me' (135–6), which he now incorporates into his account. Yet the enduring impression, as many critics have observed, is of a blurring of consciousnesses and identities: Spearing remarks that 'as the events are narrated, there seems to be no barrier between Hoccleve's [i.e. the poet-narrator's] consciousness and the Old Man's; they might as well be different versions of the same person'.[43] The technique can be regarded as a further development of the 'compositional freedom' to which Spearing attributes a great part of the appeal of such framed first-person forms as the *dit*, prologue, and dream poem. Here, however, the 'preconceived design' against which Hoccleve wishes to advertise his difference seems to be the dream poem itself.

Hoccleve's personification of his poet-narrator's *thoght* also marks a deliberate departure from convention. Despite the absence of a seasonal setting, the syntax of the *Regiment*'s opening stanza, with the deferral of its subject until the final line of a single, syntactically inverted sentence, still betrays

---

[43] Spearing, *Medieval Autographies*, p. 148. For readings of the Old Man as an alter ego or mirror for Hoccleve's poet-narrator in the *Regiment*, see also Anna Torti, *The Glass of Form: Mirroring Structures from Chaucer to Skelton* (Cambridge, 1991), p. 104; J. A. Burrow, *Thomas Hoccleve* (Aldershot, 1994), p. 20; Larry Scanlon, *Narrative, Authority and Power: The Medieval Exemplum and the Chaucerian Tradition* (Cambridge, 1994), p. 303; Knapp, *Bureaucratic Muse*, p. 89; and Jenni Nuttall, *The Creation of Lancastrian Kingship: Literature, Language and Politics in Late Medieval England* (Cambridge, 2009), pp. 63–4.

the influence of the opening of the *General Prologue* to the *Canterbury Tales*. Somewhat unexpectedly, the subject of the sentence, when it eventually arrives, is not the textual first person, but 'Thoght' who has 'me byreft of sleep the force and might' (7). The positioning of *thoght* as the subject of this first sentence, granting to the inward wits an agency that is separate and potentially antagonistic to the poet-narrator, announces the technique of 'small-scale personification' that Spearing judges to be 'one of the hallmarks of his [i.e. Hoccleve's] style'.[44] Personification allegories representing vices, virtues, or aspects of the human psyche are instrumental to what Stephan Kohl describes as 'medieval character portrayal'.[45] Spearing draws attention to the potential relationship between the *Regiment* and *Piers Plowman*, where personification is similarly localised in episodes such as the marriage of Mede in Passus II or figures like Falseness, Favel and Gyle.[46] The Dialogue with the Old Man is unusual, however, not only for the appearance of personification allegories without a dream or similar otherworldly state, but also for the fluid status of these personifications themselves. Hoccleve's adoption of a select number of literary strategies from the allegorical dream poem demonstrates the purposefulness of his imitation and refusal of the genre.

The second stanza of the Dialogue with the Old Man describes the oppressive relationship between the poet-narrator and the incubus-like *thoght*, with whom no man 'was bet than I aqweynted' (13). Early in the poem, *thoght* frequently appears as a personification of anxiety understood as external to, and impinging upon, the poet-narrator – 'thoght, my cruel fo' (73).[47] Yet even in these opening stanzas, the term *thoght* is also used to denote the poet-narrator's power of cognition ('my thoght', 36), to typify 'thoghty' (80) or 'thoghtful' men (81, 99), and as the plural noun 'thoghtes' (119). As the dialogue between the poet-narrator and the Old Man proceeds, these latter senses of *thoght* come to predominate, though Hoccleve continues to exploit the slippage between metaphor and abstract noun in lines such as 'But ay among, fadir, thoght me tormentith / So sharply [...] / That it my wit foule hyndreth and apeirith' (1825–7). The personified *thoght* never appears in the *Regiment* proper.[48] With one eye to

44 Spearing, *Medieval to Renaissance*, p. 119.
45 Kohl, 'More Than Virtues and Vices', pp. 116–17.
46 On Hoccleve's repeated use of the personified Favel in the *Regiment*, see John M. Bowers, *Chaucer and Langland: The Antagonistic Tradition* (Notre Dame, 2007), p. 199. Compare Hoccleve's personification of his poet-narrator's wayward *wit* in the 'Complaint', lines 59–60, 64, 232–3 and 247–9.
47 Compare the *Regiment*, lines 42, 107–12, 201–3 and 267–80.
48 *Thoght* is used only in a verbal sense and as a plural noun in the *Regiment* proper, with the exception of lines 4060, 4597, 4997, 5005 and 5055, where *thoght* denotes cognition or memory. The closest Hoccleve comes to a usage resembling the personified *thoght* of the opening of the Dialogue with the Old Man is in the section 'De pace', where 'tranquilitee of thoght' (5055) is prescribed as the third of three 'Thynges that leden men to pees' (5034).

the 'þouȝtfull maladie' expounded by the poet-narrator of Hoccleve's *Series* (C 21), one might interpret this movement from an allegorical to a psycho-somatic presentation of *thoght* in Hoccleve's *Regiment* as articulating an analogous shift from a derivative, depersonalised narrating persona – that is, the thought-afflicted poet-narrator of the *Book of the Duchess* – to a textual first person with quasi-autobiographical, even quasi-psychoanalytical, referentiality. This is not the ironised narrating persona of Machaut, nor the recognisable but still anonymous poet-narrator of the Prologue to Chaucer's *Legend*. When the *Regiment* is read in the context of other dream poems, it becomes clear that Hoccleve is working both with and against them in order to craft an earnest and ostensibly unguarded 'cheere' that might be acceptable to the Lancastrian regime.

Hoccleve's re-appropriation of features of the dream poem in the context of moral-political instruction – most notably, its quasi-autobiographical references to the poet-narrator – emphasises his poet-narrator's credentials as an advisor rather than a poet. The *Regiment* does not seem to lead readers to assume that the poet-narrator's bumbling is a sign of the author's skill, as they do with Chaucer; instead, the apparently honest and open revelation of humble circumstances and character seems to underwrite his capacity for giving honest and open advice. He does not dissemble when describing his abilities in the way that other poet-narrators in dream poems sometimes do. If his poetry is good, it is because he has followed his poetic father's example. If the advice he gives is sound, it is because he has paid careful attention to the advice being offered. If he has been able to follow this advice – especially that offered by the Old Man – and amend his living, then surely Prince Henry will find it easy to follow the sage counsel the *Regiment* conveys. Paradoxically, by conspicuously eschewing the largely anonymised poet-narrators of Chaucer's early dream poems and superseding the Machaut-style persona of the Prologue to the *Legend*, Hoccleve's use of form advertises both his affiliation to and his departure from his poetic father. As the Dialogue with the Old Man draws to a close, three increasingly particularised referential moments occur: the revelation of the poet-narrator's name, the *Regiment*'s first eulogy for Chaucer, and Hoccleve's resolution to compile the rest of the work. Hoccleve's self-naming is one of three famous conjurings of Chaucer in the *Regiment*; yet it can also be understood as an important moment of poetic self-determination midway through Hoccleve's literary career.[49]

The conclusion to the Dialogue with the Old Man reprises the allegorical literary commission of the *Legend*, though with an interest in authorial self-promotion more overt than Chaucer's autocitation by means of Alceste. Following an extended discussion of the proper reasons for marriage (1555–764), the Old Man finally returns to 'the emprise / That I first took' (1768–9) –

---

49 Simpson, 'Presence and Absence'.

that is, his promise to offer the poet-narrator some comforting advice 'Whanne I thee mette and sy thyn hevynesse' (1770). His first suggestion, that the poet-narrator 'Conpleyne unto his excellent noblesse, / As I have herd thee unto me conpleyne', writing 'in Frenssh or Latyn thy greef cleer' (1849-50, 1854), is unattractive to the indigent clerk. The poet-narrator's surely disingenuous claim that he is ill-equipped to write in French or Latin – 'of hem ful smal is my taast' (1859) – incurs a rebuke, 'thanne foule hastow in waast / Despent thy tyme' (1860-1), with echoes of the ironic charges of misdirected clerkly labour made against Chaucer's poet-narrators in the *House of Fame* (614-60) and the Prologue to the *Legend* (F369-416).

As in Chaucer's poems, where the humorous derision of the poet-narrator is followed by his identification as the historical author's textual double, the Old Man goes on to at last ask the poet-narrator's name: '"What shal I calle thee, what is thy name?"' (1863).[50] The poet-narrator replies: '"Hoccleve, fadir myn, men clepen me." / "Hoccleve, sone?" "Ywis, fadir, that same"' (1864-5). The revelation of the poet-narrator's name immediately triggers his recognition by the Old Man, not on account of his own reputation but that of his master, Chaucer:

> 'Sone, I have herd or this men speke of thee;
> Thow were aqweyntid with Chaucer, pardee —
> God have his soule, best of any wight!' (1866-8)

Though 'Hoccleve' may claim that he 'in Latyn / Ne in Frensshe neithir canst but smal endyte' (1870-1), he must, with so illustrious a teacher, be able to write *in English*! The Old Man instructs him to seek out and translate for Prince Henry 'any tretice / Growndid on his estates holsum-nesse' (1949-50). 'Hoccleve' assents, but, as in the moment of his initial recognition by the Old Man, his first consideration is for the decease of Chaucer, 'the honour of Englissh tonge [...] / Of which I wont was han conseil and reed' (1959-60). Following the poet-narrator's lament for 'my masitir deere and fadir reverent, / My maistir Chaucer, flour of eloquence' (1961-2), the Dialogue with the Old Man ends by sealing the narrative frame, a ubiquitous feature of fifteenth-century dream poems. 'Hoccleve' returns home and takes up his pen to begin writing to the prince:

> Recordyng in my mynde the lessoun
> That he me yaf, I hoom to mete wente.
> And on the morwe sette I me adoun,
> And penne and ynke and parchemeyn I hente
> And to parfourme his wil and his entente
> I took corage, and whyles it was hoot,
> Unto my lord the Prince thus I wroot: (2010-16)

---

[50] Such identifications occur by name in the *House of Fame* (729) and by the attribution to the poet-narrator of further works written by the historical author in the Prologue to the *Legend* (F417-41).

Unlike in Chaucer's dream poems, the text that the poet-narrator now proposes to write is not the account of his encounter with the Old Man that we have just read. In the Dialogue with the Old Man, the text which the reader is asked to believe that the poet-narrator is about to put to parchment is the *Regiment* proper. The transition from the Dialogue with the Old Man to the Prologue to the *Regiment*'s didactic core enacted by the phrase 'thus I wroot' is a transformative moment for Hoccleve's poet-narrator: he becomes, in effect, not only the implied author of the Dialogue with the Old Man but the compiler of the *Regiment in toto*.[51] This transition resonates most with the ending of Chaucer's Prologue to the *Legend*: 'And with that word my books gan I take / And right thus on my legend gan I make' (F578-9). Though his interlocutor is an Old Man rather than the God of Love and Alceste, Hoccleve uses this same device of the intradiegetic literary commission in order to present a textual double of himself who is a capable writer, a successor to Chaucer, and a man receptive to good advice, but who is also a maker of books able to marshal his poetic resources in order to produce literary works that address specific political circumstances. He has taken a form that, even when partially personalised, is enclosed – 'This was my sweven; now it is doon' (*BD* 1334) – and has derived from it the impetus to present himself, Hoccleve, as a poet to a prince.

Writing of 'the generation of 1399' – 'the broad range of texts generated by the accession of Henry IV in the months following his return from the Continent' – Frank Grady attempts to define a '"Lancastrian" poetic' based on his analysis of three poems written in the decade before the *Regiment*: *Richard the Redeless*, *Mum and the Sothsegger*, and Gower's *Cronica tripertita*.[52] For Grady:

> Two important traits characteristic of this generation of poems are the disappearance (or in the case of *Mum* the serious curtailment) of the dream-vision as the sign of topical literary engagement with contemporary events, and the concomitant increase of interest in documentary models of discourse, particularly legal texts and representations of parliamentary activity. The two motifs are certainly related; it is logical to assume that a crisis of political authority – the deposition and its aftermath – would present a problem for political poetry trying to speak authoritatively about that crisis. Trading dreams for documents turns out to offer some political solutions.[53]

---

[51] A transformation reflected in the unique rubric at the opening of the Prologue to the *Regiment* proper in London, British Library, MS Additional 18632, fol. 58, evidently written after Prince Henry had become king: 'Verba compilatoris ad Regem' [Words of the compiler to the King].

[52] Frank Grady, 'The Generation of 1399', in Emily Steiner and Candace Barrington (eds), *The Letter of the Law: Legal Practice and Literary Production in Medieval England* (Ithaca, 2002), pp. 202–29, at p. 204.

[53] Grady, 'Generation of 1399', p. 206.

To a certain extent, Grady's conclusions are borne out in the *Regiment*. The dream-framed form – which in the case of the Dialogue with the Old Man is more directly indebted to Chaucer's dream poetry than to the political visions discussed by Grady – is too abstracted in its narrative and esoteric in its subject matter to serve Hoccleve's practical purposes in the *Regiment*. Its narrating personae are conventional, anonymous, and assume a degree of integration within the English or continental courts that Hoccleve cannot, or will not, affect. Yet the Dialogue with the Old Man does not entirely fit Grady's thesis: the framed first-person narrative with which the *Regiment* begins is a reconfiguration rather than a straightforward rejection of Chaucer's dream poetry, as Hoccleve looks to establish his own, post-Chaucerian authority during a moment of institutional upheaval. Spearing is right to discuss the Dialogue with the Old Man alongside Chaucer's dream poems and the *dits amoureux* as autography; indeed, as has been demonstrated above, the opening of the *Regiment* is closer to dream-framed first-person allegory than even Spearing suggests. Hoccleve obscures the similarity between the *Regiment* and the dream poem by reducing its visionary and allegorical aspects, and by developing its textual first person as a site for quasi-autobiographical writing. Acknowledging his imitation, but also pointed refusal, of the Chaucerian dream poem allows us to reconstruct the 'originating thought' that informed Hoccleve's design.

Part II

Reading Life

5

Hoccleve's Series *and the Unanticipated Woman Reader*

Michelle Ripplinger

At the start and end of his literary career, Thomas Hoccleve appears to pass over Christine de Pizan in favour of Geoffrey Chaucer, absorbing his adaptation of her *Epistre au dieu d'amours* into Chaucerian convention. His earliest datable work, *L'epistre de Cupide*, is a loose translation of Christine's poem. But rather than naming its primary source, which had appeared just three years earlier, Hoccleve instead invokes the authority of the dead Chaucer. Nearly twenty years later, he stages the *Series* as a palinode for *L'epistre*, just as Chaucer stages the *Legend of Good Women* as an apologetic retraction of *Troilus and Criseyde* and his translation of the *Roman de la Rose*. Since *L'epistre* serves as the impetus for this Chaucerian convention, Hoccleve often has been understood to promote Chaucer's poetic reputation at Christine's expense.[1] Even as critical debates continue to circle around the question of tone in *L'epistre* or the sincerity of the apology in the *Series*, they therefore have tended to rest on the shared assumption that he uses the woman writer to get closer to his father Chaucer, or to promote an increasingly masculine English literary culture.[2]

[1] This essay has benefited from the thoughtful engagement of Steven Justice, Jennifer A. Lorden, Maura Nolan, R. D. Perry, Spencer Strub, and the members of the UC Berkeley Medieval Studies Colloquium. I am also grateful to the editors, Jenni Nuttall and David Watt, for their helpful comments. The UC Berkeley Connect in English Graduate Fellowship provided timely support.
[2] See Diane Bornstein, 'Anti-Feminism in Thomas Hoccleve's Translation of Christine de Pizan's *Epistre au dieu d'amours*', *English Language Notes*, 19 (1981), 4–17; Julie Orlemanski, *Symptomatic Subjects: Bodies, Medicine, and Causation in the Literature of Late Medieval England* (Philadelphia, 2019), p. 247; Anna Torti, 'Hoccleve's Attitudes towards Women: "I shoop me do my peyne and diligence / To wynne hir loue by obedience"', in Juliette Dor (ed.), *A Wyf Ther Was: Essays in Honour of Paule Mertens-Fonck* (Liège, 1992), pp. 264–74, at p. 265; Karen Winstead, '"I am al othir to yow than yee weene": Hoccleve, Women, and the *Series*', *Philological Quarterly*, 72 (1993), 143–55.

Yet Hoccleve does not shape his literary career around *L'epistre de Cupide* to bolster Chaucer's poetic authority, or his own.[3] Rather than the woman writer, it is the figure of the woman *reader* that most informs Hoccleve's engagement with Christine. This female figure – defined by the tendency both to neglect deeper meaning in favour of the carnal surface and to engage in euphemistic interpretation which imputes deeper meaning where it does not belong – long has been intertwined with the convention of the palinode or poetic retraction. By attending to the history of this trope as it extends beyond Chaucer in both directions, reaching back to the Ovidian commentary tradition and forward to Christine, we can better understand Hoccleve's staging of the *Series* as a palinode, as well as the nature of his relationship to Chaucer and Christine alike. While medieval commentators defend Ovid's morally dubious poetry by deflecting blame onto the carnal-minded woman reader, Christine invokes this female figure to critique the *Roman de la Rose*, a poem that claims to encompass all of the *Ars amatoria*. Hoccleve thus not only conveys an astute understanding of how Chaucer's palinode and representations of women readers participate in these longstanding debates about the nature of interpretation and the defence of literature; he deepens the theoretical stakes by placing Chaucer in conversation with Christine.

In order to facilitate a dialogue between Chaucer and Christine, Hoccleve inflects his representations of the woman reader with critical terms that were central to late medieval debates about the nature of inter-pretation and the ethics of representation, especially those of surface and depth.[4] Most importantly for the argument at hand, Hoccleve attends to how the surface-depth paradigm which undergirds such a defence parallels and even overlaps with the figure of the carnal-minded woman reader. Like the symbol of the veil or the Augustinian kernel and chaff, the idea of the woman reader proved to be 'good to think with' as exegetes debated the application of biblical exegesis to the pagan *auctores*.[5] By theorising their textual expertise through and against the negative example of the

---

[3]   Ethan Knapp argues that Christine's gendered model of authorship allows Hoccleve to negotiate his relationship to masculine literary traditions as a married lay clerk: *The Bureaucratic Muse: Thomas Hoccleve and the Literature of Late Medieval England* (University Park, 2001), pp. 72–3.

[4]   See Rita Copeland, *Pedagogy, Intellectuals, and Dissent in the Later Middle Ages: Lollardy and Ideas of Learning*, Cambridge Studies in Medieval Literature, 44 (Cambridge, 2001), pp. 51–140. The opposition between surface and depth has latterly shaped theoretical debates over reparative reading and the hermeneutics of suspicion. The *Series* relies on the same metaphorical opposition, but uses it to pose a different set of questions. For a concise overview of 'surface' in literary theory, see Stephen Best and Sharon Marcus, 'Surface Reading: An Introduction', *Representations*, 108 (2009), 1–21.

[5]   Claude Lévi-Strauss, *Totemism*, trans. Rodney Needham (Boston, 1963), pp. 89–91. See also Misty Schieberle, *Feminized Counsel and the Literature of Advice in England, 1380–1500* (Turnhout, 2014), p. 20.

woman reader, commentators could claim to reveal the deeper moral meaning which she could not see. It is within this context that Hoccleve structures the plot of the *Series* around its reception by women, first presenting the 'Tale of Jereslaus's Wife' as an indirect apology to women whom he neglected to anticipate in *L'epistre de Cupide* and then worrying that the 'Tale of Jonathas' will anger women before concluding with an envoy which imagines a specific historical woman reader, Joan Beaufort. But whereas Chaucer invokes the idea of the woman reader to promote an understanding of the narrative surface as something we might look at rather than merely through, Hoccleve looks to Christine to articulate a concern raised by Chaucer's turn away from moralisation toward fictive play. He seems to worry: what if there is nothing *but* surface?

The Unanticipated Woman Reader, the Moralised Ovid and Chaucer

By retracting earlier works, both Chaucer and Hoccleve engage with a literary convention that takes shape alongside the idea of the woman reader, specifically in Ovid's medieval reception and the *accessus Ovidiani*.[6] During Ovid's lifetime, the *Ars amatoria* provoked debate about the moral dangers posed by its salacious content. In a subsequent defence of that work, Ovid reports or pretends that misunderstandings of his poetry could be traced back to women readers he had not expected, Roman matrons (*Tristia* II.245–62).[7] Whatever they read, Ovid insists, these women read carnally, fixating on erotic possibilities whether named or not. When reading Lucretius's *De rerum natura*, for instance, married women cannot make it past the first line of the poem without wondering, to put it delicately, *how* Venus became the head of Aeneas's line. While 'all poems can increase her delinquent skills!' and furnish material that will turn her toward vice 'if wrongdoing's her bent' (*Tristia* II.256–8), Ovid claims his poetry cannot harm anyone if approached 'in the proper spirit' (*Tristia* II.275). Since the third book of the *Ars* is addressed to women, the unanticipated nature of these women readers is an acknowledged fiction. But by eliding women from that poem's intended audience, Ovid not only defends himself against concerns about his illicit poetry. He deflects the accusation of immorality onto the unanticipated woman reader. If a reader fails to see the deeper meaning, it is because of her own carnal-minded interpretive impulses, not because he intended it to be read that way.

[6] For a concise overview of Ovid's late medieval reception, see Andrew Galloway, 'Ovid in Chaucer and Gower', in John F. Miller and Carole E. Newlands (eds), *A Handbook to the Reception of Ovid* (Oxford, 2014), pp. 187–201, at pp. 190–2.
[7] All citations of Ovid's works are cited parenthetically by work and line number. Translations are from Ovid, *The Poems of Exile: Tristia and the Black Sea Letters*, trans. Peter Green (Berkeley, 2005).

Amidst twelfth- and thirteenth-century debates about which authors belonged in the schools, the *accessus* – scholastic 'introductions' for schoolroom and commentary use – seized on the idea of the unanticipated woman reader in order to accommodate Ovid's poetry to a new interpretive context. Often (although not always) perceived as didactic rather than ironic, the *Ars* did not pose a threat to laws regulating sexuality as it had in Augustan Rome, but rather to the medieval classification of literature under the ethical branch of philosophy.[8] Since no 'Life of Ovid' comes down from antiquity, medieval commentators could defend Ovid's authority as an ethical poet, at least in part, by constructing his biography as a repentant narrative. While the commentary tradition accurately views the *Tristia* and *Ex Ponto* as appeals for mercy which result from the *Ars*, it passes over evidence internal to the *Ars* which confirms that it was composed after the *Heroides*; the *Heroides* is thus made retroactively into a palinode for the *Ars*.[9] The earliest and most comprehensive example of the *accessus ad auctores*, preserved in a twelfth-century manuscript (Munich, Bayerische Staatsbibliothek, Clm 19475), describes the *vita auctoris* in terms of Ovid maturing from his youthful indiscretions, including the error of having 'taught Roman married women about illicit love affairs with his writings'.[10] In addition to claiming that Ovid wrote the *Heroides* as an 'example for [Roman married women] in order that they may know which women they ought to imitate in loving and which not', the *accessus* aligns that narrative of poetic reform with a corresponding exegetical program.[11] It encourages all readers, male and female alike, to eschew carnal-mindedness by interpreting Ovid's poetry in a moralised hermeneutic mode. So understood, the negative example of the woman reader, carnal-minded and error-prone, works in concert with the *vita* to moralise and even Christianise Ovid's poetry, an

---

[8]   For an account of how Ovid was read 'under the covers' in the Middle Ages, see Vincent Gillespie, 'The Study of the Classical Authors: From the Twelfth Century to c. 1450', in Alistair Minnis and Ian Johnson (eds), *The Cambridge History of Literary Criticism*, vol. 2, *The Middle Ages* (Cambridge, 2005), pp. 145–235, at pp. 186–206. On the medieval Ovid in Chaucer, see Marilyn Desmond, *Ovid's Art and the Wife of Bath* (Ithaca, 2006), pp. 35–54.

[9]   A. J. Minnis and A. B. Scott, with the assistance of David Wallace (eds), *Medieval Literary Theory and Criticism, c.1100–c.1375. The Commentary Tradition* (Oxford, 1988), pp. 25–9; Alessandro Barchiesi and Philip Hardie, 'The Ovidian Career Model: Ovid, Gallus, Apuleius, Boccaccio', in Philip Hardie and Helen Moore (eds), *Classical Literary Careers and Their Reception* (Cambridge, 2010), pp. 59–88. On the chronology, see Adrian S. Hollis (ed.), *Ovid: Ars Amatoria: Book I* (Oxford, 1977), pp. 150–1; James C. McKeown (ed.), *Ovid: Amores: Text, Prolegomena and Commentary* (4 vols, Liverpool, 1987), vol. 1, pp. 74–89. On commentaries to the *Heroides*, see Ralph J. Hexter, *Ovid and Medieval Schooling: Studies in Medieval School Commentaries on Ovid's Ars Amatoria, Epistulae ex Ponto, and Epistulae Heroidum* (Munich, 1986), pp. 137–209.

[10]   Stephen M. Wheeler (ed. and trans.), *Accessus ad auctores: Medieval Introductions to the Authors* (Kalamazoo, 2015), p. 89.

[11]   Wheeler (ed. and trans.), *Accessus ad auctores*, p. 89.

interpretive approach which would culminate in the *Ovide moralisé* and Pierre Bersuire's *Ovidius moralizatus* at the height of his medieval reception.[12]

It is this moralised hermeneutic mode that Chaucer resists rather than endorses when he fashions his poetic career after the *vita Ovidiana*. In the moralised Ovid, it is carnal-minded women readers whose misinterpretation elicits a corrective palinode; but Chaucer inverts that repentant narrative. Rather than apologising because his youthful amatory verse has drawn women readers into love affairs, Chaucer instead must apologise because his earlier work has *deterred* readers from them.[13] More than simply offering an ironic parody of the moralised Ovid tradition, this inversion in turn bolsters his resistance to that convention's underlying assumptions about literature's moral dangers. Rather than blaming or correcting women, as Ovid and scholastic commentators had done, Chaucer revalues the woman reader and her supposed hermeneutic faults.[14] In the *Canterbury Tales*, for instance, the Wife of Bath not only overhears Jankyn's antifeminist book which includes excerpts from 'Ovides Art' (*CT* III.680). As Chaucer's most explicit representation of the unanticipated woman reader, she also 'mis-tells' the Ovidian myth of Midas: truncating the tale's conclusion in which the reeds reveal Midas's secret, the Wife attributes the failure to keep silent to Midas's wife rather than his barber.[15] But whereas some critics have objected that the Wife misreads by reframing the tale as an exemplum warning that women 'kan no conseil hyde' (III.980), the incompatibility between her moral and Ovid's narrative is precisely the point.[16] The moralised Ovid traditionally glosses the ass's ears as evidence of Midas's inattention to deeper meaning. Yet by directing those who want to hear the 'remenant of the tale' to Ovid (III.981), the Wife invites readers to notice that she has reversed Ovidian commentators' warning against carnal-minded reading. Rather than subjecting Midas's foolish inattention to deeper meaning to scrutiny, her truncated version of the tale instead critiques readers who

---

[12] On the ethical Ovid tradition which begins with Arnulf of Orléans in the twelfth century, see Jamie C. Fumo, 'Commentary and Collaboration in the Medieval Allegorical Tradition', in John F. Miller and Carole E. Newlands (eds), *A Handbook to the Reception of Ovid* (Oxford, 2014), pp. 114–28, at pp. 118–19.

[13] Galloway, 'Ovid in Chaucer and Gower', p. 191.

[14] Chaucer consistently represents women, the Wife of Bath included, as resistant to 'a single, solid, univalent meaning'. See Carolyn Dinshaw, *Chaucer's Sexual Poetics* (Madison, 1990), p. 51.

[15] Karla Taylor, 'The Motives of Reeds: The Wife of Bath's Midas and Literary Tradition', in Brian W. Gastle (ed.), *Later Middle English Literature, Materiality, and Culture: Essays in Honor of James M. Dean* (Newark, 2018), pp. 25–41.

[16] D. W. Robertson, Jr, for instance, describes the Wife as 'hopelessly carnal and literal' in her reading: *A Preface to Chaucer: Studies in Medieval Perspectives* (Princeton, 1962), p. 317. See also Lee Patterson, '"For the Wyves love of Bathe": Feminine Rhetoric and Poetic Resolution in the *Roman de la Rose* and the *Canterbury Tales*', *Speculum*, 58 (1983), pp. 656–95, at pp. 657–8.

are so eager to accept the antifeminist moralisation that they neglect the narrative. Or to put it another way, whereas commentators claim to redress women's hermeneutic faults through moralisation, the Wife of Bath calls attention to the reductive potential of doing so. If commentators can impose a predetermined moralisation regardless of the story's content, Chaucer suggests, their textual authority begins to look less like an ability to reveal deeper meaning than a determination to see what they want to see.

In his 'Dialogue', Hoccleve similarly crafts for himself a neo-Ovidian *vita* by retracting an earlier work. But rather than preserving Chaucer's inversion of the convention, he intensifies the role of the unanticipated woman reader by placing her at the centre of the poem's plot as the story of its own composition.[17] At the beginning of the debate over *L'epistre de Cupide*, the Friend warns Thomas that he has angered women by representing them in an unflattering light. The Friend therefore instructs him to compose a palinode on their behalf:

> Thow woost wel, on wommen greet wyt and lak
> Ofte haast thow put. Bewaar lest thow be qwyt.
> Thy wordes fille wolde a quarter sak
> Which thow in whyt depeynted haast with blak.
> In hir repreef, mochil thyng haast thow write
> That they nat foryeue haue ne foryite.
>
> Sumwhat now wryte in honour and preysynge
> Of hem. So maist thow do correccioun
> Sumdel of thyn offense and misberynge. (*D* 667–75)

Whereas Chaucer must appease a God of Love angry that his representations of women have deterred 'wise folk' from love (*LGW* F331; G257), Thomas must appease women who are 'swart wrooth' that his representations of women reflect poorly on them (*D* 756).[18] The Friend's instructions to Thomas thus depart from Chaucerian convention, in which the dreamer-narrator's representations of unfaithful women ostensibly have deterred men from love affairs. True, Thomas offers two counterarguments derived from Chaucer: he claims both that he was not the author and that the poem is not an attack on women.[19] But unlike Chaucer, he does not argue that those deterred from love have misconstrued the poem. Instead, he deflects the charge of misinterpretation onto

---

[17] James Simpson describes the *Series* as 'a poem whose single unifying plot is the story of its own composition': 'Madness and Texts: Hoccleve's *Series*', in Julia Boffey and Janet Cowan (eds), *Chaucer and Fifteenth-Century Poetry*, King's College London Medieval Studies, 5 (London, 1991), pp. 15–29, at p. 20.

[18] *Riverside Chaucer*, p. 597.

[19] His first counterargument recalls the self-defence offered in the *General Prologue* (I.760–2). The second defence, derived from the Prologue to the *Legend*, is that the poem is not an attack on women: Lee Patterson, '"What is me?": Self and Society in the Poetry of Thomas Hoccleve', *Studies in the Age of Chaucer*, 23 (2001), 437–70, at p. 447.

women readers in particular. Conceding that 'sumwhat ther is therin / Þat sowneth but right smal to hir honour' (*D* 757–8), Thomas insists that women are so preoccupied with whether the poem disparages them that they fail to recognise that the 'book concludith for hem' (*D* 779). They shirk the interpretive labour necessary to distinguish between a statement an author makes *in propria persona* and a dramatic utterance, a distinction they would find in the poem's conclusion if they read it. Such interpretive faults are not reserved for women – the Friend himself fails to read the poem 'fully to the ende' (*D* 783) – but the 'Dialogue' nevertheless aligns carnal-minded misinterpretation with women even as it frames the subsequent tale as an attempt to quell women's anger.

In addition to reframing his palinode as a response to women's hermeneutic faults, Hoccleve reconfigures the sense of authorial surprise that women might read works which were not intended for them. Instructing Thomas to compose a palinode for women who overheard his earlier poem and took offence, the Friend advises Thomas that he should nest this apology to women in a book he owes Duke Humphrey. Perplexed, Thomas asks 'what lust or pleisir / Shal my lord haue' in reading the 'Tale of Jereslaus's Wife' (*D* 701–2), but the Friend insists that this indirect approach will please women and the Duke alike. He advises Thomas to feign ignorance about the fact that women will read this book for two reasons: first, it will enable him to translate a flattering tale of a woman's devotion to her husband from the *Gesta Romanorum* without suspicion that it is a calculated effort to regain women's approval, and second, it will increase the Duke's 'lust or pleisir' since he enjoys 'daliance' with ladies (*D* 701, 706).[20] The Friend's advice thus not only recalls the unanticipated women readers who prompt the palinode in the commentary tradition, but also attempts to harness the expectation that a male author will not anticipate women readers to lend further credence to the apology. These women do not merely encounter a work which was not intended for them and take offence, thereby prompting Thomas to issue a retraction; rather, the Friend advocates a compositional plan which will give them the impression that they overhear the retraction as well.

At the same time that Thomas's palinode acknowledges the conventional function of that device as a corrective to the unanticipated woman reader's carnal-minded misinterpretation, the Friend's claim that the book will enable the Duke to enjoy women's company paradoxically threatens to counteract it. A Middle English word which can denote conversation but also 'sexual union', the Duke's enjoyment of 'daliance' with women has provoked suspicion on more than one occasion.[21] John V. Fleming,

---

[20] For a discussion of the poem's multiple audiences, see David Watt, *The Making of Thomas Hoccleve's Series* (Liverpool, 2013), p. 40. Sebastian J. Langdell argues that the Friend imagines the book as a 'conversation piece': *Thomas Hoccleve: Religious Reform, Transnational Poetics, and the Invention of Chaucer* (Oxford, 2018), p. 30.

[21] *MED* 'daliaunce' (n.), 3.

for instance, felt compelled to note that the Duke merely enjoys '*innocent companionship with the ladies*', a clarification which acknowledges the euphemistic potential lurking in that description.[22] The multivalence of 'lust' and 'pleisir' bolsters this interpretive possibility. In disclosing the desire to fool women into believing they are unanticipated readers of the apologetic retraction, the Friend's advice that Thomas should include his apology to women in a book for a man not only amplifies the unanticipated nature of the woman reader. It also creates a spectacularly well-timed readerly effect. For, in the exact moment the Friend advises Thomas to compose a palinode that will redress carnal misinterpretation, we as readers of the *Series* find ourselves engaged in – or at least, alerted to the possibility of – the very same hermeneutic fault which prompts the need for the palinode in the first case. Not unlike Roman matrons wondering about Venus's maternity, we wonder if the Duke might use the book for less than virtuous purposes. Rather than correcting women readers' carnal-mindedness, then, the nested palinode renders that interpretive impulse into an object of readerly reflection. By alluding to or feigning a deeper meaning that is itself carnal, Hoccleve prompts readers to consider the instability of the moral defence of fiction, to ask how fictive interpretation might be defended if *not* as intellectual labour. Most importantly for the argument at hand, it is the amplification of the role of unanticipated woman reader that enables him to raise such concerns which bear on Chaucer's turn away from moralisation toward fictive play.

The *Vita Ovidiana*, the *Querelle de la Rose* and Christine de Pizan

Anxious about the potential loss of deeper moral meaning, Hoccleve is not alone in raising concerns about new literary attitudes which theorised interpretation as fictive play rather than intellectual labour, nor in doing so in terms of the woman reader. Since his palinode hinges on *L'epistre de Cupide*, it is therefore no coincidence that when Christine critiques the *Roman de la Rose*, the most sustained vernacular engagement with the *Ars amatoria*, she objects to Jean de Meun's euphemistic subversion of allegory by invoking this female figure.[23] A. J. Minnis has shown that scholastic literary principles from the medieval commentary tradition, most relevantly the *accessus Ovidiani*, 'determined some of the parameters of the debate' in the *Querelle*, and that these terms were shared by both proponents and opponents of the *Rose*.[24] What has not been previously recognised is that the idea of the woman reader determines some of these parameters.

[22] John V. Fleming, 'Hoccleve's "Letter of Cupid" and the "Quarrel" over the *Roman de la Rose*', *Medium Ævum*, 40 (1971), 21–40, at p. 25 (my emphasis).

[23] On Jean de Meun's 'anti-allegory', see Suzanne Conklin Akbari, *Seeing through the Veil: Optical Theory and Medieval Allegory* (Toronto, 2004), pp. 78–113.

[24] A. J. Minnis, *Magister Amoris: The Roman de la Rose and Vernacular Hermeneutics*

The woman reader shapes the arc of the *Querelle*, less through her presence than through her systematic erasure. Rather than defend the *Rose* by echoing Ovid's criticism of women's carnal misreading, Jean's defenders remove women readers from the *vita Ovidiana* altogether. In a letter to Christine written in late summer 1402, Pierre Col claims that it was jealous Roman husbands, not their wives, whose anger at the *Ars* precipitated Ovid's exile and his supposed recantation in the *Remedia*. He even goes so far as to exclude women from Ovid's audience, anticipated or otherwise:

> Ovid, when he wrote the *Art of Love*, wrote in Latin, which women do not understand. So he gave it only to the assailants in order to teach them to attack the castle. That was the goal of his book, and without speaking through personages (but he [Jean de Meun], like Ovid, gave all his teachings). Because of this, and by means of the most exceptional jealousy of Roman husbands, he was exiled – what am I saying, 'by means of'! – certainly it *was* the beginning, middle and end explaining why he was exiled – yes it was, the very great and cruel jealousy of Roman husbands![25]

Whereas Ovidian commentators disparage women's hermeneutic abilities, Col takes an extravagant step further, denying that Roman women could read at all. David F. Hult speculates that the facetious suggestion that Roman women could not read Latin may be 'a way of calling into question Christine's knowledge of Latin and therefore weakening her credentials', but the denial of Roman women's literacy also circumvents the female anger on which the repentant narrative of the *vita Ovidiana* had hinged.[26] If Ovid's audience included only men, Col can claim with a flourish that Jean makes amends with women readers by composing the *Rose* 'in a language that is common to men and to women, young and old, namely, in French'.[27] Jean displaces Ovid as the poet who apologises to women readers, since the *Rose* not only furnishes male readers with an instruction manual about how to assault women but also provides 'a greater advantage to the guards of the castle, by having taught them through which point of entry it was taken (so as to protect themselves henceforth by blocking the opening through which it happened or by posting better guards there)'.[28]

Christine redirects the arc of this debate. But she does so not by re-inserting the woman reader into the *vita Ovidiana* but by removing her still more completely from it. Rather than advancing the obvious counterargument that Ovid addresses the third book of the *Ars* to women or that Jean de Meun addresses his *apologia* for the *Rose* to 'dames honourables',

---

(Oxford, 2001), p. 255.

[25] David F. Hult (ed. and trans.), *Debate of the Romance of the Rose* (Chicago, 2010), pp. 149–50. For the French, see Eric Hicks (ed.), *Le Débat sur le Roman de la Rose* (Paris, 1977).

[26] *Debate of the Romance of the Rose*, p. 150, n. 154.

[27] *Debate of the Romance of the Rose*, p. 149.

[28] *Debate of the Romance of the Rose*, p. 149.

Christine extends Col's erasure of the woman reader from the *vita Ovidiana* to the *Rose*.[29] In an argument which complements Jean Gerson's claim that Ovid was exiled for the *Ars* but not even the *Remedia* could redeem him, she insists that the conclusion to the *Rose* effectively excludes women by obliging them to stop reading:

> what is the use of praising a work that one could not permit to be read or spoken of in a proper manner at the tables of queens, princesses, or worthy gentlewomen – who would be obliged to cover their faces, blushing with shame? And if you wish to make excuses for the author by saying that it pleased him to use these metaphors in a fanciful tale to express the goal of love, I respond to you that he is not telling us anything out of the ordinary![30]

In contrast with Col's claim that Jean includes the women readers Ovid overlooked, Christine finds that he excludes them all the more effectively. In a later letter written in October 1402, she elaborates her objection to euphemism, critiquing those who defend Jean by claiming that he:

> doesn't ever designate the indecent things that are found there by their literal names! And indeed he does not! But what does that matter? He names them with readily intelligible figurative language – six times more enticing, more piercing, and more enrapturing for those inclined to such things than if he had named them by their literal names.[31]

While Christine recognises that the *accessus* tradition aligns the woman reader with a carnal-minded hermeneutic, she uses that association to contend that the *Rose* amplifies rather than redresses the concern that this reader might read with an eye toward sexually explicit content. Women will blush and hide their faces not because they do not understand the deeper significance of the euphemistic religious language in the poem's final scene, but because they do: the deeper meaning alleged is not deep at all, is not 'anything out of the ordinary'.

Once one has pulled back the surface to reveal the thinly veiled deeper meaning of the final *gradus amoris*, one does not find an inaccessible spiritual truth, like those that Ovidian commentators provided to redeem the *Ars*, but an explicit description of the sexual violence that Ovidian commentary had attempted to neutralise in the first place. So understood, the historical woman reader whom Hoccleve erases from his neo-Ovidian palinode *herself* erases the figure of the woman reader from Jean de Meun's adaptation of the

---

[29] Félix Lecoy (ed.), *Le Roman de la Rose* (Paris, 1965), line 15195. For a discussion of the relationship between the *apologia* and commentary tradition, see Minnis, *Magister Amoris*, pp. 226–8.

[30] *Debate of the Romance of the Rose*, pp. 60–1.

[31] *Debate of the Romance of the Rose*, p. 169.

Ovidian biography. That is, whereas Jean and his defenders claim that the *Rose* renders Ovid's amatory content palatable for men and women alike, Christine points out that his poem fundamentally misconstrues the moral-ising terms used to justify literary fiction: to replace Ovid's amatory content with euphemistic representations of sexual violence is to miss the substance of the moral objections which had been made against such material. Rather like Hoccleve's nested palinode, Christine's description of the *Rose* as a work which excludes women from its audience raises a question that Chaucer's turn away from scholastic moralisation begs. If Chaucer elevates fictive play by suggesting that one need not favour 'sentence' at the expense of 'solaas' (*CT* I.798), Christine objects that such a readerly stance trivialises the terms in which interpretation traditionally had been justified. If interpretation is a game offering mere pleasure, then it is nothing. And it is on this point that Hoccleve enables Christine to speak back to Chaucer.

'The Tale of Jereslaus's Wife' and the Clerk's Apology to Women

By staging his *L'epistre de Cupide* as the work that prompts the Chaucerian palinode, Hoccleve invokes the figure of the woman reader to enter a larger literary-theoretical conversation in which Christine seems to answer Chaucer. In step with her worry about the empty centre that might be left if we cease theorising interpretation as labour rather than mere play, the narrator Thomas devotes much of his 'Complaint' to expressing his desire for interpretive depth. Part of the fascination of the *Series* is that Thomas imagines himself exhibiting the same problems as literary texts in Ovid and Christine. Urging the public that they should not determine whether he has recovered from his 'þouȝtful maladie' based on his outward appearance (C 21), he uses exegetical metaphors such as mist, darkness, and blindness to suggest that truth does not lie in evidence directly available to the senses: 'Uppon a look is harde men hem to grounde / What a man is. Therby the sothe is hid' (C 211–12). Whereas Thomas articulates his desire for the public to plumb his depths, unlock the truth, see past the cloudy mists, or perhaps most memorably to taste by engaging in conversation, the Friend literalises these metaphors, including the biting or chewing associated with *ruminatio*.[32] He couples this anti-hermeneutic stance with the directive that Thomas should compose a poem to appease angry women readers. Although Thomas initially resists the Friend's advice, it is the spectre of a threatening audience of women readers that prompts him to abandon his desire for depth

---

[32] The Friend warns Thomas, for instance, that 'Ioie hastow for the muse / Vpon thy book, and therin stare and poure, / Til þat it thy wit consume and deuoure' (*D* 404–6), a reconfiguration of *ruminatio* which transfigures Thomas's textual labour into a monstrously self-cannibalising process rather than one which provides satiating knowledge.

and the accompanying exegetical metaphors. At the Friend's behest, Thomas translates a tale from the *Gesta Romanorum* which describes a virtuous Roman empress who remains faithful to her husband. Since women readers cannot penetrate beyond the surface of the text, this tale seemingly eliminates the need for interpretive labour altogether. It is all surface.

As the Friend's advice to avoid strenuous interpretive labour suggests, the 'Tale of Jereslaus's Wife' constitutes a significant departure from the conventional device of the palinode which reveals the deeper moral meaning which women are too literal to see. The Friend responds to Thomas's distrust of false appearance by selecting a tale in which what you see is what you get. At the beginning of the tale, Jereslaus marries:

> The doghtir of the kyng of Vngarie,
> A fair lady to euery mannes ye.
>
> And for þat beautee in womman allone
> Withouten bontee is nat commendable,
> Shee was therto a vertuous persone,
> And specially pitous and merciable
> In all hir wirkes, which ful couenable
> And pertinent is vnto wommanhede. (*FIR* 6–13)

The subordinating conjunction suggests that Jereslaus's wife is virtuous *because* she is beautiful. The tale flattens her into a surface, literalising the exegetical metaphor that makes interpretation like stripping or penetrating a woman's body. For, although Jereslaus's brother hopes he will be able to uncover a misalignment between her appearance and inner nature by causing her to be unfaithful to her husband, he finds when he literally strips her bare that there is no more he can do: stripped, she remains as faithful as her beautiful appearance says she should be. The wife is so incapable of dissimulation, in fact, that she conceals her identity from Jereslaus and her four male betrayers only by covering her face with a veil. The scene in which she removes the veil from her face to reveal her identity recalls another key exegetical metaphor in which an integument must be pulled back to reveal deeper meaning: even the symbol of figural interpretation is literalised.

Unlike Jereslaus's wife, the brother-in-law, steward, thief-servant, and shipman all dissimulate. Whereas female transparency causes the wife's facial expressions to reflect her internal emotions, as evidenced by the correspondence between her 'sorwe of herte and cheer of heuynesse' when her husband departs (*FIR* 57), the brother-in-law counterfeits outward displays of emotion.[33] Feigning sadness as he lies about abandoning the wife, he 'bleew and blustred and made heuy cheere' (*FIR* 240). In this respect, the

---

[33] Although the narrative aligns 'hir wo and hir heuy contenance' (*FIR* 63), she does at one point put on an appearance, if only 'As fer as the boundes of honestee / Requeren' (*FIR* 477–8). This misalignment between her outward appearance and character in turn triggers one of the tale's antifeminist asides (*FIR* 491).

tale recalls the gendered terms in which *L'epistre de Cupide* itself pillories false appearance. The adaptation of Christine's poem defends women by claiming that 'What they been inward shewith owtward signe' (*LC* 343). Since 'Ful hard is it to knowe a mannes herte, / For outward may no man the truthe deeme', *L'epistre* suggests that women are 'betrayed by fals apparence' (*LC* 36–7, 42). As the warning to women that 'blerid is thyn ye' suggests (*LC* 105), it in turn invites interpretive labour in these gendered terms. Although the 'Tale of Jereslaus's Wife' constructs a similar gendered binary in which the wife's beauty reflects her virtue but the appearance of her four male betrayers conceals their sinfulness, it departs from *L'epistre* in that its narrative eliminates male doubleness and the corresponding need to see past it: these men ultimately are punished with diseases which close the gap between appearance and character – leprosy, blindness, deafness, and so on (*FIR* 694–718). These diseases render the men's sinfulness visible; and by the same logic, when they openly confess their sins, their bodies are healed, thereby rendering the internal process of repentance visible. The plot reverses Thomas's insistence that one should not judge a man based merely on a look, unfolding such that it brings outward appearance into alignment with inner nature.

How odd, then, that although the tale circumvents the need to look beyond false appearance, the Friend nevertheless insists that Thomas must conclude the tale with a moralisation, a proceeding that should be redundant when the moral point sits on the surface. At first glance, the Friend's insistence that Thomas cannot omit the moralisation seems to contradict his earlier advice that Thomas should not 'muse longe in an hard mateere' (*D* 496). These are terms, after all, in which exegetes defended fiction by describing interpretation as labour rather than mere play. In heeding the Friend's advice to compose a palinode, Thomas agrees that 'If I lightly nat cacche may th'effect / Of thyng in which laboure I me purpose, / Adieu my studie! Anoon my book I close' (*D* 502–4). But when the Friend fetches the closed book so that Thomas can translate the moralisation, it is, as so many modern critics have noted, remarkably bland.[34] It does not seem like work at all. What I want to suggest, however, is that the blandness of the moralisation, the fact that it elicits boredom rather than shock, is a deliberate poetic effect. That boredom is not ours but Hoccleve's, as the prose moralisation's allusion to another apology to women makes clear.

Like the staging of the *Series* as a palinode, the prose moralisation recalls another key moment in Chaucer's works which contains an implicit apology to women, Petrarch's moralisation of the Griselda story at the end of the

---

[34] Vincent Gillespie suggests that the blandness bolsters the Friend's role as an agent of orthodoxy in a Lancastrian political climate where 'dullness and predictability are a state to be aspired to'. Unpublished lecture, quoted in Sebastian James Langdell, '"What World is This? How Vndirstande Am I?": A Reappraisal of Poetic Authority in Thomas Hoccleve's *Series*', *Medium Ævum*, 78 (2009), 281–99, at p. 290.

Clerk's Tale. In his Prologue, the Clerk refuses to name Boccaccio as his source and instead claims that he has translated the tale from Petrarch. Revivifying Petrarch only so that he can be reinterred, the Clerk couples his lament over Petrarch's death with the observation that 'alle shul we dye' (*CT* IV.38). As Jonathan Stavsky notes, the 'Tale of Jereslaus's Wife' reproduces this phrase nearly verbatim.[35] After narrating the protagonists' deaths, Thomas concludes his tale with a version of this phrase: 'And whan God list, also dye shul we' (*FIR* 952). Whereas the tale up to this point has been presented as a tale about a faithful wife, in keeping with the neo-Ovidian palinode which frames the tale as an apology to women upset by *L'epistre de Cupide*, this concluding phrase encourages a different mode of interpretation which the moralisation subsequently develops. It invites all readers, men and women alike, to interpret the tale in an exemplary mode rather than as a literal representation of women as such. Indeed, it recalls the Clerk's claim that Petrarch wrote his story:

> [...] nat for that wyves sholde
> Folwen Grisilde as in humylitee,
> For it were inportable, though they wolde,
> But for that every wight, in his degree
> Sholde be constant in adversitee
> As was Grisilde. (IV.1142–7)

In step with the Clerk's insistence that Petrarch did not intend the tale of Griselda to be an example to 'wyves' but rather to 'every wight', the generalised claim that we all will die anticipates the prose moralisation reframing the tale as an example for all readers. It turns away from questions of gender by offering a string of generalised imperatives, such as 'Let vs therfore do as dide þat lady' and 'So sholde we do' (*FIR* 1041–2).

As a device that compensates for the unpalatable descriptions of Walter's violence against Griselda, Petrarch's moralisation has been aligned with and reinterpreted as an apology to women. The husband-narrator who addresses *Le Ménagier de Paris* to his bride cites Petrarch's moralisation to defend his inclusion of the tale in his book.[36] Just as Petrarch informs Boccaccio that he retold this story 'not so much to encourage the married women of our day to imitate this wife's patience, which to me seems hardly imitable', the husband insists that he translates the tale not because he hopes that his wife will behave like Griselda but rather to illustrate how 'men and women' should 'suffer patiently the tribulations that God, immortal, eternal, and

---

[35] Jonathan Stavsky, 'Hoccleve's Take on Chaucer and Christine de Pizan: Gender, Authorship, and Intertextuality in the *Epistre au dieu d'amours*, the *Letter of Cupid*, and the *Series*', *Philological Quarterly*, 93 (2014), 435–60, at p. 460, n. 54.

[36] See Gina L. Greco and Christine M. Rose (trans.), *The Good Wife's Guide (Le Ménagier de Paris): A Medieval Household Book* (Ithaca, 2012), pp. 1–43, at p. 37.

everlasting, sends them'.[37] In addition to insisting that all readers, men and women alike, should learn through the 'example of this poor woman', he invokes Petrarch's authority by way of making an apology to his wife:

> I apologize if the story contains excessive accounts of cruelty, in my opinion more than is fitting, and I don't believe it was ever true. But the story is thus, and I must not amend or change it, for someone wiser than I compiled and recounted it. Since others are familiar with it, I very much wish that you also may be familiar with it and be able to converse about such things as everyone else does.[38]

In coupling his apology with a 'noon auctor' defence and humility topos, the husband-narrator protests too much. The more he insists he does not want his wife to behave like Griselda, the more he calls that claim into question, especially since he presents the tale alongside a wide range of instructional materials for his young bride. Crucially for the argument at hand, however, it is Petrarch's moralisation that bolsters the husband-narrator's apology to his wife and the concomitant claim that he does not intend the tale to be read literally.

While Thomas's prose moralisation conveys an awareness that Petrarch's turn away from questions of gender could be parsed as an apology to women as the husband-narrator had done, the framing of the *Series* renders that implicit apology not only redundant but also self-undermining.[39] After all, the 'Tale of Jereslaus's Wife' is *itself* presented as an apology to Thomas's angry women readers. If Jereslaus's wife should not be understood as an exemplar for women, but rather for all, men and women alike, as the moralisation suggests, then the tale ceases to flatter women, as the palinode initially sought to do. The application of a moral which implies a second apology thus throws the flatness of the tale into sharp relief. It calls attention to the stark contrast between the smooth groove of the 'Tale of Jereslaus's Wife' as a tale intended to flatter women in virtue of its surface-level meaning and the interpretive complexity of the *Clerk's Tale*, a tale which has become, as Anne Middleton describes it, the 'supreme test of its readers' interpretive powers'.[40] So understood, the two competing apologies create a recursive critical loop that places readers in a position analogous to Thomas at the

---

[37] Aldo S. Bernardo, Saul Levin and Reta A. Bernardo (trans.), *Letters of Old Age* X–XVIII (New York, 2005), p. 668; *The Good Wife's Guide*, p. 118.

[38] *The Good Wife's Guide*, p. 119.

[39] Scholarship has tended to view the moralisations as redundant: Eleanor Johnson, *Practicing Literary Theory in the Middle Ages: Ethics and the Mixed Form in Gower, Chaucer, Usk, and Hoccleve* (Chicago, 2013), p. 290; Winstead, "'I am al othir to yow than yee weene'", pp. 147–8. For a contrary view, see Stavsky, 'Hoccleve's Take on Chaucer and Christine de Pizan', p. 460, n. 56.

[40] Anne Middleton, 'The Clerk and His Tale: Some Literary Contexts', *Studies in the Age of Chaucer*, 2 (1980), 121–50, at p. 121.

beginning of the *Series*, eager for depth but worried there might be nothing but surface. Whereas Christine worries that euphemism trivialises the terms in which exegesis had been justified by taking the unpalatable content which the interpretive process should neutralise as its goal, the bland moralisation conveys a complementary worry that a decorum that neutralises unpalatable content altogether leaves the labour of interpretation nothing to work on. If interpretation is a smooth groove that eliminates the need for apology, it is also nothing.

'The Tale of Jonathas' and the Apology to Lady Westmorland

As if in response to the circular logic of this recognition, the *Series* concludes with an antifeminist tale which warrants an apology to women. Yet as Thomas exasperatedly tells the Friend, the 'Tale of Jonathas', a story from the *Gesta Romanorum* that broods over how the false Fellicula deceives the young Jonathas and steals his inheritance, threatens to reignite the anger of the women whom he has been attempting to appease:

> This þat yee me now reede is al contrarie
> Vnto þat yee me red han heerbefore.
> Yee seiden, syn Y many an aduersarie
> Had of wommen, for Y mis had me bore
> To hem or this, yee redden me therfore
> Humble me to hem, and of grace hem preye,
> But this reed haldith al anothir weye. (FMM 50–6)

Thomas objects to the contradictory nature of the Friend's advice. Appealing to the revised exegetical metaphors which he adopted at the Friend's behest, he worries the story will cause women to see him as a 'double man', since it will make a 'neewe smoke now vp reyse' (*FMM* 40, 57). The Friend responds by abandoning his earlier advice that Thomas must safeguard against women's hermeneutic faults by translating a tale which flatters them at the narrative level, instead placing the ethical onus on women readers to look beyond the carnal surface.[41] He insists that virtuous women will not be offended by the tale or take it personally, a deft rhetorical move which silences women's objections before they can be articulated. If a woman reader takes issue with the tale, that objection redounds on *her* moral character, 'For, who so dooth, ful suspect is the signe' (*FMM* 67).

Addressing a male audience, this time in earnest rather than as part of an elaborate ruse to flatter women readers, the 'Tale of Jonathas' inverts the gendered hierarchy which described false appearance in the first tale.

---

[41] I owe the phrase 'ethical onus' to Holly A. Crocker: 'Engendering Affect in Hoccleve's *Series*', in Glenn D. Burger and Holly A. Crocker (eds), *Medieval Affect, Feeling, and Emotion* (Cambridge, 2019), pp. 70–89, at p. 84.

Whereas the 'Tale of Jereslaus's Wife' represents men as duplicitous, this tale represents Fellicula as the 'welle of deceyuable doublenesse' (*FMM* 590). Like the four men who betray Jereslaus's wife by performing inauthentic emotions, Fellicula feigns sadness and remorse in order to steal Jonathas's inheritance. After stealing his ring, for instance, she 'wepte, and shewid outward cheer of wo, / But in hir herte was it nothyng so' (*FMM* 244–5). In step with the 'Tale of Jereslaus's Wife', the narrative proceeds to rectify this misalignment between her appearance and inner nature by literalising exegetical metaphors – but in this case, it has a virulently antifeminist result. Near the tale's conclusion, the injured Fellicula seeks help from Jonathas who has gained renown as a doctor in her land. Jonathas interprets Fellicula's body as if it were a text: 'He sy hir vryne and eek felte hir pous' (*FMM* 604).[42] Yet rather than diagnosing her external symptoms as evidence of the body's internal functions, this prognostic exercise instead moves toward eliminating the literal barrier between her exterior and interior. Since he wants Fellicula to suffer for her sins, Jonathas gives her the water which 'his flessh from his bones before / Had twynned' (*FMM* 655–6), as well as the fruit:

> And as blyue in hir wombe gan they frete
> And gnawe so þat change gan hir herte.
> Now herkneth how it hir made smerte.
> Hir wombe opned and out fil eche entraille
> That in hir was. (*FMM* 661–5)

In a violent literalisation of the exegetical metaphor that describes interpretation in terms of the penetration of a woman's body, Jonathas closes the gap between Fellicula's outward appearance and inner nature once and for all.[43] Although the gnawing which evokes *ruminatio* changes her heart, it does not stop there; it proceeds to open her gut and spill her entrails, killing her. Unlike the 'Tale of Jereslaus's Wife' which punishes the four male betrayers through a redemptive process in which their sinfulness causes their bodies to be plagued by diseases which open confession subsequently heals, Fellicula's death forecloses such a possibility.

In spite of its antifeminist bent, the 'Tale of Jonathas' concludes with a dedication to a woman reader.[44] As the envoy in Hoccleve's autograph manuscript, Durham, University Library, MS Cosin V. III. 9, states:

---

[42]   Medieval medical discourse construes pulse and urine primarily as prognostic rather than diagnostic: Faith Wallis, 'Signs and Senses: Diagnosis and Prognosis in Early Medieval Pulse and Urine Texts', *Social History of Medicine*, 13 (2000), 265–78; see also Orlemanski, *Symptomatic Subjects*, pp. 217–48.

[43]   For a related discussion of Fellicula's insides bursting out, see Spencer Strub's essay in this volume, as well as Taylor Cowdery, 'Hoccleve's Poetics of Matter', *Studies in the Age of Chaucer*, 38 (2016), 133–64.

[44]   In his essay in this volume, R. D. Perry argues that the envoy is not a necessary component of the *Series*, an 'incompleteable' text. Our arguments are not incompatible; I argue that the dedication to Joan Beaufort amplifies a point implicit in the moralisation itself.

Go, smal book, to the noble excellence
Of my lady of Westmerland, and seye
Hir humble seruant with al reuerence
Him recommandith vnto hir nobleye
And byseeche hir on my behalue and preye
Thee to receyue for hir owne right,
And looke thow in al manere weye
To plese hir wommanhede do thy might. (FMM 733–40)

Hoccleve does not direct his 'litel bok' to kiss the steps of Virgil, Ovid, Homer, Lucan, and Statius (*Troilus and Criseyde* V.1786–92). Instead, he directs his 'smal book' to Chaucer's niece Joan Beaufort, countess of Westmorland, second wife of Ralph Neville, first earl of Westmorland, and daughter of John of Gaunt and Katherine Swynford. Although it may seem surprising that a tale detailing a woman's punishment for deceiving a man should be dedicated to a woman, the placement of the dedication immediately after the moralisation calls attention to its implicit apology. Unlike the moralisation attached to the 'Tale of Jereslaus's Wife' which contradicts the palinodal frame by providing an unnecessary second apology to women, the moralisation of the 'Tale of Jonathas' indirectly reassures women readers that Fellicula's death should not be interpreted as an act of violence against women as such, since Jonathas represents 'a Cristen man' and Fellicula 'his wrecchid flessh' (FMM 700–1).

But rather than addressing Thomas's fears about the threatening audience of women readers, the dedication to this *specific* woman calls attention to the conscious inadequacy of the moralisation to defuse the graphic description of Fellicula's death. Unlike the *vita Ovidiana* which neutralises Ovid's salacious content by revealing the deeper moral meaning which the woman reader cannot see, the biography or life of this historical woman reader has the inverse effect: it instead lends further texture to the narrative surface. As the wife of the earl of Westmorland, Joan Beaufort persuaded her husband to disinherit his eldest son in favour of *her* eldest son, who later would marry Chaucer's granddaughter.[45] Though a tale that describes a woman's punishment for stealing a man's inheritance may seem to be a 'spectacularly tactless choice', its tactlessness proves to be the point.[46] At the exact moment the moralisation seeks to counteract the tale's representation of violence against women, the dedication reinforces how the narrative resists the turn away from questions of gender. If not an apology *per se*, the address to the 'smal bok' not only shows Thomas anticipating a woman eavesdropping and then attempting to pre-empt her anger by asking her to read 'in al manere weye' (FMM 739). It also simultaneously alerts readers to how the tale could be read as a commentary which reflects poorly on

[45] K. B. McFarlane, *The Nobility of Later Medieval England* (Oxford, 1973), p. 67. See also Patterson, '"What is me?"', p. 450.
[46] The phrase belongs to Patterson, '"What is me?"', p. 450.

her. It invites all readers, women and men alike, to inhabit her interpretative stance as an unanticipated woman reader of an antifeminist tale that would be sure to offend her in particular, whether or not it concludes with a moralisation.

Even when read 'fully to the ende' (D 783), then, the Series sustains the recursive critical loop between Thomas's initial desire for hermeneutic depth and the worry that maybe there is nothing but surface. But to extend this twin desire and worry to his audience, Hoccleve does not simply imitate Chaucer. The allusions to Chaucer's palinode and envoy combined with Joan Beaufort's genealogy may suggest that the woman reader should be understood as a Chaucerian convention, a confused attempt to 'create a Chaucerian atmosphere'.[47] However, Hoccleve reimagines Chaucer's palinode as an entry point into a larger debate about the nature of interpretation and the defence of fiction, a critical conversation in which the figure of the woman reader long had played a central role. Whereas Ovidian commentators claim to reveal the deeper moral meaning which the woman reader cannot see, and Chaucer drives readerly attention back to the narrative surface as a viable site for ethical speculation, Hoccleve turns to Christine. By placing Chaucer's revaluation of the idea of the woman reader in conversation with this particular historical woman reader, he allows her to speak back to Chaucer. It is by engaging with Christine, in other words, that Hoccleve asks us to reflect on the Chaucerian defence of poetic wit and fictive play, even as we remain alert to its potential risks and limits.

---

[47] Jill Mann, *Apologies to Women: Inaugural Lecture Delivered 20th November 1990* (Cambridge, 1991), p. 21.

6

Hoccleve, Swelling and Bursting

Spencer Strub

What goes out of the body, out of its pores and openings, points to the infinitude of the body proper and gives rise to abjection. (Julia Kristeva)[1]

This essay focuses on a metaphor for emotional experience that is both entirely conventional in late medieval poetry and so reflexive and widespread as to be nearly synonymous with the experience itself: the sense that a strong emotion swells, often in the chest, until it bursts out as tears, speech, or even the act of writing.[2] Hoccleve reproduces this metaphor throughout his poetic career, but it enjoys particular pride of place in the *Series*: the collection begins and ends with swelling and bursting. These moments, defined as they are by their ambivalent relationship to originality – a cliché that nevertheless conveys an embodied particularity – call to mind the question past critics repeatedly posed about the *Series*: is it a work of fifteenth-century convention, or does it relate an account of experience locatable in the hard facts of a person's body and brain? This question has long since been superseded, its implied binary demolished by John Burrow, who sensibly pointed out that 'convention and autobiographical truth' need not 'be taken as incompatible alternatives'.[3] In James Simpson's reading, the singularity of the *Series* emerges from the agonistic play between unique personal circumstance and the well-worn tracks of literary tradition.[4] But

---

[1]   Julia Kristeva, *Powers of Horror: An Essay on Abjection*, trans. Leon S. Roudiez (New York, 1982), p. 108.

[2]   For a related analysis of medieval swelling, see Sarah Baccianti, 'Swelling in Anger: Somatic Descriptors in Old English and Old Norse Literature', in Mary C. Flannery (ed.), *Emotion and Medieval Textual Media* (Turnhout, 2018), pp. 51–73, which I encountered too late in the editorial process to fully engage with here.

[3]   J. A. Burrow, 'Autobiographical Poetry in the Middle Ages: The Case of Thomas Hoccleve', *Proceedings of the British Academy*, 68 (1982), 389–412, at p. 393. Jerome Mitchell made something of the same case earlier: see *Thomas Hoccleve: A Study in Early Fifteenth-Century English Poetic* (Urbana, IL, 1968), pp. 1–19.

[4]   James Simpson, 'Madness and Texts: Hoccleve's *Series*', in Julia Boffey and Janet Cowen (eds), *Chaucer and Fifteenth-Century Poetry*, King's College London Medieval Studies, 5 (London, 1991), pp. 15–29.

Hoccleve's repertoire of swelling feelings suggests another way in which originality can emerge from the common property of convention. In the *Series*'s pivotal moments of swelling and bursting, the confrontation between the hard facts of autobiography and warmed-over poetic commonplace renews convention, 'making it new' by making it unsettling.

The first constituent poem of the *Series* is framed by the narrator Thomas's effusive sorrow:

The greef aboute myn herte so sore swal,
And bolned euere to and to so sore
That nedis oute I muste therwithal.
I thou3te I nolde kepe it cloos no more,
Ne lete it in me for to eelde and hore,
And for to preue I cam of a womman,
I braste oute on þe morwe and þus bigan. (C 29–35)

Much of this essay will maintain a close, even obsessive attention on this stanza, because it encapsulates a uniquely Hocclevean mode of authorial self-presentation. Hoccleve's narrator is fallible, vulnerable, and internally divided; at the same time, he is unbridled and self-asserting, and the power and fragility of the voice are in a sense two sides of the same coin. As I will discuss below, the *Series* repeatedly returns to these dynamics, especially as they are instantiated in images of swelling and bursting. Most importantly, it ends with a scene of bursting that grotesquely echoes and rewrites this opening; as I will discuss at the end of this essay, that moment is crucial for understanding how the *Series* maps paths of identification running from reader to author to narrator to character.

The swelling heart is a local instance of a dynamic in Hoccleve's poetry that has already been widely noted: the migration of Chaucerian character-making back into the authorial persona.[5] Hoccleve inherits the swelling heart from Chaucer's characters, who are clearly marked as fictional thanks to the distancing mechanisms of dreams, historical distance, or inset storytelling. In Chaucer, the swelling heart signals either a character's helplessness before the pathological excess of their own affect or the compulsive emotional force provoked by a threat to a person's face or standing. Hoccleve borrows this figure for the narrating persona that shares his name and life. This overactive interiority is installed too close to the voice of the poet himself, thus investing that voice with an interlinked sense of necessity and vulnerability that threatens the careful delineation between narrative matter and authorial commentary.

But the swelling heart also suggests a second dimension of the *Series*, less often noted in criticism. The Hoccleve-narrator's language of sorrow, swelling, and release is echoed across the constituent poems of the *Series*.

---

[5]   On this dynamic in Hoccleve's poetry, see especially D. C. Greetham, 'Self-Referential Artifacts: Hoccleve's Persona as a Literary Device', *Modern Philology*, 86 (1989), 242–51.

These resonances point to the immanent design that underlies the *Series*'s framing fiction of piecework material contingency.[6] That design depends on promiscuous lines of identification: almost everyone who suffers in the work, whether virtuous or wicked, suffers in ways reminiscent of Thomas's self-descriptions; these paths of identification are strongly gendered, as Thomas (and Hoccleve behind him) presents himself as both 'feminised' and punishingly misogynist. The suffering itself, described in terms familiar from everyday emotional experience, provides a broader structure of identification for a community of readers beyond those invoked in the interstitial framing material. Though the *Series* did not achieve that readership in the fifteenth century, its postmedieval reception has been defined by such acts of identification: acts of *feeling with* that depend on the play of convention and lived reality anchored in figures like the swelling heart.

Swelling and Bursting in the Fifteenth Century

Metaphors of swelling and bursting are part of our everyday account of the emotions. They inform idiomatic expressions like 'I blew my top' – which is to say, 'I grew so upset that the anger inside me expanded so much that it burst out into public speech' – as well as more flexible expressions like 'my heart bursts' or 'my heart swells', which can be attached to named emotions like love, joy, sorrow, or pity. Such phrases can be neutral, used by convention or out of a desire to describe the felt experience of pride or sorrow. But they can also convey a moral judgement. I might say 'I blew my top' regretfully, describing an inappropriate loss of self-control; I might say of another person that 'he's puffed up with pride', describing a socially unacceptable level of self-regard. Such moralisations are culturally contingent, but the conceptual metaphor underlying them can be found across cultures and time periods.[7]

---

[6] For the fullest account of the *Series* as a work that narrates its own material making, see David Watt, *The Making of Thomas Hoccleve's Series* (Liverpool, 2013).

[7] Zoltán Kövecses has argued that the central metaphor for anger in Chinese, Japanese, Hungarian and English is '(hot) fluid in a container', which allows speakers to conceptualise – in addition to the psychophysical sensation of anger – 'intensity (*filled with*), control (*contain*), loss of control (*could not keep inside*), dangerousness (*brim with*), expression (*express/show*)'. Seething, boiling, and bursting are aspects of the metaphor: Zoltán Kövecses, 'The "Container" Metaphor of Anger in English, Chinese, Japanese and Hungarian', in Zdravko Radman (ed.), *From a Metaphorical Point of View: A Multidisciplinary Approach to the Cognitive Content of Metaphor* (Berlin, 1995), pp. 117–45, at pp. 119–20. Such metaphors may reflect the legacy of humoral theory, as Gail Kern Paster has suggested, but their deep history and presence across cultures point to a broader intuitive sense of the embodiment of emotion: *The Body Embarrassed: Drama and the Disciplines of Shame in Early Modern England* (Ithaca, 1993), pp. 6–7.

Medievalists are probably most familiar with Leslie Lockett's account of the Old English vernacular 'hydraulic model' of the mind, in which emotion is *literally* thought to cause swelling, boiling, and tightness in the breast, which was understood to be the seat of feeling and thought.[8] That corporeal literalism is specific to Old English, but poetic analogues can be found in many literary traditions. For Homer, *thumos* or anger grows and presses in the chest.[9] In the Hebrew Bible, the narrow-minded moralist Eliphaz the Temanite upbraids Job for allowing his spirit to swell up against God and vent itself in speech. Eliphaz asks, 'What bolneth' – that is, swells (*tumet* in the Vulgate) – 'thi spirit aȝens God, that thou brynge forth of thi mouth siche wordis?'[10] The spirit swells, the mouth speaks. Job blew his top.

In the fourteenth and especially fifteenth century, figures of swelling and bursting were part of a standard literary repertoire for the representation of emotion. Outside of the *Series*, Hoccleve tends to describe swelling emotion in condemnation. In 'To Sir John Oldcastle', Hoccleve describes Oldcastle's disobedience to the church as the act of a 'hy herte, bolnynge in errour' (49).[11] The heart that 'bolneth' is a common trope in Middle English writing; it most often bolneth with pride, which is implied here by Oldcastle's 'hy' – i.e. proud – 'herte'.[12] In a gloss on 1 Corinthians 8:1 in the *Scale of Perfection*, for example, Walter Hilton says that 'knowynge aloone bolneth up the hert into pride, but medle it with charité and thanne turneth it to edificacion'.[13] Hilton goes on to explain that 'this knowynge aloone is but water, unsavery and cold', which becomes wine when offered up in prayer and blessed by divine grace – a Eucharistic metaphor only made possible by the fluid dynamics of swelling pride. And indeed, two hundred lines after invoking Oldcastle's 'hy herte', Hoccleve advises him to cast the 'flood of pryde [...] out of thyn herte' (260).

---

[8] Leslie Lockett, *Anglo-Saxon Psychologies in the Vernacular and Latin Traditions* (Toronto, 2011).

[9] See the analysis in Aristotle, *On Rhetoric: A Theory of Civic Discourse*, trans. George A. Kennedy (New York, 2007), II.ii.2 (p. 116). On the *Rhetoric* in late medieval England, see Rita Copeland, '*Pathos* and Pastoralism: Aristotle's *Rhetoric* in Medieval England', *Speculum*, 89 (2014), 96–127. On *thumos*, see D. L. Cairns, 'Ethics, Ethology, Terminology: Iliadic Anger and the Cross-Cultural Study of Emotion', and Christopher A. Farone, '*Thumos* as Masculine Ideal and Social Pathology in Ancient Greek Magical Spells', both in Susanna Braund and Glenn W. Most (eds), *Ancient Anger: Perspectives from Homer to Galen* (Cambridge, 2003), pp. 11–49 and pp. 144–62.

[10] Josiah Forshall and Frederic Madden (eds), *The Books of Job, Psalms, Proverbs, Ecclesiastes, and the Song of Solomon according to the Wycliffite version* (Oxford, 1881), p. 20.

[11] Furnivall and Gollancz (eds), *Hoccleve's Works*, p. 10. On the sources and clerical posture of this poem, see Jenni Nuttall, 'Thomas Hoccleve's Poems for Henry V: Anti-Occasional Verse and Ecclesiastical Reform', *Oxford Handbooks Online* (2015), published online at 10.1093/oxfordhb/9780199935338.013.61.

[12] On forms of 'hy' as synonym for 'proud', see *MED* 'heigh', 5.

[13] Walter Hilton, *The Scale of Perfection*, ed. Thomas H. Bestul (Kalamazoo, 2000), Book 1, lines 83–6 (at p. 35).

Unsurprisingly, other sinful emotions can swell, too. In lines Hoccleve adds to *L'epistre de Cupide*, unattested in Christine de Pizan's original, the deception of Eve is named as a consequence of the 'enuyous swellyng þat the feend our fo / Had vnto man in herte' (*LC* 358–9). Langland's Envy anticipates Hoccleve's Satan, complaining that 'al my brest bolneþ for bitter of my galle' (V.120).[14] Left famished by the indigestible bad feelings in his gut, Envy asks:

> May no sugre ne swete þyng aswage my swellyng,
> Ne no Diapenidion dryue it fro myn herte,
> Ne neiþer shrifte ne shame, but whoso shrape my mawe? (V.122–5)

In Langland's treatment, the pressures of affect become the movement of stuff in the gut which in turn becomes the burden of unrepented sin. Hoccleve's swelling Satan and bulging Oldcastle, though simpler, depend on a similar dynamic. These imbalanced emotions are equated with an imbalanced movement of breath and fluid in the chest, which in turn produces bodily distention or deformity. Emotional disturbance and sicknesses of the body cleave quite closely to each other in this discourse: literary and religious writers share words like 'bolnyng' with medical texts on boils, haemorrhoids, ulcers, and cancer, and references to emotional swelling have a tendency to slide into depictions of bodily distention and infection.[15]

Like the swelling of an ulcer or fistula drained by a surgeon's incision, the swollen breast might be eased by careful purgation: thus Envy's desire for a stomach pump in *Piers Plowman* and Hoccleve's advice that Oldcastle open the floodgates of his heart. But it might also be managed by the wilful control that places a disordered interiority back under proper governance. The drama of this conventional metaphor depends on the clash between the swelling pressure of feeling and the restraint of the will. A long tradition, originating in Stoic thought but persistent in later Christian penitential writing, holds that when one wilfully assents to the first movements – the earliest bodily promptings – of certain emotions, one sins.[16] So when Satan or Oldcastle swell with envy or pride, they have already assented to the welling feeling and their will is thus perverse and captured by sin. (For Satan and a heretic, it can hardly be otherwise.) But other strong emotions can be harder to assess, especially when they seem to be transplanted into bodily movements of fluid and air. Anger – sometimes good, sometimes bad – is

---

[14] *Will's Visions of Piers Plowman and Do-Well: Piers Plowman: The B Version*, rev. edn, ed. George Kane and E. Talbot Donaldson (London, 1988), p. 313.

[15] *MED* 'bolnen', 1, 3, 4. For medical uses, see John Arderne, *Treatises of Fistula in Ano*, EETS OS 139 (New York, 1910), where the word is used throughout. See especially p. 57, which describes haemorrhoids as a product of swelling 'melancolious blode' such 'þat ouþer þe blode bresteþ out or þer ar gendred bolnygȝ of diuerse spiceȝ and schapeȝ'.

[16] See Barbara Rosenwein, *Generations of Feeling: A History of Emotions, 600–1700* (Cambridge, 2016), pp. 18 and 69–71.

often the emotion around which these questions play out. The *Parson's Tale*, translating Peraldus recapitulating Aristotle, describes anger as 'the fervent blood of man yquyked in his herte, thurgh which he wole harm to hym that he hateth. / For certes, the herte of man, by eschawfynge [*inflaming*] and moevynge of his blood, wexeth so trouble that he is out of alle juggement of resoun' (*CT* X.535–6). With sudden anger – a venial sin, not a mortal one – reason's control is usurped by this movement of blood; the proper relation between soul and body is knocked out of alignment by hot blood gathering in the chest. When Aquinas discusses sexual pleasure, he finds that it is not a sin *per se*, but defective nonetheless, because it represents 'ligamentum rationis', the binding of reason.[17] The same term might apply to the sudden compulsion that swelling and bursting emotion provides.

This language of disorder, necessity, and control could translate from the microcosm of the individual soul to broader social arrangements. Vegetius's *De re militari*, which Thomas proposes (and decides against) translating for Humphrey, duke of Gloucester in the 'Dialogue' (561), discusses the danger of *tumultus*, disorder, and internecine strife in a diverse army. In a scornful comment typical of a certain style of Roman martial masculinity, Vegetius says such upset is most common among those who have lived 'otiose delicateque' [idly and softly]. Vegetius proposes 'medicina' for this 'vulneri': appointing a tribune to govern the disorderly host. Extrapolating from the rather thin metaphor of wound and medicine in Vegetius's fifth-century Latin, the fifteenth-century English translation and paraphrase *Knyghthode and Bataile* renders this *tumultus* as a swelling salved by the imposition of order and purpose:

Sumtyme amonge an ooste ariseth roore.
Of berth, of age, of contre, of corage
Dyuers thei are, and hoom thei longe sore,
And to bataile thei wil, or out of wage.
What salue may this bolnyng best aswage?
Wherof ariseth it? Of ydilnesse.
What may aswage it best? Good bisinesse.
With drede in oost to fight thei are anoyed,
And speke of fight, when theim were leuer fle,
And with the fode and wacch their are acloyed.
'Where is this felde? Shal we no batail see?
Wil we goon hoom? What say ye, sirs?' 'Ye, ye!'
And with her hed to fighting are thei ripe
Al esily, but he the swellinge wipe.
A remedie is, when thei are asonder,
The graunt Tribune, or els his lieutenaunt,
With discipline of armys holde hem vndir

[17] St. Thomas Aquinas, *Summa theologica*, trans. Fathers of the English Dominican Province, 4 vols (Allen, 1981), 1a–2ae, qu. 34, art. 1 ad. 1 (p. 68).

> Seuerously, tech hem be moderaunte,
> To God deuout, and fait of werrys haunte.[18]

Knyghthode and Bataile substitutes a typical slice of fifteenth-century conventional wisdom for Vegetius's Roman clichés: according to these stanzas, the common mob of soldiers must be governed harshly by a strong leader, who will teach the individual soldier to be moderate, devout, and fit for war. This conventional wisdom is buttressed, however, by the poet's transformation of Vegetius's wound into a much more intricate bodily metaphor. As in Vegetius, the collective emotion of a group of soldiers is represented as a pathology in a single body, its remedy as a single medical intervention. But the fifteenth-century English argot of swelling and bursting supplies *Knyghthode and Bataile* with considerably more specificity. The inset drama of bored soldiers plotting mutiny ends by warning that they are 'ripe' to fight unless their swelling is 'wipe[d]'. Both terms carry a technical meaning in medical discourse: the ripe pustule is ready to burst; the wound left behind is wiped or cleansed by the surgeon.[19] The entire sequence, that is, is structured by the metaphor of the 'bolnyng' and its salve.

These lines suggest the ease with which that pathological swelling could be made to refer to social, bodily, or emotional disorder. Because of this flexibility, the figure enjoyed wide purchase in fifteenth-century English writing.[20] Moreover, swelling was understood to be symptomatic, disclosing deeper problems, and was easily assimilated into the discourse of the body politic. The language of politics and medicine in fifteenth-century English writing made such metaphorical transformations all the easier: according to Guy de Chauliac's surgical encyclopedia, for example, 'bocches' (boils) are produced by 'malice of þe gouernance' of the body.[21] But in all of these cases, swelling is *bad*. An infected sore or plague bubo does not bode well for the patient, demanding medical intervention. Likewise, the body politic that swells with bad feelings is sick; its boils need to be lanced by truth-telling or tough justice. Hoccleve draws on the same metaphors in the *Series*, but they are used differently: no restraint, no judgement, no surgeon or 'discipline of armys'. Instead, the *Series* dwells on a single person's experience, and his swelling is both a wound and an affirmation.

---

[18] R. Dyboski and Z. M. Arend (eds), *Knyghthode and Bataile*, EETS OS 201 (London, 1935), p. 44 (lines 1174–87). For the Latin, see Vegetius, *Epitoma rei militaris*, ed. Alf Önnerfors (Stuttgart and Leipzig, 1995), III.3–4 (pp. 110–11, lines 214–28).

[19] *MED* 'wipen', 2; 'ripe', 5.

[20] For political uses of the figure, see, for example, John Lydgate, *Fall of Princes*, ed. Henry Bergen, EETS ES 121–4 (London, 1924–27), IX.2996–7 (p. 1003), and *Mum and the Sothsegger*, in Helen Barr (ed.), *The Piers Plowman Tradition* (London, 1993), lines 1119–26 and 1380–1 (pp. 177 and 187), among others.

[21] Margaret S. Odgen (ed.), *The Cyrurgie of Guy de Chauliac*, EETS OS 265 (London, 1971), p. 277 (lines 7–9).

The *Series* and Its Sources

Hoccleve's earlier poetry, however, is closer to the norm. Satan and Oldcastle's bad swellings belong to a recognisable convention, a shorthand description of emotional experience. Put simply, the *Series* expands that shorthand and identifies the poetic voice with that experience. The prologue to the 'Complaint' famously begins with an autumnal parody of the *General Prologue* to the *Canterbury Tales*:

> Aftir þat heruest inned had hise sheues,
> And that the broun sesoun of Mihelmesse
> Was come, and gan the trees robbe of her leues,
> That grene had ben and in lusty freisshenesse,
> And hem into colour of ȝelownesse
> Had died and doun throwen vndirfoote,
> That chaunge sanke into my herte roote.
>
> For freisshly brouȝte it to my remembraunce
> That stablenesse in this worlde is ther noon.
> There is noþing but chaunge and variaunce. (C 1–10)

These lines are a homage – a way of marking Hoccleve's debts, of borrowing a little of Chaucer's star-power, and of flattering readers capable of recognising the allusion. But the changes it makes to its source are important. As a number of critics have recognised, by opening in 'the broun sesoun' rather than the spring, and by looking to the 'herte roote' and the leaves underfoot rather than the whole of England moving in pilgrimage, Hoccleve presents the *Series* as a *Canterbury Tales* reimagined: depressive rather than merry, belated rather than new, solitary rather than communal.[22] As in the *Tales*, global seasonal changes are correlated with a shift in affective temperament. Unlike the *Tales*, that change in temperament is located in the narrator himself, linked to a physiological change (the change sinking into the 'herte roote', a Chaucerian term in itself), and offered as evidence of a propositional claim ('stablenesse in this worlde is ther noon').[23] The collocation of falling leaves and depressive heart thus amounts to what D. C. Greetham has described as the 'consistent reflection of the self in the

---

[22] On this manner of poetic self-presentation, see the foundational article by David Lawton, 'Dullness in the Fifteenth Century', *ELH*, 54 (1987), 761–99.

[23] Chaucerian poetry links the 'herte roote' with cognition, especially memory: the Wife of Bath says that 'whan that it remembreth me / upon my yowthe [...] / It tikleth me aboute myn herte roote' (CT III.469–71). In the dubiously Chaucerian *Romaunt*, the Lover declares that a 'ful gret savour and a swote / Me toucheth in myn herte rote' when he remembers the sight of Beauty (1025–6): *Riverside Chaucer*, p. 698. Guillaume de Lorris places the feeling in the 'cuer', not its root: Guillaume de Lorris and Jean de Meun, *Le Roman de la Rose*, ed. and trans. Armand Strubel (Paris, 1992), line 1007 (p. 90). But other references in Chaucer (in the *Legend of Good Women* at F1993 and in the *Romaunt* at 1662 and 2037, pp. 122 and 140) refer to depth of feeling independent of memory.

world and the world in the self' in Hoccleve's poetry, the facts of interiority ratifying the facts of the outside world.[24] But it also more simply establishes that the depths of the heart are one of the stages on which the narrative action of the *Series* will unfold.

The final stanza of the prologue reinforces the point. As I noted above, it turns from sinking 'chaunge' to a drama of swelling and bursting. The physical movement narrated in this stanza merits close attention. In the two opening lines of the stanza, 'greef' swells twice: it 'so sore swal' and 'bolned euere to and to so sore' (29–30).[25] The rest of the stanza is given over to it bursting out. Thomas must come out with it, he cannot keep it in, and so he comes out the next day and produces the 'Complaint' – presented here as a monologue and only later, in the 'Dialogue', shown to be written. Editors disagree on how to construe these lines: Ellis glosses 'nedis oute I muste' as 'I must (burst) out', while Burrow suggests 'I absolutely had to come out with it', adding that 'oute' is 'a stressed form of the adverb out'.[26] Elsewhere in Hoccleve's poetry, the verbal *outen* refers to the act of speaking; the *Middle English Dictionary* suggests that this is a usage unique to his corpus.[27] Regardless, the final line of the stanza – 'I braste oute on þe morwe and þus bigan' (35) – maps Thomas's urgent composition onto the culmination of the drama of swelling affect that has preceded it. The line tweaks the convention: neither words nor affect come bursting out, but Thomas himself. As Julie Orlemanski has argued, these lines serve as 'compositional alibi', recasting the act of writing 'as both a flourish of self-creation and the gushing of embodied affect'.[28] The grief-swollen Thomas blows his top, and both he and the 'Complaint' come rushing out.

One way of reading the prologue is as an act of self-assertion. At the same time, it narrates a process by which interiority – the 'herte roote', the 'remembraunce' – is conjured up and immediately broken down, sent bursting out into poetry. Criticism has rightly emphasised how Hoccleve's poetry simultaneously asserts and fragments the narrating subject, especially by means of these kinds of vivid bodily metaphors. Jennifer Bryan, for instance, finds an 'ineradicable split between inside and out' in the *Series* and the *Regiment*, a split 'which can only be remedied, in stop-gap fashion, through compelling the inner to confess itself over and over again'.[29] For

---

[24] Greetham, 'Self-Referential Artifacts', p. 245.

[25] Burrow removes the first 'sore', added interlineally in Oxford, Bodleian Library, MS Selden Supra 53, but unattested in other manuscripts: J. A. Burrow (ed.), *Thomas Hoccleve's Complaint and Dialogue*, EETS OS 313 (Oxford, 1999), p. 74, note to C 29.

[26] Ellis (ed.), 'My Compleinte', p. 116; Burrow (ed.), *Complaint and Dialogue*, p. 74, note to C 31.

[27] *MED* 'outen', 1b.

[28] Julie Orlemanski, *Symptomatic Subjects: Bodies, Medicine, and Causation in the Literature of Late Medieval England* (Philadelphia, 2019), p. 224.

[29] Jennifer Bryan, *Looking Inward: Devotional Reading and the Private Self in Late Medieval England* (Philadelphia, 2011), p. 199.

Bryan, those dynamics of concealment and exposure can also be seen in a Hocclevean poetics of sickness and wounds. Robyn Malo in turn locates those dynamics in the ambiguous image of confessional vomit.[30] David Watt has shown how Thomas's disordered interiority in the *Series* aligns with a collective predicament: like all of England, Thomas is sick with the poison of heresy and in need of reform; his swollen heart echoes Oldcastle's.[31] Extending Watt and Bryan's arguments, Sebastian Langdell has argued that the wounds that Hoccleve invokes in the *Series*, the *Regiment of Princes*, and his devotional poems map a process of probing and revelation meant to offer individual and collective spiritual therapy.[32] What each of these readings shares is a sense of the layering of singular body and collective problem, a layering consistent with the metaphorical life of the bursting boil in fifteenth-century England discussed above: if Hoccleve really describes England with his own infection, he does so in the spirit of Gower's 'In Praise of Peace' and *Mum and the Sothsegger* before him and the *Fall of Princes* and *Knyghthode and Bataile* to come.[33] Regardless of whether one reads Hoccleve as fragmented subject, confessing sinner, or microcosm of the realm, the solution is clear: what's inside must be pushed out, perhaps by purgative force. Doing so provides either a temporary remedy for the speaker's moral or physical ills or an admonitory example for a broader community of readers, or both.

The prologue's swelling and bursting fits naturally enough into these readings of Hoccleve's persistent but permeable barriers between inside and outside. 'Greef' comes pressing out. If Thomas keeps it in, it will 'eelde and hore', a doublet that links the festering of stoppered emotion with the *Series*'s broader fixation on ageing. The eventual act of speaking is therefore self-preserving, but it's also explicitly self-asserting: Thomas bursts forth 'for to *preue* I cam of a womman'. Orlemanski suggests that this line lends Thomas's subsequent bursting forth a 'suggestion of self-parturition'.[34] The line has multiple resonances, however. As with other Hocclevean key terms like 'taste' and 'assay' – and sometimes 'ransack' and 'grope' – 'preuen' denotes the knowledge gained from bodily experience.[35] Amy Appleford has suggested that this line echoes the Office of the Dead.[36]

---

[30]   Robyn Malo, 'Penitential Discourse in Hoccleve's *Series*', *Studies in the Age of Chaucer*, 34 (2012), 277–305, at p. 298.

[31]   Watt, *Making of Thomas Hoccleve's Series*, pp. 138–43.

[32]   Sebastian Langdell, *Thomas Hoccleve: Religious Reform, Transnational Poetics, and the Invention of Chaucer* (Liverpool, 2018), pp. 138–97.

[33]   John Gower, 'In Praise of Peace' (ed. Michael Livingston) in R. F. Yeager (ed. and trans.), *The Minor Latin Works* (Kalamazoo, 2005), pp. 114–15; on *Mum* and Lydgate, see n. 19; on *Knyghthode and Bataile*, see n. 17.

[34]   Orlemanski, *Symptomatic Subjects*, p. 224.

[35]   *MED* 'preven', 1, 2, 4, 5. On taste and assay, see Taylor Cowdery, 'Hoccleve's Poetics of Matter', *Studies in the Age of Chaucer*, 38 (2016), 133–64.

[36]   Amy Appleford, 'The Sea Ground and the London Street: The Ascetic Self in Julian of Norwich and Thomas Hoccleve', *Chaucer Review*, 51 (2016), 49–67.

Elsewhere, the tag that a person 'cam of a womman' can describe Christ's humanity or a more broadly shared human condition.[37] So one point of the 'Complaint' is to furnish evidence of his humanity or manhood; the swelling, emoting body is the first article of this evidence. Dissolution and self-assertion work together.

Even as Thomas's emotional experience is aligned with an argumentative defence of his personhood or his masculinity, these lines leave us with a sense of someone not quite in command of the things moving within him. That queasy ambivalence is one major accomplishment of the 'Complaint', underlined by the exchange with the Friend in the 'Dialogue' that definitively casts the complaining Thomas as an unreliable narrator. But that sense of disrupted control lends the poetic voice a new urgency. Bryan argues that the Hocclevean solution to the split between inside and out is 'compelling the inner to confess itself over and over'.[38] In these lines, the pain produced by the pressure of affect provides the force of compulsion; it makes the 'Complaint' seem *necessary*. Orlemanski rightly terms the final moment of bursting as 'only partly agential'.[39] Though Thomas's agency is foregrounded in the last stanza of the prologue – there are five 'I's in seven lines – the swelling soreness has causal priority. This way of making a narrator, in which the act of speaking is at once emphatically associated with the first person *and* ascribed to a force of necessity that seems beyond the volition of that first-person speaker, is a gambit that Hoccleve uses elsewhere, as in a tongue-in-cheek self-defence in the *Male Regle*:

> Ey, what is me, þat to myself thus longe
> Clappid haue I? I trowe þat I raue.
> A, nay, my poore purs and peynes stronge
> Han artid me speke as I spoken haue. (393–6)

In this case, the Hocclevean narrator is *artid*, compelled, to speak by his poverty and his pain. It is a kind of joke, a begging-poem wink at the reader, but it is also characteristic of the Hocclevean poetic voice, whose fiction of urgency and immediacy is predicated on a close focus on the narrating 'I' and the sense of that I's imperfect control over himself. As Isabel Davis observes of Thomas in the *Male Regle*: 'his poetry is a release of the self but also an account of his mental and bodily disintegration'.[40] In this moment, as in the swelling and bursting at the start of the 'Complaint', disintegration and release are almost one and the same: the relief of speech depends on forces that seem to come from outside the speaker's will. And in the case of the 'Complaint', both disintegration and release are identified with the poem itself.

[37] *MED* 'womman', 1b, c.
[38] Bryan, *Looking Inward*, p. 199.
[39] Orlemanski, *Symptomatic Subjects*, p. 224.
[40] Isabel Davis, *Writing Masculinity in the Later Middle Ages* (Cambridge, 2007), p. 153.

This way of constructing a poetic voice – as wounded, divided, and never-theless assertive – is Hoccleve's innovation. The sense that the voice emerges unbidden from the upwelling sorrow of the speaker lends a useful instability to the poem that follows, a point of productive disruption analogous to the veiled allusion and *praeteritio* that Steven Justice argues produces an 'effect of historical immediacy' in the *Piers Plowman* tradition.[41] It is, I hasten to add, a fictional effect, regardless of the biographical reality of the illness related in the 'Complaint': the evidence from the autograph and holograph manuscripts shows a scribe-poet 'concerned, in the main, with being under-stood', to borrow Aditi Nafde's judgement.[42] Unsurprisingly, Hoccleve finds the raw material for this effect in Chaucer's poetry, where the bursting heart belongs mostly to love-discourse, where it is halfway insulated from the moral judgement that attends such effusions elsewhere. In love poetry and love debate, the swelling heart simply marks the intensity of a person's feeling. Lovers are not necessarily *commendable*, but one can hardly blame them for their condition. Diagnosis and culpability are held off, albeit only provisionally, in the literature of love.

In *Troilus and Criseyde*, for instance, Troilus sorrows after the Trojan Parliament decides to send Criseyde to the Greek camp: 'in his brest the heped wo bigan / Out breste' (IV.236–7).[43] Troilus's distress seems to anticipate Thomas's in some ways: like the scene Thomas sees in the first stanza of the 'Complaint', Troilus is compared to a winter's tree bare of leaves, and in subsequent lines, to a 'wylde bole' (239), a description that Hoccleve revives when Thomas complains that 'men seiden I loked as a wilde steer' (120). So the lovesick and bereft Troilus may provide a model for Thomas at the start of the *Series*. As A. C. Spearing has pointed out, 'in borrowing from Chaucer', Hoccleve's narrator routinely exposes 'in himself the vulnerabilities that Chaucer reveals in third persons'.[44] Nicholas Perkins has argued that the *Regiment of Princes* is 'haunted' by the intertext of *Troilus and Criseyde*. The poem clearly plays in the background of the *Series* as well.[45]

But Troilus is *all* vulnerability, lacking the bold self-assertion that Thomas gets from his overpowering emotion. There is a closer analogue in the *Merchant's Tale*, where Proserpina concludes her debate with Pluto on the fate of May and January thus:

---

[41] Steven Justice, 'Literary History and *Piers Plowman*', in Andrew Cole and Andrew Galloway (eds), *The Cambridge Companion to Piers Plowman* (Cambridge, 2014), pp. 50–64, at p. 62.

[42] Aditi Nafde, 'Hoccleve's Hands: The *Mise-en-Page* of the Autograph and Non-Autograph Manuscripts', *Journal of the Early Book Society*, 16 (2013), 49–74, at p. 72.

[43] Troilus bursts out again in the following lines, at IV.257 and 373.

[44] A. C. Spearing, *Medieval Autographies: The 'I' of the Text* (Notre Dame, 2012), p. 180.

[45] Nicholas Perkins, 'Haunted Hoccleve? *The Regiment of Princes*, the Troilean Intertext, and Conversations with the Dead', *Chaucer Review*, 43 (2008), 103–39.

'I am a womman, nedes moot I speke,
Or elles swelle til myn herte breke. [...]
I shal nat spare, for no curteisye,
To speke hym harm that wolde us vileynye.' (CT IV.2305–6, 2309–10)

The accusation that women jangle, or speak too much, prompts Proserpina to speak out, despite what 'curteisye' would demand.[46] Affect's pressure forces Proserpina to ignore the silencing norms of courtesy. The language here is strikingly similar to the end of the prologue to the 'Complaint': 'nedis oute I muste' echoes 'nedes moot I speke'; 'I cam of a womman', 'I am a womman'. Hoccleve certainly would have been familiar with this scene; Thomas's vulnerability, necessity, and self-assertion might be traced back here.[47]

The similarities also make it easy to identify the meaningful *differences* between the Chaucerian source and Hoccleve's poem. Unlike Thomas, so markedly lonely and adrift at the start of the *Series*, Proserpina presents her speech as a necessity brought about by patterns of identification rather than isolation: she *must* speak, because she is a woman, and must respond to women's defamation; if she did not, she would swell until her heart breaks. Thomas speaks to prove that 'I *cam of* a womman', not because 'I *am* a womman' – a moment characteristic of a poet who, in Catherine Batt's words, both 'imagines himself in those very spaces traditionally understood as "feminine"' and stages 'a complementary "masculinization" [...] of what medieval writings often conceptualize as feminine'.[48] The start of the 'Complaint' takes a line from the 'defence of women', but turns it into a defence of Thomas. The citation and disavowal of Proserpina fits Hoccleve's larger patterns of gendered identification and disidentification, an uneasy current running throughout the *Series*.[49]

Troilus and Proserpina offer ambivalent models from which to assemble a form of self-presentation. Troilus's extreme emotion is an illness; his 'heped wo' has left him 'neigh ded for smert' (IV.373). His sorrow recalls his earlier lovesickness. In Troilus's case as in Thomas's, sorrow becomes manifest in the suddenly permeable male body; the rational self is divided and usurped

---

[46] On jangling and women's speech, see Susan E. Phillips, *Transforming Talk: The Problem with Gossip in Late Medieval England* (University Park, 2007), especially pp. 106–17 on Chaucer and jangleresses.

[47] Simon Horobin has suggested that Hoccleve might be behind the rewriting of the Merchant-Squire and Squire-Franklin links in Hengwrt: 'Thomas Hoccleve: Chaucer's First Editor?', *Chaucer Review*, 50 (2015), 228–50, at p. 247.

[48] Catherine Batt, 'Hoccleve and ... Feminism? Negotiating Meaning in *The Regiment of Princes*', in Catherine Batt (ed.), *Essays on Thomas Hoccleve* (Turnhout, 1996), pp. 55–84, at p. 61.

[49] On gender and the *Series*, see Karen Winstead, '"I am al othir to yow than yee weene": Hoccleve, Women, and the *Series*', *Philological Quarterly*, 72 (1993), 143–55; and Holly A. Crocker, 'Engendering Affect in Hoccleve's *Series*', in Glenn Burger and Holly A. Crocker (eds), *Medieval Affect, Feeling, and Emotion* (Cambridge, 2019), pp. 70–89.

by the outward expression of inward feeling.[50] Proserpina's speech, on the other hand, links her honour with the unbridling of emotion – but only in the context of a *fabliau* narrative given a misogynist gloss by the Host as a story of feminine 'sleightes and subtilitees' (*CT* IV.2421). And behind both of these figures sits the threat of the *ligamentum rationis* and the perverse will, the sense that the 'Complaint' is ultimately an unrestrained outburst.

Bursting by Design

Despite its outrushing emotion, in search of a sympathetic audience, the 'Complaint' remains a lonely poem. Thomas's grief comes from his isolation and resentment, his sense that his friends have misunderstood his illness and his health. Although the 'Dialogue' shatters this diegetic isolation, its exchange simply seems to isolate Thomas further; it accentuates the duck-rabbit quality that makes it hard to establish whether the 'Complaint' is meant to be a genuine defence of Hoccleve's wellness or evidence of his continued illness – a quality introduced by his swelling outburst and intensified by the Friend's cautious advice: 'Kepe al that cloos for thin honours sake' (*D* 28).[51] Unlike Chaucer or Lydgate, Hoccleve tends to avoid peopling a crowd; both the frame narration and inset stories in the *Series* are defined by solo monologues and dyads like Thomas and the Friend in the 'Dialogue' and the disciple and his successive interlocutors in 'Learn to Die'.

But a shared vein of suffering – defined in terms of named emotion and sensory experience – nevertheless draws the characters in the collection together. The three poems of the *Series* that follow the opening frame of the 'Complaint' and 'Dialogue' seem to lose focus on Thomas; as Orlemanski puts it, 'not only does Hoccleve's body no longer interrupt his rhetorical agenda [...] but he henceforth declines to make it the topic of his remarks'.[52] But the pain, pressure, and disintegration that the 'Complaint' locates in Thomas himself recur in the collection's inset characters. The disciple and the 'image' of a dying young man with whom he speaks in 'Learn to Die' are quite clearly meant to refract aspects of Thomas, whose involvement is itself a kind of bridge for readerly involvement in the work.[53]

---

[50] Sealy Gilles, 'Love and Disease in Chaucer's *Troilus and Criseyde*', *Studies in the Age of Chaucer*, 25 (2003), 157–97, at p. 188.

[51] For a claim that Thomas remains ill, see Matthew Boyd Goldie, 'Psychosomatic Illness and Identity in London, 1416–1421: Hoccleve's *Complaint* and *Dialogue with a Friend*', *Exemplaria*, 11 (1999), 23–55.

[52] Orlemanski, *Symptomatic Subjects*, p. 242. Compare Boyd Goldie, 'Psychosomatic Illness', p. 52: 'the central topos of psychosomatic illness as it relates to contemporary discourse becomes more and more distant' after the 'Complaint' and 'Dialogue'.

[53] See Christina von Nolcken, '"O, why ne had y lerned for to die?": *Lerne for to Dye* and the Author's Death in Thomas Hoccleve's *Series*', *Essays in Medieval Studies*, 10

Other resonances across the separate poems collected in the *Series* are equally important, even if less obvious. The Thomas of the 'Complaint' presents himself as a tribulated old man. (In the *Male Regle*, written fifteen years earlier, the Hoccleve narrator is already calling himself old.) He ends the poem with a prayer of thanksgiving for the gifts that have purified him, including 'myn elde and of my seeknesse' (410). Hoccleve revisits the tribulations of old age on the villains of the third poem in the *Series*, the 'Tale of Jereslaus's Wife', who are struck by turn by leprosy; blindness, deafness, and 'the tremblynge / Of palesie' (*FIR* 704–5); podagra and gout (*FIR* 713); and 'the franesie' (*FIR* 715). They suffer, in other words, from the manifold indignities of living in an ageing and ailing body, described in terms reminiscent of the Thomas of the 'Complaint'. The movement of suffering (ultimately relieved by confession, in Thomas's case as in some of these villains') from speaker to characters might be seen as a kind of penitential-therapeutic process.

The most marked and revealing example of this migration of suffering is also the most disquieting. The final poem in the *Series*, the 'Tale of Jonathas', revisits the image of swelling and bursting once more in a new key with the spectacular death of Fellicula. Fellicula is a convenient villain, named in the Latin title as a *muliere mala*, a wicked woman, who betrays, robs, and nearly kills the innocent Jonathas. The poem ends with a cruel comeuppance: after being fed the same poisons with which she had afflicted Jonathas:

> And as blyue in hir wombe gan they frete
> And gnawe so þat change gan hir herte.
> Now herkneth how it made smerte.
> Hir wombe opned and out fil eche entraille
> That in hir was. Thus seith the book sanz faill. (*FMM* 661–5)

The body horror in this scene is not original to Hoccleve's telling. Both Hoccleve and his *Gesta Romanorum* source probably reflect Judas's death in Acts 1:18.[54] But Fellicula's death as described here, at the end of the *Series*, is carefully adapted so as to recall Thomas's own bursting woe at the start. Hearts change: as 'change gan [Fellicula's] herte', so 'chaunge sanke into [Thomas's] herte roote'. Pain follows: 'herkneth how it hir made smerte', the narrator tells us, just as Thomas tells us he swells 'so sore'. This scene is also a misogynist's parody of childbirth, like the opening of the 'Complaint' with a cruel edge.

(1993), 27–51; and Steven Rozenski, '"Your Ensaumple and Your Mirour": Hoccleve's Amplification of the Imagery and Intimacy of Henry Suso's *Ars moriendi*', *Parergon*, 25 (2008), 1–16.

[54] An analogue in the Middle English version of the *Gesta Romanorum* in London, British Library, Additional MS 9066 likewise describes how, after the villainous lover (unnamed in this version) confesses her wrongdoing and eats Jonathas's poisonous fruit, 'her bely opened, and all her guttes went out': S. J. H. Herrtage (ed.), *The Early English Versions of the Gesta Romanorum*, EETS ES 33 (London, 1879), p. 193.

As Taylor Cowdery puts it, this image 'answers the many earlier instances in the *Tale* where Fellicula manufactured a conceit of speech [...] to mask the truth of her actions'.[55] In the end, a true inwardness comes spilling out into the world, whether it's every entrail or the emotional record of the 'Complaint'. The parallel is revealing: an unwilled eruption, a breakdown, nevertheless reveals – as Cowdery suggests – a material truth, delivered urgently, painfully. If there *is* a therapeutic arc to the *Series*, whether penitential or consolatory, then this scene might offer the final containment of the irruptive and assertive emotion in the prologue: the violence has definitively moved from the narrator to a character, the unstable self-disclosure replaced with a calmer sense of poetic control and punishment. The violence of this punishment, visited upon a woman whose defining characteristic is her sexual availability – she is introduced as a 'a morsel of plesance' (FMM 159) – amounts to a classic retributive patriarchal fantasy.[56] In her reading of the *Series*, Orlemanski suggests that Hoccleve comes to prop up his tottering masculinity by offering himself up as a typical henpecked man 'within the familiar conventions of antifeminism, where men's downtroddenness stabilises gender solidarity'.[57] Fellicula's fate points to the violence that ultimately underlies that gender solidarity – fuelled, as Holly Crocker has suggested, by the supposedly rational anger of aristocratic masculinity.[58]

But as Crocker also notes, Hoccleve's 'version of male subjectivity is always provisional'.[59] In this case, his self-representation and his misogyny are ultimately inseparable. Rewriting Thomas as Fellicula is a form of containment and moralisation, but Hoccleve also *identifies with* Fellicula. Thomas's self-presentation borrows from Proserpina's; Fellicula's characterisation borrows from Thomas's. Fellicula is a creative figure, a tale-teller attentive to her audiences; Thomas (and Hoccleve behind him) is himself 'a morsel of plesance' as a writer of commissioned works, facilitator-for-pay of another's desire. Of course, the Thomas of the 'Complaint' and 'Dialogue' is Jonathas as well: he is both the gut-spiller and the virtuous sufferer. Hoccleve punishes Fellicula for this identification. But the punishment is itself the culminating act of identification, a grotesquely literalised version of the passive-actant exploding self that launches the entire collection. In the prose moralisation that follows the 'Tale of Jonathas', Fellicula is identified as an allegory for the flesh – an allegoresis that aligns with a thousand years

---

[55] Cowdery, 'Hoccleve's Poetics of Matter', p. 153.
[56] The fantasised death of Fellicula calls to mind the dissolving misogynistic violence in the fascist narratives analysed by Klaus Theweleit, *Male Fantasies*, trans. Stephen Conway with Erica Carter and Chris Turner (2 vols, Minneapolis, 1987), vol. 1 (*Women, Floods, Bodies, History*).
[57] Orlemanski, *Symptomatic Subjects*, p. 244.
[58] Crocker, 'Engendering Affect', p. 82.
[59] Crocker, 'Engendering Affect', p. 79.

of misogynist tradition *and* transforms Fellicula into a universal, whose failings are inevitably Thomas's too.

The ambivalent case of Fellicula helps clarify what Hoccleve gets from his swelling and bursting. The swelling heart is an enduring bodily figure for the central innovation of Hoccleve's long poems, their willingness to depict the narrating persona as divided and open, a voice always on the edge of abjection. The linked qualities of necessity, sickness, and immediacy turn inherited Chaucerian humility into a genuine drama, worthy of readerly attention in and of itself. The effect is in some ways similar to that of Langland's decision to restage the dream vision over and over again, turning a closed fictional form into an open-ended and inconclusive one. In *Piers Plowman*, the reiterative dream visions allow for multiple partial, provisional acts of questioning and learning.[60] Hoccleve's swelling heart and uncontrollable voice could be understood as purely affective reflexes of the formal and intellectual gambits that *Piers Plowman* pioneers. The *Series* runs on vulnerability and identification rather than ethical frustration and shame, but like *Piers*, it produces a novel picture of the self out of literary forms seemingly worn out by overuse.

The *Series* is usually thought to represent itself as the product of contingency, a book about medieval book-making in all its randomness and constraint: after the opening frame poems, it narrates its emergence from piecemeal commissions and sudden exemplar deliveries. The paths of identification in the *Series* suggest how traces of a unifying design run through these contingencies. The *Series* cultivates vulnerability and abjection in its opening moments: *Thomas cannot do otherwise but speak*, because his emotion presses on him so much that his interiority must come spilling out. This odd mixture of passivity and semi-volitional excess remains continually in sight as the collection unfolds, whether it manifests as gouty confessing villains, as a fearful man confronting his dying image, or as Fellicula, punished for her fiction-making with explosive interiority. The opening lines' invitation to witness Thomas, half-captive to his own suffering, is reiterated in these later moments, providing a thread of emotional experience that runs through the fictions of commission that structure the compilation as a whole.

Equally importantly, however, these repeated moments of suffering and bodily perforations establish points at which a reader can empathise with character, narrator, and author. A reader, from the beginning, must account for Thomas's interiority, receiving his 'Complaint' as the compulsive expression of an anxious and grief-pressed person; as the collection goes on, the circle of perspectives expands, recasting the same dynamics in different persons. This movement from sick particularity to broader shared

---

[60] The definitive statement on the relationship between innovation and expectation in *Piers Plowman* remains Anne Middleton, 'The Audience and Public of *Piers Plowman*', in David Lawton (ed.), *Middle English Alliterative Poetry and Its Literary Background: Seven Essays* (Cambridge, 1982), pp. 101–23.

experience is how the *Series* works: Thomas's failings, his account of a divided self, and his swelling compulsion to speak are dramatisations of being in the world made accessible in part by being grounded in instantly recognisable bodily expressions of extreme emotion. Those expressions are open to moral judgement and are available for punitive transformation, as Hoccleve's treatment of Fellicula suggests. But swelling and bursting is nevertheless something the reader is made to feel, too, turning a lonely collection into felt communion.

7

'Ransakid' by Death: Body, Soul and Image in Hoccleve's 'Learn to Die'

Stephanie Trigg

What is Death, what does it do to us, and who are we when it appears? In Hoccleve's 'Learn to Die', Death appears variously as an abstract concept, a speaking voice, a powerful spiritual agent, a series of physical symptoms and as a social and ethical event. And even when Death is personified, the gendering of that personification moves back and forth between male and female. This essay considers Hoccleve's fluid and variable representations of Death, and the ways in which they challenge our understanding of the relation between body and soul, and between literal and figurative language. Hoccleve offers a suggestive indication of this complex and layered understanding of death as a forceful agent in his startling image, early in the poem, of the young man as 'ny ransakid' by death (*LTD* 92). Forensic examination of this phrase can help us understand some of the problematic representations of death and dying in the poem, as Hoccleve takes us from the Disciple's desire for knowledge to a dramatic rendition of the power of feeling, across a range of bodily and mental affects, and back and forth between the four speakers: Sapience, the Disciple, the Ymage and an uncharacteristically restrained narrative observer.

'Learn to Die' is unique in the sequence of the six works that constitute the *Series*, given the absence of both the familiar, confessional first-person narrator and the framing companionship of the narrator's friend. Part Four begins very abruptly: the first conjunction of its rubric ('[...] et incipit ars vtillissima sciendi mori') refers back to and completes the *explicit* of the preceding text ('Explicit moralizacio [...]'), and the text begins with the first words of the dialogue, without any narrative frame or introduction. Hoccleve is following his source, Henry Suso's *Horologium Sapientiae* (ii.2), quite closely in structure, in content and in the naming of the first two speakers: Sapience (*sapientia*) and the Disciple (*discipulus*). But without any kind of narrative frame, and in the absence of the two familiar speakers, Hoccleve and his Friend, the effect is disorienting.[1] As Amy Appleford

---

[1]   For Suso's *Horologium Sapientiae*, see Pius Künzle (ed.), *Heinrich Seuses Horologium*

argues, this text seems to start anew, 'isolated from the social context that frames most of the other poems'.[2]

Amicable and dialogical drama is a familiar and intriguing feature of much of Hoccleve's poetry. Whether in his imagination, gazing into a mirror, or conversing with human or spiritual interlocutors, Hoccleve often stages powerful encounters between himself, others and other versions of himself. Such encounters – in the *Regiment of Princes* and the 'Dialogue' in the *Series*, for example – propel and enliven the drama of argument and intellectual debate. They provide narrative and conversational energy, as well as psychological points of orientation. Dialogues ease the comprehension of readers – and listeners – by orienting them to different perspectives as the discussion passes back and forth between different people. The dialogic form facilitates ethical, emotional and cognitive engagement with the issues being discussed, allowing readers to measure and match their own comprehension and anticipation of issues and their own feeling responses. Hoccleve's dialogues also invite us to develop a deeper understanding of his narrative voice as a relative constant across a range of texts and genres. In the *Series*, this voice emerges with greater clarity in relationship with the supportive counsel and advice of the 'Friend', who mediates many of Hoccleve's textual relationships with his social world. Taylor Cowdery describes the 'permeable frame' of the *Series* as a whole and emphasises the role of the Friend in these scenes: 'The reader, in the persona of the Friend, repeatedly crosses this frame by entering and exiting the poem, and Hoccleve draws attention both to the space and the seams of his writing.'[3] The discussions and exchanges between Hoccleve and his Friend are an essential structural element in the *Series*, offering a form of continuity in the fabric and texture of the very different narrative genres of its component parts, as well as contributing to our sense of Hoccleve's own narrative subjectivity and what Holly A. Crocker describes as his 'quotidian masculinity' as it takes shape in these various dialogues.[4] The absence of these voices in the beginning of 'Learn to Die' thus underscores the 'social isolation' described by Appleford.

In the absence of both the Friend (who appeared toward the end of the previous poem to bring Thomas the missing moralisation of the story of the Roman empress) and the familiar voice of Hoccleve as the narrator, the opening dialogue of 'Learn to Die' either seems to take place between two new characters, or perhaps even implies that there is no substantive

---

Sapientiae, Spicilegium Friburgense, 23 (Freiburg, 1977), pp. 526–40.

[2] Amy Appleford, *Learning to Die in London, 1380–1540* (Philadelphia, 2015), p. 134.

[3] Taylor Cowdery, 'Hoccleve's Poetics of Matter', *Studies in the Age of Chaucer*, 38 (2016), 133–64, at p. 147.

[4] Holly A. Crocker, 'Engendering Affect in Hoccleve's *Series*', in Glenn D. Burger and Holly A. Crocker (eds), *Medieval Affect, Feeling, and Emotion* (Cambridge, 2019), pp. 70–89, at pp. 70–1.

difference between Sapience's interlocutor (who is not named as the Disciple until line 87) and Hoccleve himself.

Even though the familiar Hocclevian autobiographical voice is subdued in this poem, a number of critics stress the importance of 'Learn to Die' as a penitential text that offers a more spiritually restored and integrated subject than the psychologically and socially broken narrator of the 'Complaint'. They suggest we might read 'Learn to Die' as the profound culmination of Hoccleve's *Series* as a penitential form.[5] In this reading, Hoccleve seems to present the fullest image of himself as an integrated subject, or at least in the process of being restored to a form of spiritual health after the trauma of psychological illness and social trauma recounted in the 'Complaint'.[6] Scholars disagree about the relative importance of Hoccleve's artistic, poetic achievement for that recuperation, but some critics certainly draw attention to this penitential poem as an important site of the making of Thomas Hoccleve as a narrative subject.[7] This essay, however, focuses on the dissemination and dispersal of narrative voice and subjective identity in the poem to develop a reading of this text as a radical experiment with the borders and boundaries of the physical, spiritual and cognitive domains of the self; the differences between private and public emotional practices; and the distinction between the living, the dead and the imagined.

'Learn to Die' opens with a very formal address, in high rhetorical style and elaborate syntax:

'Syn all men naturelly desire
To konne, o eterne Sapience,
O universel prince, lord and syre,
Auctour of nature, in whos excellence

---

[5] For example, David Watt, '"I This Book Shal Make": Thomas Hoccleve's Self-Publication and Book Production', *Leeds Studies in English*, 34 (2003), 133–60; Robyn Malo, 'Penitential Discourse in Hoccleve's *Series*', *Studies in the Age of Chaucer*, 34 (2012), 277–305; Ashby Kinch, *Imago Mortis: Mediating Images of Death in Late Medieval Culture* (Leiden, 2014), p. 74. David Watt focuses on the way the design of the text reflects the centrality of 'Learn to Die' in the *Series*, in his *The Making of Thomas Hoccleve's Series* (Liverpool, 2013).

[6] Appleford (*Learning to Die in London*, p. 106) writes, for example, of the *Series*: 'the poetic sequence sketches a program of interior asceticism, self-examination, and conversion that rests on a *continuation* of his break with society and withdrawal from the political world'. See also the discussion in Nicholas Perkins, '"Heer Y die in thy presence": The Rewriting of Martyrs in and after Hoccleve', *Review of English Studies*, 69, issue 288 (2017), 13–31, at p. 26.

[7] Ethan Knapp offers a different emphasis on Hoccleve's writerly self, writing that 'Hoccleve presents in the *Series* [...] not a narrative of recovery and consolation but a sophisticated meditation upon the irresolvable fragmentation of the self and the intricate connections between his poetic project and the specific cultural milieu of the Privy Seal': *The Bureaucratic Muse: Thomas Hoccleve and the Literature of Late Medieval England* (University Park, 2001), p. 163.

Been hid all the tresors of science,
Makere of al, and þat al seest and woost,
This axe Y thee, thow lord of mightes moost [...]' (1–7)

After two stanzas, Sapience responds and addresses the speaker as 'sone myn' (15). The first speaker is not named as 'the disciple' until line 87, when the narrator speaks in his own voice for the first time.[8] The Disciple requests greater understanding across a range of topics, from Sapience's 'tresor of wisdam and the konnynge / Of seintes' (8–9), to 'science' (12) and other 'sotil matires' (13). Sapience discourages him from 'savouring' too high, however, and instead promises to teach him the 'excellent swetnesse' (38) of learning how to die: that is, how to make a good death. This is a four-stage process of learning how to live, how to receive God in the form of the Eucharist and how to love and honour God. The Disciple embraces this project enthusiastically but is curious about how it might be possible to teach about death, since it is simply an absence of life: 'Syn deeth noon hauynge is but a pryuynge' (35). However, in the next line, the Disciple immediately represents Death not as an absence but as a powerful and active female personification: 'For shee man reueth of lyf the swetnesse' (36). Sapience completes the stanza by flipping the meaning of 'swetnesse' – redefining it as the pleasure of instruction – and introducing a feminised 'art to lerne for to dye' as the remedy for death:

'Sone, the art to lerne for to dye
Is to the soule an excellent swetnesse,
To which Y rede thow thyn herte applie.
There is noon art þat man can specifie
So profitable ne worthy to be
Preferred artes all as þat is shee.' (37–42)

Like *mors*, the Latin word *ars* is feminine and this grammatical fact seems to facilitate the use of the pronoun 'shee', encouraging the reader, very early in the poem, to think nimbly and move between death and the art of dying as paired feminised abstractions.[9]

The Disciple and Sapience both use feminine pronouns for Death in this opening dialogue. Elsewhere in the poem, Death is described more neutrally, without the use of pronouns, as in 'dethes galle' (47), but at other times the metaphors are more striking, where the pronoun makes Death easier to visualise as a more fully realised female personification: e.g. 'whan deeth cometh for to cacche hir pray' (52). Death here is a female

---

[8] Suso names Sapience's interlocutor rather earlier, in the third paragraph (*Horologium Sapientiae*, ed. Künzle, p. 527, line 30).

[9] At the same time, we may observe that *Sapientia* is also a feminine noun in Latin but is gendered masculine in Hoccleve's text ('O eterne Sapience, / O universel prince, lord and syre', lines 2–3): grammatical gender does not always lead to a correspondingly gendered characterisation.

hunter, with a net, perhaps, or a weapon of some kind. Several lines later, Sapience refers to Death as a woman who desires to tame or restrain the male subject with a 'bridle'.

'Deeth wolde han ofte a brydil put on thee,
And thee with hir led away shee wolde,
Nadde the hand of Goddes mercy be.' (71–3)

A bridle on a horse is a familiar figure for the restraint of passion, but the word can also refer to a cord, braid or ribbon (*MED* 'bridel' n. (3)). In conjunction with the idea of Death's desire to lead the Disciple away, we may even imagine the golden chains of late medieval tournament rituals, when knights are 'led' into the arena by women holding golden or silken chains.[10] Hoccleve is modifying Suso's text here, using a more emphatic feminine pronoun in a metaphor that, like the earlier image of Death as a hunter, evokes some of the familiar courtly diction of female seduction and male subjection.

Throughout 'Learn to Die', Hoccleve moves between male and female pronouns in his figurative personifications of Death. The most extended reference to Death in the feminine in Hoccleve's 'Learn to Die' comes from the Disciple in his first impatient response to the *ymage*, when he acknowledges that death comes to everyone:

'Euene to alle is dethes iugement.
Thurghout the world strecchith hir paiement.

Deeth fauorable is to no maner wight.
To all hirself shee delith equally.
Shee dredith hem nat þat been of greet might,
Ne of the olde and yonge hath no mercy.
The ryche and poore folk eek certainly
Shee sesith. Shee sparith right noon estaat.
Al þat lyf berith with hir chek is maat.

Ful many a wight in youth takith shee
And many anothir eek in middil age
And some nat til they right olde be.
Wendist thow han been at swich auantage
Þat shee nat durste han paied thee thy wage,
But oonly han thee spared and forborn,
And the prophetes deid han heerbeforn?' (153–68)

Death here is an impartial, fearless and merciless judge who spares no one as she 'pays' their wage. Ellis draws attention to the fact that Hoccleve has added the image of Death as a chess player (at line 161) to Suso's text. This allusion might suggest a courtly context, or might even allude to Fortune as

---

[10] See, for example, Stephanie Trigg, 'Women in Uniform: Dress and Performance in Medieval Court Culture', in Holly A. Crocker and D. Vance Smith (eds), *Middle English Literature: Criticism and Debate* (New York, 2014), pp. 180–90.

she is figured as a chess player in Chaucer's *Book of the Duchess* and in other medieval texts and traditions.[11]

Even though these images of death as female are not developed in any more detail, they can still trail suggestive associations. As Emily Francomano comments, in her discussion of the personification of Wisdom in medieval and early modern literature, bodies, 'even when portrayed as literary tropes, partake of complex systems of cultural symbolism'.[12] Hoccleve's Death is not gendered female as comprehensively as Lady Meed or Holy Church are in *Piers Plowman*, but the suggestion of the bridle and the idea of capturing her prey present a more layered gendering of Death than as a simple function of the grammatical gender of 'mors' in Latin, as Ellis suggests in his note.[13] It is also worth observing here that other Middle English translations of Suso, such as that in Oxford, Bodleian Library, MS Douce 322, and the two other translations edited by Elizabeth Westlake (Lichfield, Lichfield Cathedral, MS 16 and Oxford, Bodleian Library, MS Bodl. 789, titled 'To Kunne Deie'), do not feminise Death.[14] This comparison suggests that Hoccleve's choice of female pronoun does not follow inevitably from the gendering of the Latin word, but represents a more motivated or deliberate – if not consistent – choice, one that goes beyond grammatical gender to invoke other social and cultural connotations, and one that invites comparisons with other active female personifications such as Nature.[15] In other lines, the gendered associations with the feminine pronoun are not so strong, and the emphasis lies more securely on the effect on the unwary (or 'undisposed', as at lines 181, 474, 526, 546, 590 and 814) subject who is unprepared to die: 'For shee vnreedy fynt hem when she sleeth' (68).

I will return to this question of death as gendered in the latter part of this essay. For now, I note that personification is only one of the techniques Hoccleve uses to conceptualise death. The most significant, of course, is the structural dialogue he adapts from Suso's text, when Sapience introduces a third figure into his discussion with the Disciple, inviting him to make

---

[11] We may note here that Hoccleve drew on Jacob de Cessolis's *De ludo saccorum* as a source for the *Regiment of Princes*.

[12] Emily C. Francomano, *Wisdom and Her Lovers in Medieval and Early Modern Hispanic Literature* (Basingstoke, 2008), p. 18. See more generally Francomano's discussion of the critical history of the 'gendered dynamics of personification allegory', pp. 12–19.

[13] Ellis (ed.), '*My Compleinte*', p. 227, nn. 52 and 54.

[14] Elizabeth Westlake, 'Learn to Live and Learn to Die: Heinrich Suso's *Scire Mori* in Fifteenth Century England' (unpublished doctoral thesis, University of Birmingham, 1993, 2 vols), vol. 1, p. 1. For the Lichfield translation, see vol. 2, pp. 299–323, and for 'To Kunne Deie', see vol. 2, pp. 329–53. For an earlier account of the influence of Suso's text in England, see Roger Lovatt, 'Henry Suso and the Medieval Mystical Tradition in England', in Marilyn Glasscoe (ed.), *Medieval Mystical Tradition in England, 1982* (Exeter, 1982), pp. 47–62.

[15] See Kellie Robertson, *Nature Speaks: Medieval Literature and Aristotelian Philosophy* (Philadelphia, 2017), pp. 17–18.

a mental picture of a young man on the point of death. Suso writes, in Colledge's translation: 'So consider this similitude of a dying man, who as he is dying is talking to you'.[16] Suso's phrase is 'similitudinem hominis morientis'.[17] Hoccleve translates more expansively, complicating the word 'similitude' with two options 'liknesse' and 'figure': 'Beholde now the liknesse and figure / Of a man dyynge and talkyng with thee' (85–6). Hoccleve uses these two words *liknesse* and *figure* twice each in this stanza, but subsequently uses the word *ymage* to refer to the young man, reverting to the word 'liknesse' only after the *ymage* has died.[18] In the critical tradition and in Ellis's edition, the *ymage* is often described as a kind of *alter ego* of the Disciple, as if he were confronting his own death; and certainly the *ymage* offers himself as an 'ensaumple and [...] mirour' (295) for the Disciple. Nevertheless, it is the Disciple who seems to become an *alter ego* for Hoccleve himself, both as the narrator of this text and the more fully developed narrative voice of the *Series* as a whole. But these shadowed and layered versions of the self are not clearly demarcated in the poem and, indeed, Ellis reminds us that 'the unstable boundaries between the real and the fictional, or between acts of meditation and divine revelation' are a familiar feature of late medieval mystical writing. He suggests that Suso's presentation of the 'imaginative projection' of the young man is clearer and less ambiguous than Hoccleve's, that Hoccleve's poem actively capitalises on the confusion.[19] Some of that confusion stems from the ontological or phenomenological uncertainty in which Hoccleve seems to delight. At the same time, as Ashby Kinch remarks, 'Suso scrambles the distinction between what is seen and what is simulated'.[20]

Hoccleve is adamant that the *ymage* of the young man is the product of a deliberate act of cognition and meditation. The Disciple works hard to follow Sapience's command to 'Beholde now the liknesse and figure / Of a man dyynge and talking with thee' (85–6), and his success is marked by the repetition of those words in the description of this mental act:

---

[16] *Wisdom's Watch Upon the Hours*, trans. Edmund Colledge (Washington, DC, 1994), p. 234.

[17] *Horologium Sapientiae*, ed. Künzle, p. 528, lines 3–4. The *circa* 1430–40 Lichfield translation of Suso (Lichfield Cathedral, MS 16) uses the word 'symylitude' here.

[18] See Steven Rozenski, Jr, '"Your Ensaumple and Your Mirour": Hoccleve's Amplification of the Imagery and Intimacy of Henry Suso's *Ars moriendi*', *Parergon*, 25 (2008), 1–16, for a discussion of Hoccleve's terminology in translating from Suso.

[19] Ellis (ed.), '*My Compleinte*', p. 228, nn. 88–90.

[20] Cf. Kinch, *Imago Mortis*, p. 10: 'A fascinating rhetorical feature of the text cinches the point: at a decisive juncture when the dying man insists that they conduct their exchange on sympathetic, personal terms, Suso changes the name by which he refers to the dying man from 'Similitudo Mortis' to 'Imago Mortis'. Suso theorises the *Imago Mortis* as the concept that allows us to move "similitude" to "reality," and thus to experience a mediated death as though it were unmediated.'

> The disciple of þat speeche took good cure
> And in his conceit bysyly soghte he,
> And therwithal considere he gan and see
> In himself put the figure and liknesse
> Of a yong man of excellent fairnesse [...] (87–91)

The Disciple turns his mind inward and seeks attentively ('bysyly soghte he') the appropriate cognitive pathways until he sees the *ymage* put 'in himself' by Sapience.[21] David Watt draws attention to the way these stanzas dramatise rhetorical and conceptual progression as encouraging a ruminative form of contemplation, since he argues there is an initial disjunction between what Sapience commands – an image of a dying man – and what the Disciple first sees – an attractive young man Watt argues is 'the mirror image of himself'.[22] When the following stanza describes the young man as 'ny ransakid' (92) by death, Watt suggests this twist encourages the reader to see the Disciple first as misreading or misunderstanding Sapience's instructions and then fulfilling them in an exemplary way.

As the ensuing dialogue proceeds, the voice of the young man moves from despair at his situation to the visions of hell opening up before him, to the exhortation of the Disciple to amend his life and prepare for death, but the dialogic drama comes to a sudden end when the *ymage*, after rehearsing the tormented speech of the souls in hell he sees rising before him, gasps out a kind of last will and testament, and in an astonishing performative speech act, abruptly dies: 'For a memorie leue Y this sentence / To thee, and heer Y die in thy presence' (739–40). At the moment of death, the *ymage* simply stops speaking and disappears from the narrative. There is no visual description of the moment of death or the fading of an apparition; and this seems to affirm he is a mental construct of a man dying, rather than a ghostly apparition. The Disciple trembles, afraid, 'broght to the deeth almost' (748). And yet at this moment, he turns around ('Aboute he torned him', 743), and addresses Sapience again. This decisive turning around suggests that while the figure of the young man had its origins in the Disciple's internal cognitive and imaginative activity, by the end of this section, it is as if the figure had indeed become externally realised in some way, *outside* the mind and under the Disciple's physical gaze, in a fashion more reminiscent of other late medieval encounters between the living and the ghostly dead. That is, for all the poem's initial insistence that the figure of the young man is a mental construct, the *figure* is drawn in such a powerful and lively way, he seems to take a more material form as if the Disciple were standing at his deathbed. The young man even appears to call on the Disciple as a witness ('heer Y die in thy presence'), conjuring up a familiar deathbed scene where relatives, friends and perhaps a priest observe

---

[21] Watt, *Making of Thomas Hoccleve's Series*, pp. 189–90.
[22] Watt, *Making of Thomas Hoccleve's Series*, p. 190.

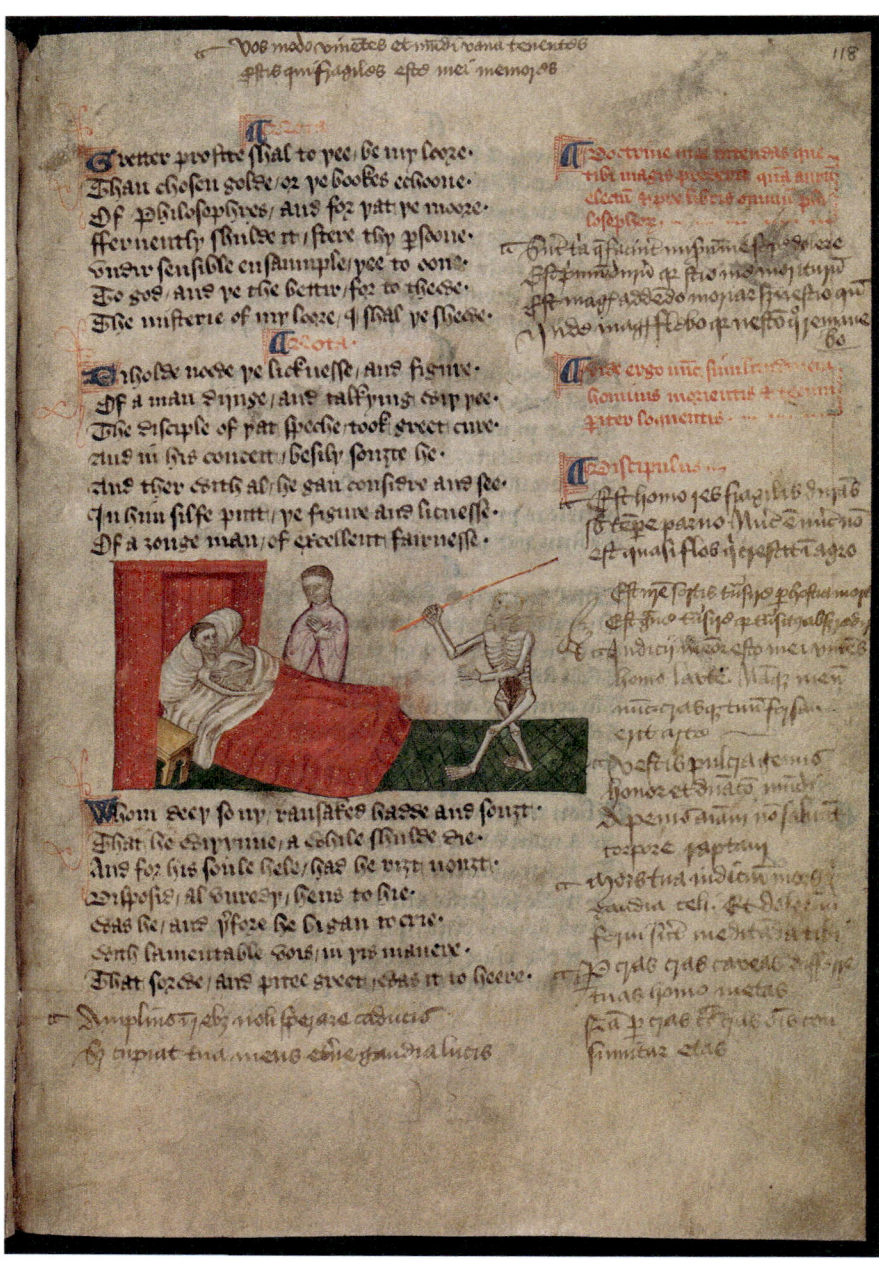

Figure 7.1. Oxford, Bodleian Library, MS Selden Supra 53, fol. 118r. Reproduced by permission of the Bodleian Libraries, University of Oxford.

the moment of the soul's passing. Death here is conceptualised as a social and emotional practice; and in this practice, it is the subjectivity of the dying man that is the central point of focus, as he now seems to summon the Disciple as a witness. Who has imagined whom?

Bringing a further dimension to the complex situation here, we may also observe that the Disciple addresses the *ymage* three times as *freend* (151, 467, 514), and even begs for his friendship (502–10). This distinctive form of address has the effect of echoing the amicable conversations between Hoccleve and his Friend elsewhere in the *Series*; and also of suggesting the *ymage* is indeed another person with social and emotional needs, not just an intellectual or cognitive abstraction. As Simpson remarks, the text 'presents images of extraordinary and tormented solitude, but the effect of this in the *Series* as a whole is to reconstruct friendships and readerships through the imagination'.[23] The complexities are manifold here, as Hoccleve uses a range of terms and rhetorical strategies to experiment with the powerful effects of personification, whereby an abstract concept such as Death can be seen both as an embodied, personified agent and as a body that can die; and as a *figure* and *likeness* that can be both self and other. The scene of death is both crowded, and social.

That sociality is a feature of the illustration that appears in the Selden manuscript (Figure 7.1), which shows the Disciple with two different images of death.[24] As David Watt shows, this image is carefully placed between the two stanzas discussed above, the stanza where Sapience instructs the Disciple to see such a figure in his mind, and then the key stanza that describes this figure as 'ransakid' (92).[25] As Watt writes, as 'the reader's eyes move from the textual depiction of "a yonge man /of excellent fairnesse" in the last line of the first stanza, they must cross over the image of a young man positioned centrally in the miniature before the reader passes to the second stanza'. For Watt, the contrast between the two stanzas is reinforced by the placing of this miniature in the Selden manuscript.[26] In this image there are three figures: the young man on his deathbed, the Disciple standing next to him; and Death, as a third body, in the form of an animated skeleton, walking briskly towards the bed with a red spear about to pierce the body. Kinch points out that this illustrator has drawn the young man and the Disciple with similar facial features and haircut: the visual conventions of the living and the dead confronting each other are very strong here, and imply that the illustrator has interpreted the young man as an *other* to the Disciple in some way.[27] Similarly, this visual tradition of representing Death in skeletal

---

[23] James Simpson, *Reform and Cultural Revolution. The Oxford English Literary History*, vol. 2, *1350–1547* (Oxford, 2002), pp. 430–1.

[24] Oxford, Bodleian Library, MS Selden Supra 53, fol. 118r.

[25] Watt, *Making of Thomas Hoccleve's Series*, pp. 193–6.

[26] Watt, *Making of Thomas Hoccleve's Series*, p. 193.

[27] Kinch, *Imago Mortis*, p. 69. Watt also remarks on the similarity of their hair and faces:

form, armed with a spear, or with a bell, accords with many of the ways Hoccleve describes the actions of Death as an external entity: a being that comes to perform a piercing or penetrative action of some kind on the living body.[28] This imagery can be feminine (as in the hunting imagery we considered above), or masculine: at line 290 the young man sees a masculine figure of Death as a hunter or warrior approaching with bow and arrow ('deeth his bowe hath for me bent').

Hoccleve's gendering of death, then, is inconsistent and uncertain, even insouciant. At times he offers sharp visual images or culturally laden associations; at other times gender distinctions fade into the background as ontological questions about identity, the relation between body and soul, the nature of the figure of the dying man, and the identity of the poem's various speaking voices come to the fore. The poem proceeds uncertainly in this regard, with varying degrees of urgency and precision.

A further layer of complexity emerges, too. If the Disciple imagines or sees the *ymage* in different ways throughout the poem, then so too does the *ymage* also conceptualise Death in different ways, as an abstraction, but also as a personification that is in turn male, female and neutral. When the *ymage* of the young man first begins to speak, he addresses Death directly, but his terminology and the pronouns are neutral. The thought of death is 'ful of bittir wo' (108); and he is conscious that 'cruel deeth' comes suddenly (114). Then he sees that Death has ambushed him, and comes with iron chains to apprehend him, 'As a man dampned wont is to be drawe / To his torment' (121–2). The young man clasps his hands and seeks in vain for a place to hide. Perhaps worst of all, he hears the 'vois horrible of deeth' (129), who addresses him directly:

'Thow dye shalt. Reson noon ne kynrede,
Frendshipe, gold ne noon other richesse
May thee deliure out of dethes duresse.

'Thyn eende is comen; comen ys thyn eende.
It is decreed. Ther is no resistence.' (131–5)

Death speaks in a fearsome and horrible voice and uses short sentences, and simple repetitive phrases, but is not perceptibly gendered here. Death also speaks of death in the third person, referring to 'dethes duress'.

Ellis points out in his notes that, in Suso's text, lines 134–5 are perhaps spoken by the young man, rather than Death as such. He also writes, 'Hoccleve follows Suso in making capital out of the difficulty of distinguishing the speakers from one another, especially the disciple from his *alter ego*, the fictionalised *imago mortis*', but he adds that 'confusion as to their identity

---

'This [...] suggests that the image of the dying man is the disciple's projection of himself having endured adversity' (*Making of Thomas Hoccleve's Series*, p. 196).

28 See, for example, Oxford, Bodleian Library, MS Douce 322, fol. 19v (Figure 7.2).

does not greatly affect the overall meaning of the work'.[29] The narrator of
'Learn to Die' does not seem to be firmly differentiated from the Disciple,
for example, while the narrator's voice is not characterised in any fullness.
We might read through the structure of the 'Complaint' and propose that
the narrator's voice shares continuities with the 'Hocclevian' voice we find
in the 'Complaint', or indeed in *La Male Regle* or the *Regiment of Princes*,
but we would be hard-pressed, I think, to identify any shared characteristics
of that narrative voice. James Simpson assumes that the Disciple is 'a *young*
seeker after wisdom' (my emphasis) but Hoccleve's text suggests that the
Disciple has been nearly apprehended by Death many times, and that he is
'wrappid [...] in synnes olde' (75), and thus may share more affinities with
the narrator than with the young *ymage*.[30] Sapience address him as 'sone'
(15), but this need not be a sign of youth.

If this conflation of voices and identities produces 'capital', in Ellis's
phrase, it is a form of ethical as well as poetic capital. Any confusion that
results has the effect of reinforcing the point about the universality of death;
it also encourages us to reflect on the poetic and symbolic traditions through
which we imagine our own death and that of others; how we routinely
imagine death as an external, and as an embodied figure.

I turn now to consider in detail a phrase that helps us approach the richly
ambivalent understanding of death as an agent. It is the narrator, in one
of his rare moments of commentary, who describes the image of the young
man that the Disciple finds in his mind: 'Whom deeth so ny ransakid had
and soght / Þat he withynne a whyle sholde dye' (92–3).[31] This powerful
and resonant word, 'ransakid', has an extensive range of senses and uses in
Middle English: its associations can help us tease out the way Hoccleve's
conceptual vocabulary weaves together body, mind, affect and feeling. As
we have already seen, the nature of 'death' as a rhetorical affect is hard to
pin down in the poem: Hoccleve's choice of word offers an equally broad
range of physical, material and cognitive meanings.

There is no direct equivalent of this phrase in Suso, who writes: 'There
appeared before his eyes the likeness of a most handsome young man, who
had been warned by death ['morte praeventus'] that he was very soon to
depart for the next world'.[32] Other instructive comparisons emerge from
other fifteenth-century translations of the Suso text. Appleford discusses

---

[29] Ellis (ed.), '*My Compleinte*', p. 228, notes to lines 134–5.
[30] Simpson, *Reform and Cultural Revolution*, p. 430.
[31] See the discussion above of the 'liknesse and figure' that Sapience instructs the
Disciple to discover in his mind.
[32] *Wisdom's Watch*, p. 244. Benjamin P. Kurtz observes that the 'simple clause, *qui morte
preuentus*, is converted into a fairly vivid line (92): "Whom deeth so ny ransakid had, &
soght;" and *iocundo* becomes a "herte wont vn-to gladnesse" (v.109)': 'The Relation of
Occleve's *Lerne to Dye* to Its Source', *Proceedings of the Modern Language Association*, 40
(1925), 252–75, at p. 272.

the version of 'Learn to Die' in Oxford, Bodleian Library, MS Douce 322, owned by William Baron.[33] At this point, the Douce manuscript version translates: 'a feyre ȝonge mon, þe which was sodenly overcome with deeþ [...] and had not disposed for þe helþe of his sowle'.[34] Similarly, the Lichfield translation uses the phrase 'sodeynly y-take with deth' at this point, and 'To Kunne Deie' places the emphasis on the urgency of the situation: the image of the fair young man is taken by death 'in ful schorte tyme'.[35] Hoccleve's 'ransakid' is both more savage, and more ambiguous than either of these alternatives. It is a significant and dramatic departure from the original; and Hoccleve seems to be making a particular point about the harrowing of body and soul that he is envisaging here.

The word 'ransack' is drawn from Old Icelandic *rannsaka*, a compound of *rann* 'house' and *soekja* 'seek'. The modern English 'ransack' is quite close to the word's original meaning – the frenzied searching of a house to steal its property; but the *Middle English Dictionary* testifies to a more comprehensive range of senses and usages. Certainly, the word preserves its original sense when it is used to mean 'search' or 'plunder', but it is not used only of houses or baggage. It can be used of the human body, in a variety of contexts, military to medical. It can also be used to describe the intellectual processes involved in studying Scripture, for example, or the provisions of a will. That is, to 'ransack' a text might be another way of describing close reading, or the kind of interrogative process I am enacting here. (The verb *serchen* has a similar range of meanings and, as I will show, it is sometimes used in apposition to *ransacken*.) The primary senses of 'ransacken' range from violent physical and military action, to more curative and recuperative associations. The word also has a range of figurative senses that describe intellectual and cognitive activity; and it is these two axes of possibility – literal or figurative; violent or recuperative – that I suggest Hoccleve is exploiting in 'Learn to Die'.

The primary sense of *ransacken* suggests a forceful, even violent action, like 'plunder'. It can mean to clear earth of weeds, or to search a battlefield. In Chaucer's *Knight's Tale*, for example, having defeated the Thebans, Creon and his soldiers did as they pleased:

To ransake in the taas of bodyes ded,
Hem for to strepe of harneys and of wede,
The pilours diden bisynesse and cure
After the bataille and discomfiture. (*CT* I.1005–8)

In this example, *ransake* means to search through the pile of bodies, but also to strip them of their clothes and gear; to ransack *in* and *under* the body's carapace of armour. It is an invasive and penetrative word, associated with

[33] Appleford, *Learning to Die in London*, p. 105.
[34] Appleford, *Learning to Die in London*, p. 122, n. 98.
[35] Westlake, 'Learn to Live and Learn to Die', vol. 2, p. 301, lines 61–2; p. 329, line 19.

the violence of dispossession, with stripping the valuable gear off the outside of a body.

The *Cursor Mundi* uses the word for violent physical assault, namely the distressing scourging of Christ on the cross: 'By his heued & bi his hare / Forþ his maister þai drogh / & ronsaked him vnrekenli'. Other variations for 'ronsaked' in other manuscripts at this point (e.g. 'rugged', and 'lugged') suggest that despite the word's popularity and frequency, it is still a word that might seem shocking and inappropriate in some way, an idea that is reinforced by the modifier *unrekenli*.[36] Alternatively, in Malory's *Morte Darthur*, to ransack, even in the field of battle, can be salvific and recuperative. After the battle of Sessoyne, Arthur ransacks the battlefields; that is, he searches for those of his knights who are still alive:

> And than relevys the kynge with his noble knyghtes and rensaked over all the feldis for his bold barouns. And tho that were dede were burryed as their bloode asked, and they that might be saved there was no salve spared nother no deyntés to dere that myght be gotyn for golde other sylver.[37]

Ransacking here is not pillaging but the painstaking search for the bodies of Arthur's followers. Another set of meanings describes an equally physical act, but one that aims to heal, rather than destroy. To ransack a wound, for example, is a familiar term from medieval medicine, where it is used in unambiguously fleshly terms, though the *Middle English Dictionary*'s example here is allegorical: 'Hou schulde a leche þis mon releeue, But ȝif he miȝte ronsake þe wounde?'[38]

A more famous literary example describes the ransacking of an ailing body. In Malory's *Morte Darthur*, Sir Urry has been brought to Arthur's court, suffering from enchanted wounds that will not heal. King Arthur 'softely handeled hym', but the wounds start to bleed again.[39] Then one hundred and ten knights of the Round Table examine the knight and 'serch' him. Finally Sir Lancelot is summoned. He is reluctant because the enchantment specifies that the wounded knight 'shulde never be hole untyll the best knyght of the worlde had serched hys woundis'; Lancelot fears his

---

[36] 'By his heued & bi his hare / forþ his maister þai drogh / & ronsaked him vnrekenli [Vsp: rugged; Trin-C: lugged]': Richard Morris (ed.), *Cursor Mundi (The Cursur o the World): A Northumbrian Poem of the XIVth Century in Four Versions*, EETS OS 99 (London, 1874–93), p. 904, lines 15821–3.

[37] Sir Thomas Malory, *Works*, ed. Eugene Vinaver, rev. P. J. C. Field, 3rd edn (3 vols, Oxford, 1990), vol. I, p. 224.

[38] Carl Horstmann and Frederick James Furnivall (eds), *The Minor Poems of the Vernon Ms (with a few from the Digby MSS. 2 and 86)*, EETS OS 98 (London, 1892–1901), p. 684, lines 39–40.

[39] Malory, *Works*, vol. III, p. 1147.

adultery with the Queen will be manifest through his failure.[40] So he prays for God's grace:

> And than sir Launcelot prayde sir Urré to lat hym se hys hede; and than, devoutly knelyng, he *ransaked* the three woundis, that they bled a lytyll; and forthwithall the woundis fayre heled and semed as they had bene hole a seven yere. And in lyke wyse he *serched* hys body of other three woundis, and they healed in lyke wyse. And than the laste of all he *serched* hys honde, and anone hit fayre healed.[41]

The word 'ransacked' here is used as a synonym for 'searched': but both examples seem to invoke putting one's hands into the wounds, or 'handling' them as Arthur had done, probing under the skin in a way that violates the boundaries of the physical self, that activates Urry's innards and perhaps helps bleed out impurities. Yet it is Lancelot's ransacking alone, blessed by God, that is successful.

This brings me to the most striking example of a body invaded by another hand, from the N-Town Nativity play, in which Salome the midwife expresses doubts about the miraculous Virgin birth. In the N-Town play, Mary challenges her and invites her to 'ransack' her still virginal body: 'Towch with youre hand and wele asay: / Wysely ransake and trye the trewthe owth / Whethyr I be fowlyd or a clene may'.[42] Even though this action is undeniably physical, it is also intimately linked with the interpretative testing of the prophetic texts, and in the context of performance, of the New Testament story. The physical testing of the Virgin body seems modelled on the example of St Thomas, who similarly tests, by penetrating, the wounded body of Christ.

When used in its figurative senses, at the other extreme from its associations with warfare and the tangled clutter of armour, weapons and bodies, to *ransack*, in the sense of 'search', is often used to describe more purely cognitive processes of reading and analysis. The object of this kind of ransacking can be a literal text: the Scriptures, or a will, for example. Sir John Falstoff writes in his will that he asks his executors to 'ransakyn besyly and discussyn soo discretly in here remembraunce'.[43] Richard Rolle suggests a man should 'amend his life and sithyn ransake godis witnessyngis. that is, his wordis, to knaw thaim'.[44] The English translation of the Acts of the Apostles similarly describes those converts who 'toke Goddes worde

---

[40] Malory, *Works*, vol. III, p. 1145.

[41] Malory, *Works*, vol. III, p. 1152 (my emphasis).

[42] Douglas Sugano (ed.), *The N-Town Plays* (Kalamazoo, 2007), No. 15, *Nativity*, lines 251–3.

[43] James Gairdner (ed.), *The Paston Letters, AD 1422–1509* (6 vols, London, 1904), vol. 3, p. 159.

[44] H. R. Bramley (ed.), *The Psalter, or Psalms of David and Certain Canticles: With a Translation and Exposition in English by Richard Rolle of Hampole* (Oxford, 1884), p. 401.

wiþ grete desire, iche daye ransakande þo holy scriptures'.[45] At the other semantic extreme, there are several examples of the word being used to describe a kind of textual or interpretative excess, an immoderate degree of interpretation and textual scrutiny. For example, in *The Fire of Love*: 'ransake we not to mykyll þo þingis þat we in þis lyfe may not consaue'.[46] Or, where reasoning is seen as inferior to contemplation: 'how dore ȝe þan ransake & seche wiþ ȝoure reson in þe wordes & þe dedes of Beniamyn?'[47]

To *ransack* is a word that is possibly even associated with the critique of Lollardy. Certainly, Hoccleve himself uses the word in this fashion in his poem to Oldcastle:

> Yee that nat sette by preestes power,
> Crystes rebels and foos men may you calle.
> Yee wade in presumpcioun to fer.
> Your soules to the feend yee foule thralle.
> Yee seyn: 'A preest in deedly synne fall,
> If he so go to messe, hy may not make
> Crystes body.' Falsly yee erren alle
> That holden so. To deepe yee ransake. (321–38)[48]

Implicit here is the sense that to *ransake* represents a form of textual and interpretative violence, a violation of some kind; going beyond, or too deeply in an inappropriate way, which might lead to heretical thought.

The *Middle English Dictionary* also gives us many examples of *ransack* that demonstrate the word has a robust conceptual life, too. Medieval writers ransack selves, sins, spiritual sickness, minds, hearts, lives, and consciences. In this forensic sense of community civic and spiritual investigation, sins and crimes can equally be the objects of ransacking.[49] More common is the sense of *ransaken* as examining one's life, one's mind, one's heart or one's conscience, as in these examples from fifteenth-century sermons: 'Euery man shuld fully ransake vp all is liff' or 'Ransake vp þi mynde and wisely

---

[45] A. C. Paues (ed.), *A Fourteenth Century English Biblical Version* (Cambridge, 1904), p. 170 (Acts of Apostles 17.12).

[46] R. Harvey (ed.), *The Fire of Love and The Mending of Life or The Rule of Living. The First Englisht in 1435, from the De Incendio Amoris, The Second in 1435, from the De Emendacione Vitae, of Richard Rolle, Hermit of Hampole, by Richard Misyn* (London, 1896), p. 16, line 19.

[47] Phyllis Hodgson (ed.), *The Cloud of Unknowing and Book of Privy Counselling*, EETS OS 218 (London, 1958), p. 159, line 18.

[48] M. C. Seymour, ed., *Selections from Hoccleve* (Oxford, 1981), pp. 61–74, at p. 69.

[49] For example, 'To him was comitted to ransake all þe greuous crimes or synnes þorw-oute þe diosise': J. J. Munro (ed.), *John Capgrave's Lives of St. Augustine and St. Gilbert of Sempringham and a Sermon*, EETS OS 140 (London, 1910), p. 66, lines 2–3.

examond þi nown conscience'.[50] Similarly, 'Euery day ransake þin herte; euery day examyne þin herte'.[51]

As I suggested above, 'ransaken' and 'serchen' share a similar range of meanings, applicable to a wide variety of objects: bodies, minds, texts, and wounds. There is a further comparable verb, 'gropen', that Hoccleve uses earlier, in the 'Dialogue', when he outlines to his Friend his plan to translate Suso's text. Such an act will be beneficial for himself and others, he suggests; while God has opened his path to mental health, there is still spiritual work to be done:

> For where my soule is of vertu al lene,
> And þoruȝ my bodies gilte foule and vnclene,
> To clense it sumwhat by translacioun
> Of it shal be myn occupacioun.
>
> For I not oonly but, as that I hope,
> Many another wiȝt eke therby shal
> His conscience tendirly groope,
> And wiþ himsilfe acounte and recken of al
> That he hath in this liif wrouȝt, greet or small,
> While hy tyme hath [...] (D 214–23)

The idea of tenderly 'grooping' one's conscience is an image that draws on physical activity to describe a spiritual and intellectual practice that can be undertaken carefully and gently, but in a way that can also be painful and intensive. This range of verbs – to seek, to grope, to ransack – all combine these possibilities of mental and physical scrutiny.

Returning to Hoccleve's 'Learn to Die', we recall that the *agent* of the verb 'ransaken' is not a confessor, a scrupulous soul, a physician or a courtly knight. It is Death itself who 'ny ransakid had and soght' (92) the young man. It is easy to see how the rival semantic associations of this verb (physical and figurative; violent and recuperative) combine here to produce a richly suggestive image. We may see Death as a ravaging, violent attacker, but perhaps also as a proactive physician or a scrupulous confessor. So, too, when we read that Death has 'souȝte' the young man, we may read this not just as Death simply looking for the young man, but similarly probing and examining both body and soul, just as the Disciple has mentally 'soghte' (88) the *figure* and *likeness* of the young man with equal seriousness and intent 'in his conceit'. When Death ransacks the young man so closely ('ny'), we may powerfully imagine Death as an external, embodied form of human agency, probing or penetrating the dying body, just as the Selden manuscript (Figure 7.1 above) shows Death approaching the dying man

[50] Woodburn O. Ross (ed.), *Middle English Sermons. Edited from British Museum MS. Royal 18 B XXIII*, EETS OS 209 (London, 1960, orig. 1940), p. 100, line 35, and p. 103, line 4 (sermon 17).
[51] C. Horstmann (ed.), *Yorkshire Writers: Richard Rolle of Hampole, an English Father of the Church, and his Followers* (2 vols, London, 1895–96), vol. 2, p. 367.

Figure 7.2. Oxford, Bodleian Library, MS Douce 322, fol. 19v.
Reproduced by permission of The Bodleian Libraries, University of Oxford.

with a red spear held aloft. Even more dramatically, in the fifteenth-century Carthusian miscellany, BL Addit. MS. 37049, an abridged English version of Suso's text is introduced with a full-page illustration (fol. 38v) that shows Death in the act of penetrating the dying man's body with his spear, having approached much closer, and ransacking, we might say, into the body itself. Death speaks here in a banderole that reads, 'I have sought the many a day for to haue the to my pray.' As in Hoccleve's poem, the voice of Death is an important auditory affect. Nowhere is the sound of Death made more visible than in Bodleian Library, MS Douce 322, fol. 19v (Figure 7.2), another manuscript containing Suso's text, where an image of Death holding a spear and a bell is surrounded by the word 'death'. The word appears nineteen times, in four variant spellings ('dethe', 'deth', 'deþe', and 'deþ'), as if Death rings out the sound of his or her own name.

In any case, the agency of Death in Hoccleve's poem is significant. In all the other examples of ransacking we have considered, while the object, text or being that is ransacked can take many different material, physical, conceptual and cognitive forms, the agent is always human. Given Hoccleve's unusual alternation of male and female pronouns, this agency may also be conceived as male or female, or indeed, as deliberately ambiguous or gender fluid.

Elsewhere, Hoccleve presents Death as clearly feminine in the *Regiment of Princes*, when he is lamenting the death of Chaucer. Hoccleve first presents Death as a male figure who 'slaughters' Chaucer (1967) and 'slays' Gower (1975), but several stanzas later he writes of 'hir vengeable duress' (2083), and her lack of mercy in taking Chaucer before another poet had emerged to take his place (2094). 'Shee mighte han tarried hir vengeance a whyle / Til that sum man had egal to thee be' (2101–2), he writes. R. F. Yeager argues that this feminised image of Death is Hoccleve's way of making a pointed political critique of the ineffectual courts of Richard II and Henry IV.[52] Yet Yeager takes the rhetorical argument several steps further by coining the name 'Lady Deeth', a name he even evokes in the title of his essay, 'Death is a Lady: The *Regiment of Princes* as Gendered Political Commentary'. The imposition of such a strongly gendered and courtly identity for death has little support from the text of the *Regiment*, however; it represents an extreme instance of the desire to build a fully realised personification out of a gendered allusion.[53]

In 'Learn to Die', in any case, the feminine imagery associated with death is far from courtly, especially as the moment of the young man's

---

[52] R. F. Yeager, 'Death Is a Lady: *The Regiment of Princes* as Gendered Political Commentary', *Studies in the Age of Chaucer*, 26 (2004), 147–93; see also Nicholas Perkins, 'Haunted Hoccleve? The *Regiment of Princes*, the Troilean Intertext, and Conversations with the Dead', *Chaucer Review*, 43 (2008), 103–39, at p. 114.

[53] Yeager also claims this female gendering of Death is unique to the *Regiment*, ignoring the feminisation of death in this opening of 'Learn to Die': 'Death Is a Lady', p. 149.

death throes approaches. The *ymage* speaks movingly about the approach of Death, who hastens to pierce and wound his limbs:

Lo, deethes strook haastith me hens to fecche.
My members shee so thirlith and distressith
That nature overcome is, shee witnessith. (684–6)

At this point, the question of Death's gender seems less significant than the *ymage*'s consciousness of the physical, sensory and emotional affects that threaten him. Chains confine him; the lamentations of the dead and the sorrows of hell surround him (99–100); Death has stolen on him unawares and bound him (119), and caught him in the snare (317). He cries with hands clasped together (124); he weeps (183); his heart is plunged into despair (227); his eyes grow dim and dark (228); salty tears flow down his cheeks (261–3); and he burns in anticipation of the horrors that await him:

'See how my face wexith pale now,
And my look ful dym and heuy as leed.
Myn yen synke eek deepe into myn heed,
And torne vpsodoun, and myn hondes two
Wexen al stif and starke and may nat do.' (654–8)

The *ymage* of the young man unprepared for death is also tormented because none of his accomplishments leave any trace or mark on the world. His riches are but shadows, or like a messenger running fast, or a ship that leaves no trace on the ocean once it has passed, or the passage of a bird through the air, or an arrow shot from a bow. It 'Twynneth the eir' (*LTD* 212) but the air closes up again immediately and leaves no trace, like the body he currently inhabits. As he concludes that stanza:

'Continuelly Y stynted for to be,
And tokne of vertu shewid noon in me.

I am consumed in my wikkidnesse.
Myn hope is as it wer a wolle-loke
Which the wynd vp reisith for his lightnesse,
Or smal foom þat desparplid is, and broke
With tempest, or as with wynd waastith smoke,
Or as mynde of an oost þat but a day
Abit, and aftir passith foorth his way.' (216–24)[54]

I draw attention here to the paradoxes. The dying man is only an *ymage*, a likeness of a young man on the point of death, but his emotions are expressed in decidedly bodily terms (his tears, his clenched hands, the fearful sights and sounds of the dead that haunt him). Yet three stanzas lament the body's *lack* of impact on the world and the ephemerality of his faith, like a lock of wool twisting in the wind. Hoccleve's insistence on

---

[54] Hoccleve uses the more homely 'wolle-loke' for Suso's image of dust blown by the wind.

the material, somatic affects of fear and despair on the body show us how closely cognition and feeling are linked in this striking image of human nature *in extremis* when insufficient care has been taken to prepare the soul for death, when body, soul and mind can be so easily 'ransacked' at the moment of death. The Disciple, and the poem's readers, are invited not just to observe and learn from this image of Death, but to feel and imagine the physical, emotional and spiritual torments of this destruction of self. Hoccleve's representation of Death is particularly powerful here; she is not simply a personification of an event but an active agent with the capacity to reach into the human body in a way that compels the realisation that in this moment of crisis, when death is upon us, it can be difficult to tell body, soul and mind apart.

Importantly, too, this deathbed scene is resolutely social, with the subjectivity of the dying man at the centre. For example, the *ymage* addresses a company of youthful people, as if the context is not just for the narrator alone, but as if addressing his deathbed room:

'O alle yee þat heer been present,
Yee that floure in youthes lusty grennesse,
And seen how deeth his bowe hath for me bent,
And tyme couenable han to redresse
þat your vnruly youthes wantonnesse
Offendid hath, considereth my miserie.' (288–93)

Sometimes he addresses the narrator, his interlocutor, with the singular *thow*, or as *frend*, as we saw above, but at other points, like this, he speaks to a plural company, as also at line 456, 'Reewe eek on me, yee alle, and pitee haue'. At this moment in any public narration, gestures of pointing or nodding to individuals would be extremely powerful; and even if this poem were read in silent isolation, this form of address would still evoke a more public deathbed scene than the simple apparition of the solitary figure first introduced by Sapience.

My point here is that while Hoccleve pays careful attention to the allegorical mechanics by which Sapience inserts a figure of the dying man into the Disciple's mind, the emotional practices around medieval death and dying, and the social habitus of the medieval deathbed, where death is public and communal, are inescapable. Death has a lesson to teach, and it must be public. It cannot be contained simply inside the mind of one single Disciple. The readership for such lessons is inevitably plural and public; and the teaching moment is irresistible. The 'making' of an individual's lesson about death seems necessarily or inevitably to involve the making of a community's lesson as well.

Hoccleve closes the poem in a penitential mood. He does not complete his translation of Suso's text. He says this first part is 'enough' for his 'small konnynge and symple art' (924) but his second last stanza offers a powerful message from Sapience which is both urgent and abrupt:

'Weel thee dispose and reedy make thee
To dye, lest the tyme be thee reft
Or þat tho be waar, for no certeintee
Haast thow therof. Thow art nothyng pryuee
Therto. Deeth is nat fer: right atte yate
Shee is. Be reedy for to dye algate.' (905–10)

One of the reasons the discourse and conversation of the *ymage* is so disturbing is the immediacy with which he relates the process of dying, as an embodied and affective process that is designed to make the Disciple *feel* and *sense* the proximity of death more urgently. As Sapience explains in the first part of the poem, the Disciple has himself been close to death many times but God has stayed his hand out of mercy, in consideration of the Disciple's sins. But now the time is more urgent, and a 'sensible ensaumple' (82), glossed by Ellis as a 'sensory example', is now required to make a deeper impression on the narrator.

In 'Learn to Die', Hoccleve makes a profound and personal argument without putting his own highly developed narrative autobiography at the affective or poetic centre of the work. Instead, he works with a series of translated and imagined dialogic voices and images in a way that seems to embrace ambiguity and complexity, inviting the reader to contemplate the problem of imagining death on a number of different levels. These productive ambiguities also underpin the relationships between thinking and feeling in the poem, and the vexed questions of whether Death is primarily something that happens to the body or the soul, and indeed, whether Death is an agent, and meaningfully male or female. The unusual concept of Death 'ransacking' the human subject brings together these physical, conceptual and emotional contradictions; but through the word's rich and varied associations, Hoccleve also suggests that while Death may be both violent and invasive, it may also offer a kind of recuperative healing. In this poem, readers are constantly and emphatically warned that Death may come at any moment; but at the same time the poem also helps us apprehend the many different ways we may apprehend death – physically, cognitively, spiritually, and emotionally.

Part III

Writing Life

8

Hoccleve's Formulary *and the Matter of*
Everyday Life

Taylor Cowdery

Roland Barthes once argued that literary realism arises when a writer
includes within his text certain trivial details and mundane events, not
to denote an extratextual reality, but to connote its intratextual illusion.[1]
But is this the only kind of realism that a literary text may project? The
work of Thomas Hoccleve offers us an occasion to revisit this question.
For more than forty years, critics have struggled to reconcile the realistic
aspects of Hoccleve's work – its eye for detail, its concern with local
place, and its autobiographical elements – with its resistance to the kind
of realism that Barthes describes.[2] Again and again, Hoccleve's poems
produce the illusion of the real within the diegesis of their textual frames,
only to break that diegesis by calling attention, repeatedly, to the material
things, actual persons, and historical places that lie beyond its scope.[3] J.
A. Burrow says it best, perhaps, when he claims that Hoccleve is interested
less in the construction of 'imaginary worlds' within his texts than with the
realistic evocation of what lies beyond them, 'the non-imaginary worlds
of public and private life'.[4] In Burrow's view, Hoccleve may be a realist,

---

[1]   Roland Barthes, 'The Reality Effect', trans. Richard Howard, in *The Rustle of Language*
(Berkeley, 1989), p. 148.
[2]   The classic accounts of Hoccleve's realism are J. A. Burrow, 'Autobiographical Poetry
in the Middle Ages: The Case of Thomas Hoccleve', *Proceedings of the British Academy*,
68 (1982), 389–412; and J. A. Burrow, 'Hoccleve's *Series*: Experience and Books', in R. F.
Yeager (ed.), *Fifteenth-Century Studies: Recent Essays* (Hamden, CT, 1984), pp. 259–73. See
too D. C. Greetham, 'Self-Referential Artifacts: Hoccleve's Persona as a Literary Device',
Modern Philology, 86 (1989), 242–51.
[3]   This is especially true of the *Series*, on which see especially James Simpson, 'Madness
and Texts: Hoccleve's *Series*', in Julia Boffey and Janet Cowen (eds), *Chaucer and Fifteenth-
Century Poetry*, King's College London Medieval Studies, 5 (London, 1991), pp. 15–28;
and Laurie Atkinson, '"Why þat yee meeued been / can I nat knowe": Autobiography,
Convention, and Discerning *Doublenesse* in Thomas Hoccleve's *The Series*', *Neophilologus*,
101 (2017), 479–94, at pp. 485–8.
[4]   J. A. Burrow, 'Hoccleve and Chaucer', in Ruth Morse and Barry Windeatt (eds),

but his realism is always in service to what actually happened. When we hear a knock upon his door, we can assume that someone is really there.[5]

This essay extends Burrow's argument in two ways. First, it suggests that Hoccleve's peculiar style of realism may have been inspired by the specific kinds of reading and writing he did at the office of the Privy Seal, where he worked as a clerk for more than forty years.[6] The depictions of reality found in the documents that Hoccleve copied out bear a striking resemblance, as we will see, to the picture of late medieval life that he gives us in the poems: quotidian, exacting in detail, and full of local colour. Second, it argues that our best guide to the influence of the Privy Seal upon Hoccleve can be found in a book that is often discussed but little read. This is the *Formulary*, a massive collection of more than eleven hundred writs, grants, letters patent, and extracts that the poet assembled between 1423 and 1426, at the very end of his bureaucratic career.[7] Because it is a compilation of templates intended to ease the writing of new documents by future Privy Seal clerks, the *Formulary* appears at first to be an anonymous and impersonal text. It reuses the same rote *formulae* ('nous vous mandons', 'de notre grace', 'amicus noster dilectus') and the same blank placeholders ('un tiel', or 'A. de B.' and 'C. de D.') again and again, so much so that previous critics have often cast it as an emblem of the impersonal and rigid quality of bureaucratic writing

---

Chaucer Traditions: Studies in Honour of Derek Brewer (Cambridge, 1990), p. 56.

[5] This is one of Barthes' examples of the reality-effect; in a scene from Michelet's *Histoire de France*, he argues, we are told that there is a 'gentle knock at a little door', not because it is significant, but because it adds texture to the scene. See Barthes, 'Reality Effect,' p. 140.

[6] For Hoccleve's biography, see J. A. Burrow, *Thomas Hoccleve* (Aldershot, 1994). For his career at the Privy Seal and discussion of that office more generally, see A. L. Brown, 'The Privy Seal Clerks in the Early Fifteenth Century', in D. A. Bullough and R. L. Storey (eds), *The Study of Medieval Records: Essays in Honour of Kathleen Major* (Oxford, 1971), pp. 260–81; Ethan Knapp, 'Bureaucratic Identity and the Construction of the Self in Hoccleve's *Formulary* and La Male Regle', *Speculum*, 74 (1999), 357–76; Helen Killick, 'Thomas Hoccleve as Poet and Clerk' (unpublished PhD dissertation, University of York, 2010), pp. 62–100; Helen Killick, 'The Medieval "Side-hustler": Thomas Hoccleve's Career in, and out of, the Privy Seal', in Gwilym Dodd and Craig Taylor (eds), *Monarchy, State and Political Culture in Late Medieval England: Essays in Honour of W. Mark Ormod* (York, 2020), pp. 144–64; Malcolm Richardson, 'Hoccleve in His Social Context', *Chaucer Review*, 20 (1986), 313–22; and Sebastian Sobecki, 'The Handwriting of Fifteenth-Century Privy Seal and Council Clerks', *Review of English Studies*, 72, issue 304 (2021), 253–88.

[7] For an overview of the formulary genre in medieval literary culture, see especially Malcolm Richardson, 'The *Ars dictaminis*, the Formulary, and Medieval Epistolary Practice', in Carol Poster and Linda C. Mitchell (eds), *Letter-Writing Manuals and Instruction, from Antiquity to the Present* (Columbia, 2007), pp. 52–66 (esp. pp. 60–2). For discussion of English formularies broadly contemporaneous with Hoccleve, see especially Killick, 'Thomas Hoccleve as Poet and Clerk', pp. 72–5; Emily Steiner, *Documentary Culture and the Making of Early English Literature* (Cambridge, 2003), pp. 54–60; and David Watt, *The Making of Thomas Hoccleve's Series* (Liverpool, 2013), pp. 160–5.

itself.[8] But the *Formulary* is actually an extraordinarily specific book, one that depicts late medieval life with a clarity and detail that cuts against its anonymous appearance. For this reason, it is not really a 'book of forms', as its editor, Elna-Jean Bentley, once put it.[9] Rather, it is a book of anecdotes touching upon the social and material currents that animate late medieval English society – or, still more precisely, a book of lightly anonymised scenarios, set within that society, that Hoccleve and his fellow clerks might adapt to write about late medieval reality as it was differently lived.

This chapter will read the *Formulary* in two ways. First, I explore the kinds of bureaucratic documents that might have caught Hoccleve's eye, not because of their 'traditional textual patterns' or standardised forms, but because of the real people, places, and events they describe.[10] Many of these items speak directly to topics that Hoccleve considers in his poetry. The second part of the essay considers how the *Formulary* may have provided the poet with certain opportunities for literary invention. Aspects of Hoccleve's realism – in particular, his self-presentation as an abject petitioner, his figuration of power in bureaucratic terms, and his depiction of setting – all have their corollary in the literary tropes of the Privy Seal office. It is well known that Chaucer looked to the *fabliau* and the *Roman de la Rose* for literary techniques that would connote a sense of realism.[11] Hoccleve, instead, seems to have rooted his verisimilitude in a more everyday tradition of writing – and so it is to that tradition, and the *Formulary*, that we must turn to understand his own attempt to hold the words of his poetry 'cosyn' to their deeds.[12]

The *Formulary* and Hoccleve's Life

Walking around the city, getting dinner at an inn and listening to the chit-chat of passers-by in the streets: these are some of the experiences that Hoccleve describes in his verse, and the ones that appear to be drawn directly from his experience of late medieval London. In a memorable passage from the *Male Regle*, for example, the poet describes the pleasure he takes in hiring river taxis to ferry him across the Thames. One evening, on

---

[8] See especially Ethan Knapp, *The Bureaucratic Muse: Thomas Hoccleve and the Literature of Late Medieval England* (University Park, 2001), pp. 181–6; and Watt, *Making of Thomas Hoccleve's Series*, pp. 144–85.

[9] Elna-Jean Young Bentley, 'The *Formulary* of Thomas Hoccleve' (unpublished PhD dissertation, Emory University, 1965), p. xxxvi.

[10] Matthew Clifton Brown, '"Lo, Heer the Fourme": Hoccleve's *Series*, *Formulary*, and Bureaucratic Textuality', *Exemplaria*, 23 (2011), 27–49, at p. 35.

[11] For the literary sources of Chaucer's realism, see especially Charles Muscatine, *Chaucer and the French Tradition: A Study in Style and Meaning* (Berkeley, 1957), pp. 11–97.

[12] *Riverside Chaucer*, p. 35 (CT I.742).

the way home from a King Street tavern and likely a bit drunk, he makes his way to a 'brigge', or pier, where he is accosted by the different 'bootmen' who want him as a fare.[13] As he writes,

> With hem I was itugged to and fro,
> So wel was him þat I with wolde fare,
> For riot paieth largely eueremo.
> He styntith neuere til his purs be bare.
>
> Othir than maistir callid was I neuere
> Among this meynee, in myn audience.
> Methoghte I was ymaad a man for euere,
> So tikelid me þat nyce reuerence
> Þat it me made larger of despence
> Than þat I thoghte han been. (MR 197–206)

Hoccleve's characteristic blend of self-deprecation and detail (the back-and-forth tugging, his inebriated delight in being called 'maister', and the playful suggestion that, at least for the evening, the boatmen serve as his 'meynee') lends this passage a wonderful realism. It's easy to assume that a late-night commute in London could unfold in just this way, and contemporary records seem to back up the assumption. As Claire A. Martin has documented, the passenger-transport industry on the Thames was, by the turn of the fifteenth century, both extensively developed and scantly regulated: one could certainly take a ferry across the river, or hire a taxi to do the same, but the price one paid was likely to be determined by such factors as the pliability of the traveller and the competition of other boatmen for the same fare.[14] What is more, rich men made more frequent use of river transport than the poor. The abbot of Faversham, for instance, maintained his own boat and dock for travel back and forth between London and Kent, and so the pleasure that Hoccleve takes in his taxi ride likely stems from his knowledge that it is an activity usually reserved for the well-to-do.[15]

We should not assume too quickly, however, that this passage draws merely upon Hoccleve's personal experience of city travel – for there is also evidence that it was inspired, at least in part, by writing rather than life. Some of this writing was literary: as Eva Thornley observed long ago, the *Male Regle* is a satirical inversion of many of the tropes of Middle English

---

[13] For discussion of Hoccleve's itinerary in the *Male Regle*, and confirmation that 'brigge' does indeed mean 'pier' in this instance, see Paul Strohm, *Theory and the Premodern Text* (Minneapolis, 2000), p. 9.

[14] Claire A. Martin, 'London: The Hub of an English River Transport Network, 1250–1550', in Valerie Allen and Ruth Evans (eds), *Roadworks: Medieval Britain, Medieval Roads* (Manchester, 2016), pp. 249–70. As Martin notes, the industry was 'relatively unregulated before 1555' (p. 270). For further discussion of the business of passenger transport across the Thames, see pp. 264–9; for discussion of matters of regulation and jurisdiction, see pp. 253–6.

[15] Martin, 'English River Transport Network', p. 250.

penitential poetry, and this passage, which skewers Hoccleve's vanity and self-importance, is no exception.[16] But another kind of writing, modelled most clearly by the *Formulary*, may also have shaped his depiction of this little scene on the Thames. Consider, for instance, two items from Hoccleve's compilation, nos. 78 and 470. Each is a grant of forfeiture by Deodand, and each describes an accident on the London waterways in which passengers fell out of a boat and drowned, leaving the boat without a legal owner.[17] Here is the text of the second grant:

> The king to the bailiff or sheriff [*gardein*] of the Thames [*de lewe de Thamise*] in the port of our city of London, greetings. From our special grace we have granted to A. de B. and C. D. a boat that you transferred to our hands by Deodand [*un bateau par vous pris en notre main come Deodand*], because E. F. of the village of G. fell out of [*cheist hors*] the same boat and drowned [*noya*] in the port of our aforesaid city on such-and-such a day [*tiel jour*], as we have been informed. Therefore, we command that, if it is indeed the case that the aforesaid E. fell into the Thames out of the aforesaid boat and drowned in the aforesaid port and that the same boat was, for this reason, transferred by you into our hands, as was said above, you should hand over [*facez liverer*] the same boat to the aforesaid A. and C. as a gift from us [*a avoir de notre doun*], if, as was said before [*avant come*], the same boat now belongs to us [*a nous appartient*] due to the aforesaid cause. And we wish to inform you that by these letters [*par cestes*] you are released from further obligation [*deschargez*] with respect to us [*envers nous*]. Issued etc.[18]

When one reads this document against the final aim of the *Male Regle*, which is to secure Hoccleve's 'yeerly' payment of ten pounds, currently in arrears, from 'th'eschequeer' (*MR* 420–1), one is presented with a series of amusing questions. Did Hoccleve have such accidents in mind when he compared the London boatmen to the sirens who draw unlucky boat-passengers to their deaths (see *MR* 225–64)?[19] Was he thinking of lax consumer

---

[16] See Eva Thornley, 'The Middle English Penitential Lyric and Hoccleve's Autobiographical Poetry', *Neuphilologische Mitteilungen*, 68 (1967), 295–321.

[17] For the legal definition of Deodand, which designated animate or inanimate things that caused the death of a person as forfeit to the law, see Frederick Maitland and Frederic William Pollock, *The History of English Law before the Time of Edward I*, 2nd edn (2 vols, Cambridge, 1909), vol. 2, pp. 473–4. For a discussion of the practice of Deodand as it evolved in medieval England, see Anna Pervukhin, 'Deodands: A Study in the Creation of Common Law Rules', *American Journal of Legal History*, 47 (2005), 237–56.

[18] Bentley, 'Formulary', pp. 455–6 (item no. 470). Subsequent references to the *Formulary* will be given parenthetically by the number of the item in Bentley's edition and, if I have quoted the text, the page number on which the quotation appears.

[19] Strohm holds that the allegorical valences of the boatmen in this passage are inspired, at least in part, by Hoccleve's inability to resist their call to open his 'purs' (*MR* 199); see Strohm, *Theory and the Premodern Text*, pp. 17–18.

protections when he ruefully noted how expensive the ride was?[20] Did he resent that he was not among the royal servants who had received similar gifts of forfeiture from the king, such as John Ellis, a 'yeoman de chambre' whom the other grant of Deodand names as the recipient of a vessel involved in a nearly identical accident?[21] Was Hoccleve, in short, asking the Exchequer for his own boat?

This last possibility seems rather unlikely, but my point is that the *Formulary* contains a wealth of information that can help us contextualise the local and historical colour of Hoccleve's poetry. Over the course of its many pages, we hear often of places with which Hoccleve was familiar; of people that he knew or likely wished to know; and of events and happenings that shaped, both directly and indirectly, the everyday circumstances of his life. Moreover, the common ground between the *Formulary* and Hoccleve's circumstances did not go unnoted by the poet, for at those moments when it touched topics relevant to his life, he appears to have inserted his own initials, 'T. H.', into the document at hand. There are eleven such documents in the *Formulary*, and while it is possible that the 'T. H.' to which they refer is not Hoccleve but some other individual with a similar name, item nos. 219 and 982–3 very likely name the poet.[22] The first is a grant to the Exchequer ordering it to release funds to 'notre ame clerc, T. H.' for the purchase of ink, wax, and parchment on behalf of the Privy Seal, while the latter two are templates for wills made out in the name of 'T. H.'; this individual is probably Hoccleve because the wills contain sentiments and phrases that recall passages from his poetry. Four more documents, nos. 159–61

---

[20] Martin notes that just such regulation to regulate boat prices was introduced in 1372, to limit the amount charged for taxi passage between London and Westminster to no more than two pennies (when the boat was partly full) or three pennies (when it was full), and in 1437, to limit the amount that a ferryman, rather than a taxi-boat, could charge for passage across the river to no more than half a penny; see 'English River Transport Network', pp. 266, 266, n. 75, and 266, n. 77. Given Hoccleve's account, however, we must doubt whether this legislation was much enforced.

[21] Bentley, 'Formulary', p. 71 (item no. 78); Bentley identifies the anonymous recipient of this boat, 'A. de B.', as 'Johan Elys, yeoman de chambre', on the basis of a parallel record in the Calendar of the Patent Rolls (see p. 71, n. 2).

[22] These documents are, as numbered in Bentley's edition, item nos. 139, 159, 160, 161, 179, 200, 219, 567, 659, 982 and 983. Ethan Knapp had previously identified ten of these documents; to my knowledge, this is the first time that no. 659 has been discussed as an item that contains his initials; see Knapp, 'Bureaucratic Identity', pp. 368–9 and 368, n. 42. For details on these items, and further discussion of their contents, see the appendix. Sebastian Sobecki has recently discovered a new Hoccleve holograph, Cambridge, Trinity College, MS O.7.43, that contains excerpts from the *Formulary*, including three of its 'T. H.' items. The find corroborates my claim that the presence of these initials in the *Formulary* is deliberate and not the product of happenstance. See Sobecki, '"Gens sans argent": A New Holograph Manuscript by Thomas Hoccleve', forthcoming in *The Library*, 24 (2023).

and 567, are letters of protection (again, made out for a person with the initials 'T. H.') and are relatively straightforward with respect to the legal sureties they afford.

The last four documents, nos. 139, 179, 200 and 659, are more eclectic. Item no. 139 is a letter of recommendation that names 'dilectum clericum nostrum T. H.' as the Crown's candidate for taking over a now-vacant parish church that had once been held by 'W. de B.', now deceased. Item nos. 179 and 200 are writs, both of which concern properties whose management has passed, for various reasons, into the king's hands: in the case of the first, 'T. H.' is the escheator who has determined that, having died without drawing up a will, the son of 'J. F.' should inherit his manor; while in the case of the second, 'T. H.' is the clerk who is named as steward and receiver, the 'custodem ac receptorem', of one of the king's castles and its incomes. Finally, item no. 659 is a lengthy account of a dispute between several parties, including John de Whitteby, a prior recently deposed from his post at the Gilbertine house in Watton, and the newly appointed prior of that house. 'T. H.', in this letter, plays the hapless new appointee, who is driven from the monastery after John arrives 'ovec grand nombre de gens', breaks down the door, and chases him off the grounds 'par force et armes' (p. 679).

Why did Hoccleve choose to include his initials in these eleven documents – or at the very least, in the three items (nos. 219 and 982–3) in which these initials almost certainly refer to him? The presence of Hoccleve's name in many of them is very strange: the poet never served, after all, as a steward to a castle or as a prior, and there is no evidence that he ever travelled in Picardy with a letter of royal protection in hand. But it is somewhat easier to reconstruct Hoccleve's motives in the case of document nos. 982 and 983, both of which are wills that contain strikingly similar phrases to what one finds in 'Learn to Die'. Like that poem, both wills stress the importance of preparing for one's last moments ahead of time, when one is 'saluti anime', or of sound mind (no. 982; p. 1046), and when one still possesses a 'recenti memoria', or memory for present things (no. 983; p. 1046), so that one can 'dispose and make plans' for one's 'goods, in such a way that one might do good by ceding possession of them' to some Christian authority (no. 982; p. 1046). The wills also stand out because they are, to the best of my knowledge, the only two wills contained in the *Formulary* – a fact that only heightens the strangeness, and provocation, encoded in Hoccleve's apparent decision to make them out in his own name. Hoccleve had recently been at work on the *Series* when he composed the *Formulary*, and, as Sebastian Sobecki has demonstrated, he had also been a recent beneficiary in the will of his newly deceased colleague and friend, John Bailey.[23] It should not surprise us, then, that phrases from both wills recall what Hoccleve says

---

[23] Sebastian Sobecki, *Last Words: The Public Self and the Social Author in Late Medieval England* (Oxford, 2019), pp. 65–73. Sobecki further suggests that Bailey's sudden death may have been an inspiration for the production of the *Series* (pp. 74–8).

about dying and preparation for death in the *Series*. For in that poem, too, Hoccleve tells us he is of sound mind – that his 'wit' has 'hoom come aȝein' (*C* 64) – and he also stresses, in the guise of Sapientia, the importance of 'correct[ing]' one's 'lyf' while one is 'yong' and 'haast strengthe and force' (*LTD* 825–6).

The presence of these two wills does not, of course, mean that Hoccleve drew upon the *Formulary* directly when he composed the *Series*. For one thing, the *Formulary* likely post-dates that work; for another, it is an imperfect and selective sample of the thousands of documents that Hoccleve copied out across his career.[24] What the wills do suggest, however, is that Hoccleve paid attention – in some cases, very close attention – to what he read and wrote during his days at the office, because it is the matter of these wills, their specific details and sentiments, that seems to have caught his interest. Brought face-to-face with a situation, person, or event that spoke to his own circumstances, he projected himself into the text under his pen – and, in some cases, chose to record that moment of identification by replacing the initials of the named party with his own.

Why would Hoccleve have felt spurred to identify, at times, with what he read and wrote while at work? In certain cases, he may have felt a personal kinship with the places, persons, and situation described in the letter at hand. Many items in the *Formulary*, for example, touch upon the business of the Privy Seal and its clerks. Some of these have to do with its run-of-the-mill operations: regular payments for supplies are listed (e.g. no. 219), as are grants for livestock and coal to be used by its officers (nos. 594 and 609). But some items deal with more unusual matters. One document, for example, records a livery for robes that are to be provided to the clerks at Christmas – or, more precisely, for the upcoming Christmas, 'contre la feste de Noel prochein venant' (no. 403; p. 396).[25] Other items describe

---

[24] We know that countless other Privy Seal letters in the poet's hand survive, and so it is almost certain that he read many similar documents long before he wrote out these particular wills. Linne Mooney and Helen Killick have done invaluable work in their attempts to excavate the broader scope of Hoccleve's labours at the Privy Seal office. Mooney, for example, has identified 145 documents that are in the poet's hand contained in the National Archives, while Killick has identified a further 913; see Mooney, 'Some New Light on Thomas Hoccleve', *Studies in the Age of Chaucer*, 29 (2007), 293–340; Killick, 'Thomas Hoccleve as Poet and Clerk', pp. 36–8 and 187–230; and Killick, 'Hoccleve's Career in, and out of, the Privy Seal'. The *Formulary* is thus best understood not as a representative *epitome* of the poet's bureaucratic work, but as a curtailed and unrepresentative selection of it.

[25] Compare item nos. 23 and 67 in the appendix to Burrow, *Thomas Hoccleve*, pp. 38 and 49, for similar documents found on the rolls. Burrow suggests that the allowance for cloth at Christmastime was 'customary' (p. 13), though he offers no corroboration for the claim. It seems more likely to me that the clerks could expect such liveries as a special gift from time to time, and indeed, the two liveries Burrow lists were enrolled many years apart from each other, in late 1407 and *circa* 1425, respectively.

the role that the Privy Seal sometimes played in certifying the results of certain royal inquests – in murder investigations (no. 340) and cases of forfeiture (no. 334) – and also in stranger cases. One writ is addressed to a 'visconte', or sheriff, in Chester, and orders him to summon John Brokhouse, son of the late William Spense, to prove John's age 'en la pleine veritee', and then to send word of the age back to the Privy Seal, under letter close (no. 323; p. 318); a second writ, addressed to the justice of Chester, instructs him to investigate why certain trees have been cut down in one of the king's forests, and, having ascertained the truth of the matter, to send his findings back to the Privy Seal (no. 339). When one considers such documents alongside others that discuss the promotion of certain individuals with connections to the office – as we know from item nos. 745 and 746, the one-time keeper of the Privy Seal, Henry Ware, was recommended for the position of bishop of Chester, with the Privy Seal itself employed in the drafting of letters to that effect – it seems likely that Hoccleve would have read some of what he copied out with a degree of professional interest, or even professional identification.

In one respect, then, Hoccleve may have noted what he read because it had to do with his career and circumstances at work. But some of the documents that crossed his desk would likely have caught his eye even if they had little to do with, say, the provisioning of Christmas robes for him and his friends. Indeed, many items in the *Formulary* deal with topics that were of pressing concern to him personally – for instance, the granting of benefices, annuities, and corrodies. Two of the 'T. H.' items, nos. 139 and 567, either recommend or reassert the election of a clerk to some kind of benefice; and, in the case of the second document, a letter of protection for a clerk who has been appointed a prebend at a cathedral chapter, we are presented with a scenario that speaks directly to a passage in the *Regiment of Princes*, where Hoccleve warns that, in the election of the head of a 'chapitre of a chirche cathedral', the king should honour the choice of the canons, lest 'the man' elected to the post lack 'habilitee' (2906–16). 'To kynges lettres geven is credence', he warns Henry: 'Beeth waar how that yee wryte in swich mateere, / lest that yee hurte and mayme conscience' (2927–9). Countless other documents describe, in turn, the award of state incomes, not on the basis of merit, but on the basis of personal connections to the Crown. Item no. 251, for example, instructs the treasurer to pay the annuity of John Langrigge, a friend of the king, before he pays the annuities of others, while others concern the distribution of extravagant gifts: a grant of 'mille et CC floryns de lescu ou la value dicelx en autre moneye courrante en notre roiaume' to one 'A. de B.' for 'bon service' (no. 256; p. 251), or a grant of 'mille mille marcs par an' to one of the king's brothers or brothers-in-law, who is said to require it for the maintenance of his country estate (no. 55; p. 49). In light of the poet's many comments about his poverty, about the delays that so often accompanied the payment of his own annuity, and about his longing for a clerical income – 'I gazid longe first and waytid faste / Aftir sum benefice', he tells us, 'and whan noon cam, / By procees I me weddid atte laste' (*RP* 1451–3) – one must imagine that copying out these letters was a little painful at best, and humiliating at worst.

Still other items treat eclectic topics that sometimes reappear in the digressions and asides scattered across Hoccleve's poetry. One writ, for example, asks any number of local bishops for their list of available benefices. Young graduates of Oxford and Cambridge, it explains, are facing a difficult job market, 'because they do not have the resources needed to sustain themselves nor to obtain the necessary books, nor do they have any hope [*ne nestoient en espoir*] of being advanced to benefices of Holy Church, because they cannot accept benefices [*ne purroient accept benefices*] on the orders of our very holy father, the Pope' (no. 683; p. 704). This recalls a moment in the *Regiment of Princes*, when the poet laments the terrible situation in which new university graduates have found themselves: 'so many a worthy clerk famous / In Oxenforde and in Cambrigge', he writes, 'stonde unavaunced', but this does not stop 'Favel' from giving his followers countless 'chirches and provendres', to God's displeasure (*RP* 5272–6). A second writ is addressed to the master of the wardrobe and specifies, at astonishing length, the materials that the king's tailor, John Dyndon, will require to make new clothes for the monarch – to name only a few, 'drap si bien dor', 'leyn de diverse colours', 'pelure et linure', 'linge toil', 'lyntheux', and, naturally, many 'autres noz necessaires' (no. 399; p. 391). This again recalls the *Regiment*, where the Old Man complains about rich men who 'walke in gownes of scarlet / Twelve yerdes wyde, with pendaunt sleeves doun / On the ground' (422–4). The Old Man's specific target, he tells us, is those petty bourgeois who seek, through their dress, to emulate their lords (442–8) – but the behaviour of grandees also comes under indirect fire, for if lords were to wear simple clothing 'as men dide in olde tyme', the Old Man explains, then 'al this costlewe outrage' would surely be 'refusid' (507–11).

So far, this essay has traced moments where the *Formulary* and Hoccleve's literary writings treat the same matter or topic. Naturally, there are limitations to this approach: it is hard to determine what is the chicken and what the egg in any given parallel, nor can we be sure that the parallel is the result of more than happenstance. Nonetheless, a third category of documents in the *Formulary* offers compelling evidence that Hoccleve did draw consciously upon the specifics of what he read at the Privy Seal when he sat down to write his own poetry. These documents, which are contained in the section of the *Formulary* entitled 'Exordies et Extraitz dez Lettres', are a series of Latin *dicta* that seem to recall the various sayings listed towards the end of many *ars dictaminis* handbooks: little aphorisms, commonplaces, and phrases that one could use to elevate the style of a letter.[26] But where the handbooks typically organise such *dicta* according to the rhetorical technique or form of expression that each one exemplifies, they seem instead to be grouped on the basis of topic in the *Formulary*.[27] For instance, aphorisms on anxiety and worry, on patience and fortitude (nos. 941–6), and on worldly instability are placed side by side (see, respectively, nos. 892–94, 941–6, and 948–55) – and at certain moments, the rubrics to the *Formulary* make the topical logic of the groupings clear. Just so, 'Nota de detractione' is followed by several items that discuss slander (nos. 1032–7), and 'Nota de lingua lubrica' does the same with respect to several items as well (nos. 1038–41).

Hoccleve's decision to group the extracts by topic rather than trope may offer us insight into the mode of reading he employed in his research for this section of the book: when he went on the hunt for extracts, it seems that he was paying attention to matter and sense rather than form and rhetoric. What is more, his attention to the matter of these *dicta* may also explain why he seems to have latched onto their sentiments, rather than their form, when he reused some of them in his poetry. Nearly twenty-five years ago, Burrow noted one extract that obviously speaks to Hoccleve's personal concerns in the *Regiment*: 'Expectantes excruciat dilatio promissorum', or in his translation, 'delay in delivering promised things torments those that await them' (no. 892; p. 1030).[28] But there are many others, too. Elsewhere in the *Regiment*, for example, the poet complains of the pain suffered by anyone who must 'keepe him cloos and holde his pees, / And nat out shewe how seek he inward is' (*RP* 253–4); this strongly recalls item no. 899: 'He is truly sad [*verus siquidem dolor*] who is afflicted in secret but cannot bear witness [*testimonium*] to his sadness' (p. 1031). Another passage, which asserts that God knows of 'inward' penance 'by any outward tokne resonable' (*RP* 320–1), also reworks a commonplace found in the extracts, item no. 998: 'The outer works of man [*opera hominis extrinsica*] show what his intentions, his feelings, and the extent of his love [*caritas*] might be' (p. 1049). The poet's claim that he 'so sore swal' about his heart that he had to 'braste oute' with his lament in the 'Complaint' (29–35) recalls item no. 1030: 'I am burdened by sins, dragged down by the weight of the body, wrapped in continual cares, infected by worldly desires, weak, anxious,

---

[26] See chapters 6 and 7 of John of Garland's *Parisiana poetria* for an example of such a collection of extracts: *Parisiana poetria*, ed. and trans. Traugott Lawler (New Haven, 1974). But see too Watt, *Making of Thomas Hoccleve's Series*, pp. 179–80, who suggests that Hoccleve's collection of aphorisms may owe as much to sermon-*florilegia* as it does to letter-writing manuals.

[27] In John's letter-manual, chapter 6 (which specifies the rhetorical tropes that its examples demonstrate) and chapter 7 (which includes extracts for specific contexts and occasions) do just this: *Parisiana poetria*, pp. 110–273.

[28] Burrow, *Thomas Hoccleve*, p. 5 and p. 5, n. 15.

and bursting [*erumpuosus*]' (p. 1056).[29] The idea that, once it is 'purgid' in a furnace, 'golde' becomes 'finer and clenner' (*C* 358–9) refigures item no. 887: 'Just as the virtue of gold [*virtutis aurum*] is tempered [*excoquitur*] in a furnace of tribulations and shines again [*relucet*], so too is the virtue of many tested through the miseries of others' (p. 1030). And, finally, the advice, in the 'Dialogue', that one must 'make a iust and trewe reckenynge' before the end of one's life, when 'Sharpnesse of peine is therto greet hinderinge' (*D* 230–1), brings to mind a phrase from one of the two 'T. H.' wills that we considered above, where Hoccleve says it is 'difficult, at the painful end of one's life [*laborantibus in extremis*], on account of the pricks of a death that is to come, to retain properly in one's higher mind [*superne mentis emeoriter retinere*] and make arrangements for [*disponere*] many and diverse things as well as a healthy man is able to do' (no. 982; p. 1046).

The *Formulary* and Literary Invention

What should we make of these verbal echoes? In one respect, they indicate that Hoccleve paid minute attention to what he copied out at the Privy Seal, even down to the level of the word and the phrase. But these echoes also point towards a second way that Hoccleve's career influenced his literary work. This is the obvious debt that his poetry displays to the formal and literary conventions of bureaucratic writing, and, in particular, to the way that bureaucratic documents, in their aggregate, represent social reality as a collage, or even a *bricolage*, of different places, persons, and things.[30] In the *Series* and *Regiment of Princes*, especially, Hoccleve's segmented narrative forms, preference for local settings, and interest in 'the extra-textual conditions' of his poems all correspond to certain tropes of representation in the *Formulary*.[31]

Consider, for instance, the way that the *Formulary* represents setting. In the many letters that concern the Pale of Calais, we learn in detail about the far-off city that was the logistical heart of the English war effort – but

---

[29] Amy Appleford has argued that this passage in the *Series*, and in particular its claim that Hoccleve was 'born of a woman', are derived from the Mass for the Dead: 'The Sea Ground and the London Street: The Ascetic Self in Julian of Norwich and Thomas Hoccleve', *Chaucer Review*, 51 (2016), 49–67 (esp. pp. 61–7). I find Appleford's argument very convincing, but as Spencer Strub has observed in his essay in this volume, Hoccleve's particular idiom in this passage (e.g. 'bursting' and 'swelling') probably stems from tropes and figures that were ubiquitous in medieval medical and pastoral discourse.

[30] Critics have often used this term, originally coined by Claude Lévi-Strauss in *The Savage Mind* (1962), to describe the structure of Hoccleve's poems. See, for example, Sarah Tolmie, 'The Professional: Thomas Hoccleve', *Studies in the Age of Chaucer*, 29 (2007), 341–73, at p. 356; and Jane Griffiths, '"In Bookes Thus Writen I Fynde": Hoccleve's Self-Glossing in the *Regiment of Princes* and the *Series*', *Medium Ævum*, 86 (2017), 91–107, at p. 95.

[31] Simpson, 'Madness and Texts', p. 23.

only one piece at a time. Documents focus alternately upon the central castle of the city, its port, its marketplace, the city centre, and the march that surrounds it, which itself contains more castles, some in considerable disrepair (see items 294, 298, and 299). Throughout these spaces, different people and different things come and go. Merchants from Flanders arrive to sell food and goods within the city limits, to the consternation of local officials (no. 662); 'W. B., marchant de Br.', imports wine to slake the thirst of the city, and somehow forgets to pay customs (no. 292); and food is distributed to the hungry soldiers who guard the walls (no. 288). Most of all, Calais expands and contracts, with a systolic and diastolic rhythm, over the course of the letters. Soldiers now have their wages withheld, and now receive a Christmas bonus (nos. 544, 528); some begin a forty-day home leave, while others return from it (no. 305); and the very size of the garrison grows and shrinks depending upon the year: we are told, in one document, that war pay is cancelled and the number of troops will be reduced because of a truce (no. 302), only to be informed, in the very next item, that the war once again requires an increase in the number of soldiers at Calais, and that hazard pay is to be distributed once again (no. 303).

What is remarkable about these letters is that Calais can only be half-glimpsed in any one of them. In the same way that one comes to know a large city only through repeated excursions to its different neighbourhoods, one comes to know Calais in a piecemeal fashion through the *Formulary*, by means of the different letters that detail its many people, places, and activities. This recalls Hoccleve's own tendency to represent urban settings in pieces – or, more precisely, to depict city life as a series of snapshots. We see him eating, drinking, and embarrassing himself 'at Poules Heed' (*MR* 143); walking into London through 'Westmynstre yate' (*MR* 178); spending the night 'at Chestres In, right faste by the Stronde' (*MR* 5); going 'amonge the prees' in 'Westmynstir Halle' and 'in Londoun' (*C* 72–3); and observing the various kinds of activities that take place in all of these locations: the ploughing of the fields around the city (*RP* 981–5), the work of the tanners, furriers, drapers, and tailors in its suburbs and streets (*RP* 472–90), the labour of 'artificeres' working through heat and sweat (*RP* 1009–12), and, of course, the work that Hoccleve himself does at the Privy Seal office.[32] Like the representation of Calais in the *Formulary*, Hoccleve's London is too big to depict in its totality. Unlike Chaucer, Hoccleve never gives us a panoramic description of all the 'smale foweles' who chirp in the springtime season upon the city walls, or a wide-angle view of the countless 'palmeres' who leave its gates to 'seken straunge strondes' each time May comes around (*CT* I.9–13). Instead, he gives us local details and partial impressions, because he knows that a marketplace looks one way in the morning and quite another

---

[32] Chester's Inn was likely rented for the clerks so that they would not have to make the long journey home after working late; see Burrow, *Thomas Hoccleve*, p. 7.

in the evening – that London itself is, as Matthew Boyd Goldie puts it, 'fragmented, discontinuous, contradictory'.[33] To read Hoccleve is thus to experience urban life as a flipbook: we watch the city move and change from page to page, place to place.

The documents of the *Formulary* do not, however, merely describe places or persons. Instead, they prescribe certain actions to be done – and most of the time, they do so through the use of lists that convey both the scope and the depths of the king's power. Sometimes, they represent this power bluntly, through the astonishing privileges they grant to their recipients: the guardianship of 'isles de Jereseye, Gerneseye, Serk et Aureneye, et de noz soubgiz, habitantz en icelles' (no. 60; p. 53), for example, or the control of the whole county of 'Benauges' in the south of France (no. 138). Other writs, in turn, vest apparently ordinary people with extraordinary powers. One document, addressed to the constable of Dover, grants him the temporary authority to commandeer commercial ships so that soldiers and archers might be brought across the Channel, post-haste, to Calais (no. 549). But still more remarkable are those moments where royal power commands ordinary things to be done, but on an extraordinary scale. In one item, for instance, the warden of the king's parks is ordered to provide the royal furrier, Richard Hunte, with fifty dozen conies (no. 500), while in another, the steward of the armoury is instructed to manufacture two tons of new arrows 'pur la sauve garde' of the country (no. 508; p. 482). A third item provides the reader with a dizzying list of the lands, rights, and privileges that a certain person, 'R. S.', is to receive upon taking possession of his new country estate, a gift from the king:

> [...] the fiefs [*feez*] of knights, benefices [*avoesons*] of churches, abbeys, priories, hospitals, chantries, chapels, rights of judgment [*gardes*], dowries [*mariages*], relief-payments [*reliefs*], forfeitures, escheats, fisheries [*pescheries*], moors, marshes, parks, hunting-chases [*chaces*], warrens, woods, markets [*feires*], marches, ferry-crossings [*feries*], mills and lakes [*estanks*], grants of freedom [*franchises*], privileges [*libertees*], releases from customs [*frankes custumes*], services of free tenants and of serfs [*neifs*], jurisdiction over acts of theft upon the manor [*infangtheof*], jurisdiction over tenants committing crimes beyond the manor [*outfangtheor*[34]], forfeitures occurring by land and by sea, along with shipwrecks upon the sea [*wrek de meer*], chattel-properties of fugitives and felons, in addition to all the hamlets, dependencies [*membres*], tenement lots [*parcelles*], subsidiary buildings [*appurtenances*], and customary practices [*usages et custumes*] pertaining to the aforesaid manor. (no. 55; pp. 49–50)

---

[33] Matthew Boyd Goldie, 'Psychosomatic Illness and Identity in London, 1416–1421: Hoccleve's *Complaint* and *Dialogue with a Friend*', *Exemplaria*, 11 (1999), 23–55, at p. 37.
[34] *Sic* in Bentley but should read 'outfangtheof'; the final 'r' is likely a transcription error.

What stands out here is not what the king's letter commands, but the vast extent of the king's power, which extends to all aspects of the manor, from the big to the small – everything from shipwrecked goods that lie off its coast to the deer that run through the woods upon the property.

Power, in the *Formulary*, is thus represented as a thing that is at once bureaucratic and sublime. When considered on its own, the scope of its force and reach is almost unimaginable, but when one considers how it is enacted, one is struck both by its concern with the most trivial of things and by the mundane process of its operation. This paradox seems to have made an impression on Hoccleve, who often figures the operation of power – even supernatural power – in bureaucratic terms within his poetry. In his playful verses to Henry Somer, for instance, the power of the summer season brings life, not through the miraculous quickening of the earth, but through its 'heruest' of coin that the Exchequer divvies up between the king's servants (27). In the *Male Regle*, health is restored, not through 'medecyne', but through the 'coyn' that the Crown disburses (*MR* 446). In *L'epistre de Cupide*, the power of love is administered, not through the emotions, but through a letter that Cupid addresses to 'our ministres echoon' (464), complete with the Middle English version of the closing *formulae* for a writ: 'Fulfillid be it, cessyng al delay. / Looke ther be noon excusacion' (470–1). And in the *Regiment of Princes*, the Virgin Mary is said to employ the pen of her personal secretary, rather than her personal relationship with God, in order to levy her might. As Hoccleve suggests, perhaps Mary might intercede on Chaucer's behalf, since he once wrote so many lines in praise of her:

> O now thyn help and thy promocioun!
> To God thy sone make a mocioun,
> How he thy servant was, mayden Marie,
> And lat his love floure and fructifie. (*RP* 4988–91)

It seems that even the Virgin – whom Hoccleve elsewhere twice calls an 'advocate' – must go through the proper channels if she is to make her will felt.[35]

At first glance, Hoccleve's figuration of the superhuman and the divine in bureaucratic terms would seem to confirm Knapp's view that the *Formulary*, and the bureaucratic culture that gave rise to it, led the poet and his fellow clerks to see themselves as alienated from a fundamentally 'impersonal' operation of power.[36] Indeed, one could even claim that, in Hoccleve's eyes, power was a concept so abstract, and so divided from any individual who wielded it, that the only suitable idiom for its representation was in fact the language of bureaucracy. Cupid, he seems to imply, really ought to wield a pen instead of a bow and arrow. But this line of argument obscures the fact that, in the *Formulary*, figures of power often characterise their

---

[35] See *RP* 4984, and Furnivall and Gollancz (eds), *Hoccleve's Works*, p. 53 (line 40).
[36] Knapp, 'Bureaucratic Identity', p. 369.

friends, lieges, and allies in personal or even intimate terms. We read, for example, of a young woman detained on suspicion of theft, but ordered to be released 'for the compassion that we have regarding her poverty' (no. 474; p. 458), and of the king's command that the legal case of a poor man, which has long stalled in court, be expedited. The man, we are told, has already suffered 'the great destruction [*grand avientisement*[37]] of his poor estate', and so he ought to bear no further hardships because of legal delay (no. 486; p. 469). A still more empathetic tone can be heard in a letter of protection that the king orders to be drafted for a poor woman, 'Johane R. de C.', whose business takes her to various courts around the country, and who, because she presumably travels alone, often fears for her safety. As the letter says,

> Because our vassal [*lige*], a poor woman, Johane R. de C., must pursue [*eit a pursuire*] many affairs of business in several of our courts and elsewhere within our realm, and because she fears greatly [*par tant*] for the damages, perils, and burdens which may befall her [*que lui purront*], being, as she is, made light in body [*de legier estre faiz de son corps*] and, besides this, from those who wish her ill [*par ses maleveullans*]; for these reasons, we have thus taken the aforesaid Johane, while she pursues her aforesaid business, into our special protection and defense. For this reason, we command you that, to the same Johane and her friends and property [*chateux*], you neither do nor allow to be done, so far as it is possible for you, any harm, trouble, burden, damage, or unreasonable hindrance [*nempeschement contre raisoun*], during the time when she pursues her aforesaid business. (no. 568; pp. 549–50)

Here, the specificity with which the letter details Joan's fears, and the specificity with which it appeals to its reader – she is, the letter tells us, a small person, only 'light in body' – give the document an almost tender tone. Though it is the product of an immense bureaucratic operation, it takes pains to solicit our pity for poor Joan, who must rely upon this scrit for protection as she travels the country, selling whatever she can.

Documents like these recall aspects of Hoccleve's own self-representation in his poetry: again and again, he calls himself poor, old, friendless, and dull.[38] These features of Hoccleve's *persona* have received plenty of prior critical attention, but the specific tropes Hoccleve uses for his self-representations can be found not only in Gower and Lydgate but in the *Formulary* as well.[39] Consider, for instance, the poet's anxious prediction of what his life will be like once he retires from his state position.

---

[37] *Sic* in Bentley but should read 'anientisement'; the 'v' is likely a transcription error.

[38] For discussion of this conventional mode of self-representation in Hoccleve, see David Lawton, 'Dullness and the Fifteenth Century', *ELH*, 54 (1987), 761–99 (esp. pp. 762–4).

[39] Compare especially Robert Meyer-Lee, *Poets and Power from Chaucer to Wyatt* (Cambridge, 2007), pp. 88–123.

Service, I woot wel, is noon heritage;
Whan I am out of court anothir day,
As I moot whan upon me hastith age
And that no lenger I laboure may,
Unto my poore cote, it is no nay,
I moot me drawe and my fortune abyde,
And suffre storm aftir the mery tyde. (*RP* 841–7)

Hoccleve's 'poore cote', here, is his fearful projection of what life may be like if he is not granted a corrody, or assisted with some other arrangement, when he is no longer able to work.[40] As it turned out, the poet's worries were unfounded, but this passage adopts many of the tropes and conventions of the grants for such livings recorded in the Privy Seal records.[41] One *Formulary* grant, for example, earmarks lodging at Windsor Castle and a per diem for an old knight, who has served the king faithfully, labouring 'long in our wars [*longement travailez ad en noz guerres*] and elsewhere', but who cannot 'labour anymore, and possesses nothing by which to live or support himself' (no. 699; p. 723). A second grant, this one addressed to the king's almoner, is still more telling: here, we learn of a certain 'A. B.', who, on account of working 'for his whole life as one of our poor beadsmen [*poures oratours*]', has been granted both a place to live in his old age and 'two pennies for his sustenance each day' (no. 665; p. 688). Like the old knight, Hoccleve characterises himself as a man who can work 'no lenger' (*RP* 844), and who, with the exception of an annuity for which it is 'hard' to get 'paiement' (825), has no resources with which to support himself. Like the faithful beadsman, in turn, he stresses his 'long servyse' (818) and exclusive employment in the offices of the Crown, and worries that, once he is 'out of court' (842), he will have no one to take care of him.

Did Hoccleve have grants like these in mind when he painted his bleak little pictures of life after work? Maybe, maybe not – but either way, these echoes of the *Formulary* within his verse should not surprise us, any more than we should be surprised by echoes of Calais in his representations of London, or the echo of royal decrees in his portrayal of Cupid and his ministers. Hoccleve, after all, worked for his whole life at the Privy Seal, and even if the writing he did at the office differed from his literary writing, evidence for the cross-pollination of the two is everywhere in his poetry. Did he find, in this daily work, a set of techniques that he could adapt for his own depictions of late medieval life? No doubt, the gritty representation of his poverty and need, his vivid impressions of London, and the bits of dialogue that he reports, filled with 'the tang and cadences

---

[40] See Killick, 'Thomas Hoccleve as Poet and Clerk', pp. 115–16, for discussion of the kinds of support clerks could, and could not, typically expect after retirement.
[41] Hoccleve was granted a corrody to Southwick Priory on 4 July 1424; for his petition for the corrody, and the grant of the same, see item nos. 63 and 64, in the appendix to Burrow, *Thomas Hoccleve*, p. 48.

of popular speech', do not add up to realism in the sense that Barthes imagines.[42] But their effect is all the more real because, like the documents of the *Formulary*, their very fragmentation suggests the way that everyday life is lived: a series of passing impressions, feelings, and thoughts that the mind loosely strings together, from one moment to the next.

Conclusions

Hoccleve wasn't the only Middle English poet with an office job, and he wasn't the only one to write about it in his poetry. At one point in Chaucer's *House of Fame*, a garrulous eagle scolds the poet for spending so many of his hours, at work and at home, in front of a book. As the eagle says:

> when thy labour doon al ys,
> And hast mad alle thy rekenynges,
> In stede of reste and newe thynges
> Thou goost hom to thy hous anoon,
> And, also domb as any stoon,
> Thou sittest at another book
> Tyl fully daswed ys thy look;
> And lyvest thus as an heremyte,
> Although thyn abstynence ys lyte.[43]

With its self-deprecating imagery and preposterous setting, the passage is, in one respect, obviously comic: a terrified poet is carried miles above the earth by the force of his imagination, all while weathering a string of insults from a bird who wants him to spend less time reading. But in another, more telling respect, this passage also suggests that, even if he believed that his work at the Customs House and the writing he did at home were 'mutually legitimating', as Robert Meyer-Lee has argued, Chaucer felt that there was a split – or at least, that there ought to have been a split – between his clerical occupation and his literary vocation.[44] Even if the 'rekenynges' he did at the office could be wittily compared to the metrical labour he did at home, he seems to have believed that their conflation was as absurd as an eagle holding forth on the principles of sound, astrology, and grammar.

If Hoccleve felt this way, he never quite said so. There is little question that, like many of us, he found his job difficult: it was a kind of labour, as he puts it, that wore out the eyes, made the back ache, and unsettled the

---

[42] The phrase belongs to Derek Pearsall: see his 'The English Chaucerians', in D. S. Brewer (ed.), *Chaucer and Chaucerians: Critical Studies in Middle English Literature* (London, 1966), 201–39, at p. 224.

[43] *Riverside Chaucer*, p. 356 (HF 652–60).

[44] Robert Meyer-Lee, 'Literary Value and the Customs House: The Axiological Logic of the *House of Fame*', *Chaucer Review*, 48 (2014), 374–94, at p. 393.

stomach and bowels (*RP* 1016–22).[45] Anyone who has spent hours before a laptop can relate. But as the many office jokes and bureaucratic allusions in his poetry make clear, Hoccleve also knew that the work he did at the Privy Seal had much in common with the work that he did off the clock.[46] I thus suggest three further avenues for the future study of Hoccleve's *Formulary*, which remains our best guide to the labour he did in Westminster. First, a longer and more detailed account of the *Formulary* would likely discover more parallels with Hoccleve's poems. We already know, thanks to the work of Linne Mooney, Helen Killick, and Sebastian Sobecki, that the palae-ographic and linguistic evidence offered by the *Formulary* can be used to date his literary works, reconstruct the circumstances of their composition, deepen our knowledge about his likely patrons, and even account for aspects of his idiom.[47] But the matter of the *Formulary* – to put it bluntly, what the text says – has largely been ignored by scholars, and it might offer new insights into everything from Hoccleve's formal predilections to his motives in writing, as he sometimes does, about eclectic topics.

Second, the *Formulary* still has a great deal to tell us about Hoccleve's sense of his own identity, and, in particular, about the obvious tension between collaboration and individuality that characterises so much of his work.[48] Indeed, we often find in Hoccleve a strange combination of these two impulses: an immersion in the corporate and anonymous culture of bureaucracy that gives rise, as Knapp has argued, to an 'interest in the self as its own end', or an embrace of the collaborative culture of scribal labour that finds its corollary, as David Watt has suggested, in Hoccleve's attempt to reform his own 'memory' and 'moral character', in the same way that one would emend a book.[49] The *Formulary* can help us to address these questions anew because it is obviously the product of both tendencies. On the one hand, it is partly an autograph manuscript, and one that contains allusions both to Hoccleve's poetry and to his name; but on the other, it

---

[45] For discussion of Hoccleve's attitude towards his job, see especially James Simpson, 'Nobody's Man: Thomas Hoccleve's *Regement of Princes*', in Julia Boffey and Pamela King (eds), *London and Europe in the Later Middle Ages* (London, 1995), pp. 149–80.

[46] For further discussion and some examples of these jokes, see the chapter on Hoccleve in my book, *Matter and Making in Early English Poetry: Literary Production from Chaucer to Sidney* (Cambridge, forthcoming).

[47] See Linne Mooney, 'A Holograph Copy of Thomas Hoccleve's *Regiment of Princes*', *Studies in the Age of Chaucer*, 33 (2011), 263–96, for the use of the *Formulary* in dating Hoccleve's work and identifying his hand; Killick, 'Thomas Hoccleve as Poet and Clerk', especially pp. 161–72, for her discussion of how the language of the *Formulary* may have shaped Hoccleve's idiom in his verse; and Sobecki, 'Handwriting of Privy Seal and Council Clerks', pp. 23–7, for discussion of Hoccleve's rather informal hand and its implications for patronage.

[48] For an account that usefully relates this aspect of Hoccleve's work to his formal predi-lections, see the essay by R. D. Perry contained in this volume.

[49] Knapp, 'Bureaucratic Identity', p. 370; Watt, *Making of Thomas Hoccleve's Series*, p. 145.

is mostly anonymous in form, and displays the traces of at least four other scribes, whose hands appear sporadically throughout its pages.[50]

Finally, more work on the *Formulary* may reveal that, upon closer inspection, it is a more literary document than it seems. Other formularies, after all, were often sites for autobiographical writing and imaginative invention, and many items in the *Formulary* refer the reader to other, similar documents found elsewhere in its pages, suggesting that Hoccleve put together his collection in a through-composed way.[51] Still more intriguing is the fact that Hoccleve sometimes seems to have worried that the sentiments of the *Formulary* might be taken as a reflection of his own views. At one point in the extracts, for example, Hoccleve includes a short *dictum* that seems to address the reader directly, on the heels of several preceding aphorisms that concern the dangers of backbiting and slander. As he writes:

> Let it be known that, with respect to these things, I speak them out of love [*loquor quoniam diligo*], and, lest perhaps an envious eye should bring forth the detraction of a wicked tongue [*improbe lingue aliquid*] with respect to such things, let it be broken apart [*frangatur*] once the page has been read.[52]

If Hoccleve felt the *Formulary* was an entirely impersonal document, it is unlikely he would feel compelled, even out of superstition, to include a note defending his intentions.

One thing, in any event, seems clear enough: Hoccleve paid attention to what the documents in his *Formulary* said, and this means that he did not view it as a mere collection of empty ciphers and fill-in-the-blank cribs. Instead, he seems to have appreciated the *Formulary* for what it truly is: a window onto the material currents that ran beneath, and indeed animated, late medieval life. Much of it is mundane, but this is precisely the point. For as Hoccleve knew well, the matter of everyday life is not something we merely experience. Instead, it is something we produce, and that is produced for us, by the forces of administration that the *Formulary* so meticulously tracks.

---

[50] See my discussion in the appendix below for the hands in London, British Library MS Additional 24062. For Hoccleve's autograph manuscripts, see especially Rory G. Critten, *Author, Scribe, and Book in Late Medieval English Literature* (Cambridge, 2018), pp. 36–75.

[51] Item no. 464, for example, refers the reader to nos. 483 and 516; no. 484 refers the reader to nos. 463 and 516; no. 172 seems to refer the reader to no. 4; and no. 635 seems to refer to a letter, now missing, that contained a similar situation. For the autobiographical possibilities offered by the formulary genre, see Steiner, *Documentary Culture*, p. 58; and Knapp, *Bureaucratic Muse*, pp. 32–3.

[52] This is item no. 1040 (quotation on p. 1058); the preceding items to which it seems to refer are nos. 1032–9.

Appendix: Documents in the *Formulary* that Mention 'T. H.'

Eleven items in the *Formulary* mention an individual with the initials 'T. H.'. To encourage future work upon the book, I have rendered these documents into English below. My translations are based upon the text found in Elna-Jean Bentley's edition of the *Formulary*. I have not been able to consult the physical manuscript (London, British Library MS Additional 24062) but I have corrected Bentley's text against a microform copy, noting those instances where she seems to have made an error in transcription. There is considerable dispute about the hands of the *Formulary*. Until recently, all of the items below were thought to have been composed in Hoccleve's hand, but Sebastian Sobecki has argued that item nos. 159, 160 and 161 are in fact the script of Henry Benet, and that no. 567 is also written in a hand that is not Hoccleve's own.[53] Most scholars agree that the date of the *Formulary* manuscript is late, and that Hoccleve likely worked on it into the early 1420s, and perhaps even after his retirement from the Privy Seal in 1424.[54] Finally, I should note that the foliation of the *Formulary* presents some problems. As Linne Mooney has noted, the pencilled folio numbers found in the manuscript – which are typically located on the lower left-hand corner of each recto, just below the last line of the main text – are irregular and inconsistent. In some cases, these numbers count blank *folia*, while in other cases, they do not.[55] To avoid confusion and allow for easier reference to the manuscript, I have noted both the true foliation of the manuscript,

---

[53] Scholars since Bentley had held that most of the *Formulary* was copied in Hoccleve's hand, but that a second hand, which she termed 'Hand B', had copied some of the documents (no. 138, the marginal note to no. 4, some of the letters patent, and several of the missives). Sobecki has argued, instead, for a much wider range of hands in the manuscript: in addition to Hoccleve, William Alberton, and Henry Benet, he argues that two other, as yet unidentified hands participated in the composition of the *Formulary*. See Sobecki, 'Handwriting of Privy Seal and Council Clerks', pp. 15–16; and compare Mooney, 'Holograph Copy', pp. 265–7, for a different account.

[54] Bentley argues for the very end of Hoccleve's career, after 1423 and even after being granted his corrody on 4 July 1424, which typically signals that a clerk has retired. Mooney suggests that, while a late date holds for certain items, other portions of the book, especially fols 105r–8v, were written earlier in his career, at least before 1413. According to Killick, documentary evidence suggests that Hoccleve did not in fact retire after receiving his corrody; see Killick, 'Thomas Hoccleve as Poet and Clerk', pp. 156–7 and p. 156, n. 48.

[55] For discussion, see Mooney, 'Holograph Copy', p. 267, n. 15. Going by increments of roughly ten, here is the actual foliation of the manuscript, counting all pages, as compared with the pencilled foliation found on its pages: 1r = 1r; 11r = 7r (now off by 4); 21r = 17r; 30r = 26r; 40r = 36r; 50r = 45r (now off by 5); 60r = 55r; 70r = 64r (now off by 6); 80r = 74r; 90r = 84r; 100r = 94r; 110r = 104r; 120r = 114r; 130r = 123r (now off by 7); 140r = 133r; 150r = 143r; 160r = 153r; 170r = 163r; 180r = 172r (now off by 8); 190r = 182r; 200r = 192r; 210r = 201r (now off by 9); 218r = 208r (now off by 10).

which is based upon my own count of its pages, and the irregular pencilled foliation, which I've marked off in brackets.

Document 139: London, British Library MS Additional 24062, fol. 37v [numbered 33v]; ed. Bentley, 'Formulary', p. 138. Titled 'Presentatio', and included in the section of Hoccleve's book entitled 'Au Chaunceller – Presentations et Permutations'. Anglo-Latin. This letter of recommendation nominates 'T. H.' to a position (presumably, of rector) at a parochial church recently left vacant by the death of its prior holder, 'W. de B.'. No date specified.

> The King to his Chancellor, greetings. We command you that, to the parochial church in the diocese of B. L., which, due to the death of W. de B., formerly the rector of the same, is now left vacant and awaits, by reason and as is said, our recommendation [*presentacionem*] for the guardianship [*custodie*] of the lands and estate [*terre et heredie*] of W. de S., deceased, which he held from us while alive but which are now again in our hands [*in manu nostra existentis*], you should put forward for this position the name [*nomine presentetis*] of our beloved clerk, T. H., through letters made in the requisite form [*in forma debita*] under our great seal.

Document 159: London, British Library MS Additional 24062, fol. 39v [numbered 35v]; ed. Bentley, 'Formulary', p. 154. No title. Included in the section of Hoccleve's book titled 'Au Chanceller Sauf Conduytz, Commissions, Protections et autres Garranz Overtes issanz souz le Prive Seal, nient Faisantz Mention de lestile de Chanceller'. Anglo-Latin. This letter of protection promises 'T. H.' safety for his travels to parts of France, and specifies that he will be part of the retinue of a certain relative of the king. No date specified.

> Let there be a state of protection [*protectio*], with the clause volumus [*cum clausula volumus*[56]], that will last for a period of one year [*per unum annum durature*[57]], for T. H., who, to do our bidding [*in obsequium nostrum*], is about to depart to parts of France, and will remain in our service while there in the retinue of so-and-so [*talis*], our beloved and faithful relative.

Document 160: London, British Library MS Additional 24062, fol. 39v [numbered 35v]; ed. Bentley, 'Formulary', p. 154. No title. Included in the same section of Hoccleve's book as Document 159, above, and Document 161, below. Anglo-Latin. This letter of protection is in effect an abbreviated version of the letter above; it describes the same circumstances for the travels of 'T. H.' and offers the same protections. No date specified.

---

[56] A letter of protection 'cum clausula volumus' absolved the bearer of almost all pleas and legal suits filed against him or her during the period specified in the letter.

[57] durature MS; should likely be 'duratura'; compare item no. 160 below, which has 'protectio [...] per unnum annum duratura'.

Let there be a state of protection [*protectio*], with the clause volumus [*cum clausula volumus*], that will last for a period of one year [*per unnum annum duratura*], for T. H., who, in our service [*in obsequio nostro*], will remain in parts of France in the retinue of so-and-so [*in comitiva talis*].

Document 161: London, British Library MS Additional 24062, fol. 39v [numbered 35v]; ed. Bentley, '*Formulary*', p. 154. No title. Included in the same section of Hoccleve's book as Documents 159 and 160, above. Anglo-Latin. This letter of protection differs from the other two, in that it suggests that 'T. H.' will take up residence at a castle in Picardy held by a certain knight, and also specifies that its protections extend beyond those naturally afforded by the castle. No date specified.

Let there be a state of protection [*protectio*], with the clause volumus [*cum clausula volumus*], for T. H., who in our service is about to depart to regions in Picardy [*partes Picardie*] and will dwell [*moraturus*[58]] there in the retinue of such-and-such a knight [*talis custodis*] of such-and-such a castle [*talis castri*], but beyond the secure protection [*super salva custodia*] offered by the same castle, for one etc. [*per unnum etc.*].

Document 179: London, British Library MS Additional 24062, fols 43r–v [numbered 38r–v]; ed. Bentley, '*Formulary*', pp. 170–1. Headed 'Liveree de terres et tenementz prise primerement la foialtee'. Included in the section of Hoccleve's book headed 'Lettres au Chanceller de Diverses Natures'. Anglo-Latin. This writ informs us that the king has ruled that 'N.', the son of 'J. F.', now deceased and having left his manor without a clear heir, should inherit the manor. The escheator (or person responsible for determining that there was no heir and that the property should revert to the king, who will then determine who will take control of it) is named in this letter as 'T. H.'. No date specified.

The King etc. to his Chancellor, greetings. By information gained through an in-person examination of T. H., our escheator in the county of S. [*escaetore nostro*[59] *in comitem S.*], that was held and pursued [*captam [...] retornatam*] in our chambers and on our orders, we know that J. F., now deceased, held in his dominion and by fief [*in dominico suo et de feodo*] in the aforesaid county on the day when he died the manors of C. and N., with rights pertaining to the same [*cum pertinenciis*], together with rights to the benefices of the churches of the same manors [*una cum advocacionibus ecclesiarum eorumdem*], from royal bequest, from right [*de nobis ut de honore*], and from P., due to his military service; and also that N., the son

---

[58] Though 'moraturus' properly means 'stay behind' or 'delay', the context makes it clear that T. H. will physically live in the retinue of this knight, but not within the castle; hence, the protection specified extends beyond ('super') the safety afforded by the fortifications.

[59] *nostro* MS; Bentley has 'notro'.

of the same J., is his nearest heir [*heres eius propinquior*] of the whole estate; we have thus accepted the fealty owed to us [*ceperimus homagium* [...] *nobis* [...] *debitum*] by the aforesaid N. for the aforesaid manors and benefices, and we have returned possession [*reddiderimus*] of the aforesaid manors and the aforesaid benefices to him, along with the rights pertaining to the same. We command you that, with the pledge of the same N. having been accepted [*fidelitate* [...] *capta*] in this matter [*in hac parte*], you release possession to him [*liberari demandetis eidem*] of the said manors and the aforesaid benefices, with the rights pertaining thereto, through letters made in the requisite form [*in forma debita*] under our great seal, exactly as it should be done according to the law and customary practice of our English kingdom. Issued etc.

Document 200: London, British Library MS Additional 24062, fol. 46v [numbered 41v]; ed. Bentley, 'Formulary', p. 192. No title. Included in the section of Hoccleve's book titled 'Lettres au Chanceller de Diverses Natures'. Anglo-Latin. This grant, which is written in a very obscure style, designates 'T. H.' as the steward and receiver ('custodem et receptorem') of a certain castle, its lands, and its incomes. No date specified.

H. etc. to our Chancellor, greetings. Because we have the greatest trust in the loyalty and prudence of our beloved T. H., clerk [*de fidelitate et circumspectione*[60] *dilecti nobis T. H., clerici*], we have appointed this same T. H., for however long it will please us, as the steward and receiver [*custodem et receptorem*] of all the incomes [*proficuorum*] which we have recently allocated from our funds [*de monetis*] to our castle, E. [*ad castrum nostrum E. de novo fieri ordinaverimus*]. For the accomplishment of our wishes, let it be done [*continget*] that the steward of our coin [*custodem cuneorum nostrorum*] in that place carries out the following orders [*ordinanda ita*] with respect to our aforesaid monies: that, regarding all expenditures [*de exitibus illis*], he should render a faithful account to us [*fidelem compotum nobis reddat*], and that, afterwards, the assayer of our money [*assaiator monete nostre*[61]] in the aforesaid town should, through the supervision and auditing of our banker [*per supervisum et contrarotulacionem*[62] *campsoris*], confirm to us that the necessary diligence is being exercised [*percipiendum*[63]] in those offices [*in officiis illis*] with respect to those allotted [*assignatorum*] the customary pledges and fees [*vadia et feoda consueta*[64]]. This we command to you etc. Issued etc.

[60] circumspectione MS; Bentley has 'circumspectionem'.

[61] An 'assaiator' is an assayer of coin, who ensures that it is of the proper weight and physical composition; presumably, the king wishes to be certain that the money received from his renters has not been falsified.

[62] Literally, the action performed by a comptroller, who checks over financial records and their copies to ensure that no mistakes have been made.

[63] 'Percipiendum' seems to refer, in other legal contexts, to the concept of 'necessary diligence', which is how I have translated it here.

[64] 'Vadia et feoda' seems to concern the right of T. H. to be recognised, by the tenants

Document 219: London, British Library MS Additional 24062, fols 50r–v [numbered 45r–v]; ed. Bentley, '*Formulary*', p. 214. Headed 'Pur paier tiele somme pur parchemyn, ynke et cire etc. despenduz en loffice du prive seal'. Included in the section of Hoccleve's book headed 'As Tresorer etc. de lEschequer'. Anglo-French. A grant to the Exchequer ordering it to release funds to 'T. H.' for the purchase of ink, wax, and parchment on behalf of the Privy Seal; Burrow notes several documents of a similar kind recorded in the rolls.[65] No date specified.

> The King to the treasurer and stewards [*chamberleins*] of our Exchequer, greetings. We command that you make payment [*facez paier*] of a certain sum [*tiele somme*] for parchment, ink, and red wax to our beloved clerk, T. H. [*a notre ame clerc, T. H.*], so that he might purchase these from such-and-such a person, a haberdasher of London,[66] and put them to use [*despenduz*] in the office of the Privy Seal from a such-and-such a day, such-and-such a year thenceforward [*de tiel jour, tiel an, en cea*]. Issued etc.

Document 567: London, British Library MS Additional 24062, fol. 113r [numbered 107r]; ed. Bentley, '*Formulary*', pp. 548–9. Headed 'Protection bone'. Included in the section of Hoccleve's book headed 'Lettres patentes'. Anglo-Latin. A wide-ranging letter patent for protection, granting a clerk, 'T. H.', the right to take up the office and draw the income associated with the prebend (or cathedral benefice) of a college of canons in a cathedral of 'L', without molestation from his rivals or, for that matter, from anyone else. The letter is striking in the range and depth of the protections it affords T., which suggests that his election to the post was perhaps controversial. No date specified.

> The king to each and every one of his justices [*justicariis*], landowners [*loca tenentibus*], administrators [*prepositis*], sheriffs, mayors, bailiffs, ministers, officials and to all our other faithful liegemen and subordinates, up to and including freemen [*tam infra libertates quam extra*]: to all present who receive this letter, greetings. So that our loyal clerk, T. H., ecclesiastical canon [*canonicus ecclesie*] of Cathedral L., and prebendary [*prebendarius*] of the prebend [*prebende*] of T. in the same place, might be able, in point of fact [*realiter*], to take up and possess the prebend which has been given to him by our agreement [*ex collatione nostra*] under our royal laws, as determined by the judgment handed down [*redditum*] in our court and on

---

of the castle manor, as their landlord; the 'feodum' is the fee, or right to lease the land from the landlord, while the 'vadium' is the pledge made to the landlord.

[65] See item nos. 13, 19, 22, 24, 31, 35, 39, 43, 50, 56, 62 and 68 in the appendix to Burrow, *Thomas Hoccleve*, pp. 33–49, and pp. 4–5 for discussion of this item in the *Formulary*.

[66] According to Killick, this 'haburdassher de Londres' was either William Surcestre (before 1417) or Walter Lucy (after that time); see 'Thomas Hoccleve as Poet and Clerk', pp. 90–1.

our behalf, we, wishing that our same clerk might remain in peace [*in pace consonere*] in his possession of his prebend obtained [*adepta*] in accordance with our ecclesiastical law [*canonice*], free from any impediment [*absque impedimento*], and for the sake of the bodily safety [*securitate corporis*] of the same T. and against the malice and injury of anyone and everyone who might presume to molest or impede the same T. or his agents [*procuratores suos*] from taking possession of his prebend or its profits and emoluments [*proficuis et emolumentis*], or those who, in an act of reckless audacity [*ausu temerario*], might seek to weaken [*enervare*] the laws of our crown in this region, hereby bestow upon the same T., upon the aforesaid prebend, its fruits, returns, and profits [*fructusque redditus et proventus*], and upon whatsoever agents, ministers, and servants of the aforesaid prebend exist in any place whatsoever, up to and including freemen, the royal defence of our honourable goodwill [*regio munimine dignis favoribus*], and we take and place him under our protection, defence, and special royal oversight [*tuitionem nostram regiam specialem*], and we enjoin and command [*injungimus et mandamus*] you and any agent of yours who might be busily sought out [*vobis et cuilibet vestrum districtius quo peterimus*] that you protect, take in hand, and defend [*manuteneatis protegatis et deffendatis*] the same T. and his aforesaid prebend, its fruits, returns, and profits, including whatever agents, ministers, and servants of that prebend there might be, up to and including freemen, neither bearing against them [*inferrentes eis*] nor allowing to be borne against them, so far as is possible, any injury, molestation, condemnation [*dampnum*], violence, hindrance [*impedimentum*], or any other sort of trouble [*gravemen*]. And if there is any forfeit or injury [*quid [...] forisfactum vel injuriatum*] to these persons or to their property that we would not wish, you must make it so that it is set right for them [*quod eis*[67] *[...] corrigi faciatis*], with no debt of goodwill [*sine dilectione debite*]. In witness of which matter etc. Issued etc.

Document 659: London, British Library MS Additional 24062, fols 140r–v [numbered 133r–v]; ed. Bentley, '*Formulary*', pp. 678–81. Headed 'Pur cesser de tortz et grevances faire'. Included in the section of Hoccleve's book titled 'Omnegadrium'. Anglo-French. An eclectic document that describes a rather messy dispute between several parties. It seems that a certain malcontent prior, John de Whitteby, made life so miserable for the nuns at his priory in Watton that he was removed from his post by the leader of his order.[68] John then went to the Archbishop of York, secured his support and favour, returned to Watton Priory with a band of armed men, forced his way back into the priory, and beat and punished the nuns for several weeks, all while

---

[67] *quod* eis MS; Bentley has 'ad eis'.
[68] The reference to Sempringham below indicates that the parties involved in this dispute, with the obvious exception of the archbishop of York, were members of the Gilbertine Order, which was primarily an order for nuns, but also included canons regular, lay brothers, and lay sisters. Many of its houses were double monasteries, as Watton Priory was.

refusing entry to the leader of his order. The document names 'Brother T. H.' as the new prior of Watton, and he is presumably John's successor; 'T. H.' is forced out of his post when John returns and breaks back into the priory. No date specified, but because John de Whitteby was named as prior of Watton in 1394, the dispute almost certainly took place after that time.[69]

The King etc. to the honourable father in God, the Archbishop of York,[70] primate of England, greetings. From the grievous complaint [*complainte*] of the master, prior, nuns of the order of Sempringham, and especially from the recluse nuns [*las noneignes recluses*] of the priory of Watton in the county of York [*en contee dEverwik*], we have heard the following.[71] At the time when their most recent [*nadgairs*] chapter meeting [*chapitre*] was held at Sempringham by the said master and priors, a certain John de Whitteby [*Johan Whitby*], then the prior of Watton, for his acts of disobedience, misdeeds, and thefts [*pur ses desobeissances, mesfaitz et mesprisions*], which were done by him against the said nuns of Watton, and which included taking away from them [*souztreant de les*[72]] their victuals and clothes [*lour vivres et vestres*] during the time when he was prior, was duly removed and discharged from his position as prior, by the deliberation and common agreement [*commun assent*] of the said master and priors, who held standing office [*esteanz*] at the aforesaid meeting [*au chapitre susdit*]. The said John, after his removal from office, departed and, going against his due obedience [*sa obedience*], went outside the priory of Chicksands, within which he had been instructed and ordered to remain by the said master. The said John then went to you [*se vynt [...] a vous*] so that he might seek your help and assistance in this situation, and, through this help and assistance, returned to the priory of Watton with a great number of people [*ovec grand nombre de gens*], forced his way inside [*se intrusa en icelle*] and compelled, by force, brother T. H., the prior of that place [*compella par reddure frere T. H., priour illoeques*], to give up his post there [*de cesser de mesme son estat*], which he held at that time by the assignment of the aforesaid master. The said John then broke open [*debruser*], by force and arms, the gates of the church [*les huys de leglise*] of the same nuns of Watton, and beat [*batre*] any of the nuns who were nearby and hurt them terribly [*desfoibler horriblement*], and did not allow them to hold masses for three weeks and more. To correct and redress these aforesaid

---

[69] The rolls name John de Whitteby as prior of Watton as of 4 February 1394; see Bentley, 'Formulary', p. 678, n. 1.

[70] Given that this dispute took place after 1394, and assuming that John didn't manage to stay out of trouble for more than ten years, the archbishop named in this letter is likely either Thomas Arundel (in office 1388–96), Robert Waldby (1397–98), or Richard le Scrope (1398–1405).

[71] The jurisdiction of this case is interesting; the priories of Sempringham and Chicksands were located in the diocese of Lincoln, while those of Watton and Malton were located in the diocese of York.

[72] *deles* MS; but this should presumably be separated into two words: 'de les'. According to the *Anglo-Norman Dictionary*, 'les' can refer to a feminine plural object.

acts of disobedience, misdeeds, and harms, the said master instructed his obedientiary [*son obediencer*] to visit the aforesaid priory of Watton, because the said master did not, for fear of his life, visit the same priory. By the force of the same directive [*par vertue de mesme la commissioun*], the aforesaid prior of Malton performed the orders of the said master, his superior; and, for this reason, you afterwards wrongfully summoned [*somondre torteuousement*] the aforesaid prior of Malton and his canons and servants to appear before you, and then improperly did to them very great wrongs by cutting off [*par sequestratioun*] their incomes [*fruytz*], suspending their churches, and excommunicating [*excommengementz*] their persons, in contravention of their monastic exemption [*contre lour exemption*] and privileges; and, when the said prior of Malton showed you your letters of legal release [*voz lettres de dimmissioun*[73]] issued under your seal, you took them back into your possession [*les retenistes devers vous*], and made such threats [*manaces*] to the aforesaid prior and his canons that no man of the law in those parts, nor any other man, would dare to be of counsel to them [*ose destre de lour conseil*], and that the same prior and canons did not dare to persist in their case [*nosent demorer en leur ruesoun*], for fear of your aforesaid threats. At all of this, we feel very great displeasure and very great astonishment. And so [*par quoy*], we command and charge you firmly, on the faith and allegiance that you owe to us, to do the following: if things have occurred as they were said to have occurred [*si ensy est come avant est dit*], then you must allow [*soeffrez*] the aforesaid master, either in his own person or by his representatives, depending upon his wishes [*sicome lui plera*], to visit the aforesaid John and all his other subjects, both for the reason of the good governance of the rule and order of Sempringham, and for the amendment of the condition and governance of the aforesaid priory of Watton and the recluse nuns in it, without any hindrance being done [*sanz aucune maintenance faire*] either by you or by any other in the county, in prejudice and breach [*lesioun*] of their aforesaid exemption. Moreover, you must henceforth cease [*cessez desore*] from doing such wrongs and such harms and from making such threats [*tielx tortz, grevances, et manaces faire*] to the aforesaid prior and canons of Malton and their servants; and, if nothing that was done to them was misrepresented by the manner of what was said above [*si riens eiez envers eux mespris par manere come dessus est dit*], then you must redress and make it right without delay [*le facez sanz delay corriger et redresser*], in such a way that, from henceforth, we do not hear complaints about you [*nous neons desore plainte de vous*] with respect to the aforesaid matters. For if we do [*par quoy*], we must then determine [*il nous covendra*], with the opinion and deliberation of our counsel, to ordain another sort of redress [*autre remede*] for the aforesaid religious in this matter, to maintain peace and

---

[73] This phrase is difficult; it literally means 'letters of resignation', but given that a monastic exemption seems to be the topic of discussion here, I suspect that 'lettres de dimmissioun' refers to legal documents stating that the archbishop formally discharges his authority over the Gilbertines because of that exemption.

tranquillity between them and all our other lieges [*noz lieges*] in those parts. Issued etc.

Document 982: London, British Library MS Additional 24062, fols 196v–7r [numbered 188v–9r]; ed. Bentley, '*Formulary*', pp. 1045–6. No title. Included in the section of Hoccleve's book titled 'Exordies et Extraits'. Anglo-Latin. This is a will made out in the name of 'T. H.'. In many respects, it is unexceptional, but it does place a striking emphasis both upon proper preparation for the end of life, well ahead of the moment of death, and upon the sound mind and memory of the person whom it names. Both themes, of course, recur in the *Series*, and especially in 'Learn to Die'. No date specified.

In the name of the father etc. Because it is difficult at the painful end of one's life [*laborantibus in extremis*], on account of the pricks of a death that is to come, to retain properly in one's higher mind [*superne mentis memoriter retinere*⁷⁴] and make arrangements for [*disponere*] many and diverse things as well as a healthy man is able to do with respect to the same [*valeat de eisdem*]; and because it is expedient to all Christians [*universis expedit Christianis*], while their memories of all their goods are reliable and sound, to dispose and make plans [*disponere et ordinare*] for these goods, in such a way that one might do good by ceding possession of them [*cedere valeat*] for the salvation of our souls; therefore, considering the things noted above, sound in mind [*saluti anime mee*] and wishing to make provisions while I am healthy [*cupiens salubriter providere*] for the disposition of the goods and property [*rerum et bonorum*] that the lord God mercifully deemed to provide me in my life, I, T. H., compose my will in the form that follows, and lay it out thus [*dispono*]. First of all, etc.

Document 983: London, British Library MS Additional 24062, fol. 197r [numbered 189r]; ed. Bentley, '*Formulary*', p. 1046. No title. Included in the section of Hoccleve's book titled 'Exordies et Extraits'. Anglo-Latin. This will is similar to the will translated above, but it is more homiletic in tone: where the first will is utilitarian, this one takes time to meditate, in rather elevated Latin, upon the meaning of death and its relation to the fall. Here as above, 'T. H.' makes the explicit claim that his memory is strong enough, at present, to dispose of his possessions with reliable legal intention. No date specified.

In the name of the father, etc. When they slipped out [*labentis*] of the state of innocence, our first parents' deadly fall replaced [*commutavit*], in an unhappy exchange [*infelici commercio*], immortality with mortality, and poured out [*derivavit*], upon their descendants, the streams of dreadful refreshment [*dire refectionis rivulos*], with the result that the human race

---

⁷⁴ *memoriter* MS; Bentley has 'emeoriter'.

has, by reason of that original disease [*originalis contagii*], been propagated from an infected root up to the very present. By the divine will, then, the moment of one's undoing [*resolutionis* [...] *discrimina*[75]] and its justice have been suffered by all those who have followed [*paterentur* [...] *decetero*], because the human race was compelled to walk an unsteady path [*motas semitas incedere*]; and so I, T. H., considering the matter carefully, and wishing, while I still possess the benefit of a strong memory [*recenti gaudeo memoria*] for the composition [*ad* [...] *condendum*] of my last will and testament, have decreed my last will to proceed and be declared in this way. First of all, etc.

---

[75] 'Discrimina resolutionis' is a bit obscure; it literally means something like 'the dividing lines of [our] loosening', but seems to refer here to the moment when one's body passes into death (when it 'loosens' or 'relaxes' out of animation).

9

Hoccleve's Feet: The Kinaesthetic Imaginary in Hoccleve's Writing

Helen M. Hickey

Hoccleve's distinctive literary persona is vivified to a remarkable extent by the images of his body that appear throughout his writing. Whereas other poets mention their physical characteristics in passing – Will refers to his length in *Piers Plowman* and Chaucer jokes about his weight in the *House of Fame* – Hoccleve writes a great deal about his body's shape and its constituent parts: head, brain, eyes, mouth, veins, heart, back, stomach, hands, legs, and feet. The motility of Hoccleve's body features throughout his writing, yet most critics have either ignored it or subordinated it to the self-referential persona he so frequently describes.[1] When Hoccleve's body does receive attention, it is often read as a droll illustration of his self-conscious state.[2] Thus Hoccleve criticism reflects a broader practice in literary analysis which typically reads the body as a prop or a signifier for some other concept. This chapter takes a different approach. Following Guillemette Bolens, it aims 'to explore the interpretive value of kinesic intelligence in reading gesture in literary narrative'. Readers' perceptions, according to Bolens, are based on their embodied knowledge and on their kinaesthetic

---

[1] For scholarship on Hoccleve's body as a prop for political and professional commentary see J. A. Burrow's claim that Hoccleve's personal details, many including the state of his body, are playful entries to entertain potential patrons, in 'Autobiographical Poetry in the Middle Ages: The Case of Thomas Hoccleve', in his *English Poets in the Late Middle Ages: Chaucer, Langland and Others* (Farnham, 2012), Pt V, pp. 223–46, at p. 243. Nicholas Perkins argues that Hoccleve is primarily a political poet who reminds the king of his contractual obligations to the needs of his body politic as voiced through a coherent subject, in *Hoccleve's Regiment of Princes: Counsel and Constraint* (Cambridge, 2001), pp. 143–50. Antony Hasler's critique in 'Hoccleve's Unregimented Body', *Paragraph*, 13 (1990), 164–83, is an astute psychoanalytic-based reading of Hoccleve's 'body' in the Prologue to the *Regiment*.
[2] Hasler puzzles over why Hoccleve's degenerating labouring body is presented playfully: 'Hoccleve's Unregimented Body', p. 163.

memory of the motor sensation of kinesis, of what a body *in action* feels like and how it behaves.[3]

Rather than tackling Hoccleve's entire body from a kinesic perspective, this chapter focuses on feet. Feet perform steps or *pas*; they dance, jump, run, walk, shuffle, stroll, kick, hop, stomp. These various movements make different demands on the body and convey different meanings. This chapter concentrates on the way that feet walk, trot, and 'pricke or prance' in four of Hoccleve's poems: the *Series*, the Prologue to the *Regiment of Princes*, the *Male Regle*, and the ballade addressed to Henry V which begins 'Victorious Kyng'. The pedestrian movements in these poems vary in pace and character, but they all invite readers to assess and recognise various spiritual, physical, emotional, and cognitive states.[4] Reading Hoccleve's pedestrian imagery according to the principles of kinesic intelligence set forth by Bolens, I hope to track these various states and extend our appreciation of Hoccleve's poetic technique, which is less pedestrian than these images might suggest.

Pre-amble

Whereas modern studies of gesture in medieval literature privilege hands and facial expression in their interpretive scheme, Hoccleve and his readers would have been comfortable using feet to represent other states of being.[5] Both static and dynamic images of feet serve a range of allegorical functions in medieval texts. For example, in medieval religious discourse and philosophies of the body politic, pedestrian imagery is often used allegorically to explore the soul's faculties.[6] In a long-established patristic tradition, Philippe

---

[3] Guillemette Bolens, *The Style of Gestures: Embodiment and Cognition in Literary Narrative* (Baltimore, 2012), pp. 1–2. Bolens (p. 1) follows Ellen Spolsky's definition of 'kinesic intelligence', which is 'the human capacity to discern and interpret body movement, body postures, gestures, and facial expressions in real situations, as well as in our reception of visual art' (cited from Spolsky's 'Elaborated Knowledge: Reading Kinesis in Pictures', *Poetics Today*, 17 (1996), 157–80, at p. 157). 'Kinaesthesis' is 'the sense of muscular effort that accompanies a voluntary motion of the body or the sense or faculty by which such sensations are perceived' (*Oxford English Dictionary*). 'Kinesics' are body movements and gestures which convey meaning non-vocally (*Oxford English Dictionary*).

[4] Christian Keysers, *The Empathic Brain: How the Discovery of Mirror Neurons Changes Our Understanding of Human Nature* (Lexington, 2011).

[5] See J. A. Burrow, *Gestures and Looks in Medieval Narrative* (Cambridge, 2009).

[6] For an excellent summation of this tradition, see John Freccero's 'Dante's Firm Foot and the Journey without a Guide', *Harvard Theological Review*, 52 (1959), 245–81; and Siegfried Wenzel, *The Sin of Sloth: Acedia in Medieval Thought and Literature* (Durham, NC, 1967). Augustine used this image several times, as did Bernard of Clairvaux, Aelred of Rivaulx, Guibert de Nogent, Brinton and Wyclif. See Wenzel, *Sin of Sloth*, p. 237, n. 66. John of Salisbury, in the *Policraticus*, likens the community to a human body whose parts are interdependent; the head represents the king, the feet represent the artisans and

de Vitry, following Augustine, states that feet and their movements illustrate two faculties, the *pes intellectus* [foot of intellect] and *pes affectus* [foot of emotion]: 'Our spirit has two feet – one for the intellect and the other of the affect, or of cognition and love – and we must move both so that we might walk the right way.'[7] These spiritual and quotidian concerns merge in the image of what Vincent Gillespie calls 'the mystic foot'.[8] Christian commentators portrayed the image of the soul journeying towards heaven as a person walking along a road undertaking the pilgrimage of life. This soul's journey consists of putting one foot (the *pes intellectus*) ahead of the other (the *pes affectus*), which lags behind hesitantly. Further, the right (*dexter*) foot performed the active or agile function to instigate walking while the left (*sinister*) or resting foot provided stability to the other.[9] This allegory's structure and the process of interpretation it encourages both privilege the intellect over the emotions or the body as the location of meaning.

By inviting readers to subordinate corporeal feet to their spiritual significance, the foot imagery used in theological contexts seems to confirm Ethan Knapp's observation that allegory is a 'peculiarly disembodied thing [...] examined against a smoothly ideational background'.[10] However, this line of interpretation assumes that reading itself is mainly an intellectual activity. This essay, in contrast, insists that reading is a physical activity that sits at the crossroads of neurophysiological and sociocultural parameters of human interaction. According to Bolens, images of the body in motion evoke a response that is grounded in the reader's kinesic intelligence.[11] When encountering a description of one foot striding confidently while the other lags behind, many readers are likely to undergo what James Simpson calls 're-cognition' in an embodied sense: 'We know because we

---

peasants 'who erect, sustain and move forward the mass of the whole body': *Policraticus*, ed. and trans. Cary J. Nederman (Cambridge, 1990), pp. 63, 67.

[7] Wenzel, *Sin of Sloth*, p. 108.

[8] Vincent Gillespie, 'Mystic's Foot: Rolle and Affectivity', in his *Looking in Holy Books: Essays on Late Medieval Religious Writing in England*, Brepols Collected Essays in European Cultures, 3 (Turnhout, 2011), pp. 243–76. See also Sarah Brazil, 'The Materiality of Metaphors: Why the *Affectus* Needs Shoes in *The Doctrine of the Hert*', in Mary Flannery (ed.), *Emotion and Medieval Textual Media* (Turnhout, 2018), pp. 177–93.

[9] Freccero, 'Dante's Firm Foot', pp. 252–6, discusses the firm versus agile foot. Augustine, after Pliny and Aristotle, assumed the agile foot was on the right.

[10] Ethan Knapp, 'Towards a Material Allegory: Allegory and Urban Space in Hoccleve, Langland, and Gower', *Exemplaria*, 27 (2015), 93–109, at p. 93. Knapp situates late medieval allegory within the challenge of interpreting the representation of crowds and urban space in Hoccleve's *La Male Regle*, arguing that both the representation of the anonymous crowd and that of urban space help shape medieval allegory in Hoccleve's poems. His observations of the 'prees' (C 139) are focused through a lens of social banishment and the feelings and thoughts evoked by that banishment. In my view, Hoccleve's moving body helps shape allegory.

[11] See note 3.

knew.'[12] Paradoxically, then, the allegory of the soul's journey depends on the reader's kinesic intelligence concerning what it means to walk in order to encourage them to privilege the intellect over embodied knowledge.

Images of feet in motion can therefore help readers both to recognise (or re-cognise) how a spiritual journey might feel and to alter their feelings. In a late medieval sermon based on Paul's letter to the Ephesians (5.2) and called 'Ambulate', the imagery shifts from the foot's anatomy to the foot's movement to the mood associated with the body parts being used for their proper purpose:

> In þis fote ben v toes. Þe firste tooe is often tyme / to þenke on God. The second too ys oft tyme to speke *and* tell of hum to othur men. The þride toe ys gladdely to here speke of God. The iiij too ys to flee þinges þat God hateþ. The v too ys for to do þinges þat shuld plese God. On þis fote of loue shulde we goe to-Godwarde, aftur þe techynge of þe holy apostell Seynt Poule, ad Ephesios, quinto, Ambulate in dileccione— goye in loue of God.[13]

The toes stand in as counting tools: they serve as prayer beads, catechistic reminders of correct spiritual emotion (love) and action (preaching). Embedded as they are in a long sermon on the spiritual importance and allegorical function of walking, the toes remind the faithful that the five actions they represent are as fundamental to the spiritual journey as the toes are to walking. In the sense that the passage focuses on the need to walk in the love of God, the sermon echoes an approach taken by the cleric Thomas Bradwardine, in his *Summa de causa Dei*. Quoting Aristotle, Avicenna, and Averroes, Bradwardine grounds within the body all the passions of the soul (*animae passiones omnes esse cum corpore*): gentleness, fear, compassion, understanding with joy and love and hate speak to those who suffer anything of the body.[14] Although these writers consistently use the body to signify spiritual matters, they also suggest that corporeal imagery offers privileged access into what Raymond Williams calls 'structures of feeling', those

---

[12] Simpson refers to the knowledge we bring to reading so-called 'new' literature that re-cognises rather than discovers: 'Cognition is Recognition: Literary Knowledge and Textual "Face"', *ELH*, 44 (2013), 25–44, at p. 25.

[13] W. O. Ross (ed.), *Middle English Sermons* (London, 1940), p. 77.

[14] Thomas Bradwardine, *Summa de causa Dei* (London, 1618), p. 532 (book 2, chapter 18): 'Idem 1 (Aristotle) *de Anima*. 14. videntur, inquit, animae passiones omnes esse cum corpore; puta mansuetudo, timor, misericordia, con dentia, adhuc gaudium, et amare et odire; simul enim his patitur aliquid corpus. Super quod dicit ibi Auerroes in *Comment*, quod omnia accidentia animae concupiscibilis fiunt cum alteratione et transmutatione in corpore' [These things are seen, he says, that all the passions of the soul are with the body; for example, gentleness, fear, compassion, understanding with joy and love and hate; at the same time, they are speaking to those that suffer anything of the body. Further, Averroes, in his *Commentary*, says that all the accidents of the concupiscible soul take place with an alteration and transmutation in the body].

processes of 'affective elements of consciousness and relationships' as they are 'actively lived and felt, [and] through the body'.[15] Although Hoccleve is occupied with secular concerns in addition to religious ones, his pedestrian imagery has a great deal in common with the imagery employed by medieval theological writers insofar as it provides access into the 'structures of feeling' through which consciousness and relationships are both experienced and potentially shared through the body.

Walk

What is it to walk? It is to place one foot forward with the other leg and foot muscles launch-ready for lift-off before relegating the forward foot to the rear position, in a steady if not an even rhythm.[16] To walk is to experience time, space, measurement, and pace in an embodied way.[17] For Bolens and her mentor, Maurice Merleau-Ponty, perception is a bodily phenomenon: 'Perception is irreducibly intentional and bodily, sensory and motor, and so neither merely subjective nor objective, inner nor outer, spiritual nor mechanical.'[18] Hoccleve invites readers to imagine perception as embodied when he depicts himself walking through and by topographic places: Chester's Inn, the office of the Privy Seal, the River Thames, and London and Westminster streets, pavements, bridges and other amorphous cartographic spaces such as the outer suburban fields. These scenes remind readers that walking requires multiple sensory engagements. The senses of vision, smell, and hearing work together with the sense of touch – the feeling of feet on the pavement – to help Hoccleve to avoid stepping on rubbish, to navigate uneven surfaces, or to wade in mud. While he is walking, Hoccleve overhears or actively listens for gossip, sees his acquaintances flee from him on the street. Walking in Hoccleve's poetry is 'itself a form of circumambulatory knowing', beating out a pattern of lived time and space that invites readers to perceive the rhythm of his walk as part of the world he describes.[19]

---

[15] Raymond Williams, *Marxism and Literature* (Oxford, 1977), p. 132. See also Nicholas Watson, 'Desire for the Past', *Studies in the Age of Chaucer*, 21 (1999), 59–97, on the role and importance of feeling and emotion in motivating our research.

[16] See Michel de Certeau, *The Practice of Everyday Life* (Berkeley, 1988), for a model of social practice, especially in the chapter on 'Walking in the City', pp. 90–114.

[17] According to Andrew Gordon, footprints are a 'widely shared symbol of located knowledge': 'The Renaissance Footprint: The Material Trace in Print Culture from Durer to Spenser', *Renaissance Quarterly*, 71 (2018), 478–529, at p. 479.

[18] Taylor Carman, *Merleau-Ponty*, 2nd edn (Abingdon, 2019), p. 76.

[19] Tim Ingold, 'Culture on the Ground: The World Perceived through the Feet', *Journal of Material Culture*, 9 (2004), 315–40, at p. 331. As Ingold also writes in the same article: 'It is in the very "tuning" of movement in response to the ever-changing conditions of an unfolding task that the skill of walking, as that of any other bodily technique, ultimately resides' (p. 332).

In the 'Complaint', Hoccleve's feet pound the pavement while journeying to work each day as he ruminates about his imagined social rejection; the rhythmic *pas à pas* pulsates in the background. Routine plodding movement accompanies rueful rumination as Hoccleve struggles but fails to escape feeling cheated because his labour in the office is unappreciated by others:

As that I oones fro Westminstir cam,
Vexid ful greuously with þouȝtful hete,
Thus thouȝte I, 'A greet fool I am,
This pauyment adaies thus to bete,
And in and oute laboure faste and swete,
Wondringe and heuinesse to purchace,
Sithen I stonde out of al fauour and grace.' (C 183–9, my emphasis)

These lines allow readers to empathise with Hoccleve's emotional responses through our kinaesthetic intelligence. The imagery invites readers to recognise the sensation of touching stone underfoot while simultaneously realising that we are often oblivious to that sensation, especially when our steps are driven by preoccupied thoughts and troublesome feelings. Thus readers draw on visceral knowledge of what it means to pound the pavement in order to understand that anxious thoughts activate the sympathetic nervous system, driving flight, fight, or freeze responses, and all of the corporeal changes those responses entail.[20] The flight response propels rushed or agitated bodily movements even if the 'injury' is psychological, such as perceived social rejection.

While the association between feet and rhythm might seem like an obvious one to make in the context of an essay about verse, readers are not the only ones to use their kinesic intelligence while reading Hoccleve's feet as a sign of his unregulated body. As he overhears others speaking in the 'Complaint', he notices that others regard his feet as compelling evidence that he has not yet recovered from his 'wilde infirmitie'. He recalls that others say, 'My feet weren ay wauynge to and fro' (C 131). Hoccleve's choice of 'waving' is jarring to the modern reader who pairs waving with hands and arms, not feet. But in Hoccleve's poem 'waving' means 'moving' in a particular way: swaying, wandering or being unable to stand still, which are actions associated with feet rather than hands (*Middle English Dictionary*, 1(a)). Thus the 'waving' feet reveal the seriousness of his illness to others by suggesting that his proprioceptive and cognitive abilities have failed as his feet seem to be operating independently of his will (C 155–68). The specific diction used by those whom Hoccleve overhears creates imagery that shapes the reader's perception that he is unable to control his body adequately. Readers are then given access to the process whereby Hoccleve's thoughts about those who imagine his feet to be out of his control ultimately compel him to make many a 'saute' (C 162) to his mirror when he returns to his

---

[20] Bolens, *Style of Gestures*, p. 57.

room, leaping anxiously to see if he can perceive the signs of illness in his expression. Thus his waving and jumping feet convey to others information about his state of mind: whatever else it reveals about him, the movement of his feet in these scenes reveals the intensity of his distress.

Whereas Hoccleve beats the pavement in a repetitive, purposeful, gloomy pace on his way to work in the *Series*, he rushes between work and the taverns he visits in *La Male Regle*. The many inns in Westminster advertised their services with long poles projecting above the door surmounted by a bunch of evergreen leaves, and these visual cues spur Hoccleve to 'hye' (126) or rush to one of the taverns in the unincorporated district instead of going home to the hostel. The body's appetites override rational thought and compel him to speed, boosted by craving and the promise of a respite from the routine of work. He writes of rushing to the Paul's Head often, and Hoccleve implies that dashing to taverns was another defining quality of that identity. Once inside, though, Hoccleve scrupulously controls his body. He claims this is because he is so afraid of getting into a fight:

> But oon auauntage in this cas I haue:
> I was so ferd with any man to fighte,
> Cloos kepte I me. No man durste I depraue
> But rownyngly I spak, nothyng on highte. (169–72)

Given his compulsion to reach the tavern, Hoccleve's ability to self-regulate some of his physical impulses in the interior of the tavern comes as a surprise. Amidst the noise, Hoccleve seems to find an inner quietness reminiscent of Augustine's exhortation in Trevisa's Middle English translation of Bartholomaeus Anglicus's *On the Properties of Things*:

> Therfore Austyn seith that reste hath ke(n)de inclinacioun toward the myddel, and therfore it is heed and disposicioun of gaderinge and oneynge of parties in here owne place. Therefore al that is ordeyned to reste by kynde is acountid more nobil and more worthi whanne it is fynalliche in reste than it is whanne it is in meuynge, as the ende is more worthi than thinges that beeth ordeyned for the ende.[21]

In *La Male Regle*, Hoccleve's dash to the tavern is comically juxtaposed with the quietude he finds within the tavern and himself in the company of fellow clerks. The juxtaposition of these two states takes full advantage of the reader's kinesic intelligence, for readers know through experience that the physiological states brought about by rushing through the streets and quietly sitting are very different indeed, if only at the level of the heart's rhythms. This poem thus reminds readers to employ their knowledge of

---

[21] M. C. Seymour (ed.), *On the Properties of Things: John Trevisa's Translation of Bartholomaeus Anglicus, De Proprietatibus Rerum: A Critical Text* (3 vols, Oxford, 1975–88), vol. 1, p. 340.

movement when considering the change of pace that takes place early in the *Regiment of Princes*.

In the *Regiment*'s Prologue, impulsive walking while alone gives way to a meandering stroll with a companion. Unable to sleep, Hoccleve rushes from Chester's Inn at daybreak to an unspecified 'feeld' in the outer suburbs to wade 'herte-deep' in 'wo' (*RP* 117–19). Hoccleve does not wander alone for long, for he is interrupted by an old man:

> By that I walkid hadde a certeyn tyme,
> Were it an hour I not, or more or lesse,
> A poore old hoor man cam walkyng by me,
> And seide, 'Good day, sire, and God yow blesse!' (*RP* 120–4)

From this point on, the two amble together. The gentle rhythms and pace of a dialogic meander are a stark contrast to the poem's frenetic opening and are the ideal kinesic image for the introspective examination that Hoccleve undergoes until the Old Man interrupts the stroll to 'sitte adoun' as his legs ache – a penance for his rebellious youth that resembles the one that Hoccleve describes in *La Male Regle* (*RP* 808–12). We hear that the Old Man, who now invites Hoccleve to slow down, also once sped to the tavern when 'folk wel reuled dressid hem to bedde / In tyme due by reed of nature' (*RP* 624–5). Thus the *Regiment* emphatically repeats the pattern established by *La Male Regle*, establishing an appropriate contemplative state by changing the pace of the feet and the heart.

The time and space through which they walk are also significant. Their walk begins at dawn, loops back and ends at the White Friars church between Fleet Street and the Thames, east of Chester's Inn, just in time for Hoccleve's 'mete' in the Privy Seal (*RP* 808–12, 2006–9) and the Old Man's daily worship, the 7:00am 'Carmes messe' (*RP* 2007–8). Although daily mass attendance and the writing of a *Regiment* may seem unrelated, both engage in an economy of need and habit: spiritual, financial, and quotidian. Moreover, the endpoint of their slow walk suggests that the Old Man is a member of the Carmelite Order, which had a reputation for its learning, engagement with book production and collection, and anti-Wycliffite polemics. Carmelites also enjoyed an extensive affiliation with English royalty from Edward II onward.[22] They were confessors and spiritual advisors to Richard II, Henry IV, Henry V (the *Regiment*'s dedicatee), Henry VI, and probably Humphrey, duke of Gloucester. Stephen Patrington (the provincial

---

[22] Bruce P. Flood Jr, 'The Carmelite Friars in Medieval English Universities and Society, 1299–1430', *Recherches de théologie ancienne et médiévale*, 55 (1988), 154–83; James Hamilton Wylie, *The Reign of Henry the Fifth* (3 vols, Cambridge, 1914–29), vol. 1, pp. 236–57; Valerie Edden, 'The Mantle of Elijah: Carmelite Spirituality in England in the Fourteenth Century', in Marion Glasscoe (ed.), *The Medieval Mystical Tradition in England, Ireland, and Wales. Papers Read at Charney Manor, July 1999: Exeter Symposium VI* (Cambridge, 1999), pp. 67–84.

of the Order) had confessed John of Gaunt, was confessor to Henry IV and would become confessor to Henry V until 1414. Patrington's royal annuity of £69 10s. 6d. underlines his status. Thomas Netter of Walden succeeded Patrington as prior provincial and was Henry V's confessor after 1414 then Inquisitor-General. The Church considered Netter's three-volume defence of the faith, *Doctrinale Antiquitatem Fidei Catholicae Ecclesiae*, so crucial that it was the official articulation on Wycliffism as heresy.[23] Netter had been an official assessor at Sir John Oldcastle's trial in 1413 and was present at Badby's 'show' trial in 1410. Badby's execution by burning (attended by Prince Henry) is an event that the Old Man and Hoccleve spend a great deal of time discussing as they walk together.[24]

Although the reader only hears about the Old Man's association with the Carmelites at the end of the Prologue, Hoccleve himself would have been accustomed to the sight of the mendicant Carmelite Friars out walking, and he knew of their role as confessors to the Lancastrian kings as well as their anti-Wycliffite reputation. An entry in his *Formulary* grants Patrington linen for his confessor role: 'Pur liverer naperie au confessour, come ad este accustumee es temps dautres roys. Roy etc. Nous vous mandons que a notre chier en dieu, e(tienne) p(atryngton), notre confessour, facez liverer de temps en temps tancome il sera ainsi notre confessour naperie' [To deliver linen to a confessor, as has been customary in the time of other kings, King etc. We order you to deliver napery from time to time to our beloved in God, S(tephen) P(atrington), our confessor, for as long as he will be our confessor].[25] Nonetheless, Hoccleve's confession in the *Regiment* appears to be focused on secular matters: work, money worries, and Chaucer's death. The Old Man's spiritual advice is more broadly conceived: he pleads with Hoccleve to abjure arguably the most dangerous heresy of the era, one that challenges the hierarchy of state and Church. The remedy for work and money worries must be the avoidance of certain types of thought, and that avoidance was the Carmelites' dogged speciality. Yet the *Regiment* also suggests that the Old Man might have more in common with Badby than he would like to admit. His purse holds a needle, thread and a leather thimble,

[23] Thomas Netter, *Doctrinale Antiquitatem Fidei Catholicae Ecclesiae* (3 vols, Venice, 1757–59; repr. edn, Farnborough, 1967); Kevin J. Alban, *The Teaching and Impact of the 'Doctrinale' of Thomas Netter of Walden (c.1374–1430)*, Medieval Church Studies, 7 (Turnhout, 2010), p. 15; Johan Bergström-Allen, 'Promoting and Policing Religious Speculation: The Vernacular Literature of the Carmelite Order in Medieval England' (unpublished doctoral thesis, Université de Lausanne, 2017), p. 192.

[24] Wylie, *Reign of Henry the Fifth*, p. 241; James Hamilton Wylie, *History of English under Henry the Fourth* (3 vols, London, 1844–1914), vol. 3, p. 439; Peter McNiven, 'Badby, John (d. 1410), Lollard heretic' (*Oxford Dictionary of National Biography*). The *Regiment* was composed in 1410–11. It is likely that Hoccleve knew of *Piers Plowman*, a poem that provides a model of roaming widely in the world to seek knowledge and question belief.

[25] Elna-Jean Young Bentley, 'The *Formulary* of Thomas Hoccleve' (unpublished dissertation, Emory University, 1965), item 406.

which are appropriate for a poor mendicant friar but were also the tools of the trade for Badby, who was a tailor.[26] The conjunction between heretic hunter and his prey is strangely menacing when Badby's burning supplies the metaphorical backdrop to the *Regiment*'s perambulations. The Old Man's destination, mass at the Carmelites or Whitefriars, is significant as it suggests that the Old Man's enquiries into Hoccleve's spiritual beliefs may have been more of an inquisition and that their walk together may have been less haphazard than it initially seemed.

The stroll and topics under discussion may seem to meander, yet their apparent digressions and ultimate destination provide insight into the approach Hoccleve takes to the *Regiment*'s sources and dedicatee. The Old Man and Hoccleve seem to embody the roles of the writer and recipient of one of his main sources, the *Secreta Secretorum*.[27] Just as the *Secreta* ostensibly records Aristotle's advice to Alexander the Great on quotidian matters like diet, sleep, and rest, the Old Man provides advice in their dialogue.[28] The pace of their walking is also connected to Hoccleve's cautious approach to incorporating his two other primary sources, as Hoccleve worries that he may not be able to reach 'the steppes clergial / Of thise clerkes thre' (*RP* 2150–1). He implies that his ignorance has slowed his progress so far, and he ends the Prologue by praying 'the Crois of Cryst my werk speed and avance' (*RP* 2156). The hope is that his pace may quicken again as he turns his perambulation with the Old Man into a preamble to reading material suitable for Prince Henry. It also seems to mark the culmination of the Old Man's words at the beginning of their time together, at which point he commands Hoccleve to 'walke at large out of thy prisoun' away from distress, anxiety, insomnia, and agitated movement (*RP* 277).[29] Having rushed aimlessly into a field (*RP* 117) after

---

[26] The Carmelite Friars were called the 'stragulati fratres', which broadly translated means 'embroidered or part-coloured friars', due to their custom of sewing strips of cloth together to make up their garments. The Order decided to adopt the white cloak in the thirteenth century. See C. T. Martin, *The Record Interpreter: A Collection of Abbreviations, Latin Words and Names used in English Historical Manuscripts and Records* (London, 1892), p. 260.

[27] See Derek Pearsall, 'Hoccleve's *Regement of Princes*: The Poetics of Royal Self-Representation', *Speculum*, 69 (1994), 386–410, at p. 407. The Old Man has been seen as Hoccleve's *alter ego*, as a dialogic *amicus* figure as a type of anti-Lady Philosophy to Boethius (as Lady Philosophy does not confess to sins of youth), or as Age personified. In my view, circumstantial evidence indicates he is most likely to be an exemplary confessor and, plausibly rather than possibly, a Carmelite, a position Sebastian Langdell contests based on a lack of hard evidence in his *Thomas Hoccleve: Religious Reform, Transnational Poetics, and the Invention of Chaucer* (Oxford, 2018), pp. 158–9.

[28] M. A. Manzaloui (ed.), *Secreta Secretorum: Nine English Versions*, EETS ES 276 (Oxford, 1977).

[29] C. S. Lewis (*The Allegory of Love: A Study in Medieval Tradition* (Oxford, 1958), p. 239) wonders if the lines about Thoght in the Prologue to the *Regiment* ('That fretynge Adversarie / Myn herte made to hym tributarie / In sowkynge of the fresschest of my

enduring a sleepless night bound by troubling thoughts, Hoccleve's walk with the Old Man regulates his emotions and provides him with a sense of direction as he gets in the rhythm of writing 'a goodly tale or two' (*RP* 1902) for Henry as he began taking steps to become king.

Trot

In a much shorter (three-stanza) poem addressed to Henry after he had become king, Hoccleve asks his addressee to take appropriate steps on behalf of clerks suffering on account of the Crown's outstanding debts. Composed soon after Henry V's return from the battle of Agincourt in November 1415 and before Hoccleve's illness in 1416, the *Balade to Henry V, for Money* (which begins 'Victorious Kyng') lauds the king while appealing to him for relief from the financial suffering endured by Hoccleve and his fellow clerks. Hoccleve reminds Henry that long service and loyalty are the hallmarks of 'your seruantz of the olde date' (20). He also expresses his fear that unless the king showers his clerks with his 'rial largesse' (5), they will be forced to 'trotte vnto Newgate' (8).[30] To 'trot' is to move faster than a walk but slower than a run. It is characterised by a shortened stride, a brisk, staccato gait, and even-paced rhythms that clip the road. 'To be trotted', though, carries a sense of enforcement; to be hurried along under pressure from another. To be trotted to Newgate would be serious enforcement indeed. Both the destination and the enforced trot signal the threat of public shame, humiliation, and social mockery. Read with attention to the enforced trotting, Hoccleve's *Balade* challenges King Henry to intervene on behalf of Hoccleve and his fellow clerks by staging the discomfort that the march to Newgate might create for all associated with it.

This lyric emphasises the circumstances that might bring the clerks to Newgate rather than the misery that might await them there. Perhaps Hoccleve felt that readers could imagine conditions in the prison for themselves. After all, Newgate was one of London's foulest prisons. According to one witness later in the century, it was a 'soore streite and perillous prisone for any man to be yn'.[31] Its notoriety might help to explain why Hoccleve chose to name it as the clerks' destination rather

---

blod', 88–90) 'cry out to be re-clothed in sesquipedalian iambics?' Etymologically 'sesquipedalian' stems from long footed.

[30] Margery Bassett, 'Newgate Prison in the Middle Ages', *Speculum*, 18 (1943), 233–46, at p. 246.

[31] R. Horrox (ed.), 'Edward IV: Parliament of October 1472, Text and Translation', in *The Parliament Rolls of Medieval England*, ed. C. Given-Wilson et al. (Leicester, 2005), item 136, online at http://www.sd-editions.com/PROME. In the Parliament of Edward IV of October 1472, one Henry Bodrugan applied for bail for missing his surety meeting. He pleaded for clemency fearing that should he be incarcerated he faced certain death.

than Ludgate, the debtor's prison, which was founded in 1382. This choice is puzzling at first since Ludgate fits Hoccleve's poetic line and the rhyme scheme just as well as Newgate, and the clerks in this poem are worried about not having the money to pay their creditors.[32] Their worry was completely understandable: as the clerks knew better than anyone, the Crown was deeply in arrears in its payments of annuities and indebted to many other creditors as well. Hoccleve may have faced financial difficulties not only because his salary was falling further and further behind but also because he still had to acquire the tools of his trade – parchment, ink, and wax – from men like William Surcestre and Walter Lucy while walking through other parts of London.[33] Privy Seal clerks often experienced considerable delays in reimbursement, as shown by a note in the rolls that states that the 14 February 1417 payment covered seventeen months' worth of materials.[34] He may also have had to make excuses for the king's delay in payment to the parchmenters. At one point Walter Lucy had to wait for eight years for payment.[35] While it was possible for clerks and suppliers to petition the Crown for reimbursement, nobody ever expected the king to serve time in a debtor's prison for the Crown's insolvency. It was a different story for the clerks who may have acquired supplies by paying out of pocket or establishing credit directly. Until the money began to 'flowe' (6) from the king's coffers again, Hoccleve and his fellow clerks were condemned to live in debt. Theologically, debt was linked to loss of faith 'pro fide lesa'.[36] The debtor could therefore be punished for moral and spiritual failure and be forced to rely on the creditor's satisfaction, pity, or mercy to release them of their debts. At Ludgate, a debtor could take counteraction against their creditor as a way to delay their prosecution, but the prison's main aim was 'to secure the safe custody of inmates' bodies' until they repaid their disappointed

---

[32] See Anthony Babington, *The English Bastille: A History of Newgate Gaol and Prison Conditions in Britain 1188–1902* (New York, 1972), p. 16. The debtors in Ludgate were purported to be 'more willing to keep abode there than to pay their debts'.

[33] Linne R. Mooney, 'New Light on Thomas Hoccleve', *Studies in the Age of Chaucer*, 29 (2007), 293–340, at p. 297, n. 12.

[34] M. C. Seymour, *Selections from Hoccleve* (Oxford, 1981), p. 125, suggests that the *bille* was a petition for payment for official expenses of parchment, ink, and wax. The poem was probably written in 1416 after Henry V's return from Agincourt on 23 November 1415 and probably before Hoccleve's illness.

[35] London, The National Archives, SC/8/346/E1416 shows that Walter Lucy petitioned the king in 1421 for payment of 108s. 1d. from the Exchequer for debentures owed to him by the king while Henry was prince.

[36] Charles Johnson, F. E. L. Carter and D. E. Greenway (eds and trans.), *Dialogus de Scaccario (The Course of the Exchequer) by Richard, Fitz Nigel, and Constitutio Domus Regis (The Establishment of the Royal Household)* (Oxford, 1983), p. 117; Richard W. Ireland, 'Theory and Practice within the Medieval English Prison', *American Journal of Legal History*, 31 (1987), 56–67, at p. 57.

creditors.[37] In comparison to Newgate, though, the inmates at Ludgate were relatively free to walk about within the prison, receive visitors and food and clothes from friends and relatives. Being trotted anywhere implies a sense that others are compelling the body to move in a specific way, but the choice of Newgate over Ludgate heightens the sense of constraint that Hoccleve conveys in this stanza, for it implies that his body will be constrained upon arrival as well as *en route*.

When Hoccleve imagines being compelled 'to trotte unto Newgate', he is envisaging a scenario in which a more powerful figure constrains the length of his stride and, consequently, the contraction of leg muscles. Our kinesic intelligence can help us to feel the discomfort the clerks might have experienced when having another will imposed on their bodies through the pace of their steps. A different kinesic image here would produce a very different response. This becomes clear when we compare Hoccleve's unhappy trot to the apparently merry, unrepentant one undertaken in Chaucer's *Cook's Tale* by the incorrigible apprentice Perkyn Revelour, who was 'somtyme lad with revel to Newegate' (I. 4402).[38] Whether or not Perkyn actually revelled in his walk to Newgate, the leading of bodies to this prison did often provide entertainment for passers-by and could be accompanied by mocking music. Hoccleve's use of the word 'trotte' reminds readers that the 'revel' would have resonated differently for those who were being led to prison for circumstances outside of their control. When contrasted with the image of the cook's apprentice, the 'trotting clerks' remind the king he may well be able to use his 'special' body to impose unequal power over his citizens' ordinary bodies, but they may not feel entirely comfortable with what he is asking them to do.[39] It also reminds readers that the imposition of the king's will here depends on his control over another anonymous team of bodies, the guards who escort the culprits on their march of shame. Symbolising civic and royal authority, the guards would have flanked the trotters, dictating their speed.

The trotting of the clerks is also significant because it takes place in a public pedestrian space, one that hosted civic, ecclesiastical and royal rituals. More specifically, Hoccleve's choice of Newgate here means that he and his fellow clerks would be trotted down the same streets where Henry's glorious and lavish pageant took place after his victory at Agincourt and just before the poem was written. The prisoner's parade to Newgate wended past Westminster Abbey to the north-west perimeter of the city, which is a

[37] Margot C. Finn, *The Character of Credit: Personal Debt in English Culture, 1740–1914* (Cambridge, 2003), p. 110.

[38] Despite liberal citations throughout the rolls and *Calendar of Letter-Books*, references to London's Newgate prison occur only twice in medieval poetry: Chaucer's *Cook's Tale* and this poem by Hoccleve.

[39] Quoted in Hasler, 'Hoccleve's Unregimented Body', p. 166, from Louise O. Fradenburg, 'Spectacular Fictions: The Body Politic in Chaucer and Dunbar', *Poetics Today*, 5 (1984), 493–517, at p. 499.

similar but contrary path to the coronation procession. In effect, the trotting clerks make the Agincourt pageant in reverse. By connecting these two kinds of processions, Hoccleve draws attention to what the cost of waging war in France has yielded: victory at Agincourt and the Crown incapable of paying its creditors, even those who have served the king faithfully. The imagined trot of the Privy Seal clerks to Newgate is based on rituals of civic procession that warn against wrongdoing and poverty.[40] Accused felons, prisoners, debtors, and the poor were paraded on their way to or from prison, as medieval penal procedure demanded, as they were when pageants were underway.[41] These rituals were designed to shame those being trotted, demonstrating the power that the state had over their bodies through the pressure of a forced march, but this ritual also threatens to shame the king for not only disregarding his 'seruantz of the olde date' (20) but also needing someone like Hoccleve to remind him of his negligence. While this poem initially seems to flatter the victorious king, its flattery is calculated to generate a sense of shame if the king allows those who serve him to suffer by defaulting on the debt he owes them.[42] By projecting an image of clerks trotting to Newgate against the flow of the Agincourt pageant, Hoccleve provides the king – and the readers of this poem – with a timely reminder of the tension that these clerks are holding in their bodies, which have become stiff through unjust treatment. He also reminds the king – and his readers – that should they be dehumanised by being forced to enact, at a pace not of their choosing, a motion attributed more commonly to equine hooves, they will not bear the shame alone: it will be shared by the king in whose service they have incurred the 'indigences' that Hoccleve now asks him to 'softne and abate' (11).

'Pricke or Prance'

Writing to Henry V after his return from Agincourt, Hoccleve uses the trot to Newgate to invoke an image that potentially dehumanises the clerks. In contrast, he uses equine footwork to achieve a different effect when writing to the king's brother on the occasion of his own triumphant return from France. As he attempts to decide on appropriate material to include in a book he owes to Humphrey, duke of Gloucester, who has recently returned from Cherbourg, Hoccleve expresses his limitations in terms which pertain more to the symbolic and literal landscape of romance and military combat

[40] David Postles, 'Penance and the Market Place: A Reformation Dialogue with the Medieval Church', *Journal of Ecclesiastical History*, 54 (2003), 441–68.
[41] Ralph Pugh, *Imprisonment in Medieval England* (Cambridge, 1970).
[42] Sarah Tolmie, 'The "prive scilence" of Thomas Hoccleve', *Studies in the Age of Chaucer*, 22 (2000), 281–309, makes a similar point that Hoccleve is not afraid to criticise, albeit via comedy, his sovereign.

than they do to the writing life.[43] That seems to be exactly his point as he describes the fact that he will translate a tale he lately saw in the *Gesta Romanorum* despite the fact that his body is unfit for riding a horse:

A tale eek which I in the Romayn deedis
Now late sy, in honur and plesance
Of yow, my ladyes, as I moote needis,
Or take my way for fer into France,
Though I nat shapen be to pricke or prance,
Wole I translate and that shal pourge, I hope,
My gilt as cleene as keuerchiefs dooth sope. (*D* 820–6)

These lines, like so many others in Hoccleve's autobiographical poetry (especially the Prologue to the *Regiment*, and the 'Dialogue' of the *Series*), according to C. S. Lewis, are indebted to ideas circulating about romance convention.[44] Hoccleve invokes those conventions here to indicate that they do not apply to him. The fact that his body is 'not shapen [...] to pricke or prance' reminds readers of Hoccleve's status as an unhorsed and untravelled clerk who will never make his name through military or chivalric feats. In other words, he implies through this imagery that he will make a book for Duke Humphrey even though they inhabit such different worlds that they seem to inhabit different kinds of bodies.

The most obvious interpretation of this passage is that it is self-deprecation, a compulsive Hocclevian literary habit. These lines in the 'Dialogue' are consistent with similar scenes in the *Regiment*, where Hoccleve describes his body as ageing, aching, short-sighted, and wearied from work, or perhaps too round. It is therefore possible that Hoccleve is simply suggesting here that he is now past his prime. Perhaps once he could demonstrate equestrian prowess and hence chivalric performance, but he is no longer fit enough to perform such feats. It seems more likely, though, that Hoccleve is confessing his social misshapenness: he reminds readers that he is not equipped to perform such feats because he is not from the chivalric class. Hoccleve's depiction of his body in this passage underscores the corporeal opposition between the body of the clerk, who writes, and the body of the knight, who rides.

Moreover, the passage implies that the ideal knight's body can be distinguished from the bodies of others because it is mounted on a horse and intimately connected to its steps. The chivalric body is nearly, but not quite, that of a centaur. The relationship between horse and rider was, as Susan Crane writes, the 'most closely coordinated and densely represented

---

[43] Lewis discusses the importance of romance convention to Hoccleve's autobiographical poetry, especially the Prologue to the *Regiment* and the 'Dialogue'. He claims that the poetry is all the more interesting because it is not concerned with conventional romance (*Allegory of Love*, p. 238).

[44] Lewis, *Allegory of Love*, p. 238.

interaction between humans and animals in the late Middle Ages'.[45] In the chivalric context, human and horse bodies act as one or in concert: consider, for example, the relationships between either the Green Knight and his green horse or Gawain and his precious Gringolet in *Sir Gawain and the Green Knight*. As Noel Denholm-Young puts it, 'it is impossible to be chivalrous without a horse'.[46] The nobility of the horse is closely connected with the nobility of the knight according to a thirteenth-century tract by Jordanus Rufus: 'No animal is nobler than the horse, since it is by horses that princes, magnates and knights are separated from lesser people and because a lord cannot fittingly be seen among private citizens except through the mediation of a horse.'[47] The bodily attributes of the ideal knight stipulated by Vegetius's fourth-century military manual *De re militari* – a tract that Hoccleve considers translating for Humphrey in the 'Dialogue' – apply equally to the noble horse. One should choose a horse

> by schap of body and light chere [...] þe chere & countenaunce of visage, and principally to þe eyȝen and so to oþere membres and lymes, and þerby he may deme whiche ben able to fulfille þe office of a werriour. ffor no doute þat þe strengþe and myȝt and vertu [...] boþe of men, of hors [...] be many tokenes and signes in kinde.[48]

Men suited to the 'werk of Mars, þat is god of batayle' must have similar tokens:

> wakyng eyȝen, streyte and stalworþe nekke, brood brest, wel brawned schuldres, (strong-boned arms) stalworþ bonyd armes, longe fyngres, smal of wombe, mesurable porpocyonyd tþyes, not to grete ne to smale, anclees and feet not coumbred wiþ flesch, but wel hardid & knyt togidre wiþ sadnese of synewes. When þou fyndist þese tokenes in þy newe chosen kniȝt, take þane none hede to lengþe ne to gretnesse of body, for more profitable hit is to haue miȝti kniȝtis and stronge þan if grete and longe.[49]

Vegetius idealises the chivalric body by focusing on its attributes according to a specific scheme. Thighs must be well-proportioned with no plump or swollen feet and ankles, while the feet must be strong and sinewy. The broad breast, straight and stalwart neck, and bright eyes could refer primarily to the ideal qualities of a horse, but here they are the ideal attributes of a worthy knight's body parts, emphasising thighs, ankles and feet. The

---

[45] Susan Crane, 'Chivalry and the Pre/Postmodern', *postmedieval*, 2 (2011), 69–87, at p. 72.

[46] N. Denholm-Young, *Collected Papers of N. Denholm-Young* (Cardiff, 1969), p. 95.

[47] Cited in R. H. C. Davis, *The Medieval Warhorse* (London, 1989), pp. 107–8.

[48] G. A. Lester (ed.), *The Earliest English Translation of Vegetius' De re militari* (Heidelberg, 1988), p. 54.

[49] Lester (ed.), *Vegetius' De re militari*, p. 54.

parallel descriptions of perfect horse and knight figures have so much in common that the horse and knight seem to blend into one idealised figure.

In the 'Dialogue', Hoccleve repeatedly presents Humphrey as an idealised knightly figure who exemplifies martial superiority and amorous aspirations. Recalling his dedicatee's recent exploits in Rouen and Cherbourg, Hoccleve asserts that nobody could be better shaped both to 'pricke' and to 'prance' in France than Humphrey:

> O Lord, whan he cam to the seege of Roon
> From Chirburgh, whethir fere or cowardyse
> So ny the walles made him for to goon
> Of the town as he dide? I nat souffyse
> To telle yow in how knyghtly a wyse
> He logged him ther, and how worthyly
> He baar him. What, he is al knyght, soothly. (D 610–16)

Hoccleve seems to think this may make Humphrey more qualified than him to work directly with Vegetius's *De re militari*. After all, Humphrey possesses the qualities, knowledge and skills specified in the text, 'For he þat art wel can for the maistrie' (D 565).[50] Moreover, Humphrey seems likely to have better luck with women than Hoccleve, who recalls having infuriated the court ladies with his misogynistic English translation of Christine de Pizan's *Epistre au dieu d'amours*. He hopes Humphrey will share the book he is making with his lady friends, since 'his lust and his desir / Is, as it wel sit to his hy degree, / For his desport and mirth, in honestee / With ladyes to haue daliance' (D 703–6). Once again, Humphrey embodies a chivalric ideal that is the complete opposite of Hoccleve, who is not shaped for military exploits and seems prone to put his foot in his mouth when addressing women readers. Here, Hoccleve uses kinesic imagery in a new way. He differentiates readers with different kinds of kinesic intelligence: Humphrey, or readers like him, would know exactly how it felt to prick and prance because their bodies are made for it; readers without that experience would share Hoccleve's experience of knowing what it feels like only to be able to imagine such an experience.

Conclusion

Sebastian Sobecki has argued that Hoccleve's writing hinges on the portrayal of an 'indexical self' that is intended in the first instance 'for a specific audience with direct access to the author and full understanding of the text's

---

[50] We cannot be certain that Humphrey had read or possessed a copy at the time Hoccleve composed the *Series* but Humphrey had a Latin original, and a French version by Jean de Vignai by the 1440s. See Alessandra Petrina, *Cultural Politics in Fifteenth-Century England: The Case of Humphrey, Duke of Gloucester* (Leiden, 2004), p. 279.

fabric of allusions'.[51] Hoccleve's audience appears to be situated within his social networks and friendship groups. The close affinity to his tight-knit groups would allow him to express his embodied self and emotional life to an audience who understood his personal and political circumstances. However, his writing necessarily addresses a broader readership through its display of embodied emotion. His descriptions of himself in motion suggest that he had a sense that kinesic imagery might convey his presence as a living, breathing person within his writing. But this imagery also depends on a living, breathing reader. As Hoccleve's feet map urban space in the city and its surroundings, readers attuned to their tempo and pace can use their kinesic intelligence to imagine his emotional state. His steps punctuate or, at the very least, fuel his poetry's muscular immediacy. Hoccleve recursively and intimately employs embodied affects as metaphors for his persona's different states: moods, desires, actions, status, ill health, pains 'in every veyne and place' (RP 1025). He invites readers to walk with him as he tramples autumn leaves underfoot, struts the pavement to and from the office, dashes to the fields or hurtles to the inn. We imagine his trot as a debtor to Newgate along the streets of London and believe his self-described non-knightly role as Humphrey, duke of Gloucester's promotional amanuensis. Pedestrian movement intensifies poetic force in Hoccleve's writing as his feet mirror, illustrate, and reinforce the moods he fleshes out through his poetry, a force that readers recognise based on knowledge of their own body's kinetic/physiological responses.

---

51 Sebastian Sobecki, *Last Words: The Public Self and the Social Author in Late Medieval England* (Oxford, 2020), p. 7.

10

Curatorial Hoccleve:
Spiritual and Codicological Illumination
in the Regiment of Princes

Ruen-chuan Ma

Hoccleve has long been connected with Chaucer's literary legacy because he eulogises his predecessor in two passages in the *Regiment of Princes* (1958–74, 2077–107). His use of the terms *maistir* and *fadir* to describe Chaucer participates in what has been called a 'genealogical metaphor' of authorial lineage in late medieval literature, although Ethan Knapp has argued for that metaphor being a 'strategy for poetic usurpation'.[1] While the term 'genealogical' captures the affiliations of father and son and master and pupil (as well as the professional, bureaucratic, masculine culture that defines so many of Hoccleve's social connections), it directs our attention away from Hoccleve's use of book-related language and imagery as dominant motifs in the eulogising passages.[2] Inspired in part by Sonja Drimmer's contention that manuscript illustrations of late medieval English authors seek to establish their authorial status, this essay suggests that Hoccleve's curation of Chaucer's legacy, not least via the author portraits that accompany one of the passages in several manuscripts, is influenced by a broader material-cultural phenomenon. Hoccleve invokes the very aesthetics of reading a late medieval manuscript – the holistic impression of the page as generated by words, decoration, and illustration – as a means to secure the works and

---

[1] Ethan Knapp, *The Bureaucratic Muse: Thomas Hoccleve and the Literature of Late Medieval England* (University Park, 2001), pp. 107–9. Knapp provides an overview of scholarship on the genealogical metaphor and discusses how Hoccleve, in calling Chaucer his *maistir*, displaces and usurps Chaucer's position. Although I treat the relationship between Chaucer and Hoccleve as one of mutual reference and illumination through text and image, and not necessarily one of displacement, Knapp nonetheless offers a useful discussion of how Hoccleve's authorship depends on his attitudes toward Chaucer (at pp. 107–28).

[2] For Hoccleve's participation in these masculine cultures, see Isabel Davis, *Writing Masculinity in the Later Middle Ages*, Cambridge Studies in Medieval Literature, 62 (Cambridge, 2007), pp. 138–67.

reputations of authors beyond their lifetimes.[3] This article focuses especially on Hoccleve's use of illumination, in both a codicological and a spiritual sense, to curate literary legacy.

I refer to Hoccleve's practice as 'curatorial codicology' in order to describe it as a kind of pastoral care for the author's memory that emerges from encounters with the written word in its multimodal manuscript context. As a professional scribe, Hoccleve participated in late medieval English scribal culture and copied a number of Middle English literary manuscripts.[4] He also witnessed the development of Chaucer's afterlife through the production and circulation of codices.[5] As both author and scribe, he would have been aware of the sensory, performative, and even affective functions associated with the manuscript page.[6] Hoccleve's attitudes towards his literary *maistirs* thus intersect with his awareness of codicological curation: an interrelated network of verbal, graphical, and decorative elements on the page that can safeguard literary works and their authors, as if they are to be venerated as saints. Hoccleve's curatorial codicology sees books as vehicles for preserving renown and facilitating exaltation. Moreover, both in Hoccleve's Marian devotional poems and in other early fifteenth-century English writings, book-related language and imagery are similarly spiritually inflected. In both Hoccleve's *Regiment* and his Marian devotional poems, the word *enlumyne* connotes an inspirational, animating luminescence informed by the intersection of codicological features and religious devotion – divine light and vivid illustration. This set of meanings is well established in the medieval French and medieval Latin equivalents of *enlumyne* (*enluminer* and *illuminare* respectively), suggesting that Hoccleve, Lydgate, and other English writers were drawing on a richly evocative overlap of meanings when they used these terms.[7]

We might begin by asking to what extent the book, as a physical medium, conditions the meaning and the expression of reverence to Chaucer in the *Regiment*? What implications might the visual aesthetics of reading manuscript books have for the connection that Hoccleve makes to Chaucer?

---

[3] Sonja Drimmer, *The Art of Allusion: Illuminators and the Making of English Literature, 1403–1476* (Philadelphia, 2019).

[4] M. B. Parkes and A. I. Doyle, 'The Production of Copies of the *Canterbury Tales* and the *Confessio Amantis* in the Early Fifteenth Century', in M. B. Parkes, *Scribes, Scripts, and Readers: Studies in the Communication, Presentation, and Dissemination of Medieval Texts* (London, 1991), pp. 201–48, at pp. 220–3 and 235–6.

[5] Simon Horobin, 'Thomas Hoccleve: Chaucer's First Editor?', *Chaucer Review*, 50 (2015), 228–50.

[6] David Watt discusses 'the commercial and spiritual rewards' associated with Hoccleve's book-making labours, and I draw from this idea for further examining Hoccleve's codicological and curatorial concerns, especially those relating to page layout and illustration. See Watt, *The Making of Thomas Hoccleve's Series* (Liverpool, 2013), pp. 93–102.

[7] See *illuminare* in the *Dictionary of Medieval Latin from British Sources* (DMLBS) at logeion.uchicago.edu; and *enluminer* in the *Dictionnaire du Moyen Français* at atilf.fr/dmf/.

Hoccleve integrates words and images on the page to engage readers in remembering Chaucer and position his works as an intermediary for his predecessor's memory. The book is an apt aesthetic vehicle for Hoccleve's curatorial designs because page layout enables the juxtaposition and inter-action of words and images, encompassing a range of sites for engaging the reader's senses and shaping their encounter with authorial figures and their virtues. As with other early fifteenth-century English writers such as John Lydgate who are also discussed in what follows, Hoccleve thus emphasises the codex as a unique site of memorialisation through curation.

Manuscript illumination and features of poetic form serve as the operative devices that not only memorialise Chaucer in the *Regiment* but also ensure Chaucer's living presence after death. Addressing a personified figure of death, Hoccleve is keen to preserve the memory of the author's virtue and eloquence both by formal and figurative means. In one passage, he evokes ideas of wisdom ('universel fadir in science', *RP* 1964) and illumi-nation ('enlumynyng', *RP* 1974) to give Chaucer a revered, exalted status that transcends death:

> O deeth, thow didest nat harm singuler
> In slaghtre of him, but al this land it smertith
> But natheless yit hastow no power
> His name slee; his hy vertu astertith
> Unslayn fro thee, which ay us lyfly hertith
> With bookes of his ornat endytyng
> That is to al this land enlumynyng. (*RP* 1968–74)

In order to read the entire stanza, the reader's eye must perform the very sense of defiance that Hoccleve expresses: the ability to move past a terminal point. Hoccleve's claims of defying death are especially visible in the poetic form and the juxtaposition of sight and sound in this stanza. The syntac-tical continuity and the constant forward rhythm of the enjambments enact the defiance of death in poetic, formal terms. Enjambment occurs in almost every line, such that line breaks almost never correspond to syntac-tical breaks. For example, readers must read past 'astertith' and 'hertith' in order to see how Chaucer's 'hy vertu' remains 'unslayn' and stays alive 'with bookes of his ornat endytyng'. As a result, readers must repeatedly move past the end of the line, a visual terminal point, in order to grasp the complete meaning of the verses. This becomes particularly visible when compared to the syntactical evenness of the preceding stanza, in which every line break corresponds to a syntactical break.

Furthermore, the same stanza invites readers to apprehend Chaucer's memory through a multimodal affiliation of text and image, the sensory impression generated by the manuscript page as a whole. Hoccleve deftly combines the visual impacts of the decorative and verbal components of medieval books in the lines 'With bookes of his ornat endytyng / That is to al this land enlumynyng'. The phrase 'ornat endytyng' refers, at first glance, to the eloquence of Chaucer's writing, but it does so in explicitly decorative terms. The word *ornat* means 'ornamented' or, when referring to literature, 'embellished' with rhetorical devices. Moreover, it suggests that the 'bookes' are able to shine upon the entire land because their 'ornat endytyng' generates a kind of luminous radiance. The nationalistic undertone of these two lines recalls Gower's making of a 'bok for Engelondes sake' (24) in the Prologue of the *Confessio Amantis*, yet Hoccleve's codicological language, inflected as it is by spiritual connotations, suggests that the book can do more than serve as a physical repository or monument.[8] In the *Regiment*, the book's illumination becomes a visible feature that doubles as a metaphor for the luminescent spread of an author's renown. As the final couplet of the *rime royal* stanza, these lines end in 'endytyng' and 'enlumynyng' respectively. Hoccleve complicates their relationship by rhyming both the first and last syllables of each word – *en* and *yng* – to form a para-rhyme. The layers of rhyme generate an aural affiliation and develop the connection between the verbal and pictorial aspects of medieval book production. By devising this multimodal affiliation, Hoccleve allows the sense of ornateness to comprehend both literary composition ('endytyng') and the visual aesthetics of the manuscript page ('enlumynyng'). Hoccleve's 'bookes of ornat endytyng' become the means for making the light of Chaucer's virtue shine upon England, a means of spreading both authorial renown and spiritual illumination.

Alongside the linking of text and image enhanced by rhyming sounds and line breaks, Hoccleve incorporates the author portrait into his project of curation, drawing on the vividness of an illustration to elevate the reader's remembrance of Chaucer. He refers to 'peynture' (*RP* 4998), an ornate, decorative element on the manuscript page, and associates the lifelike representation that it provides with the renown and illumination of Chaucer's virtue. In another eulogising passage in the *Regiment*, we find that reverence for Chaucer is combined with an allusion to a portrait of the deceased author:

Althogh his lyf be qweynt, the resemblance
Of him hath in me so fressh lyflynesse
That to putte othir men in remembrance
Of his persone, I have heere his liknesse
Do make, to this ende, in soothfastnesse,
That they that han of him lost thoght and mynde
By this peynture may ageyn him fynde.

The ymages that in the chirches been
Maken folk thynke on God and on his seintes
Whan the ymages they beholde and seen,
Where ofte unsighte of hem causith restreyntes
Of thoghtes goode. Whan a thyng depeynt is

---

8 John Gower, *Confessio Amantis*, ed. Russell A. Peck (3 vols, Kalamazoo, 2000), vol. 1, p. 66.

Or entaillid, if men take of it heede,
Thoght of the liknesse it wole in hem breede. (*RP* 4992–5005)

Hoccleve refers to illustrations within a book, specifically a lifelike portrait of Chaucer ('I have heere his liknesse / Do make'), as a way of helping readers retain the dead *maistir* in their memories ('By this peynture may ageyn him fynde'). The absence of images moreover bears negative moral consequences because it limits the reader's ability for virtuous thinking ('unsight of hem causith restreyntes / Of thoghtes goode'). The medieval book becomes a means to defy death and cultivate the reader's remembrance of literary renown in both a particular and a general sense. Hoccleve actively invokes the visual and physical features of the book to structure and mediate the reader's encounter with the memory of a deceased author; this curation also invites readers to reflect on what is at stake in the remembrance of deceased authors. The defiance of death gains prominence, whether challenging a personified 'deeth' through Chaucer's enduring virtue ('hy vertu astertith') or declaring that Chaucer would be 'unslayn' from death in the previous eulogising passage, or contrasting death ('his lyf be qweynt') with a vivid, lifelike memory in this one ('of him hath in me so fressh lyflynesse') in these lines.

Hoccleve claims the visual features of medieval books as a means to defy death and maintain Chaucer's renown. When readers see Hoccleve's verses on the manuscript page alongside decoration and a portrait of Chaucer, the sense of in-person likeness and liveliness enhances the *Regiment* passages, revealing the development of Hoccleve's curation and the centrality of illumination to it. Whether with radiant decoration that reflects luminous eloquence or meditative portraits that incline readers to regard Chaucer with reverence, Hoccleve uses the trope of illumination to position himself as a caretaker of Chaucer's memory and the book as the means to safeguard it. Indeed, the reader's interactions with medieval books become essential for revivifying Chaucer's presence in the minds of readers.

Such portraits of Chaucer have survived in some late medieval copies of the *Regiment*, suggesting that Hoccleve's curation contributed to Chaucer's status as a revered author. Late medieval illuminators took Hoccleve's cue to furnish readers with an image of Chaucer as an aid for their reflection. Surviving portraits appear in three copies of the *Regiment*, and their dates range from the first to the third quarter of the fifteenth century, in addition to two known instances of excised Chaucer portraits.[9] In both London, British Library, MS Harley 4866 (Figure 10.1) and London, British Library, Royal

---

[9]   See related discussions on the Chaucer portraits in Nicholas Perkins, *Hoccleve's Regiment of Princes: Counsel and Constraint* (Woodbridge, 2001), pp. 151–7; and Derek Pearsall, 'Hoccleve's *Regement of Princes*: The Poetics of Royal Self-Representation', *Speculum*, 69 (1994), 386–410. The portraits are excised in London, British Library, MS Arundel 38 – a copy of the *Regiment of Princes* that contains the famous presentation portrait of Hoccleve and Henry, Prince of Wales – and London, British Library, MS Harley 4826 (discussed below).

MS 17. D. VI, the portraits appear in the margin alongside the eulogising passage quoted above, with Chaucer's finger pointing to the relevant lines where Hoccleve refers to the image ('I have heere his liknesse / Do make'). A third portrait appears in the margins of Philadelphia, Rosenbach Museum and Library, MS 1083/30; it was made in the eighteenth century, and its source was likely MS Harley 4866. This portrait closely resembles the portrait in MS Harley 4866 in style and appearance, with identical poses for Chaucer and similar green, diapered backgrounds.[10] It appears alongside a different passage than the other two portraits, an earlier point in the *Regiment* where Hoccleve praises Chaucer as the 'fyndere of oure fair langage' (*RP* 4978). Even though the portrait in the Rosenbach manuscript is a later copy, there are consistent visual features across all three portraits, a degree of similarity that suggests the role of *Regiment* manuscripts in shaping the iconographic representation of Chaucer. In each instance, the portrait takes up the width of the adjacent margin and its length spans multiple stanzas; the figure of Chaucer wears a dark grey robe, holds a rosary in one hand, and gestures at the written text with the other. The similarities in appearance indicate that those who copied the manuscript, those who created the portraits, and those who read Hoccleve's work likely shared expectations for an authorial appearance of Chaucer; the rosary echoes the sense of religious devotion that Hoccleve associates with seeing Chaucer's likeness in a book.[11]

By calling such portraits into being in his text, Hoccleve positions himself as an intermediary for readers to venerate Chaucer. The image of Chaucer validates Hoccleve's praise and helps realise the compelling impact of his curation – the call for illumination as a vehicle for the reader's remembrance. As the verses mention Chaucer's image, the image of Chaucer refers back to Hoccleve's verses, the very words that call the image and memory of Chaucer to the reader's mind. In the portrait in MS Harley 4866 (Figure 10.1), Chaucer's finger points at the precise stanza in which Hoccleve uses such terms as 'lyflyness', 'resemblance', and 'remembraunce', as if the portrait vividly acknowledges being mentioned in the verses themselves.[12] Hoccleve calls for an image of Chaucer in his poetry and anticipates its subsequent realisation on the page, and he therefore exploits codicological features to design a lively,

---

[10] A. S. G. Edwards discusses the possible eighteenth-century provenance of this portrait in 'The Chaucer Portraits in the Harley and Rosenbach Manuscripts', *English Manuscript Studies*, 4 (1993), 268–71.

[11] Helen Barr discusses wider implications and parallels of these Chaucer portraits in *Transporting Chaucer* (Manchester, 2014), pp. 112–15. Barr discusses the portrait in MS Harley 4866 in relation to the *Canterbury Tales* and to the portraits of pilgrims, including Chaucer as the storyteller, found in the Ellesmere Chaucer (San Marino, Huntington Library, MS EL 26 C 9).

[12] The similar portrait in Rosenbach Museum and Library MS 1083/30 also shows Chaucer's finger pointing at the text, but since the portrait does not appear adjacent to Hoccleve's mention of Chaucer's 'resemblance', the echo between text and image is lessened compared to the other two manuscripts.

resonant combination of text and image and represent his *maistir* to his readers. In a self-conscious move, he also draws attention to his own authorial position by placing himself as an evocative intermediary between readers and Chaucer's legacy of eloquence. Indeed, with the phrase 'I have heere his liknesse / Do make', he addresses readers as if he himself has the power to create and draw attention to the likeness of Chaucer for readers of the *Regiment*. If Chaucer is a saintly figure for readers to admire, then Hoccleve becomes an important intercessor, a self-proclaimed literary agent whose own verses authorise reverence and devotion through the luminescence of the page.[13]

The luminescent, formative capacity of the codex that we see in the *Regiment* becomes such a potent vehicle for Hoccleve to preserve Chaucer's memory that the removal of Chaucer's portrait reveals the reader's need for the juxtaposition of text and image. As Hoccleve himself anticipates when he eulogises Chaucer, the image forges an elevated, exalted connection between readers and the revered author. In London, British Library, MS Harley 4826, a *Regiment* manuscript produced in the second quarter of the fifteenth century (i.e. shortly after Hoccleve's death in 1426), a late fifteenth-century reader reacts angrily to the excision of a remarkable Chaucer portrait that appeared alongside the lines which compare viewing Chaucer's portrait to viewing images of holy figures in a church. The image would have run the entire vertical length of the page and occupied the entire outer margin, but it has been crudely cut out from the margins, with blotches of pigment visible at the edge of the cropped folio (Figure 10.2). In the bottom margin, adjacent to the excised image, this anonymous reader has written verses lamenting the loss:

Off worthy Chaucer
here the pickture stood
That much did wryght
and all to doo us good.
Summe furyous foole
have Cutt the Same in twayne
His deed doo shewe
He bare a barren Brayne[14]

---

[13] Sebastian Langdell discusses these passages from the *Regiment*, especially their presentation of the lifelike quality of the Chaucer portrait and its ability to generate moral authority, calling this portrait how 'Hoccleve packages his poetic approach in the form of an image': *Thomas Hoccleve: Religious Reform, Transnational Poetics, and the Invention of Chaucer* (Liverpool, 2018), pp. 116–23, at p. 123.

[14] London, British Library, MS Harley 4826, fol. 139r. According to the British Library Catalogue of Illuminated Manuscripts, the hand of the marginal verses is medieval, but several decades later than the date of the manuscript itself. The manuscript also contains a copy of Lydgate's *Life of St. Edmund and Fremund* and his translation of Aristotle's *Secreta Secretorum*. The *Regiment* ends imperfectly and is the last item in the manuscript. The transcription of the verses is taken from the Catalogue of Illuminated Manuscripts, http://www.bl.uk/catalogues/illuminatedmanuscripts/record.asp?MSID=8714&CollID=8&NStart=4826.

How þat dyuerse was mayden marie
And sir his loue floure ans sanctifie

Al þogh his lyfe be queynt þe resemblaunce
Of hym hath in me so fressh lyflynesse
þat to putte othir men in remembraunce
Of his persone I haue heere his lyknesse
Do make to þis ende in soothfastnesse
þat þei þat haue of hym left þought & mynde
By þis peynture may ageyn hym fynde

The ymages þat in þe chirche been
Maken folk þenke on god & on his seyntes
Whan þe ymages þei be holden & seen
Were oft vnsyte of hem canstith restreyntes
Of þoughtes gode Whan a þing depeynt is
Or entrailed if men take of it heede
Thoght of þe lyknesse it wul in hym brede

þit some holden oppynyon and sey
þat none ymages schuld y maked be
þei erren foule & goon out of þe wey
Of trouth haue þei scant sensibilite
Passe ovir þt now blessid trinite
Vppon my maistres soule mercy haue
ffor hym lady eke þu mercy craue

More othir þing wolde I fayne speke & touche
Heere in þis booke but osuuch is my dulnesse
ffor þat al voyde and empty is my pouche
þat al my lust is queynt wt heuynesse
And heuy spirit commaundeth stilnesse

Figure 10.1. London, British Library, MS Harley 4866, fol. 88r.
© The British Library Board.

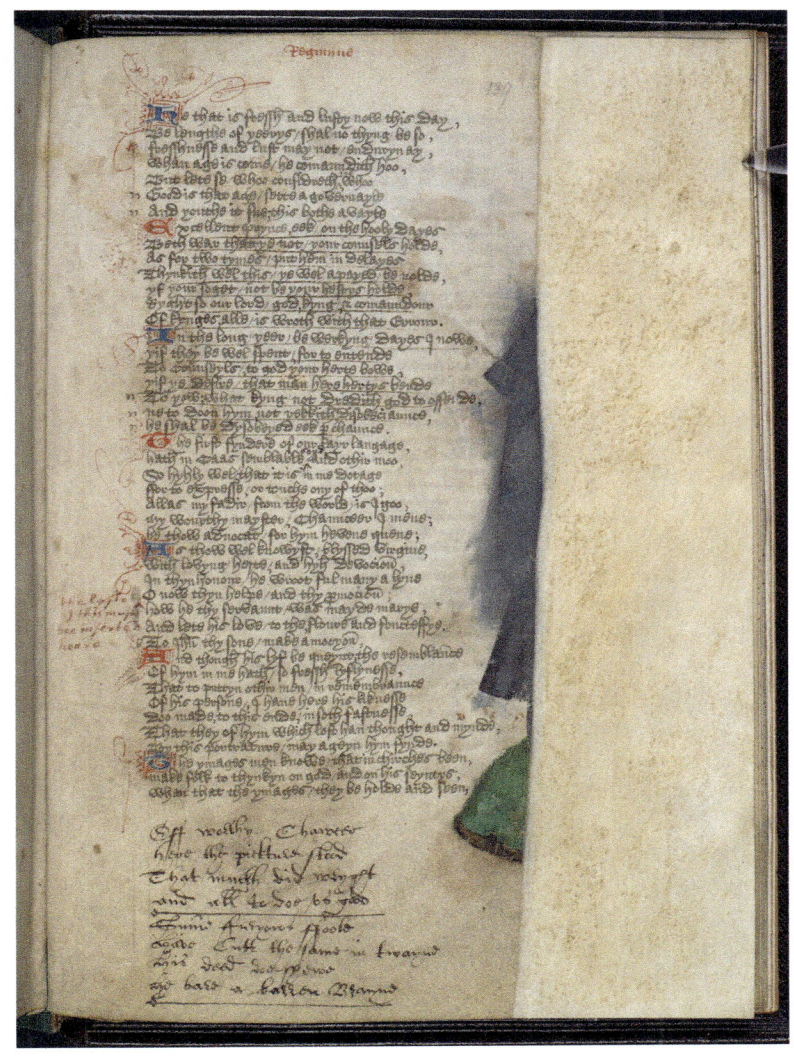

Figure 10.2. London, British Library, MS Harley 4826, fol. 139r.
© The British Library Board.

While these verses are simple, they bear witness to the sense of spiritual deprivation caused by the absence of Chaucer's image, the very 'unsighte' (*RP* 5002) to which Hoccleve refers in the *Regiment*. They associate Chaucer's own image with the ability of his writing to exert a beneficial influence on readers, and so the absence of the image amounts to the loss of this influence, to the 'restreyntes / Of thoghtes goode', such that the destruction of the portrait amounts to readers being denied Chaucer's goodness. This reader, whose late fifteenth-century hand suggests that the image was removed after the manuscript's production in the 1420s and before the end of the century, feels the absence of the image keenly and blames the 'furyous foole' for denying him access to the virtue and eloquence that Chaucer and his works represent. His frustration at the 'unsighte' of Chaucer lends support to Hoccleve's idea that readers desire meditative images as an aid for remembrance. Hoccleve specifies that both words and images are essential for readers to appreciate Chaucer's legacy, and he compares viewing an image of Chaucer in a book to viewing images of God or of saints in a church (*RP* 4999–5001). Both the textual and the iconographic representation of renowned authors help readers construct and retain their memory, and such images become a crucial platform through which Hoccleve performs memory and virtuous admiration for readers.

Hoccleve's efforts to preserve the memory of Chaucer therefore model a spiritual curation centred on a careful preservation and fashioning of Chaucer's image. In addition to reading words of praise, viewing images inclines readers towards remembrance and reverence. Hoccleve's own authorship then becomes predicated on his ability to deploy the features of the book in order to fulfil his duty to care for Chaucer's image and being. For Hoccleve, the visual aesthetics of medieval codices are essential vehicles for the maintenance of a writer's fame and renown. The tributes to Chaucer in the *Regiment* suggest that he associates the book with a sense of enduring brilliance and that he takes advantage of this sense in order to extol Chaucer and emphasise preserving the memory of his *maistir*. Furthermore, outside of the eulogising passages of the *Regiment*, Hoccleve's use of the word *enlumyne* in his wider corpus extends beyond these author portraits to encompass a wider range of decorative, illuminative features. By exploring Hoccleve's vocabulary of illumination more broadly, and by comparing the vocabulary of his fellow Middle English poets, we can set out a more comprehensive idea of codicological curation. The various pictorial elements of the manuscript page – decoration, illumination, and portraiture – combine to vivify the words of the author and generate spiritual, reverential significance.

Enlumyne has many attestations in Middle English in the late fourteenth and early fifteenth centuries and is a verb which can refer both literally to manuscript illumination, and, more figuratively, to spiritual or intellectual enlightenment, as well as to illustrious renown. In its most paradigmatic usage, Chaucer's paean to Petrarch describes him as the writer 'whos rethoryk swete / Enlumyned al Ytaille of poetrie' in the Prologue of the *Clerk's Tale*, and as Lois Ebin has argued, the close association among terms of illumination and rhetoric becomes a transformative 'critical ideal' for the poetic process of late medieval English writers.[15] Hoccleve's eulogies for Chaucer in the *Regiment* echo Chaucer's praise of Petrarch but, as we have seen, Hoccleve envisions Chaucer's writings situated in a specifically codicological setting, with Chaucer's words not simply distinguished by their rhetoric but forming visual and semantic relationships with illustrations and other features of the manuscript page. Hoccleve treats Chaucer's 'ornat endytyng' as the particular source for the 'enlumynyng' and thereby suggests that the light of Chaucer's eloquence emanates from the books themselves – that readers appreciate Chaucer's literary virtues through luminescent decoration and illustration.

Hoccleve's Marian devotional poems, directed as they are to a holy figure, provide further insight into the relationship between spiritual and codicological illumination. Their more explicitly religious purpose heightens the spiritual significance of such terms as *enlumyne*, especially the ideas of exaltation and sanctuary that the luminescence of books can impart. Several short lyrics offer meditations on the virtues and the suffering of the Virgin Mary, and some of these show a simultaneously visual and spiritual apprehension of light, facilitated by a sense of curation similar to the Chaucer passages in the *Regiment*. In one such poem, we find that Hoccleve uses *enlumyne* in both codicological and devotional contexts, referring to the divine, virtuous light embodied by the Virgin Mary:

> So that the wil fulfild be of thy sone,
> And that of the holy goost he menlumyne.
> Preye for vs, as ay hath be thy wone!
> Lady alle swiche emprises been thyne.
> Swich an aduocatrice, who can dyuyne,
> As thow right noon our greeues to redresse:
> In thy refuyt is al our sikirnesse.[16]

The word *menlumyne* is a form of *enlumyne* with an elided first-person object pronoun (i.e. 'me') attached; it refers to the light of the Holy Spirit ('holy goost') shining on the speaker. The light offers a direct connection with the Holy Spirit and thus creates the possibility of spiritual exaltation, even salvation. Later in the stanza, Hoccleve links this sense of illumination with

---

[15] *Riverside Chaucer*, p. 137 (CT IV.32–3). See Lois Ebin, *Illuminator, Makar, Vates: Visions of Poetry in the Fifteenth Century* (Lincoln, NE, 1988), pp. 3 and 20–3.

[16] The poem is headed by the rubric 'Ad beatam Virginem' in San Marino, Huntington Library, MS HM 111. It appears on fols 34r–6v. See Furnivall and Gollancz (eds), *Hoccleve's Works*, pp. 52–6. MS HM 111 is available as a digital facsimile via the Huntington Digital Library (http://hdl.huntington.org/), and in the EETS monochrome facsimile (Burrow and Doyle (eds), *Facsimile*).

a sanctuary-like sense of 'sikirnesse', that is, the spiritual safekeeping of those upon whom the divine light shines.[17] The half-line, 'our greeues to redresse', even identifies the means – spiritual consolation – by which the effects of illumination are conferred to readers.

When read alongside the *Regiment*, the nuanced connotations of the word *enlumyne* on display in Hoccleve's Marian poetry situate illumination at the intersection of literary reputation and spiritual integrity as a positive and enlightening heuristic. The redemptive potential of illumination in Hoccleve's Marian devotional poem suggests that his concept of curation, as expressed in the *Regiment*'s Chaucer eulogies, effectively transcends the mortal life of an author and confers spiritual protection on readers long beyond the author's death. Hoccleve's curation thus combines literary and divine virtues and echoes a broader medieval tradition of the reflective use of books as an act of memorialisation.[18] It endeavours to use the features of the medieval book to safeguard an author's memory – rooted in the medieval book's visual, luminescent properties – and make its virtuous spiritual benefits accessible to readers beyond the author's mortal lifetime.

This connection between the codicological and the spiritual is also invoked when Hoccleve's late medieval contemporaries, especially those of the early fifteenth century, use the term *enlumyne*. According to the *Middle English Dictionary*, the first attested uses of *enluminen* in English in relation to manuscript books appear in John Lydgate's *Fall of Princes* and in an epistolary poem written by Benedict Burgh to Lydgate, both of which date to the 1430s.[19] In the *Fall of Princes*, Lydgate describes the posthumous fame of the Roman consul Marcus Manlius:

> And for he was so victorious,
> Hymsilff allone be this hih victorye,
> This name he gat to hym & al his hous,

---

[17] *MED* 'sikernesse'. The term's meanings are complicated. It can mean certainty and security of one's physical person, as well as a spiritual sense of safety, that is, freedom from anxiety and temptation.

[18] For discussions of the broader tradition of such memorialisation, see Jesse Gellrich, *The Idea of the Book in the Middle Ages: Language Theory, Mythology, and Fiction* (Ithaca, 1985), pp. 170–7, in particular the case study based on Chaucer's *House of Fame*. Mary Carruthers also explores the close relationships between memory and the visual and physical form of books in *The Book of Memory: A Study of Memory in Medieval Culture* (Cambridge, 2008).

[19] See quotations in *MED*, entry for *enluminen*. In the case of Burgh, the relevant verses contain concepts similar to that of Lydgate, although he explicitly links *enluminen* with the medieval codex by using the phrase 'thenlumynyd boke'. It appears in London, British Library, Additional MS 29729. A published edition is available in E. P. Hammond, *English Verse between Chaucer and Surrey* (Durham, NC, 1927), pp. 189–90. The full passage is: 'thowghe they be go yet the wordis be not dede / thenlumynyd boke where in a man shall rede / thes and mo be in this londe legeble / ye be the same ye be the goldyn bible' (at p. 180, lines 25–8).

> Perpetueli to be in memorye
> And registred in the consistorie,
> In ther cronicles his name determyned,
> With goldene lettres to been enlumyned.[20]

In the last two lines of the stanza, Lydgate refers to illuminated initials ('goldene lettres') and associates their luminousness with helping to safeguard the memory of Marcus Manlius's victory. Specifically, the golden letters represent the physical form in which his name becomes 'registred' and 'determyned' – put in the form of a written record, able to be read by future readers long after his death. Lydgate effectively attributes the liveliness of heroic deeds to the codicological setting of a written work in much the same way that Hoccleve relies on Chaucer's portrait appearing on the page as a safeguard for the dead author's memory. Moreover, Lydgate also evokes the power of manuscript illumination to defy death through the permanence of its luminescent visuals. The gold letters grant a lasting presence to the words and enable them and their author to become 'unslayn', just as Hoccleve declares with regard to encountering Chaucer's image in the *Regiment*. The sensory apprehension of light and the visual salience of the written, decorated word sustain the reader's memory of deceased figures and facilitate remembrance. Lydgate's use of the word *enluminen* refers more directly to the codicological context that we see in Hoccleve's tributes to Chaucer, and it identifies the manuscript codex, specifically its ability to project a luminescent dimension, as the agent of transformation. Hoccleve and Lydgate's ideas about the book transform gold lettering, portraiture, and other features into a living presence, standing in for those who lived in the past and facilitating access to virtuous thoughts. That Chaucer's eloquence and Marcus Manlius's military prowess are celebrated in similar manners suggests that curatorial codicology enables the worship of virtues, of equivalence between great literary deeds and deeds of heroic renown.

Read in the wider context of his own works and those of his contemporaries, usage of the term *enlumyne* reveals the extent to which Hoccleve conceives of images, likenesses, and their properties in a devotional manner. A second Marian poem more explicitly affirms the spiritual benefits illumination can confer. In this instance, Hoccleve uses *enlumyne* in relation to the spread of divine grace:

> Euene as the moone a mene is verraily
> Betwixt vs and the sonne of whom hir light
> Shee takith & it vniuerselly
> Yeueth vn-to the world whan it is nyght;
> In swich a wyse god, thy sone right,
> The light of grace betook vn-to thee,

---

[20] *Lydgate's Fall of Princes*, ed. Henry Bergen, EETS ES 121–4 (4 vols, London, 1924–27), vol. 2, p. 483 (Book IV, lines 358–64).

For to mynistre it vn-to euery wight
That ther-of list enlumyned to be.[21]

These lines highlight the universality of divine light by saying that it can be given to 'the world' and to all people ('mynistre it vn-to euery wight') who wish to have it. They do so by making comparison to the illumination provided by the sun and the moon as a metaphor for lasting, universal light. Such a comparison lends a greater sense of permanence to *enlumyne*, and, when combined subsequently with the idea that grace should reach everyone, these lines suggest that lasting illumination serves as the vehicle for spiritual benefits. Illumination is to be desired because it inclines people towards good, because it becomes the lasting means by which divine grace becomes widely spread. In this Marian poem, we therefore see the full extent of Hoccleve's curation. This process of posthumous care encompasses book illumination, spiritual benefit, and divine grace, the three qualities being mutually informing and reinforcing. Reading a book and seeing its luminescent illumination and decoration affords readers access to virtuous edification, facilitated by the writerly pastoral care of Hoccleve.

Hoccleve's curation transforms the medieval book, with its luminescent and revivifying capacities, into an embodiment of eternal presence that can take on the grace of divine light. In the Marian poem that compares illumination to the light of the sun and the moon, the universality and ameliorative qualities of divine light recall the way that Hoccleve imagines that the light of Chaucer's eloquence shines upon 'al this land' (1974), and echo the images in church that make 'folk thynke on God and on his seintes' (5000) in the *Regiment*. Generated by illustrations and illuminated lettering, the light emanating from medieval books is therefore desirable not only for the spiritual benefits that it bestows on readers but also for its widespread promulgation. Such figurations invoke many of the processes involved in medieval book production and focus on the visual impact of codices – illuminated, decorated or coloured letters, pictures, ruling, and spatial organisation on the page. As deployed by Hoccleve, the book's decorative, pictorial features become points of access for readers to appreciate the deeds and virtues of deceased authors. The universality of light as a medium thus underpins Hoccleve's curation because it draws the different meanings of *enluminen* into productive resonance with each other. Both medieval books and divine grace rely on promulgation through light, and with light as the medium, they attain a universal audience, whether in terms of readership or of the recipients of grace. Throughout Hoccleve's oeuvre, the term embodies the simultaneous physicality and spirituality of the medieval book. While light itself is not a codicological feature, features of book design such as script, colour, decoration, and illumination benefit from

---

[21] Furnivall and Gollancz (eds), *Hoccleve's Works*, pp. 43–7, at p. 46. This poem appears in San Marino, Huntington Library, HM 111, on fols 28v–30v.

the association with the elevating, positive qualities of spiritual devotion; likewise, illuminating spiritual practices benefited from the glowing visual features associated with medieval books.

Hoccleve knew that his works – the *Regiment*, his Marian devotional poetry, as well as his other writing – would end up being written in and transmitted through manuscript codices. How might his awareness of the revivifying capacity of the codex be reflected in his works, specifically in the collections of verse in each of his three autograph manuscripts? While these manuscripts do not have illustrations or lavish decoration, they contain portions from the autographical *Series* and poems dedicated to specific people in the aristocratic and bureaucratic circles familiar to Hoccleve. Bearing in mind the curatorial qualities that Hoccleve associates with books, the compilations of poems in the autograph manuscripts have, at least, a personal significance and a sense of self-curation, especially since they date towards the end of Hoccleve's life. In light of Hoccleve's concern that readers should be able to remember Chaucer by the books that contain his works, we might consider how Hoccleve would want readers of his autograph manuscripts to remember him – how he deploys curatorial codicology with regard to his own literary aspirations.

11

Reading Through: *Major/Minor Hoccleve*

Sebastian J. Langdell

In his final years, Thomas Hoccleve compiled the two manuscripts of his shorter poems now housed at the Huntington Library in San Marino, California: MSS HM 111 and 744. The manuscripts evince a conservative impulse, an effort to preserve a range of material composed over Hoccleve's lifetime. Of the twenty-nine pieces included therein, only nine survive in other manuscripts from the period.[1] The earliest firmly datable poem in the manuscripts is *L'epistre de Cupide*, recorded, within the poem, as having been written in May 1402.[2] Another piece, Hoccleve's translation and adaptation of the *ars moriendi* chapter from Henry Suso's *Horologium sapientiae*, is also found in Hoccleve's *Series*, completed between 1421 and 1426.[3] The Huntington holographs follow a trend put in place by Hoccleve's predecessor Chaucer with his own *Canterbury Tales* collection: the use of one's final years to gather up the leaves of a life's work, offer whatever order is possible, and send them into the world.[4]

---

[1] For a list of the contents and their non-autograph witnesses, see Burrow and Doyle (eds), *Facsimile*, pp. xii–xvii. See also J. A. Burrow, *Thomas Hoccleve* (Aldershot, 1994), pp. 52–4. Only nine stanzas of the *Male Regle* are preserved in another manuscript: these stanzas comprise a moral ballad in Canterbury Cathedral Archives, Register O.

[2] See the poem's final stanza.

[3] Burrow posits that a draft of the 'Complaint' and 'Dialogue' would have been complete by May 1421: Burrow (ed.), *Complaint and Dialogue*, p. lix. He is less certain about the dating of the other three pieces in the *Series*, but notes elsewhere (with Doyle) that the Durham *Series* was written between 1422 and 1426: *Facsimile*, p. xx.

[4] The last part of that process is no doubt the most complex. Derek Pearsall informs us that the *Canterbury Tales* most likely existed in scattered papers at the time of Chaucer's death; it was then left up to a team of scribes and editors to determine the appropriate order of the tales and send them forth: *Life of Geoffrey Chaucer: A Critical Biography* (Oxford, 1992), p. 233. On Hoccleve's potential role in compiling the *Tales*, see Simon Horobin, 'Thomas Hoccleve: Chaucer's First Editor?', *Chaucer Review*, 50 (2015), 228–50. It is also not immediately clear for whom Hoccleve created each of the Huntington manuscripts – what the 'sending forth' entailed. And while Chaucer's *Canterbury Tales* collection is likely not as 'life-ranging' as Hoccleve's, it does include tales that circulated before the project commenced.

The contents themselves are truly various. While thematic connections do sometimes occur – such as between the first six items in HM 744, all religious poems, the first three of which are invocations in turn to God, Christ, and the Holy Spirit – there is no overarching narrative, and little by way of transitions between texts. In the same four-year span that Hoccleve was compiling the Huntington holographs (1422–26), he was also at work on the Durham *Series* and his Formulary.[5] The latter is a book of forms intended for the use of future scribes in the office of the Privy Seal. The Huntington holographs give a similar impression to the Formulary: they serve as a collection of poetic forms, exhibiting the writer's expertise in a variety of modes, from petitionary verse to poems of Marian devotion, *ars moriendi*, Cupid poetry, *envoi*, autobiographical verse, admonitions against heresy, and dedicatory verses.[6]

The collections also raise the question of how Hoccleve's poems, long and short, 'major' and 'minor', work in parallel.[7] Reading Hoccleve's shorter poems alongside his two longer works presents the reader with an opportunity to consider how a certain rhetorical strategy or narrative approach is reimagined in a different situation, or how a given word, even, can be transplanted from one rhetorical environment into another. While Hoccleve's two longer works – the *Regiment of Princes* and the *Series* – are rich enough to study on their own, they are not, of course, his only works; and often overmuch focus on one of these poems, treated in isolation, gives the reader a limited sense of what Hoccleve achieves in his work. To omit Hoccleve's shorter poems from the conversation is to severely limit the spectrum upon which the reader engages Hoccleve. Reaching outside the major poems, and into Hoccleve's shorter verse, illuminates how language functions in those

[5]   Durham, University Library, MS Cosin V. III. 9, and London, British Library, MS Additional 24062. For the dating of these manuscripts (and the Huntington manuscripts), see Burrow and Doyle (eds), *Facsimile*, pp. xx–xxi; and Burrow, *Thomas Hoccleve*, p. 26.

[6]   See also my discussion in *Thomas Hoccleve: Religious Reform, Transnational Poetics, and the Invention of Chaucer* (Liverpool, 2018), pp. 176–7.

[7]   I place 'major' and 'minor' in quotation marks to reflect on a tradition of labelling certain Hoccleve poems 'major' or 'minor'. The shorter poems in the Huntington manuscripts were edited by Furnivall and Gollancz as 'the minor poems' (*Hoccleve's Works*). The *Series* appears in this edition as 'Poems. The Durham MS.', following the poems in HM 111 and *L'epistre de Cupide*. Roger Ellis's edition ('*My Compleinte*') includes six of Hoccleve's shorter poems under the heading 'Minor Verse'; whereas, the *Series* appears under its own heading – 'The Series' – suggesting that it is 'non-minor verse'. This, indeed, mirrors a more recent critical tendency to treat the *Series* as a major work, worthy of attention on its own. David Watt's book-length study, *The Making of Thomas Hoccleve's Series* (Liverpool, 2013), is a fine example of this. We should also remember that the *Series* travels alongside the *Regiment* in all five non-autograph copies, suggesting that early editors (and perhaps even Hoccleve himself) saw the two works as complementary, or at least as two longer works that deserve to be read side-by-side.

longer works – how specific virtuosic presentations are not 'one-off' productions, but rather exist in continuity with earlier and later efforts.

Such an examination also sheds light on the religious and sacramental resonances at play in even seemingly secular presentations. The ability to read between the major and minor poems opens up religious valences in works that are often lauded for their seemingly secular accomplishments: this is the case, as I will demonstrate, with *L'epistre de Cupide*, the 'Chaucer' figure in Hoccleve's *Regiment*, and the Hoccleve-Prince dynamic in the *Regiment*. Critics have sometimes assigned Hoccleve's more overtly religious poems to the beginning of his career, presupposing that an early investment in Christianity (in sync with early priestly training) gave way to more 'secular' productions.[8] But datable religious poems indicate a lifelong engagement with Marian devotion, ecclesiastical commentary, and verse prayer and meditation.[9] Reading *through* the longer poems, into the shorter verse, indicates how even the most seemingly secular production can be sacramentally infused. Such investigations not only better illuminate the longer poems, they also affect how we see Hoccleve himself; and they allow us to better situate the 'Hoccleve' persona, to reconsider the line between fictive persona and historical person.

In order to demonstrate the usefulness of reading across the major/minor divide, I will first examine intermixtures of divine and human identity between the shorter poems and the *Regiment of Princes*, before moving on to the role of reading (within a moral context) in *L'epistre de Cupide* and the *Series*. I will then examine the role of death and 'lyflynesse' between the shorter poems, the *Regiment*, and the *Series*; and will close by considering the role of images – including the 'Hoccleve' image – in Hoccleve's shorter poems and the *Series*.

Of Gods and Men

Among the more random ingredients in the Huntington holographs – and among those that make the case for the 'book of forms' reading of the manuscripts – is the *envoi* to Hoccleve's longest and most popular poem, the *Regiment of Princes*.[10] The *envoi* serves as a useful entry point for our explo-

---

[8] See M. C. Seymour, *Selections from Hoccleve* (Oxford, 1981), pp. xv–xvi. Burrow gives the undated religious poems a 'neutral position' at the middle of Hoccleve's career (*Thomas Hoccleve*, p. 11).

[9] Hoccleve's engagement with ecclesiastical commentary is evident in 'To Sir John Oldcastle', for instance. The 'Complaint' and the Suso treatise both evidence a late interest in vernacular theology, prayer, and meditation. The assembling of the Huntington manuscripts, furthermore, indicates a late interest in preserving a range of his devotional verse, including a range of poems of Marian devotion.

[10] The *Regiment* survives in forty-three manuscripts, indicating a significant level of

rations in that it proceeds directly from Hoccleve's most 'major' work, and yet it exists in the Huntington holographs in a different form, as a different poem. The changes that Hoccleve sees fit to make to the *envoi* underscore Hoccleve's emphasis, within the body of the *Regiment*, on clarifying the limits of the prince's power, and on the prince's necessary deference to his own 'kyng and commaundour' (*RP* 4969), God. As I will show, the *envoi* also serves as a route into contemplating a particularly Hocclevian rhetorical strategy: the 'delayed signified'. This rhetorical technique allows Hoccleve to play with the space between gods and men; it indicates his agility in manoeuvring between apotheosis, playfulness, and bold critique.

The *envoi* in question – Hoccleve's revision to the *Regiment envoi* – is found towards the end of HM 111, lodged between a petitionary verse (with ending *chanceon*) to Henry Somer and another petitionary verse to Henry V. The rubric for the *envoi* informs us that the 'balade ensuyante' was placed at the end of the 'liure del Regiment des Princes', thereby linking this miscellany to Hoccleve's popular (and well-received) long poem, the *Regiment of Princes*. In the poem immediately preceding the *envoi*, Hoccleve introduces his name into the collection for the second time (see line 25), and the connection here between the personal signifier and his single most apparent claim to literary fame serves as something of an early signature to the collection as a whole.[11]

More striking, however, are the changes made to the *envoi* in question: three key changes in the final stanza, which are not present in any other surviving manuscript of the *Regiment*. Here is the final stanza of the *envoi* (and, therefore, the final stanza of the entire *Regiment*) as it appears in London, British Library, MS Arundel 38, one of the two earliest and most authoritative copies of the poem, and representative of most non-autograph copies of the *envoi*:

> Byseeche him, of his gracious noblesse,
> Thee holde excusid of thyn innocence
> Of endytynge, and with hertes meeknesse,
> If anythyng thee passe of negligence,
> Byseeche him of mercy and indulgence,
> And that for thy good herte he be nat fo

---

popularity. The *Series*, by contrast, survives in full in only six manuscripts: Burrow, *Thomas Hoccleve*, pp. 50–1. As a point of comparison with the *Regiment*'s popularity, consider that the *Canterbury Tales* exists in its complete (or near-complete) form in fifty-five manuscripts (Pearsall, *Life of Geoffrey Chaucer*, p. 231).

[11] Hoccleve also names himself in the *Male Regle* (351), the third item in HM 111. His name is also in the introductory rubric for that poem: 'Cy ensuyt la male regle de T. Hoccleue'. His name appears in one item in HM 744, the playful 'trois chaunceons' that come immediately before Hoccleve's Suso translation. He uses his name three times in the *Regiment* (1864, 1865 and 4360); and also uses 'Hoccleve' (*D* 3) – though much more commonly 'Thomas' – in the *Series*.

To thee, that al seist of loues fervence.
That knowith he whom nothyng is hid fro. (5456–63)[12]

And here is the stanza, revisited and revised, in HM 111:

Byseeche him, of his gracious noblesse,
Thee holde excusid of thyn innocence
Of endytynge, and with hertes *humblesse*,
If anythyng thee passe of negligence,
Byseeche him of mercy and indulgence,
And þat for thy good *wil* he be nat fo
To thee, þat al seist of loues feruence.
Þat knowith *God*, whom nothyng is hid fro. (17–24; my emphasis)

The italicised words are those that Hoccleve saw fit to change upon revisiting the *envoi*, over a decade after its initial composition.[13] 'Humblesse'
provides alliteration in the given line, and also offers a more directly
virtuous term for 'humility'.[14] The substitution of 'wil' for 'herte' suggests
a degree of agency for the poem itself.[15] The final change, however, is by
far the most telling: the substitution of 'God' for the initial 'he' resolves a
meaningful ambiguity. In the stanza, Hoccleve asks his poem to beseech
Prince Henry to not be a 'fo'; after all, as Hoccleve says, his poem says
everything out 'of loues feruence'. The final 'he' presents a meaningful
tension: our minds have been trained to align 'he' with 'Prince', and
the omniscience suggested in the final line would, by then, easily align
with the prince.[16] The fact that we must pause to reflect on just who this
omniscient 'he' is, and how far removed he is, in fact, from a mere human,
pivots the meaning of the very address: in the end, it does not matter if
the prince (dead after August 1422) is 'foe' to the *Regiment*, or whether or
not he understands that the poem 'seist al of loues feruence', i.e. that even
the attempts at advice and critique are well-meant. The prince may not
know. God knows.

Hoccleve's choice to substitute 'God' for 'he' in this late-period revision
draws attention to the ambiguity with which he had originally imbued
the pronoun. But it also echoes a particularly Hocclevian *modus operandi*.
This *envoi* – a different poem in HM 111, interacting with the *Regiment* in
a different way – channels the same playful (and instructive) muddling of
the divine and human that Hoccleve entertains throughout his work. To

---

[12] I also consider Hoccleve's changes to this *envoi* in *Thomas Hoccleve*, pp. 180–1.
[13] As Blyth notes in his edition, these changes are unique to the HM 111 version of the *envoi*; no *Regiment* manuscripts include these variants (p. 252).
[14] Where 'meeknesse' and 'humblesse' can both mean humility, 'meeknesse' can also mean 'wretched state, affliction', 'shame', and 'timidity': MED 'humblesse' and 'meknesse'.
[15] Hoccleve would seem to use 'wil' for 'intention' here: MED 'wille', 5a.
[16] The prince is channelled throughout the *envoi* as the clear source of power: 'his hynesse' (12), 'his magnificence' (15), 'his gracious noblesse' (17).

read through the contents of the Huntington holographs is to witness the range of gods and god-like men in Hoccleve's universe. There is the pagan god Cupid in *L'epistre de Cupide*; the 'earthly god' Health in the *Male Regle*; Lady Money in the 'trois chaunceons'; the very real God and Christ in multiple religious poems; and Sapience – divine wisdom – in Hoccleve's Suso. The Hoccleve narrator is often in a position to beg or plead, and from that vantage point, so many people appear god-like: kings, princes, patrons, noblemen who owe Hoccleve (and his associates) money. But then there is the reminder, pitched gently in the *Regiment envoi*: for all the imaginings of playful pagan gods, for all the financial and martial prowess wielded, only God is omnipotent; and each man ultimately answers to God.

Hoccleve indicates as much in the *Regiment* itself when, just before the Chaucer-portrait presentation stanzas, he asks the prince to avoid holding councils on holy days. In one of the boldest and most direct moments in the *Regiment*, Hoccleve takes the prince to task, and he is ready to remind the prince of his answerability to (and necessary deference to) his own 'kyng and commandour', God:

> Thynkith wel this: yee wel apaid be nolde
> If your soget nat by youre heestes tolde.
> Right so our lord God, kyng and commaundour
> Of kynges alle, is wrooth with that errour.
>
> In the long yeer been werk-dayes ynowe,
> If they be wel despent for to entende
> To conseiles. To God your herte bowe
> If yee desyre men hir hertes bende
> To yow. What kyng nat dredith God offende
> Ne nat rekkith do him disobeissance,
> He shal be disobeied eek, par chance. (4967–77)

I have discussed these stanzas elsewhere in the light of a contemporaneous poem, the *Crowned King*, in which an anonymous petitioner addresses Henry V on behalf of the people, and reminds the king of his answerability to that other, mightier crowned king, Christ. While Hoccleve wields this reminder sparingly, he nonetheless wields it.[17] And it is echoed in the final lines of his *envoi*: in the final line of a poem addressed to the prince, counselling the prince, imagining the prince's rise to ultimate (secular) power, Hoccleve positions God – not the prince – as the ultimate reader and interpreter of his poem.

Hoccleve's shift from 'he' to 'God' in this late revision plays out like an extended version of a rhetorical trope he exercises elsewhere: the delayed signified. The opening stanza of Hoccleve's *Male Regle* offers an early rendition of this, in which the series of superlatives end up not referring to God or Christ (as one might think), but rather to an 'earthly god', Health:

---

[17] See Langdell, *Thomas Hoccleve*, pp. 118–19.

O precious tresor inconparable,
O ground and roote of prosperitee,
O excellent richesse commendable,
Abouen alle þat in eerthe be,
Who may susteene thyn aduersitee?
What wight may him auante of worldly welthe
But if he fully stande in grace of thee,
Eerthely god, piler of lyf, thow Helthe? (1–8)

One can imagine the poem being performed aloud, with the superlatives inviting a certain interpretation, and then surprising the listener with the entrance of this 'earthly god' named Health. The trope would seem to have drawn its inspiration from Chaucer, and his similar playfulness in *Troilus and Criseyde*, as the pagan Pandarus momentarily seems to lapse into monotheism, before catching himself and clarifying what he means:

Fil Pandarus on knees, and up his eyen
To heven threw, and held his hondes highe:
'Immortal god,' quod he, 'that mayst nought deyen,
Cupide I mene, of this mayst glorifie;
And Venus, thow mayst maken melodie!' (III.183–7; my emphasis)

The 'Cupide, I mene' comes across as tongue-in-cheek, sportily winking at the fourteenth-century Christian reader and clarifying that the 'immortal god' in question is in fact the pagan god, Cupid.[18] Chaucer then adds Venus for good measure, indicating the polytheistic landscape of his fiction. Hoccleve uses the delayed signified to refer to Chaucer himself in the *Regiment*, referring to the poet first, obliquely, as 'the first fyndere of our fair langage', then as 'my fadir', and then finally clarifying:

The first fyndere of our fair langage
Hath seid, in cas semblable, and othir mo,
So hyly wel that it is my dotage
For to expresse or touche any of tho.
Allas, my fadir fro the world is go,
My worthy maistir Chaucer – him I meene [...] (4978–83)[19]

The 'tacking on' of a signified, after the build-up of an entire stanza, offers a pleasing sense of resolution. But this otherwise playful rhetorical strategy

---

[18] Hoccleve activates the same winking tone when, in *L'epistre de Cupide*, he interjects, in the voice of Cupid, that St Margaret should not be considered commendable for her virginity, because – after all – Cupid speaks on behalf of lovers, and as such he battles the defenders of chastity: 'But vndirstondith, we commende hir noght / By encheson of hir virginitee. / Trustith right wel, it cam nat in our thoght, / For ay we werreie ageyn chastitee' (428–31). Here too is the intermixture of Christian and pagan delightfully foregrounded, then comically corrected.

[19] I also entertain this stanza alongside the *Troilus* stanza – albeit in the context of Langlandian voice, religious reform, and counsel – in *Thomas Hoccleve*, pp. 120–1.

can also turn serious. In the earlier rendition of the *Regiment envoi*, the disembodied signifier 'he' presented in the reader's mind a search for a signified that unravels the distance between *any* man and the Divine. This is remedied in HM 111 with the ultimate delayed signified, and with it an end to ambiguity: *God*, I mean.

While such wordplay (and word-change) may seem relatively minor, these lexical dynamics evince the ways in which Hoccleve exercises power in his writing. A writer once known mostly for his 'meekness' and insecurity might be seen, in another light, to wield equal amounts of heart and humility, agency and will.[20]

Reading Through: The *Series* and *L'epistre de Cupide*

Hoccleve's *Series* is notable for two 'major/minor' crossovers. The first of these is the presence of Hoccleve's Suso translation, in different forms, in the *Series* and the Huntington holographs. In the *Series*, the treatise is integrated into the longer work: Hoccleve speaks of his intention to translate it in the 'Dialogue', and it appears in full after the first *Gesta* tale. In HM 744, by contrast, it exists on its own, as a 'shorter' poem, a minor piece. The other major/minor crossover is the Friend's reference to Hoccleve's short poem *L'epistre de Cupide* towards the end of the 'Dialogue' section of the *Series*. *L'epistre*, a translation and adaptation of Christine de Pizan's *Epistre au dieu d'amours* (1399), is dated May 1402. It is found in HM 744 after six religious poems, and is separated from the last piece in HM 744 – the Suso treatise – by only two short poems: five stanzas addressed to Henry V, and Hoccleve's 'trois chaunceons', involving a light-hearted rally with Lady Money. The *L'epistre* remark in the *Series* is the only time that Hoccleve refers to one of his shorter poems within one of his two longer poems.[21] Moreover, it is notable that the reference *is* to a shorter poem – written some two decades before – and not to Hoccleve's most popular (and more recent) work, the *Regiment*.[22] While there are implicit invitations to compare shorter texts with longer ones in Hoccleve's

---

[20] Furnivall characterised Hoccleve as a 'weak, sensitive, look-on-the-worst side kind of man' (*Hoccleve's Works*, p. xxxviii).

[21] The only exception here is the reference to the (impending) Suso translation within the 'Dialogue' section of the *Series*, but the reference here is of course not to the version in HM 744.

[22] It is important to remember, however, that, judging by manuscript count, *L'epistre* was the most popular among Hoccleve's shorter poems, surviving in ten manuscripts beyond HM 744. The *Series*, by contrast, survives in its entirety in only six manuscripts. (The 'Conpleynte paramont' also survives in ten non-autograph manuscripts, but is not treated therein as a stand-alone text, nor as Hocclevian.) As noted above, the *Series* is collected with the *Regiment* in all five non-autograph copies; if Hoccleve had intended for this to be the case, then a reference to *L'epistre* would link his most popular shorter poem to his most popular longer poem, through the medium of the *Series*.

oeuvre – such as the reprisal of various Hoccleve narrators between the *Male Regle*, the *Regiment*, and the *Series*; or the two *Regiment envois* entertained above – this is the sole explicit invitation to cross-reference. As I shall demonstrate, following Hoccleve's advice and revisiting *L'epistre* in HM 744, in the context of the *Series*, not only absolves him of the guilt that the Friend claims for him in the 'Dialogue'; it also complicates and underscores the devotional contexts of the *Series*. Reading *L'epistre* through the *Series* boosts Christian-devotional elements of both texts: the importance of Marian devotion to *L'epistre*, and the often complex interweavings of vice and virtue in the *Series*.

The reference to *L'epistre* arrives as Hoccleve and his Friend cast about for ideas for what to write to fulfil a commission for Duke Humphrey. The Friend suggests that Hoccleve write something to atone for past misbehaviour, namely his textual mistreatment of women. When Hoccleve notes that he is not guilty of such an offence, the Friend offers *L'epistre* as evidence:

> 'Freend, hard it is wommen to greeue, I grante,
> But what haue I agilt, for him þat dyde?
> Nat haue I doon why, dar I me auante,
> Out of wommennes graces slippe or slyde.'
> 'Yis, Thomas, yis, in th'epistle of *Cupyde*
> Thow haast of hem so largeliche said
> That they been swart wrooth and ful euele apaid.'
> (*D* 750–6; my emphasis)

In response, Hoccleve first notes – *à la* Chaucer in the Prologue to the *Legend of Good Women* (*LGW* G460–1, 525–45) – that he was 'noon auctour' in that poem, but only 'a reportour / Of folkes tales' (*D* 760–2). He then seems to remember that the work itself is not actually guilty of the offence named. After Hoccleve pushes the point, a humorous exchange ensues in which the Friend admits to never having read *L'epistre* (or at least, to not having read it to the end), and Hoccleve advises his Friend that the poem does indeed end well for women:

> Looke in the same book. What stikith by?
> Whoso lookith aright therin may see
> Þat they me oghten haue in greet cheertee,
>
> And elles woot I neuere what is what.
> 'The book concludith for hem, is no nay,
> Vertuously, my good freend, dooth it nat?'
> 'Thomas, I noot, for neuere it yit I say.'
> 'No, freend?' 'No, Thomas.' 'Wel trowe I, in fay,
> For had yee red it fully to the ende,
> Yee wolde seyn it is nat as yee wende.' (*D* 775–84)

The close reader is quickly rewarded for returning to the poem in question, and for reading it 'fully to the ende', as Hoccleve recommends. *L'epistre* serves as an implicit meditation on the practice of grouping people, texts, and deeds into binary (and seemingly clear-cut) categories of 'vice' and 'virtue'. An initial discussion of vice and virtue entertained along gender lines (male vice versus female virtue) turns, around line 351, from literary/political examples to biblical/religious ones.[23] A defence of Eve (351–420) gives way to a commendation of St Margaret (421–34), then to praise for Jesus's loyal female companions (435–48).[24]

In Hoccleve's hands, the discussion bends devotional: the playful premise of a pagan love god (Cupid) criticising male misbehaviour becomes a preface to a consideration of the place of women in biblical history. Eve's so-called sin was 'happy to mankynde' (393) in that it cleared the path for Christ's eventual coming – that is, God's descent in human form:

> God, to descharge mankynde of the weighte
> Of his [the devil's] trespas, cam doun from heuenes heighte,
> And flessh and blood he took of a virgyne,
> And souffred deeth, man to deliure of pyne. (396–9)[25]

Eve's actions are then tied not only to Christ's birth, but also to Christ's mother. Hoccleve argues that God would not have chosen to be born through Mary unless she herself was devoid of sin, and he uses phrasing that will now resonate anew:

> And God, fro whom ther may nothyng hid be,
> If he in womman knowe had swich malice,
> As men of hem recorde in generaltee,
> Of our lady, of lyf reparatrice,
> Nolde han be born. But for þat shee of vice
> Was voide, and of al vertu wel, he wiste,
> Endowid, of hire be born him liste. (400–6)

This explanation leads to a commendation of the virgin martyr St Margaret, and then to the observation that while all Christ's male companions forsook him, his female companions 'forsook him naght' (442). The entire faith of the Christian church remained, after Christ's death, in women's hands. Hoccleve (through Cupid) encourages the reader to consult 'holy writ' to prove his point, and he uses language not far from Thomas's exhortation to the Friend in the *Series* to 'Looke in the same book [*L'epistre*]' to resolve *his* error:

---

[23] The literary/political focus in the early movement of the poem does include some brief religious references (155–68, 199–200); however, the broader inclination here is certainly towards the literary/political.

[24] The St Margaret material does not appear in Hoccleve's source text.

[25] All quotations from *L'epistre* come from my own transcription of the poem as it appears in HM 744. The same is true of any other shorter poems below, unless otherwise noted.

Wommen forsook him noght, for al the feith
Of holy chirche in womman lefte oonly.
This is no lees, for thus holy writ seith.
Looke, and yee shuln so fynde it, hardily. (442–5)

Hoccleve's discussion culminates in an apostrophe that gestures to Mary above all: 'O womman, þat of vertu art hostesse, / Greet is thyn honur and thy worthynesse' (461–2). As the reader has just witnessed Mary's presence as 'hostesse' to the supreme 'vertu' (God), it is hard not to read these lines through a Marian lens.[26] The greater trajectory of Hoccleve's L'epistre tends this way: from the literary-secular to the conspicuously religious, from mere fallible men to the exemplary woman par excellence, the Virgin Mary.[27]

The positioning of L'epistre in HM 744 deepens the Marian-devotional resonances within the poem. A reader arriving at the poem in HM 744 would have first read invocations to God, Christ, and the Holy Spirit (items 1–3), before reading two poems addressed to the Virgin Mary (items 4–5) and a tale detailing a miracle of the Virgin (item 6). L'epistre arrives after this deeply devotional sequence – the longest such sequence in either holograph – and so the return to biblical and Marian material toward the end of L'epistre would feel familiar, deeply rooted. This raises the question: even given the literary and political contexts for L'epistre (the Querelle de la Rose; the deposition of Richard II and the accession of Henry IV), is it possible to read Hoccleve's L'epistre as, in some senses, a work of Marian devotion?[28] Does it use the premise of a pagan god reciting male misbehaviour to arrive at the improbable end of magnifying the name of the foremother of Christian tradition, Mary, and also to honour, albeit to a lesser extent, figures like Eve, St Margaret, and Mary Magdalene?[29]

It is worth noting, when considering these questions, that Hoccleve makes more attempts to bind the poems in HM 744 together than he does in HM 111. At the end of the third poem, 'Ad spiritum sanctum', Hoccleve unites the first three poems in the collection – the 'Trinity poems' – with three concluding lines:

To fadir, sone, and to thee, we commende
Our soules, hem to haue in gouernance.
O Trinitee, haue vs in remembrance. (68–70)

---

[26] Returning to Thomas's comment in the 'Dialogue' that the 'book concludith for [women] [...] vertuously' is instructive here: 'vertuously' is indeed the operative term, and not in the vaguely positive way that it first comes across (D 779–80).

[27] While Christine's Epistre (Hoccleve's source) does include much of the biblical material used, Hoccleve compresses it and re-sequences the greater poem to allow for the trajectory highlighted here.

[28] I consider the political and literary contexts for L'epistre in great detail in Thomas Hoccleve, chapter 2.

[29] While Eve and St Margaret are singled out by name, Mary Magdalene is left unnamed, but she is included implicitly in Hoccleve's mention of those 'wommen [who] forsook him noght' (442).

These lines bind the first three poems together quite conspicuously, an unusual occurrence in the Huntington manuscripts. The next three items are bound by their shared focus on the Virgin Mary. Then, between the final two items in HM 744, the playful 'trois chaunceons' and the heavy Suso, Hoccleve offers a linking couplet: 'Aftir our song, our mirthe, and our gladnesse, / Heer folwith a lessoun of heuynesse'. It is here that we get closest to the organising spirit of the *Series*, in which various texts are invited towards cohesion.[30] But the evidence for Hoccleve making an effort to highlight his guiding hand in this collection reinforces the sense that *L'epistre* may arrive where it does, not as a change of pace, but rather as a different route to a familiar face, a familiar theme. The preceding items give *L'epistre* a firmly religious context, and this context orients the reader's eye towards the biblical (and Marian) material at the end of the poem. The very positioning of *L'epistre* in HM 744 recasts it not exclusively as 'Chaucerian love poetry' or as 'didactic/devotional verse', but rather as a way of bridging the gap between the two.[31]

Taking Hoccleve at his word in the *Series*, and reading *through L'epistre* – reading it fully to the end – indicates those ways in which the two poems (*L'epistre* and the *Series*) speak *to* and *through* each other. Both works cast the act of reading in a moral context – that is, situated within the binary, and seemingly clear-cut, categories of vice and virtue. Both works also complicate these categories. But the *Series* goes further than *L'epistre* in highlighting the people who embrace such categorisation, and, as such, it reads as an extension of the same literary meditation. In offering a meta-narrative frame within the *Series*, Hoccleve is able to underscore the relatively superficial decision-making process involved. He achieves a distinct sense of irony by involving the Friend as a separate character with separable intentions. *L'epistre*, on the other hand, uses the blanket discussion of 'bad men' and 'good women' to move towards a religious consideration of truly (wholly) virtuous individuals. The reader is drawn from Cupid's complaint over misbehaviour in the secular world, in the direction of the divine.[32]

L'epistre also serves a very specific organising function in the *Series*: its mention serves as a spur to Hoccleve's translation of the *Gesta* narratives. It becomes a shorthand, a means of reopening a rhetorical approach, of

---

[30] The French *dit* form appears to have been a key influence in Hoccleve's approach to making the *Series*. See John Burrow, 'Hoccleve and the Middle French Poets', in Helen Cooper and Sally Mapstone (eds), *The Long Fifteenth Century: Essays for Douglas Gray* (Oxford, 1997), pp. 35–49; see also A. C. Spearing, *Medieval Autographies: The 'I' of the Text* (Notre Dame, 2012).

[31] Relevant here is Heather Blurton and Hannah Johnson's discussion of Hoccleve's role in furthering a Chaucerian-Marian tradition: 'Reading the *Prioress's Tale* in the Fifteenth Century: Lydgate, Hoccleve, and Marian Devotion', *Chaucer Review*, 50 (2015), 134–58.

[32] I consider this dynamic further, in the context of heresy and orthodox reform, in *Thomas Hoccleve*, chapters 1 and 2.

engaging with binary representations of gender, and of vice and virtue. The presence of Hoccleve's Suso translation in close proximity to *L'epistre* in HM 744 – and the close proximity between the Suso translation, the *L'epistre* reference, and the *L'epistre*-motivated *Gesta* tales in the *Series* – suggests that Hoccleve might have seen the more religious dimensions of *L'epistre* aligning with (or prefiguring) the deeply meditative and more overtly religious *ars moriendi*.[33]

Reading Through: Death and Lyflynesse

One of the most useful aspects of 'reading through' Hoccleve's poems – of the practice of seeing how the longer and shorter poems speak to and through one another – is the opportunity to see how Hoccleve reuses a certain rhetorical strategy in a decidedly different context, how a given *word*, even, can be transplanted from one rhetorical environment into another. The example given below indicates how Hoccleve's seemingly 'secular' and 'religious' works interrelate and inter-inspire; it highlights the sacramental valences at play in Hoccleve's rendering of Chaucer in the *Regiment of Princes*.

Hoccleve uses one word in particular to connect his two main presentations of Chaucer in the *Regiment*: the word 'lyfly', which is also used in the noun form 'lyflynesse'.[34] Whereas, as we have seen, the acts of reading and writing sometimes become rather fraught in the *Series*, in the *Regiment* reading and writing are often posited as enlivening and invigorating. Addressing the prince, Hoccleve says that writing the virtuous material that comprises the *Regiment* 'Wacchen [his] goost' (2146) and prevents him from sleep. As Hoccleve laments Chaucer's death, he uses similarly energising language, and indicates Chaucer's books as the vessels through which an enlivening Chaucerian 'vertu' can 'lyfly hertith' the reader:

> O deeth, thow didest nat harm singuler
> In slaghtre of him, but al this land it smertith.
> But nathelees yit hastow no power
> His name slee; his hy *vertu* astertith
> Unslayn fro thee, which ay us *lyfly* hertith

---

[33] The alignment of Christine de Pizan (as author of the *Epistre*) with the *Gesta* tales should be attended to anew following the recent discovery of Hoccleve's hand in London, British Library, MS Harley 219, which contains among its contents *Gesta* tales and Christine's *Epistre Othea*. See Misty Schieberle, 'A New Hoccleve Literary Manuscript: The Trilingual Miscellany in London, British Library, MS Harley 219', *Review of English Studies*, 70, issue 297 (2019), 799–822.

[34] I refer to Hoccleve's early references to Chaucer in the *Regiment* (1958–74, 2077–107) as the first such presentation; the portrait presentation stanzas (4978–98) constitute the second.

With bookes of his ornat endytyng
That is to al this land enlumynyng. (1968–74; my emphasis)

Chaucer's books are given a specific type of power here: they possess an enlivening, vivifying 'vertu'. 'Deeth' and 'lyflynesse' interact for the first time in the poem: as death attempts to rob 'al this land' of Chaucer, the presence of the poet's 'bookes' enables an ongoing virtue, power, and energy that transcends death.

The only other instance in which Hoccleve uses the words 'lyfly' and 'vertu' together occurs in one of the shorter poems from HM 744, 'Ad spiritum sanctum'. This is the third poem in HM 744, the poem that rounds out the opening invocations to the three persons of the Trinity. There, praying to the Holy Spirit, Hoccleve invites the 'lyfly lemes' of the Spirit to invigorate our 'slouthy hertes':

Kyndle eek and qwikne with thy *lyfly* lemes
Our slouthy hertes, of *vertu* bareyne.
Our soules perce with thy shynyng bemes.
To thy godhede thow vs knytte and cheyne.
Thy ryuer of thy lust lat on vs reyne.
Of worldly sweet venym souffre vs nat taaste,
Ne our tyme in this world misspende and waaste. (22–8; my emphasis)

The vivifying beams of the Holy Spirit serve a similarly invigorating role to the lively, vivifying nature of Chaucer's 'vertu' in the *Regiment*, as transmitted through the medium of his books. The same trajectory that the Hoccleve narrator enacts in the first section of the *Regiment* – a journey out of despair and sloth, and into newly invigorated activity – is echoed too in these lines, in which the Holy Spirit is summoned to drive sloth from the heart. Whether or not 'Ad spiritum sanctum' predates the *Regiment*, Hoccleve's similar rhetorical manoeuvring in the two texts indicates that he would use the same language to describe the sacred, enlivening effects of the Holy Spirit as he would use to describe the enlivening effects of Chaucer's works, his still-living power, and his name.[35]

Hoccleve also uses 'lyflynesse' – the noun form – twice in the *Regiment*, and these instances deepen the transcendent valences of the word. In lines 2724–6, 'lyflynesse' is used to describe the life-giving (or animating) force of the soul in a body:

Evene as *a soule is bodyes lyflynesse*,
And whan that it is twynned from a wight
The herte is deed, so farith rightwisnesse [...] (my emphasis)

The word is then used to describe the freshness of Chaucer's likeness and presence in Hoccleve's memory, towards the end of the *Regiment*:

---

[35] For further consideration of 'lyfly', see Langdell, *Thomas Hoccleve*, pp. 165–70, where the discussion expands to consider examples from Thomas Usk and the Digby 102 poet.

> Althogh his lyf be qweynt, the resemblance
> Of him hath in me *so fressh lyflynesse*
> That to putte othir men in remembrance
> Of his persone, I have heere his liknesse
> Do make, to this ende, in soothfastnesse,
> That they that han of him lost thoght and mynde
> By this peynture may ageyn him fynde. (4992–8; my emphasis)

Even without having read 'Ad spiritum sanctum', a reader encountering these lines in the *Regiment* would have a sense-history for 'lyflynesse' involving a soul-like animating force, and a vivifying quality. Both of these are undertones in Hoccleve's presentation of his image of Chaucer.

The Chaucer image has a tradition of being discussed in the context of Christian iconography, and this is of course spurred on by Hoccleve himself.[36] After presenting the image as a means of communing with Chaucer, Hoccleve immediately turns to discuss the images found in churches, thereby aligning his 'peynture' with images of 'God' and 'his seintes':

> The ymages that in the chirches been
> Maken folk thynke on God and on his seintes
> Whan the ymages they beholde and seen,
> Where ofte unsighte of hem causith restreyntes
> Of thoghtes goode. Whan a thyng depeynt is
> Or entaillid, if men take of it heede,
> Thoght of the liknesse it wole in hem breede.
>
> Yit sum men holde oppinioun and seye
> That noon ymages sholde ymakid be.
> They erren foule and goon out of the weye;
> Of trouthe have they scant sensibilitee. (4999–5009)

These lines deepen the sense that Hoccleve is inviting a para-religious context for Chaucer. Chaucer's 'lyflynesse' – repurposed here to give Hoccleve licence to create the poet's image – gives way to a discussion of Christian images, and the people (Lollards) who oppose their use. The Chaucer image is being proffered not as a religious icon in its own right, but rather as something to be received as para-religious, evocative of religious icons. The use of 'lyfly' in 'Ad spiritum sanctum' offers us a broader context for how Hoccleve might conceive of this rendition of Chaucer, and its nigh-sacramental properties.

---

[36] See, for instance, James H. McGregor, 'The Iconography of Chaucer in Hoccleve's *De regimine principum* and in the *Troilus* Frontispiece', *Chaucer Review*, 11 (1977), 338–50; Jeanne Krochalis, 'Hoccleve's Chaucer Portrait', *Chaucer Review*, 21 (1986), 234–45.

Reading Through: The Textual Image

Hoccleve reprises his discussion of how to read religious images (and his criticism of Lollards) in 'To Sir John Oldcastle', the second item in HM 111, written *circa* 1415 – about five years after the *Regiment*:[37]

> And to holde ageyn ymages makynge,
> Be they maad in entaille or in peynture,
> Is greet errour, for they yeuen stirynge
> Of thoghtes goode, and causen men honure
> The seint aftir whom maad is that figure,
> And nat worsshipe it, how gay it be wroght.
> For this knowith wel euery creature
> Þat reson hath: þat a seint is it noght. (409–16)

Hoccleve's argument here is the same as in the *Regiment*: whereas in the *Regiment*, 'unsighte of [images] causith restreyntes / Of thoghtes goode', in the later poem 'they yeuen stirynge / Of thoghtes goode'. The language, and especially the focus on 'thoghtes goode', is so similar that these two discussions come across as aligned; in fact, the 'Oldcastle' stanzas serve in some ways as an extension of the *Regiment* argument. To further his point, Hoccleve adds (in 'Oldcastle') the useful analogy of peering through a corrective glass ('a spectacle') to sharpen one's eyesight:

> Right as a spectacle helpith feeble sighte
> Whan a man on the book redith or writ,
> And causith him to see bet than he mighte,
> In which spectacle his sighte nat abit,
> But *gooth thurgh*, and on the book restith it,
> The same may men of ymages seye:
> Thogh the ymage nat the seint be, yit
> The sighte vs myngith to the seint to preye. (417–24; my emphasis)

Whereas in the *Regiment* images allow 'thoghtes goode' to 'breede' in the mind of the viewer, and they remind viewers to think about God and his saints, in 'Oldcastle' the image is more specifically positioned as a go-between, a medium meant to be *passed through*, with the end result of the viewer being reminded to pray for the given saint or holy figure.[38]

Hoccleve's own (textual) image in the earlier sections of the *Series* is presented in similar terms – not as an end in itself, but rather as a medium through which moral meaning can be attained. The 'Complaint' lays out

---

[37] Due to rebinding (and perhaps the desire to cover up for the lost leaf at the beginning of 'Conpleynte paramont'), HM 111 actually begins with two leaves of 'Oldcastle' (fols 1r–2v); the rest of the poem continues after the end of the 'Conpleynte'.

[38] As Shannon Gayk notes, Hoccleve's understanding of the image-reading process is rooted in the reader's ability 'to perceive in the sense of *perspicere*: "to see through."': *Image, Text, and Religious Reform in Fifteenth-Century England* (Cambridge, 2010), p. 58.

what is taken to be Hoccleve's recent past: his sickness and recovery, his social alienation, and his determination to view his sickness and recovery as a 'visitacioun' from God. In the 'Dialogue', Hoccleve presents his experience as a 'spectacle', and it is hard to read that stanza without hearing some resonance of Hoccleve's words to Oldcastle ('Oldcastle' having been written only about five years prior):

> The benefice of God not hid be sholde.
> Sithen of myn heele he ȝaf me þe triacle,
> It to confesse and þanke hym, am I holde,
> For he in me hath shewid his miracle.
> His visitacioun is a *spectacle*
> In wiche that I biholde may and se,
> Bet þan I dide, howe greet a lord is he. (*D* 92–8; my emphasis)

It is important to note the multiple senses of 'spectacle' that align here: spectacle can mean 'wonder' or 'marvel', but also, as we have seen, 'eyeglass'.[39] The focus in this stanza is clearly on improving spiritual eyesight ('I biholde may and *se*, / Bet þan I dide'), and so the 'eyeglass' metaphor is activated, alongside the sense of Hoccleve's sickness and recovery as a marvel or wonder – indeed, a 'miracle' (95), as he puts it. Hoccleve indicates that this spectacle is not only useful for him; rather, it should be *used* and should be *seen through*, as a means of moving others towards deeper reverence for God. Hoccleve considers it his duty to disseminate his narrative (and with it, his personal image), rather than hide it: 'The benefice of God not hid be sholde' (*D* 92).[40]

We are perhaps not accustomed to seeing Hoccleve as a constructed image, as something built and presented with skill, rather than merely translated directly from life. Certain aspects of 'Hoccleve', such as his work at the Privy Seal, align with the historical Hoccleve. But reading the *Series*, we would do well to remember Hoccleve's own lessons in reading: that to some degree, we need to look *through* the proffered image, rather than *at* it. Jenni Nuttall has warned critics to remain sceptical when it comes to the 'Hoccleve' that we entertain in his works.[41] The literary may line up with reality in Hoccleve; and it may not: 'we must always remain on guard for the ways in which Hoccleve's identity can be unexpectedly protean'. Nuttall offers as an example the relationship between the version of Hoccleve seen in the opening sections of the *Series* and the 'Hoccleve' seen in another of the short poems, a *balade* sent to Henry Somer on behalf of the Court of Good Company, the penultimate item in HM 111. As Nuttall notes, the

---

[39] *MED* 'spectacle', especially senses 1 and 3.
[40] See *D* 78–81, 92–5.
[41] See Jenni Nuttall, 'Thomas Hoccleve's Poems for Henry V: Anti-Occasional Verse and Ecclesiastical Reform', *Oxford Handbooks Online* (2015), published online at 10.1093/oxfordhb/9780199935338.013.61.

poem was written in late April 1421, around the same time that Hoccleve was finishing his initial draft of the 'Complaint' and 'Dialogue'.[42] Whereas the *Series* is marked by isolation, anxiety, and depression, 'Good Company' is cheery, sociable, and sees Hoccleve eagerly awaiting a convivial dinner party.[43] To focus overmuch on the substance of the 'Complaint' as *biography* is to miss, for instance, the rich ways in which the image of Hoccleve interacts with the image of the dying man in the Suso treatise. It is to miss the fact that, in some ways, Hoccleve may wish us to view this particular 'Hoccleve' as a devotional image, something to be *passed through* en route to prayer and contemplation. It is to miss the very idea of a Hoccleve construct, a Hoccleve *image*.

We should also keep in mind that moment in the 'Dialogue' when Hoccleve's wife enters the scene: there, too, is the glimmer of sociability amid the guise of asceticism. 'Thomas, how is it twixt thee and thy feere?' the Friend asks. Hoccleve responds, 'Wel, wel [...] My wyf mighte haue hokir and greet desdeyn / If I sholde in swich cas pleye a soleyn' (739–42).[44] Hoccleve waits some 1,100 lines to introduce his wife into the landscape of the *Series* – and, seemingly, for good reason. The 'Complaint' – and much of the 'Dialogue' – is dependent on our reading Hoccleve in a certain way: as the abject, wounded solitary, calling out (Psalm-like) for God.[45] The mention of Hoccleve's wife gestures to the fact that the Hoccleve-image that readers have entertained thus far does not necessarily accord with the historical Hoccleve. The narrator may give the impression of being a 'soleyn' – a solitary individual – but this single stanza suggests otherwise.[46] The stanza tears the fabric of the illusion momentarily, and forces the reader to pause and consider the distance between Hoccleve and 'Hoccleve'. To see the carefully crafted 'soleyn' in *Series*-Hoccleve is to consider how this image might ultimately prove useful to the design of the greater poem.[47] Why was the creation of this particular 'Hoccleve' necessary for the creation of the *Series*?

The blueprints of *Series*-Hoccleve appear in the first section of the *Regiment*, but also in the relatively early *Male Regle*, where the Hoccleve narrator first tries out the tones of barren joy:

[42] Nuttall follows the dating for 'Good Company' suggested by Burrow in *Thomas Hoccleve*, pp. 28–9.

[43] Nuttall, 'Poems for Henry V', [n.p.].

[44] 'Wyf' can of course mean 'woman' as well as 'wife'. But Hoccleve's self-identification as a 'weddid man' in the *Regiment* (1449–53) resolves the ambiguity.

[45] On the Psalmic voice in Hoccleve, see David Lawton, 'Voice after Arundel', in Vincent Gillespie and Kantik Ghosh (eds), *After Arundel: Religious Writing in Fifteenth-Century England* (Turnhout, 2011), pp. 133–51.

[46] The *Regiment* exercises a similar dynamic: we wait until line 1450 to learn that Hoccleve is not the solitary wanderer we had thought, but is in fact married.

[47] For further discussion, see Sebastian Langdell, 'Hoccleve', in Julia Boffey and A. S. G. Edwards (eds), *The Oxford History of Poetry in English*, vol. 3: *Poetry in English 1400–1500* (Oxford, forthcoming).

And now my body empty is, and bare
Of ioie, and ful of seekly heuynesse,
Al poore of ese and ryche of euel fare. (14–16)[48]

But *Series*-Hoccleve is even more resonant in Hoccleve's short poem, 'Conpleynte paramont' (the first item in HM 111), in which the Virgin Mary's very woundedness, her momentary loss of mind and self after her son's death, humanises her all the more, and makes the defining moment of Christian history all the more visceral. Mary addresses herself: 'Poore Marie, *thy wit is aweye*' (217), whereas Hoccleve remembers those 'that deemen *my wit is goon*' (207).[49] The *Series*-Hoccleve image is also felt in 'Ad filium', the second item in HM 744, where the speaker internalises the wounds of Christ's crucifixion:

I am the wownde of al thy greuance.
I am the cause of thyn occisioun
And of thy deeth, dessert of thy vengeance.
I am also verray flagicioun.
I causid thee thy greuous passioun.
Of thy torment I am solicitour –
Thow Goddes sone, our lord and sauueour. (8–14)

To internalise – *inhabit* – the wound is a Hocclevian move. His work as a scribe, as detailed in the first section of the *Regiment* (981–1029), reaches us primarily through the wounds that he bares. He presents himself there in a manner not unlike the Roman soldier, appearing in an exemplum midway through the *Regiment*, who exhibits his wounds for Caesar (a moment deeply resonant of Christ to Doubting Thomas) as a means of moving the ruler to compassion:

'My wowndes beren good witnesse ynow
That I sooth seye, and lest yee leeve it naght,
I shal yow shewe what harm have I caght,
The doute out of your herte for to dryve.'
He nakid him and shewid him as blyve. (3286–9)

We locate 'Hoccleve' in and between these images. Reading *through* these poems helps to deliver not only a firmer context for the use of given words or rhetorical manoeuvres, but also a better grounding for the creation of 'Hoccleve' himself, as an image. We are beginning to see Hoccleve as he is: deeply protean, composed of parts both real and imagined, long dead and still living.

---

[48] Cf. for instance D 246–59. Also cf. 'Conpleynte paramont': 'Of ioye am I bareyne' (40).

[49] I have also made a case elsewhere for the influence of a Deschamps poem on Hoccleve's presentation of 'lost wit' and regained sanity in the *Series*: see my *Thomas Hoccleve*, pp. 55–7.

Index

Printed and bound by CPI Group (UK) Ltd, Croydon, CR0 4YY
23/08/2022
03143334-0003